INTRA-GROUP FINANCING AND ENTERPRISE GROUP INSOLVENCY

ELGAR CORPORATE AND INSOLVENCY LAW AND PRACTICE

Series Editors: Andrew Keay, *Professor of Corporate and Commercial Law, University of Leeds, UK* and *Chief Insolvency and Companies Court Judge* Nicholas Briggs

The Elgar Corporate and Insolvency Law and Practice series is a library of works by leading practitioners and scholars covering discrete areas of law in the field. Each title will be analytical in approach, highlighting and unpicking the legal issues that are most critical and relevant to practice. Designed to be detailed, focused reference works, the books in this series aim to offer an authoritative statement on the law and practice in key topics within the fields of company law, corporate governance, corporate insolvency and personal insolvency.

Presented in a format that allows for ease of navigation to a particular point of law, each title in the series is written by specialists in their respective fields, often with insight either from private practice or from an academic perspective.

For a full list of Edward Elgar published titles, including the titles in this series, visit our website at www.e-elgar.com.

INTRA-GROUP FINANCING AND ENTERPRISE GROUP INSOLVENCY

Law and Practice

ILYA KOKORIN

Assistant Professor of Law, Leiden University, the Netherlands

ELGAR CORPORATE AND INSOLVENCY LAW AND PRACTICE

Edward Elgar PUBLISHING

Cheltenham, UK · Northampton, MA, USA

Published by

Edward Elgar Publishing Limited
The Lypiatts
15 Lansdown Road
Cheltenham
Glos GL50 2JA
UK

Edward Elgar Publishing, Inc.
William Pratt House
9 Dewey Court
Northampton
Massachusetts 01060
USA

Authorised representative in the EU for GPSR queries only: Easy Access System Europe – Mustamäe tee 50, 10621 Tallinn, Estonia, gpsr.requests@easproject.com

A catalogue record for this book is available from the British Library

Library of Congress Control Number: 2025939000

This book is available electronically in the **Elgar**online
Law subject collection
https://doi.org/10.4337/9781035330218

MIX
Paper | Supporting responsible forestry
FSC® C013604

ISBN 978 1 0353 3020 1 (cased)
ISBN 978 1 0353 3021 8 (eBook)
ISBN 978 1 0353 7044 3 (ePub)

Printed and bound by CPI Group (UK) Ltd, Croydon, CR0 4YY

CONTENTS

EXTENDED CONTENTS

PART III PRINCIPLES OF INSOLVENCY LAW AND HOW TO BALANCE THEM

PREFACE

The enterprise group is one of the primary forms of organising entrepreneurial activity. In fact, nearly every major firm operates as a corporate group. From early precursors of business groups, such as the Medici system of partnerships in the fifteenth to sixteenth centuries and the European colonial trading empires of the seventeenth century (e.g. the Dutch and English East India Companies), to the emergence at the end of the nineteenth century of the first modern groups of companies, characterised by multi-layered and hierarchical structures of ownership and control, groups have played a significant role in the economic and political life of societies.

However, the enterprise group presents a curious case, as it does not have a legal personality of its own. It combines separate legal entities, usually shielded by limited liability, with an often integrated business enterprise facilitated by intricate networks of financial arrangements. Some of these arrangements 'perforate' limited liability shields (e.g. cross-guarantees), while others closely bind the fates of separate group members (e.g. intra-group loans, centralised cash management, intercompany cross-default and ipso facto clauses). As a result, the concept of legal separateness, which underpins modern company and insolvency law, rarely aligns with present-day economic realities.

The insolvencies of corporate giants like Lehman Brothers, Nortel Networks, Oi Brazil, and more recently, Hertz, LATAM Airlines, FTX, Steinhoff and Vroon – where debtor entities are scattered across the globe – demonstrate that group entities not only 'live' together, but also 'die' or 'recover' together. If insolvency law fails to account for the economic reality of group integration, it risks undermining the value created by group synergies, as well as the organisational and financial links within a corporate group.

This book aims to rethink the treatment of groups of companies in insolvency law, arguing that insolvency law should respond to both the legal reality of entity separateness and the economic reality of group integration. It focuses on financial arrangements common among enterprise groups and explores their impact on and treatment in insolvency and restructuring of corporate groups. On the one hand, these arrangements can have a positive effect by mitigating credit risk and resulting in a lower cost of debt and greater liquidity. On the other hand, intra-group financing promotes group interdependence and could magnify the risk of contagion and opportunistic behaviour within the group. In this book, I provide a comprehensive analysis of contemporary commercial practices, case law and the legal tools offered by three prominent restructuring hubs: the UK, the USA, and the Netherlands.

The book consists of three major parts. The first introduces groups of companies, discussing their characteristics and types. It also examines how insolvency law addresses financial distress within enterprise groups and how it has evolved over time. The Global Financial Crisis of 2008 and the rise of the so-called rescue culture prompted the adoption of group-mindful solutions and tools. The second part describes the financial arrangements typically found in groups of companies, such as cross-guarantees and intra-group loans, analyses their benefits, and highlights the problems they cause in situations of financial distress. The third part explores potential solutions to these problems, delving into various legal tools that have emerged in response to the economic reality of enterprise groups and the patterns of their failures. These tools include third-party releases, extensions of enforcement stays to non-debtor group entities, and safe harbours and pre-emptive strategies to promote intra-group rescue financing.

This book is the result of a long and exciting journey – a journey of constant learning and development. I am grateful to the many people who have supported and guided me in my academic and professional pursuits. Without them, this book would not have been possible. My first words of gratitude go to Matthias Haentjens and Reinout Vriesendorp, who provided me with unwavering support and the flexibility to explore new ideas and engage in various, sometimes rather ambitious projects. I also greatly benefited from discussions with Bob Wessels, Irit Mevorach, Ray Warner, Pim Rank, Michael Veder, Branda Katan, Harold Koster, Stephan Madaus, Jeroen van der Weide, Gert-Jan Boon, Shuai Guo, Daniël Stein, Kristin van Zwieten and many other excellent professionals.

I would like to express my appreciation to Stichting Hazelhoff Van Huet and the Meijers Research Institute of the Leiden Law School, who generously co-funded my research. Finally, I would like to thank Edward Elgar Publishing and its excellent team.

In this book, developments have been taken into account until 15 November 2024.

Ilya Kokorin
Leiden, the Netherlands, 15 November 2024

ABBREVIATIONS

ABI	American Bankruptcy Institute
AktG	*Aktiengesetz* (German), German Stock Corporation Act
ALI	American Law Institute
APR	Absolute priority rule
Art.	Article
AT&T	American Telephone and Telegraph Company
BCBS	Basel Committee on Banking Supervision
BGH	*Bundesgerichtshof* (German), German Federal Court of Justice
B.R.	Bankruptcy Reporter
BRRD	Bank Recovery and Resolution Directive, Directive 2014/59/EU of 15 May 2014 establishing a framework for the recovery and resolution of credit institutions and investment firms
BW	*Burgerlijk Wetboek* (Dutch), Dutch Civil Code
CBM	Contractually binding mechanism
CCAA	Companies' Creditors Arrangement Act (Canada)
CEO	Chief executive officer
CERIL	Conference on European Restructuring and Insolvency Law
CIGA	Corporate Insolvency and Governance Act 2020 (UK)
Cir.	Circuit
CIWUD	Directive 2001/24/EC of 4 April 2001 on the reorganisation and winding up of credit institutions
CJEU	Court of Justice of the European Union
CNA	Citicorp North America
COMI	Centre of main interests
Coop	Oi Brasil Holdings Coöperatief U.A.
CPR	Civil Procedure Rules (UK)
CUP	Cambridge University Press
CVA	Company voluntary arrangement
DAO	Decentralised autonomous organisation
DCC	Dutch Civil Code

DIP	Debtor in possession
EBA	European Banking Authority
EBOR	European Business Organization Law Review
EBRD	European Bank for Reconstruction and Development
EC	European Commission
ECB	European Central Bank
ECFR	European Company and Financial Law Review
ECGI	European Corporate Governance Institute
ECHR	European Convention on Human Rights
ECtHR	European Court of Human Rights
EFTA	European Free Trade Association
e.g.	*exempli gratia* (for example)
EIC	English East India Company
EIR 2000	Council Regulation (EC) No 1346/2000 of 29 May 2000 on insolvency proceedings
EIR Recast	Regulation (EU) 2015/848 of 20 May 2015 on insolvency proceedings (recast)
EU	European Union
EUR	Euro
EWCA	England and Wales Court of Appeal (UK)
FDIA	Federal Deposit Insurance Act (USA)
FDIC	Federal Deposit Insurance Corporation
FSB	Financial Stability Board
Fw	*Faillissementswet* (Dutch), Dutch Bankruptcy Act
GFC	Global Financial Crisis
GFSA	Group financial support agreement
GMRA	Global Master Repurchase Agreement
G-SIB	Global systemically important bank
HR	*Hoge Raad* (Dutch), Dutch Supreme Court
HUP	Harvard University Press
ibid.	*ibidem* (in the same place)
i.e.	*id est* (in other words)
IHC	Intermediate holding company
III	International Insolvency Institute
InsO	*Insolvenzordnung* (German), German Insolvency Code
IP	Insolvency practitioner
IRDA	Insolvency, Restructuring and Dissolution Act (Singapore)
ISDA	International Swaps and Derivatives Association
IT	Information technology
IVA	Individual voluntary arrangement

JOR	*Jurisprudentie Onderneming & Recht* (Dutch), Jurisprudence Business & Law
KA	Key Attribute
LBHI	Lehman Brothers Holdings, Inc.
LBT	Lehman Brothers Treasury Co B.V.
LMA	Loan Market Association
MEG	Multinational enterprise group
MLCBI	UNCITRAL Model Law on Cross-Border Insolvency
MLEGI	UNCITRAL Model Law on Enterprise Group Insolvency
MPOE	Multiple point of entry
MREL	Minimum requirement for own funds and eligible liabilities
MSME	Micro, small and medium-sized enterprise
NACIIL	*Nederlandse Vereniging voor Rechtsvergelijkend en Internationaal Insolventierecht* (Dutch), Netherlands Association for Comparative and International Insolvency Law
NCWO	No-creditor-worse-off
NJ	*Nederlandse Jurisprudentie* (Dutch), reports of court decisions (Netherlands)
NPV	Net present value
OUP	Oxford University Press
PTIF	Portugal Telecom International Finance B.V.
R&D	Research and development
Rb.	*Rechtbank* (Dutch), first instance court (Netherlands)
ReO	*Restrukturierungsordnung* (German), Restructuring Regulation (Austria)
RPT	Related party transaction
SME	Small and medium-sized enterprise
SPE	Special purpose entity
SPOE	Single point of entry
SPV	Special purpose vehicle
SRB	Single Resolution Board
SRMR	Single Resolution Mechanism Regulation, Regulation (EU) No 806/2014 of 15 July 2014 establishing uniform rules and a uniform procedure for the resolution of credit institutions and certain investment firms in the framework of a Single Resolution Mechanism and a Single Resolution Fund
SSA	Secured support agreement

StaRUG	*Gesetz über den Stabilisierungs- und Restrukturierungsrahmen für Unternehmen (Unternehmensstabilisierungs- und -restrukturierungsgesetz – StaRUG)* (German), Enterprise Stabilization and Restructuring Act (Germany)
TLAC	Total loss-absorbing capacity
UCC	Uniform Commercial Code
UK	United Kingdom of Great Britain and Northern Ireland
UKSC	United Kingdom Supreme Court
UNCITRAL	United Nations Commission on International Trade Law
USA/US	United States of America
USD	US dollar
VOC	*Vereenigde Oostindische Compagnie* (Dutch), Dutch East India Company
Vol.	Volume
WHOA	*Wet Homologatie Onderhands Akkoord* (Dutch), Act on Court Confirmation of Extrajudicial Restructuring Plans (Netherlands)

TABLE OF CASES

INTERNATIONAL

Court of Justice of the European Union

Akzo Nobel and Others v. Commission, C-516/15, 27 April 2017	11.35
Estro/Smallstep, C-126/16, 22 June 2017	4.06
Eurofood IFSC Ltd, Case C-341/04, 2 May 2006	6.07
French Republic v. European Commission, Case C-559/12 P, 3 April 2014	4.19
'Private Equity Insurance Group' SIA v 'Swedbank' AS, Case C-156/15, 10 November 2016	4.31
Simona Kornhaas v. Thomas Dithmar, Case C-594/14, 10 December 2015	4.15
Sumal SL v. Mercedes Benz Trucks España SL, Case C-882/19, 6 October 2021	11.35

EFTA Court

EFTA Surveillance Authority v. Iceland, E-16/11, 28 January 2013	3.39

European Court of Human Rights

Boyadzhieva and Gloria International Limited Eood v. Bulgaria, Appl. nos. 41299/09 and 11132/10, 5 July 2018	4.23
Cipolletta v. Italy, Appl. no. 38259/09, 11 January 2019	4.55
Gratzinger and Gratzingerova v. The Czech Republic, App. no. 39794/98, 10 July 2002, 2002-VII, 399	4.23
Sunday Times v. United Kingdom, App. no. 6538/74, Judgment, 26 April 1979	4.54

NATIONAL

Australia

Lavin v. Toppi [2015] HCA 4; (2015) 254 CLR 459	5.28
Mahoney v. McManus (1981) 180 CLR 370	5.28
Opes Prime Stockbroking Ltd, Re [2009] FCA 813	8.09

Canada

Cayman Islands

Germany

Hong Kong

Ireland

India

Netherlands

Russia

Singapore

United Kingdom

United States of America

TABLE OF LEGISLATION

REGIONAL LEGISLATION

Council of Europe

European Union

NATIONAL LEGISLATION

Argentina

Australia

France

Germany

Italy

Netherlands

Russia

Singapore

Spain

United Kingdom

United States

PART I

INTRODUCTION

I

WHAT THIS BOOK IS ABOUT

1.1 SETTING THE SCENE

1.01 This book explores certain financial transactions, enterprise groups and their interaction with insolvency law. However, before diving into this fascinating yet complex interaction, I would like to introduce three 'benchmark' cases to set the tone for the rest of the book and provide a general background against which the legal issues will be analysed. These cases recount the collapses of major multinational enterprise groups – Lehman Brothers, Nortel Networks and Oi Brazil. Each case highlights distinctive features that set them apart from 'simple' single-debtor bankruptcies. Our choice of these cases has been determined by their international character, large scale, involvement of multiple stakeholders and intricate group financial arrangements. These characteristics make a group-wide resolution of financial problems more challenging but at the same time more desirable (or even necessary) to preserve and maximise value.

1.1.1 Lehman Brothers

1.02 The colossal failure of Lehman Brothers needs no introduction. For most of its lifespan, Lehman Brothers operated as a partnership. Founded in 1859, it initially engaged in the trading of retail goods and commodities. Gradually, Lehman Brothers transformed into an investment bank. In 1984, it was sold to American Express, which merged it with its financial subsidiary to form Shearson Lehman Brothers. As a result, Lehman Brothers became a wholly owned subsidiary of American Express, losing its partnership status but preserving its 134-year-old name. Yet the merger proved short-lived. In the 1990s, American Express began divesting its financial services business, and in 1994,

Lehman Brothers was spun off in an IPO as Lehman Brothers Holdings, Inc. (LBHI).

Over the 2000s, Lehman Brothers expanded its portfolio of services and pursued business opportunities in proprietary trading, derivatives, asset management, securitisation, and real estate.[1] As part of this expansion, the firm shifted from a relatively low-risk brokerage model to a high-risk, capital-intensive banking model, particularly with proprietary investments in commercial real estate, leveraged loans and private equity.[2] This crucial change in the business model rewarded excessive risk taking and leverage. It also made Lehman Brothers increasingly dependent on the confidence of its counterparties – confidence that quickly evaporated when the value of mortgage-backed securities, the primary assets held by Lehman's corporate group and used as collateral for its credit lines, sharply declined in 2007–2008. Unable to secure government funding or find a private solution, LBHI and its subsidiaries filed voluntary Chapter 11 petitions in the United States Bankruptcy Court for the Southern District of New York on 15 September 2008, listing liabilities exceeding USD 600 billion.[3] At that time, Lehman Brothers was the fourth-largest investment bank in the USA and one of the largest financial services firms in the world. **1.03**

The bankruptcy of Lehman Brothers proved to be a long-lasting battle. Court documents indicate that '[t]he chaos that ensued was unprecedented and presented the potential for highly fractious proceedings permeated by years of extended, complex and expensive litigation among competing interests and entities'.[4] One of the main reasons for this complexity relates to the group's organisational and financial structure. **1.04**

Lehman Brothers' worldwide headquarters in New York and regional headquarters in London and Tokyo were complemented by a network of offices spanning North America, Europe, the Middle East, Latin America and the Asia-Pacific region.[5] The Lehman Brothers group consisted of 2,985 legal **1.05**

1 R.Z. Wiggins, T. Piontek and A. Metrick, The Lehman Brothers Bankruptcy A: Overview, Journal of Financial Crises, Vol. 1, 2019, p. 43.

2 For an overview of the Lehman Brothers' history and reasons for its bankruptcy, see A.R. Valukas, R.L. Byman and D.R. Murray, The Rise and Fall of Lehman Brothers, in D. Faber and N. Vermunt (eds), Bank Failure: Lessons from Lehman Brothers, OUP, 2017, paras. 1.01–1.83; S.J. Lubben and S.P. Woo, Reconceptualizing Lehman, Texas International Law Journal, Vol. 49, 2014, pp. 295–325.

3 Lehman Brothers Holdings Inc. (Chapter 11) <https://dm.epiq11.com/case/lehman/info> (accessed 10 October 2024).

4 Debtors' Amended Response to Objections to Approval of Proposed Disclosure Statement, *In re Lehman Bros. Holdings*, No. 08-13555 (Bankr. S.D.N.Y. 23 August 2011).

5 Lehman Brothers Holdings Inc. Form 10-K for fiscal year ended 30 November 2007.

entities operating across some fifty countries.[6] Pistor describes the structure of Lehman Brothers as follows:

> Lehman Brothers ... developed the legal partitioning of assets with the help of corporate law into an art form. The business operated as a fully integrated global financial services provider, but its operations, liabilities, and profit centers were divided among hundreds of legal entities.[7]

1.06 This corporate complexity made the implementation of an orderly resolution challenging. The collapse of the enterprise group resulted in over seventy-five separate proceedings worldwide, with more than sixteen official representatives appointed.[8] The proceedings were not only separated by geographical lines; the legal boundaries were perhaps even more significant. While US law applied to the proceedings opened against LBHI and its US subsidiaries, insolvency laws from more than eighty jurisdictions governed non-US Lehman Brothers entities.[9] This legal fragmentation at times led to irreconcilable judgments.[10] Writing on Lehman's intra-group operations, the Basel Committee on Banking Supervision (BCBS), the primary global standard setter for prudential regulation of banks, observed that:

> The flexibility of the organisation was such that a trade performed in one company could be booked in another. The lines of business did not necessarily map to the legal entity lines of the companies. The group was organised so that some essential functions, including the management of liquidity, were centralised in LBHI.[11]

1.07 The Lehman Brothers group operated as an integrated global enterprise, with a corporate structure designed to optimise economic returns for the entire group. The vast majority of LBHI's subsidiaries were not intended to act as standalone legal entities; instead, many were incorporated as special-purpose vehicles supporting core operating companies. For example, the Dutch entity, Lehman Brothers Treasury Co B.V. (LBT), functioned as a financing company,

---

6 BCBS, Report and Recommendations of the Cross-Border Bank Resolution Group, March 2010, para. 49.

7 K. Pistor, The Code of Capital: How the Law Creates Wealth and Inequality, Princeton University Press, 2019, p. 54.

8 J. Altman, A Test Case in International Bankruptcy Protocols: The Lehman Brothers Insolvency, San Diego International Law Journal, Vol. 12, 2011, p. 464.

9 M.J. Fleming and A. Sarkar, The Failure Resolution of Lehman Brothers, Federal Reserve Bank of New York Economic Policy Review, Vol. 20, 2014 <https://www.newyorkfed.org/research/epr/2014/1412flem.html> (accessed 10 October 2024).

10 A.V. Sexton, Current Problems and Trends in the Administration of Transnational Insolvencies Involving Enterprise Groups: The Mixed Record of Protocols, the UNCITRAL Model Insolvency Law, and the EU Insolvency Regulation, Chicago Journal of International Law, Vol. 12, 2012, p. 815.

11 BCBS, Report and Recommendations of the Cross-Border Bank Resolution Group, March 2010, para. 50.

issuing notes to both professional and retail investors and on-lending the proceeds to finance the group's activities. Obligations under these notes were guaranteed by LBHI and hedged by other group members, such as Lehman Brothers Special Finance Inc. Consequently, in the bankruptcy of LBHI, two types of claims were filed: (i) LBT's direct intercompany claim, and (ii) claims of noteholders based on the cross-guarantee. Initially, LBHI dismissed LBT's claim in its entirety, citing concerns that it might lead to a double recovery by LBT's noteholders. However, after rounds of negotiations between Dutch and US parties, a settlement was eventually reached. Under this settlement, LBT's intercompany claim was recognised, while some distributions by LBHI on LBT guarantee claims were to be reallocated to holders of unsecured claims against LBHI.[12]

As indicated by LBT's bankruptcy trustees, 'LBT was incorporated solely for serving the financing needs of [LBHI] and other entities of the Lehman Brothers Group … So, economic dependency was a characteristic of LBT. It was not meant to be a[n] autonomous business entity'.[13] Another important member of the Lehman Brothers' 'family' was Lehman Brothers International (Europe) (LBIE), headquartered in London. LBIE played a pivotal role as the group's main European hub, placing notes on the market and maintaining books and records for other subsidiaries, including LBT. This internal group hierarchy was not only opaque to outsiders but also to some of Lehman's employees, who were unaware of the distinctions between various group entities or even which specific entity employed them.[14] **1.08**

The integrated character of the Lehman Brothers group was evident in the way it organised its finances. It had a centralised cash management system in which LBHI acted as a banker for hundreds of its subsidiaries, some of which could not function without cash transfers from LBHI to fund their operations. According to the report of the LBHI's examiner, Anton R. Valukas (the **1.09**

12 Modified Third Amended Joint Chapter 11 Plan of Lehman Brothers Holdings Inc. and its Affiliated Debtors, dated 5 December 2011 <https://portal-redirect.epiq11.com/LBH/document/GetDocument.aspx?DocumentId=1456969> (accessed 10 October 2024). The plan was confirmed by the court on 6 December 2011.

13 R. Schimmelpenninck and F. Verhoeven, Investigation of the causes of the bankruptcy of Lehman Brothers Treasury Co B.V., Amsterdam, 1 March 2013.

14 J. Carmassi and R.J. Herring, Corporate Complexity and Systemic Risk: A Progress Report, in A.N. Berger, P. Molyneux and J.O.S. Wilson (eds), The Oxford Handbook of Banking, OUP, 3rd edn, 2019, p. 98; C. Cumming and R.A. Eisenbeis, Resolving Troubled Systemically Important Cross-Border Financial Institutions: Is a New Corporate Organizational Form Required? Federal Reserve Bank of New York, Staff Report No. 457, 2010 <https://www.newyorkfed.org/research/staff_reports/sr457.html> (accessed 10 October 2024), observing that the Lehman legal structure 'was essentially unrelated to either its operational structure or the lines of business in which the organization engaged'.

'Valukas Report'), LBHI controlled the 'cash disbursements and receivables for itself, its subsidiaries and its affiliates'.[15] This system was designed to track all cash activities, maximise investment opportunities and minimise transaction costs, including funding, capital and tax costs. As a holding company, LBHI lent money to its operating subsidiaries 'at the beginning of each day and then swept the cash back to LBHI at the end of each day'.[16] In other words, it ran a zero-balance cash management or cash pooling system (see Figure 1.1).

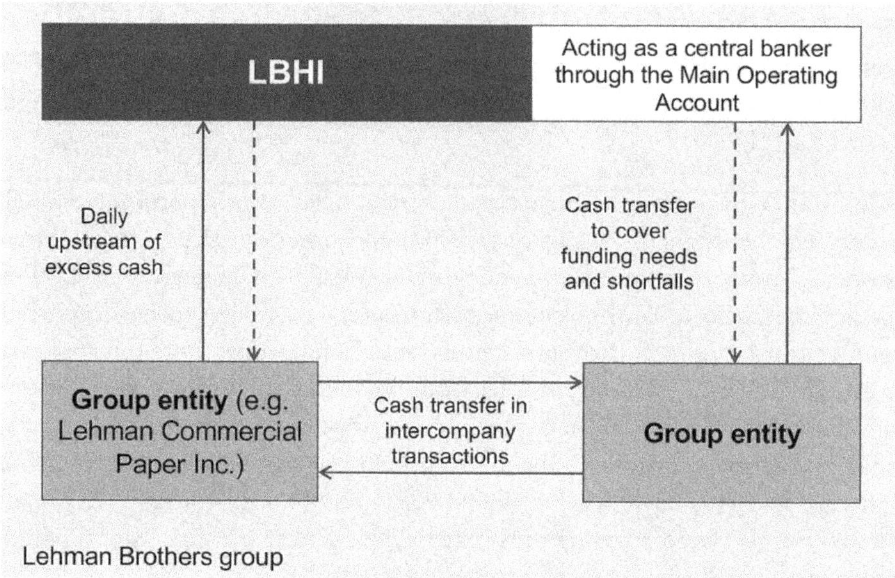

Note: This figure is based on the Valukas Report, p. 1553. Not all LBHI's subsidiaries took part in the cash management system.

Figure 1.1 Lehman Brothers cash management system

1.10 As a consequence, when LBHI filed for bankruptcy, a large portion of the group funds became part of the US proceedings and, therefore – as was generally held – unavailable to support Lehman's subsidiaries on a going concern basis.[17] On the same day as LBHI filed a Chapter 11 petition, LBIE was

15 Lehman Brothers Holdings Inc. Chapter 11 Proceedings Examiner's Report (Valukas Report), 2010, p. 1550.

16 R.J. Herring and J. Carmassi, The Corporate Structure of International Financial Conglomerates: Complexity and its Implications for Safety and Soundness, in A.N. Berger, P. Molyneux and J.O.S. Wilson (eds), The Oxford Handbook on Banking, OUP, 1st edn, 2012, p. 225.

17 R. Herring, The Challenge of Resolving Cross-Border Financial Institutions, Yale Journal on Regulation, Vol. 31, 2014, p. 870.

placed into administration in the UK, citing limitations on the transfer and receipt of payments from LBHI.

Alongside the integrated cash management system, Lehman Brothers' intra-group financing featured an elaborate system of intercompany obligations, cross-collateralisation and intra-group guarantees.[18] Following the bankruptcy filing, highly contentious disputes arose between the group members regarding the size and validity of intra-group claims and the enforceability of guarantee claims by group affiliates against LBHI as the principal debtor or guarantor. Some of LBHI's creditors proposed consolidating the insolvency estates of Lehman's entities, and in this way eliminating cross-guarantees, intercompany and joint and several liability claims, primarily for the benefit of LBHI's creditors. However, this proposal was ultimately rejected, and the corporate shields of group companies were retained. Nevertheless, the redistribution of payouts to specific creditors, including holders of senior unsecured claims and general unsecured claims against LBHI, was agreed upon based on an implied 20 per cent risk of substantive consolidation.[19] **1.11**

The resolution of intra-group claims was facilitated through separate settlement agreements reached between insolvency practitioners (IPs) appointed in different proceedings,[20] as well as the bankruptcy protocol. The latter set out a coherent and orderly process for the treatment of intercompany claims – a part of the protocol referred to as 'the heart of the Protocol'.[21] **1.12**

---

18 H.R. Miller, L.R. Fife and M. Horwitz, In re Lehman Brothers Holdings Inc. From Chaos to Consensus, Presentation from 22 June 2012, stating that USD 328 billion in claims under guarantees were filed against LBHI by affiliates and that USD 255 billion in claims under guarantees were filed against LBHI by non-affiliate third parties.

19 *In re Lehman Brothers Holdings Inc., et al.*, Order confirming modified third amended joint Chapter 11 plan of Lehman Brothers Holdings Inc. and its affiliated debtors, Chapter 11 Case No. 08-13555 (JMP) (Bankr. S.D.N.Y. 2011), explaining that litigation regarding substantive consolidation 'would require vast amounts of discovery and investigation into the operations of Lehman prior to the Commencement Date, would be extraordinarily complex and costly for all parties involved, and would significantly delay Distributions to all Creditors'.

20 F. Verhoeven, Lehman Brothers Treasury, in M. Haentjens and B. Wessels (eds), Research Handbook on Cross-Border Bank Resolution, Edward Elgar Publishing, 2019, p. 354. *Re LB Holdings Intermediate 2 Ltd* [2017] EWHC 2032 (Ch); *In re Lehman Brothers Inc.*, Case No. 08-01420 (JMP) SIPA (Bankr. S.D.N.Y. 2013), Order approving Settlement Agreement among the Trustee, Lehman Brothers International (Europe) and the LBIE administrators.

21 Debtor's Motion Pursuant to Section 105 and 363 of the Bankruptcy Code for Approval of a Cross-Border Insolvency Protocol, *In re Lehman Brothers Holdings Inc.*, No. 08-13555 (Bankr. S.D.N.Y. 2009), at 23. Negotiations over the protocol resulted in the Global Close Balance Sheet, prepared between November 2008 and January 2009. This Global Close Balance Sheet played an important role, because it 'represented the last consolidated set of books and records of the Lehman Group prior to insolvency'. A. Lehavi, Property Law in a Globalized World, CUP, 2019, p. 269. The Cross-Border Insolvency Protocol for the Lehman Brothers Group of Companies <https://www.iiiglobal.org/initiatives/iii-insolvency-protocols/> (accessed 10 October 2024).

1.1.2 Nortel Networks

1.13 Nortel Networks group (Nortel) was another multinational giant with a long history that ended in the twenty-first century. Nortel was founded in 1895 in Montreal, Canada, as the Northern Electric and Manufacturing Company. The major stake in it belonged to the Bell Telephone Company of Canada (Bell Canada), one of Canada's most prominent telecommunications enterprises. It manufactured phones, telephone switchboards, gramophones and other equipment. In 1914, it merged with Imperial Wire and Cable Company to become the Northern Electric Company (Northern Electric). In this company, 44 per cent of the share capital was owned by Western Electric, a subsidiary of the American Telephone and Telegraph Company (AT&T), while the remainder belonged to Bell Canada. Until the 1950s, Northern Electric primarily relied on designs and licences from Western Electric. As a consequence of an antitrust suit in the USA, AT&T had to sell its stake in Northern Electric to Bell Canada in 1956. Having lost access to AT&T's resources, Northern Electric began developing its own technologies and products, including electronic switching systems. In 1973, Northern Electric went public, with Bell Canada retaining a 90.1 per cent stake. The 1970s and 1980s were marked by rapid growth and expansion into foreign markets, such as the USA, Europe and the Caribbean.

1.14 In 1998, the company changed its name to Nortel Networks in order to emphasise its shift from telecommunications to data and multimedia networking. By the year 2000, Nortel had reached its peak, representing over one-third of the total value of the S&P/TSX index, employing more than 90,000 people globally, and ranking among the most valuable companies worldwide.[22] As the 2000s progressed, Nortel faced significant financial challenges, partly stemming from an aggressive acquisition strategy, a high-cost structure, a lack of financial discipline, questionable product-related decisions and operational changes impairing innovation. Moreover, the post-dot-com bubble burst era brought heightened market competitiveness, further complicating Nortel's position.[23] Nortel laid off many employees, downsized its research projects and gradually lost track of the evolving business and technological environment.

---

22 For a study of the causes of Nortel's failure, see An Overview of the Demise of Nortel Networks and Key Lessons Learned: Systemic effects in environment, resilience and black-cloud formation, Report by the University of Ottawa (Canada), 2014 <https://sites.telfer.uottawa.ca/nortelstudy/files/2014/02/nortel-summary-report-and-executive-summary.pdf> (accessed 10 October 2024).

23 Ibid., pp. 3–4. See also Nortel Networks Corporation Annual Report 2001 <https://bib.kuleuven.be/files/ebib/jaarverslagen/NortelNetworks_2001.pdf> (accessed 10 October 2024), reporting a net loss of USD 27.3 billion in 2001 and workforce reduction from appr. 94,500 employees at the beginning of 2001 to appr. 52,600 employees by the end of 2001.

This led to a gradual erosion of trust among its customers, who became increasingly doubtful about Nortel's long-term survival and its ability to keep R&D and maintenance promises – a situation often referred to as a 'black cloud'. The global recession in 2008 exacerbated the challenges faced by the once-leading telecommunications company, contributing to its downfall.

On 14 January 2009, Nortel Networks Inc. and fourteen of its subsidiaries filed Chapter 11 petitions in the United States Bankruptcy Court for the District of Delaware (jointly administered). On the same day, the ultimate corporate parent of these companies, Nortel Networks Corporation, along with its own parent company, Nortel Networks Limited, and several affiliates, filed an application with the Ontario Superior Court of Justice under the Companies' Creditors Arrangement Act (CCAA). Simultaneously, the High Court of Justice in London placed all companies of the Nortel group established in the EU into administration. In May 2009, the Commercial Court of Versailles (France) opened secondary proceedings with respect to one of them, Nortel Networks S.A.[24] Pointing out the 'gargantuan bankruptcy cases' of Nortel Networks, Judge Kevin Gross of the US Bankruptcy Court for the District of Delaware wrote: 1.15

> The how and why for the downfall are the subject of numerous books and articles and the Court will not gratuitously add its views which are not necessary to the work at hand. It is sufficient to note that even a writer of fiction would not dare to compose the story of the death of this multi-national enterprise and the harm it inflicted on tens of thousands of employees and creditors.[25]

Just like Lehman Brothers, Nortel Networks was a truly multinational enterprise with a large network of branches and subsidiaries spread across the globe. It relied on operating synergies and was managed 'on divisional lines that generally ignored geographical boundaries and corporate structures'.[26] Judge Newbould of the Ontario Superior Court of Justice described the business structure of Nortel Networks as follows: 1.16

> Nortel (a) had fully integrated and interdependent operations; (b) had intercompany guarantees for its primary indebtedness; (c) operated a consolidated treasury system in which generated cash was used throughout the Nortel Group as required; (d) disseminated consolidated financial information throughout its entire history, save for the year before its

24 On the interaction between the UK main and French secondary proceedings, see R. Dammann, Lessons to be Learned from the Nortel Case, Eurofenix, No. 82, Winter 2020/21, pp. 34-35.

25 *In re Nortel Networks, Inc.*, 532 B.R. 494, 499 (Bankr. D. Del. 2015).

26 J.L. Westbrook, Transparency in Corporate Groups, Brooklyn Journal of Corporate, Financial & Commercial Law, Vol. 13, 2018, p. 37.

> bankruptcy; and (e) created IP [intellectual property] through integrated R&D activates that were global in scope.[27]

1.17 Nortel's business was highly integrated. This integration was, in part, determined by the nature of its main assets – patents and other intellectual property developed in labs around the world and shared throughout the group. This is why, upon the onset of insolvency, the entity-by-entity allocation of ownership rights over the intangible assets among enterprise group members was difficult (if not impossible); in any case, it would have likely resulted in significant costs and protracted court battles.

1.18 The problem was solved by an agreement of all major parties to sell the key assets on a global basis, largely ignoring corporate and geographical boundaries. According to this agreement,[28] the sales proceeds were to be deposited into an escrow account. The distribution of these funds would be carried out either through the agreement of all selling debtors on a method of allocation or, in the case of disagreement, upon the 'determination of any dispute relating thereto by the relevant dispute resolver'.[29] Because of this 'unified' approach to the realisation of the group's assets, Nortel could sell its business lines for approximately USD 3.285 billion and the intellectual property for USD 4.5 billion, totalling USD 7.3 billion placed in the so-called 'lockbox' with JP Morgan in New York.[30]

1.19 However, the sale of the group's assets was only part of the story, perhaps the easiest part. Once the money was received in the escrow account, distribution issues naturally arose. These issues turned out to be very complex and divisive. The complexity was attributed to the legal separateness of group members, which underpinned the separateness of the insolvency estates of such members, as well as their liabilities. It was further complicated by the fact that some creditors – most notably bondholders and pensioners ('double claimants') – simultaneously asserted their claims against several companies within the Nortel group.[31] After failed attempts to resolve the deadlock through mediation,[32] the disputes concerning the allocation of proceeds ended up in

---

27 *Nortel Networks Corporation (Re)*, 2015 ONSC 2987, 12 May 2015.

28 The Nortel Interim Funding and Settlement Agreement (Execution version) <https://www.iiiglobal.org/initiatives/iii-insolvency-protocols/> (accessed 10 October 2024).

29 *Nortel Networks Corporation (Re)*, 2015 ONSC 2987, 12 May 2015.

30 Ibid. See L.L. Peacock, A Tale of Two Courts: The Novel Cross-Border Bankruptcy Trial, American Bankruptcy Institute Law Review, Vol. 23, 2015, pp. 543–570.

31 J.L. Westbrook, Corporate Formalism in a Global Economy, in J.P. Sarra and B. Romaine (eds), Annual Review of Insolvency Law, Toronto: Carswell, 2015, p. 311.

32 J.A.E. Pottow, Cross-border Corporate Insolvency in the Era of Soft(ish) Law, in B.E. Adler (ed), Research Handbook on Corporate Bankruptcy Law, Edward Elgar Publishing, 2020, p. 347, noting a

courts of several jurisdictions. These disputes lasted for nearly a decade, resulting in substantial expenses and creating frustration among creditors.[33]

The courts in the USA and Canada recognised that the Nortel enterprise, as a whole, developed assets in common and that it was not possible or fair to assign any of the group entities certain and calculable claims to the proceeds from the liquidation of the group's assets. Instead, a pro rata allocation method was adopted. According to this method, referred to by the US court as an 'extraordinary result', each debtor was to receive a percentage of the lockbox funds that corresponded to the percentage of the total allowed claims against that specific debtor relative to the total allowed claims against all group debtors. This method was chosen over alternatives, such as the 'revenue' and 'contribution' approach, or the ownership allocation suggested by the parties seeking more beneficial treatment.[34] The chosen method upheld the separateness of the group companies' insolvency estates from which distributions were to be made. It also maintained intercompany claims for the purposes of determining the amount of claims against the relevant debtors. **1.20**

As for intra-group guarantees, the courts in the USA and Canada concluded that there was insufficient evidence that the guaranteed creditors, such as bondholders, relied on the corporate separateness of the various companies comprising the group. They also noted that the market did not differentiate the bonds that carried a guarantee and those that did not; at least, this was not reflected in the terms of the bond documentation. As a result, it was decided that a claim that could be filed against more than one debtor, inter alia, due to a cross-guarantee, should only be calculated and recognised once. This is an unusual approach, as the main point of a guarantee, as explained later in the book, is that it effectively 'multiplies' a claim by allowing simultaneous filings against the principal debtor and a guarantor. In the case of Nortel, for allocation purposes, guaranteed claims were to be included only against the principal obligor (i.e. issuer). It was emphasised that any other approach would **1.21**

---

spectacular failure of the mediation attempts.

33 See E.J. Janger and S. Madaus, Value Tracing and Priority in Cross-Border Group Bankruptcies: Solving the Nortel Problem from the Bottom Up, University of Miami International and Comparative Law Review, Vol. 27, 2020, pp. 334-357, observing that the Nortel story represents a remarkable paradox in recent cross-border restructuring practice, standing as both the biggest success and the biggest failure. This is due to the fact that despite securing the high purchase price for the group's assets, the fight over the allocation of proceeds consumed a large chunk of the asset value, estimated at a staggering USD 2.6 billion. On Nortel's insolvency, see J.A.E. Pottow, Two Cheers for Universalism: Nortel's Nifty Novelty, in J.P. Sarra and B. Romaine (eds), Annual Review of Insolvency Law, Toronto: Carswell, 2015, pp. 333-367.

34 *In re Nortel Networks, Inc.*, 532 B.R. 494 (Bankr. D. Del. 2015), comparing the allocation dispute between the US, Canadian and EMEA parties to 'three people trying to reach the top of a mountain by pulling the others down. In other words, no one gets to the top'.

give guaranteed creditors access to the lockbox funds, representing assets of thirty-eight group entities, some of which did not provide guarantees.[35] That said, guaranteed creditors could still claim for any shortfall from an entity that has provided a guarantee in order to participate in the distribution with other creditors.[36]

1.1.3 Oi Brazil

1.22 Oi group (Oi Brazil), formerly known as Telemar, is a large fixed and mobile telephone operator in Brazil and one of the largest telecommunications enterprises in Latin America. Founded in 1998 as Tele Norte Leste during Brazil's telecommunications sector privatisation, the company was rebranded as Oi in 2007. By 2015, Oi employed 140,000 direct and indirect employees in Brazil, operated 651,000 public telephones, over one million public Wi-Fi hotspots and 330,000 kilometres of fibre optic cables.[37] Its financial problems stemmed from debt accrued through mergers and acquisitions, mounting competition in mobile and data sectors, declining demand for fixed-line services (Oi Brazil's main operational focus), and the heavy capital expenditures required for the government-mandated expansion of its fixed-line network in rural areas experiencing negative growth.[38]

1.23 Affected by Brazil's economic downturn that began in 2014 and the ensuing political uncertainty, Oi Brazil was facing unsustainable debt levels, predominantly arising from bonds governed by New York and English law. Some of these bonds were issued by the Dutch financing subsidiaries, Portugal Telecom International Finance B.V. (PTIF) and Oi Brasil Holdings Coöperatief U.A. (Coop), and were guaranteed by the group's parent, Oi S.A. The funds received by PTIF and Coop from the sale of notes to investors were on-lent to other group entities to finance their operational activities. Hence, the repayment of the notes fully depended on the financial condition of Oi S.A. and its operating subsidiaries. This type of arrangement is common among multinational groups.[39] The use of special purpose financing companies, intercompany guarantees and intra-group transfers facilitates access to foreign capital markets,

---

35 *Nortel Networks Corporation (Re)*, 2015 ONSC 2987, 12 May 2015.

36 D. Miller and M. Shakra, *Nortel*: The Long and Winding Road, in J.P. Sarra and B. Romaine (eds), Annual Review of Insolvency Law, Toronto: Carswell, 2015, p. 299.

37 *In re Oi Brasil Holdings Coöperatief U.A.*, 578 B.R. 169 (Bankr. S.D.N.Y. 2017).

38 Ibid. See also J. Leahy and S. Pearson, Oi bankruptcy spotlights Brazilian debt problems, Financial Times, 21 June 2016.

39 INSOL International Special Report, Restructuring Cross-border Groups: Key Considerations Around Foreign Tax and Finance-driven SPVs, June 2020.

reduces the cost of capital for the entire group, and enables efficient allocation of resources within it.

Following unsuccessful attempts to reach an out-of-court debt restructuring agreement with bondholders, Oi S.A. and several of its subsidiaries, including PTIF and Coop, filed for a jointly administered reorganisation proceeding (*recuperação judicial*) in Brazil on June 20, 2016. The Brazilian court accepted jurisdiction over PTIF and Coop. The centralised restructuring of the multinational enterprise group was seen by the parent company as the preferred solution over an alternative approach involving the sale of assets on an entity-by-entity basis. **1.24**

In Brazil, the principle of corporate separateness has historically been upheld. However, since 2014, courts have increasingly confirmed restructuring plans that involve the substantive consolidation of assets and liabilities of separate companies.[40] In the Oi Brazil case, the initial proposal for a reorganisation plan was also based on substantive consolidation. Nevertheless, the Brazilian court decided that the issue of substantive consolidation should be determined by the creditors of each entity. For voting purposes, the court determined that guarantees on the bonds should not be counted.[41] This is despite the fact that substantive consolidation may, and usually does, have a direct effect on distributions to guaranteed creditors. Without it, such creditors have two paths for recovery: (i) against the principal debtor (issuer), which itself has a claim against the guarantor based on an intra-group loan, and (ii) against the guarantor (ultimate borrower) who owes money to the internal lender (issuer). This dual recovery strategy is sometimes referred to as the 'double dip' because it permits the creditor to make more than one claim in relation to the same debt. **1.25**

In parallel to the centralised restructuring process in Brazil, separate bankruptcy proceedings against PTIF and Coop were initiated in the Netherlands. After months of litigation, the Dutch Supreme Court (*Hoge Raad* or HR) upheld the jurisdiction of the Dutch courts over these entities. It almost automatically tied the question of international insolvency jurisdiction to the fact **1.26**

40 S.C. Neder Cerezetti, Reorganization of Corporate Groups in Brazil: Substantive Consolidation and the Limited Liability Tale, International Insolvency Review, Vol. 30, 2021, pp. 169–190, noting the wide and unsubstantiated use of substantive consolidation in Brazil and the weakening role of limited liability and asset partitioning. See also *In re Rede Energia S.A.*, 515 B.R. 69, 100 (Bankr. S.D.N.Y. 2014), referring to the Brazilian Bankruptcy Court, which found that substantive consolidation of the Rede debtors was appropriate for plan purposes, because these debtors were 'organized as a corporate group, with a common controlling company and credit inter-dependence' as a result of loans that exist between the companies in the group and cross-corporate guarantees to third parties.

41 R.J. Cooper, F.L. Cestero and J.W. Mosier, Oi S.A.: The Saga of Latin America's Largest Private Sector In-court Restructuring, Pratt's Journal of Bankruptcy Law, Vol. 14, 2018, p. 211.

that Coop and PTIF were separate legal persons incorporated under Dutch company law.[42] As part of the Dutch bankruptcy proceedings, in May 2017, the trustee of Coop initiated an avoidance action in a Dutch court, challenging certain intra-group transfers and seeking repayment in relation to several loans made by Coop to other group entities.

1.27 When bondholders realised that there would be no compensation offered for the intercompany claims, some of them attempted to interfere in the centralised restructuring process or gain leverage via recognition of the Dutch bankruptcy proceedings as the foreign main proceedings in the USA. These attempts were unsuccessful. The US court had previously recognised the Brazilian insolvency proceeding as the foreign main insolvency proceeding under Chapter 15 of the US Bankruptcy Code. Now the bondholders were attempting to overturn such recognition. The court characterised this behaviour as an attempt to weaponise Chapter 15 'to collaterally attack both the Brazilian RJ Proceeding and the Oi Group's proposed Brazilian RJ Plan'.[43]

1.28 As the powers of the Dutch bankruptcy trustees were not recognised in Brazil, any coordination and cooperation between parallel insolvency proceedings were stalled. The trustees of Coop and PTIF were not allowed to interfere with the restructuring process in Brazil under Brazilian law, even though they may have been required to do so under Dutch law, acting in the interests of creditors, including the bondholders seeking the described 'double dip' recovery.[44] The deadlock was particularly difficult to resolve, as neither the Netherlands (outside the European context) nor Brazil had comprehensive rules on international insolvencies, let alone rules on the mutual recognition of restructuring plans.[45]

---

42 HR 7 July 2017, ECLI:NL:HR:2017:1280, r.o. 3.1, *NJ* 2018/363; HR 7 July 2017, ECLI:NL:HR:2017:1281, r.o. 3.1, *NJ* 2018/364, m.nt. F.M.J. Verstijlen.

43 *In re Oi Brasil Holdings Coöperatief U.A.*, 578 B.R. 169, 242 (Bankr. S.D.N.Y. 2017); *In re Oi Brasil Holdings Coöperatief U.A.*, 582 B.R. 358 (Bankr. S.D.N.Y. 2018), refusing to reconsider the recognition decision and denying the petition for recognition of the Dutch bankruptcy proceedings. See, however, P.J.M. Declercq, The Actions of a Distressed Investor in the Restructuring of Brazilian Telecom Group Oi SA Assessed – Villain or Essential Contributor to the Development of Law & Practice in Cross-border Restructurings/insolvencies of Groups? INSOL World, Second Quarter 2018, pp. 12–14.

44 J.H. Overduin and J.M.W. Pool, De curator in de spagaat: tussen Nederlandse taakuitoefening en het belang van een internationale herstructurering. Interview met curatoren Marcel Groenewegen (PTIF) en Jasper Berkenbosch (Oi Coop) over de voorlopige surseances en faillissementen van de financieringsmaatschappijen van Oi Telecom, Tijdschrift voor Insolventierecht, 2020/9, pp. 58–67, describing the complexities of the Oi restructuring process, based on the interviews with the Dutch trustees of Coop and PTIF.

45 In December 2020, Brazil adopted the law implementing the UNCITRAL Model Law on Cross-Border Insolvency. This law is in force as of 23 January 2021.

The restructuring plan (RJ plan) was approved at a fourteen-hour creditor meeting, held on 19 and 20 December 2017, in which more than 1,000 people gathered in a former Olympic venue in Rio de Janeiro. The plan was confirmed by the Brazilian court on 8 January 2018 and became effective on 5 February 2018. According to the plan, the bondholders of Coop and PTIF were entitled to elect to receive as recovery for the claims: (i) a package of securities and common shares of Oi, or (ii) the right to receive the full amount of their claims with a twenty-year principal grace period.[46] **1.29**

Following the approval of the RJ plan in Brazil, the composition plan was proposed in the Dutch bankruptcy proceedings. This plan effectively mirrored the terms of the Brazilian restructuring plan and was consistent with it in all material aspects.[47] Although the amount of distribution was not entirely clear, the composition plan received support from the creditors of PTIF and Coop, who agreed that their claims against various Oi group entities would receive equal treatment. The Dutch court approved this plan on 11 June 2018.[48] This marked the end of the long rivalry between parallel proceedings and provided a much-needed resolution to the complex insolvency case. Chapter 15 cases were closed in 2023. **1.30**

1.1.4 Common features of group insolvencies

Leo Tolstoy's novel Anna Karenina (1877) begins with a saying: 'All happy families are alike; each unhappy family is unhappy in its own way' (in Russian: *Все счастливые семьи похожи друг на друга, каждая несчастливая семья несчастлива по-своему*). In the same way, the three insolvency stories described above are different from each other. This concerns their individual circumstances, causes of financial distress of once-booming businesses, the behaviour of parties and the outcomes reached. Two of the three companies no longer exist. However, despite these differences, there are commonalities or similar features shared among all three cases, albeit varying in extent or degree. **1.31**

- The first feature relates to the fact that multinational enterprises are often organised as multi-layered structures, consisting of many levels of subsidiaries

46 The summary of the key terms of the RJ Plan <https://cms.law/en/content/download/342269> (accessed 10 October 2024).

47 See Advice regarding composition plan ex art. 140 DBA by Mr. J.R. Berkenbosch, 26 April 2018 <https://cms.law/nl/content/download/344103/8925087/version/1/file/Oi_Coop_Advice_Bankruptcy_Trustee_Article_140_DBA_26_April_2018_English.pdf> (accessed 10 October 2024).

48 Rb. Amsterdam 11 June 2018, ECLI:NL:RBAMS:2018:5047 (*PTIF*); Rb. Amsterdam 11 June 2018, ECLI:NL:RBAMS:2018:5048 (*Oi Coop*), *JOR* 2018/259, m.nt. W.J.M. van Andel.

performing different functions and located in different countries. This multi-layered corporate structure can result in multiple insolvency proceedings initiated against group members in different jurisdictions and subject to different laws. The coordination of these proceedings with the aim of value preservation – either through a global sale of assets, as in the case of Nortel Networks, or via a comprehensive group-wide restructuring plan, as in Oi Brazil – is problematic and costly.

- The second feature concerns the integrated nature of enterprise groups, as mentioned earlier. This group integration materialises in the manner in which the corporate group is managed and in the degree of operational and financial interconnectedness. It may also translate into the division of responsibilities within the group. For example, specific companies within the group may be tasked with raising funds from investors, as seen in the case of special purpose financing vehicles used by Lehman Brothers and the Oi group. Others could function as a group bank, collecting and re-distributing liquidity to different group entities. In highly integrated groups, the allocation of assets or liabilities to a particular group entity can be challenging due to the intermingling of assets and liabilities or the collective effort to generate enterprise value, as witnessed in the case of Nortel Networks.
- The third feature refers to the prevalence of group-specific financial arrangements. In many enterprise groups, financing is coordinated and organised at a group level with the involvement of different group entities. It is common in practice for legally separate entities to enter into transactions to reallocate funds within the group (e.g. intra-group loans, centralised cash management), or to support each other in securing external financing (e.g. intercompany guarantees, co-debtorship, provision of collateral). These transactions seek to optimise liquidity allocation within the group, maximise economic efficiency by minimising tax exposure, provide access to foreign capital markets and ultimately secure better lending terms. While the group is solvent and not in default on obligations, such financial arrangements usually do not create any problems. Yet, in situations of financial distress and insolvency, they can give rise to prolonged disputes and complicate the efficient administration and resolution of group insolvencies. Typical disputes concern the validity of pre-insolvency intra-group transfers, the calculation, attribution and enforcement of intercompany claims, access to intra-group financing, and the potential threat of substantive consolidation. Thus, both the presence of intra-group liability arrangements and the challenges they present in insolvency proceedings are significant.

1.32 These shared similarities characterising the operation and financing of groups of companies, together with the common challenges and problems arising in group insolvencies, provide a solid ground for this study. The cases of Lehman Brothers, Nortel Networks and Oi Brazil are eye-opening and representative of both the complexities of group insolvencies, unravelling power struggles between different creditors (or even countries) and the desirability or necessity of group-sensitive legal responses or solutions. Throughout this book, these cases will serve as valuable reference points.

1.2 SCOPE AND AIMS OF THIS BOOK

This book explores financial arrangements involving group entities, their creditors and other stakeholders within the context of financial distress and insolvency. Among the most common intra-group financial arrangements discussed are cross-guarantees and intra-group loans. Before analysing the challenges associated with intra-group financing and group insolvency, some general observations and clarifications regarding the scope of this book, its structure and the terms used in it are necessary. **1.33**

First, the book is a study of insolvency law.[49] This law is understood broadly to include various proceedings which seek to resolve corporate financial distress. These proceedings encompass 'traditional' or 'classical' fully collective proceedings, addressing the problem of a general default and aimed at the joint satisfaction of all the debtor's creditors.[50] It also includes proceedings that are not premised on or do not require full collectivity (e.g. Dutch WHOA schemes, English schemes of arrangement) and that may be available in the absence of insolvency. However, the focus of this book is limited to the use of these proceedings to resolve financial problems of commercial enterprises. This includes situations where a company is insolvent or imminently insolvent, and where it is technically solvent but faces a reasonable likelihood of insolvency. Therefore, this book does not address solvent procedures (e.g. the use of English schemes for takeover purposes) and procedures aimed at the discharge of debt for natural persons (e.g. English individual voluntary arrangements). **1.34**

---

49 In the UK, the term 'bankruptcy' refers to the process concerning natural persons, while 'insolvency' applies to corporations. In the USA, the term 'insolvency' describes the state of the debtor being insolvent, whereas 'bankruptcy' relates to a statutory process of dealing with a debtor under the US Bankruptcy Code, whether the debtor is a legal or natural person. In the Netherlands, the term 'bankruptcy' is commonly used to refer to the traditional bankruptcy procedure (*faillissement*) of the Dutch Bankruptcy Act, while 'insolvency' tends to reflect the debtor's financial state. In EU and UNCITRAL instruments, the term 'insolvency' is predominant, referring to both the state of financial distress and the procedure (i.e. insolvency proceedings). For an overview of the historical roots of the modern terms and a brief history of bankruptcy, see H. Rajak, The Culture of Bankruptcy, in P.J. Omar (ed), International Insolvency Law. Themes and Perspectives, London and New York: Routledge, 2008, pp. 3-25. To avoid any confusion, in this book, I will use both terms interchangeably, while accommodating national preferences when discussing specific national laws.

50 The collectivity requirement has been described as the key defining characteristic of insolvency proceedings. See H. Eidenmüller, What is an insolvency proceeding? ECGI Law Working Paper No. 335/2016, December 2016 <https://ecgi.global/working-paper/what-insolvency-proceeding> (accessed 15 July 2023), arguing that in a cross-border context, only 'fully collective' proceedings should be characterised as insolvency proceedings. For a different view, see G. Ray Warner, Comparative Collectivity: European Union and United States Approaches, International Insolvency Review, Vol. 32, 2023, pp. 156-175, referring to the collectivity requirement as 'unworkable', and noting the shift towards the fairness requirement in recognition cases.

The law of personal insolvency pursues specific policy goals and principles (e.g. fresh start), distinct from those of corporate insolvencies.[51]

1.35 I recognise that the appearance of new procedures and the possibility of using the same ones by both solvent and insolvent companies, collectively or selectively, have somewhat blurred the boundaries of what is called 'insolvency law'. There are divergent views on what insolvency law is and whether restructuring law is a part of insolvency law or whether it is a separate area of law with its own unique set of doctrines and principles.[52] I acknowledge important differences between the distinct types of procedures. That said, the broad approach advocated in this book is justified, given that the resolution of financial distress within enterprise groups and the accompanying legal tools dealing with intra-group financing can be implemented via insolvency and restructuring proceedings,[53] whether fully collective and insolvency-tested or not. Often, parallel proceedings are opened in different jurisdictions (e.g. US Chapter 11 and UK scheme of arrangement, Dutch WHOA and UK scheme of arrangement), some of which are fully collective, while others are not, but each represents a piece of one 'group puzzle'.[54] The openness of this approach reflects

---

51 See I. Ramsay, Personal Insolvency in the 21st Century: A Comparative Analysis of the US and Europe, Hart Publishing, 2017.

52 S. Madaus, Leaving the Shadows of US Bankruptcy Law: A Proposal to Divide the Realms of Insolvency and Restructuring Law, EBOR, Vol. 19, 2018, pp. 615–647, proposing to distinguish insolvency law – addressing the present common pool problem via a collective liquidation process, and restructuring law – aiming at facilitating the conclusion of a restructuring agreement and dealing with entitlements to future revenue streams. Also, S. Paterson, Rethinking the Role of the Law of Corporate Distress in the Twenty-First Century, LSE Law, Society and Economy Working Papers 27/2014, 2014, p. 3, distinguishing insolvency law that addresses 'the situation in which some or all of the existing stakeholders who finance the firm no longer wish to support it and new financiers cannot be found' and restructuring law where 'the majority of the existing financial stakeholders wish to continue to remain invested in the firm but must agree a new bargain'. In other words, whereas insolvency law imposes a collective process to maximise capital that can be redeployed in the economy, restructuring law solves the deadlock created by the hold-out position of an individual creditor who does not agree to a new bargain.

53 In literature, there are no universally recognised boundaries of what constitutes 'restructuring', its content and aims. Restructuring can be understood in the narrow sense to include only procedures where the business remains within the debtor's corporate shell. See B. Wessels and S. Madaus, Rescue of Business in Insolvency Law. Instrument of the ELI, 2017, p. 71 <https://ssrn.com/abstract=3032309> (accessed 10 May 2024). It can also be viewed more broadly, as incorporating procedures seeking preservation of the business as an organisational entity rather than the debtor's corporate shell, and therefore including a transfer of the business from the debtor to another legal entity via a going concern sale. See R. Bork, Corporate Insolvency Law. A Comparative Textbook, Intersentia, 2020, pp. 4, 165–166. Bork distinguishes 'restructuring' per se, which removes debt from the business, and 'asset-deal restructuring', which removes the business from its debt. This book generally adheres to the latter interpretation of restructuring as seeking either the rescue of the debtor company or at least of its business.

54 A good example illustrating the global resolution of financial distress is restructuring of Hertz. See J.A.E. Pottow, Love *Hertz*: Corporate Groups and Forum Selection, Texas International Law Journal, Vol. 56, 2021, pp. 155–180. On parallel restructurings, see I. Kokorin, Parallel Restructurings: Challenges and Opportunities, Tijdschrift voor Insolventierecht (TvI) 2024/12.

the versatility of the ways in which financial distress within corporate groups may be tackled.

Second, this book addresses contractual and other voluntary financial arrangements. Based on an extensive literature review and conversations with practitioners and academics, the following transactions or financial arrangements have been selected due to their prevalence in enterprise groups and importance in practice: **1.36**

- group guarantees, co-debtorship and other consensual forms of shared liability;
- intra-group loans and centralised cash management.

This selection limits the scope of my investigation in two important ways. First, I do not examine non-contractual arrangements or involuntary situations that could lead to joint and several liability of several group members. For example, I will not address the liability of a parent company in tort for actions of its subsidiaries. Like personal insolvencies, corporate torts raise unique legal and moral questions that deserve careful examination and possibly a different analytical approach.[55] Second, my primary concern lies in pre-insolvency transactions and the treatment of 'original' creditors. Consequently, 'non-original' creditors, such as distressed debt investors, and claims trading more broadly, are excluded from the analysis. The dynamics of claims trading and the role of specialised distressed investors might raise distinct policy concerns that are not inherently tied to group scenarios.[56] **1.37**

Third, the approach of this book necessitates a broad inquiry into and comparison between different national legal systems, as well as the ideas and solutions they have developed to tackle similar problems. Nevertheless, it is not the purpose of this book to propose how a given legal system (e.g. Dutch bankruptcy law) can be improved. Instead, the analysis of national laws and their application on the ground aims to provide valuable insights into legal instruments and commercial practices. These comparative insights help discover some common **1.38**

55 See H. Hansmann and R. Kraakman, The End of History for Corporate Law, Georgetown Law Journal, Vol. 89, 2001, p. 466, arguing that when it comes to corporate torts, the rule of limited liability 'induces inefficient risk-taking and excessive levels of risky activities – inefficiencies that appear to outweigh by far any offsetting benefits, such as reduced costs of litigation or the smoother functioning of the securities markets'.

56 For discussion of distressed debt trading, see L. Welling-Steffens, J.A. Ellias, S.W. van den Berg and T. Florstedt, Distressed Debt Trading – Brave New EU Legal Rules in Relation to Bold New Strategies, NACIIL 2019 report, Eleven International Publishing, 2019 <https://naciil.org/2021/08/20/reports-2019-distressed-debt-trading-brave-new-eu-legal-rules-in-relation-to-bold-new-strategies/> (accessed 10 October 2024).

threads and serve as a foundation for suggestions concerning the appropriate design of insolvency law.

1.39 The primary focus of this book is on three jurisdictions: the USA, the UK and the Netherlands. They are Western common law and civil law jurisdictions – neither too similar nor too different from each other.[57] They are sufficiently comparable from economic, social and cultural perspectives, which underpin insolvency law. Markesinis and Fedtke assert that in selecting a range of legal systems for comparative research, one should choose 'a system on the basis of its prima facie richness, development, relevance, and transplantability'.[58] The legal regimes of the USA, the UK and the Netherlands are examples of such a system, from which inspiration may be sought, at least on the subject of this book.[59]

1.40 The bankruptcy law of the USA, and specifically Chapter 11 of the US Bankruptcy Code, has influenced insolvency law reforms around the world.[60] It has been used by many non-US groups of companies seeking to benefit from its highly sophisticated and debtor-friendly provisions. In the 2000s, English schemes of arrangement[61] gradually gained popularity as a tool for group (financial) restructurings. They have been 'exported' to numerous other (mainly common law) jurisdictions, including Australia, New Zealand, Canada, Hong Kong, Ireland, Singapore and the Cayman Islands.[62] They have also served as role models or sources of inspiration for modern reforms in some European civil law jurisdictions, such as Germany and the Netherlands. The latter has positioned itself as an emerging restructuring hub, introducing a legal tool known as WHOA schemes,[63] which draw inspiration from both Chapter 11 and English schemes of arrangement. Throughout the book,

---

57 Siems describes this selection as one favoured by traditional comparative lawyers. M. Siems, Comparative Law, 2nd edn, CUP, 2018, p. 18.

58 B. Markesinis and J. Fedtke, Engaging with Foreign Law, Hart Publishing, 2009, p. 50, and continuing on p. 51 that a 'claim that the codes, laws, and judicial decisions of all systems are of intellectual value and practical utility can only be made by those who wish to be politically correct or otherwise gain some "favour" from such proclaimed open-mindedness'.

59 This does not mean that other legal systems, not covered in this book, are less relevant or inspirational.

60 It is noted that Chapter 11 deserves a prominent place in 'the pantheon of extraordinary laws that have shaped the American economy and society and then echoed throughout the world'. E. Warren and J.L. Westbrook, The Success of Chapter 11: A Challenge to the Critics, Michigan Law Review, Vol. 107, 2009, p. 604.

61 Companies Act 2006, Part 26 (schemes of arrangement). The book also discusses Part 26A (restructuring plans), sometimes referred to as 'super-schemes'.

62 For an overview of schemes in some common law jurisdictions, see J. Payne, Schemes of Arrangement: Theory, Structure and Operations, CUP, 2014, Chapter 8.

63 Act on Court Confirmation of Extrajudicial Restructuring Plans (*Wet homologatie onderhands akkoord* or WHOA). The WHOA came into force on 1 January 2021 and added new articles on WHOA schemes to the Dutch Bankruptcy Act.

references to other jurisdictions (e.g. Germany, Singapore) will also be included. These concise excursions aim to provide additional insights and perspectives on issues that may not exist or are less prominent in the chosen jurisdictions but remain of significant practical importance.

Fourth, this book draws valuable lessons from the post-financial crisis regulation of banks. In the aftermath of the Global Financial Crisis of 2008, the regulation of bank failures in various jurisdictions, including the EU and the USA, underwent fundamental changes.[64] These reforms were largely driven by the desire to effectively address the collapses of credit institutions, prevent the need for bailouts, safeguard banks' critical functions, and ensure the stability of the financial system. To achieve this, it became imperative to supervise and resolve banks, paying attention to their group structures. To the extent that bank regulation takes a group-sensitive approach (e.g. group resolution plans, group financial support agreements), it should be studied. Yet, I do not aim to exhaustively cover bank insolvencies and their regulation. Any in-depth examination of national insolvency or supranational bank resolution regimes deserves a book of its own. **1.41**

Fifth, and finally, this book does not delve into the matters of private international law, such as international jurisdiction, recognition of foreign insolvency proceedings and insolvency-related judgements, and communication and cooperation between courts and IPs. My choice to exclude these matters does not mean that they are less important or deserve less attention than those considered in this book. On the contrary, in other academic works, I have argued that the ability to deal with group financial distress in a centralised or well-coordinated manner is crucial to preserve and maximise enterprise value.[65] Furthermore, the effectiveness of some of the tools analysed in this book, like third-party releases and extended enforcement stays, hinges on their cross-border recognition. The decision to exclude private international law issues is dictated by the fact that they rest on or are supported by a distinct set of legal principles, categorised by Bork as 'jurisdictional principles'.[66] Among **1.42**

64 M. Haentjens and B. Wessels, Three Paradigm Shifts in Recent Bank Insolvency Law, Journal of International Banking Law and Regulation, Vol. 7, 2016, pp. 396–400.

65 See I. Kokorin, S. Madaus and I. Mevorach, Global Competition in Cross-Border Restructuring and Recognition of Centralized Group Solutions, Texas International Law Journal, Vol. 56, 2021, pp. 109–154; I. Kokorin and B. Wessels, Cross-Border Protocols in Insolvencies of Multinational Enterprise Groups, Edward Elgar Publishing, 2021; I. Kokorin, Contracting Around Insolvency Jurisdiction: Private Ordering in European Insolvency Jurisdiction Rules and Practices, in V. Lazić and S. Stuij (eds), Recasting the Insolvency Regulation: Improvements and Missed Opportunities, Asser Press, 2020, pp. 21–58.

66 R. Bork, Principles of Cross-Border Insolvency Law, Intersentia, 2017.

them are the principles of unity, universalism, mutual trust, cooperation and communication. Given the book's focus on substantive national law, for the purpose of maintaining coherence, I have decided to exclude private international law matters from its scope.

1.43 This book has several aims.

First, it aims to *restate, compare and explain* insolvency law as applied to intra-group financial arrangements. 'Restating' the law involves describing legal rules; 'comparing' the law entails comparing legal rules in different jurisdictions; 'explaining' the law refers to examining the legal principles and objectives underpinning these rules. All three aims are free from any evaluative judgements. There is an increasing number of studies that describe the problems characteristic of group insolvencies and the rules established to address them.[67] This book draws on these studies. It classifies different types of groups, outlines relevant legal principles, studies their manifestation in group insolvencies, examines common intra-group financial arrangements, and investigates their treatment in the insolvency laws of the UK, the USA and the Netherlands. Achieving these 'descriptive' aims should deepen our understanding of the law as it currently stands, forming a necessary foundation for the book's second category of aims.[68]

1.44 Second, the book aims to *evaluate* and *normatively assess* the law in the given context. These aims could be termed 'normative', as they seek to evaluate the current state of the law and make general suggestions or recommendations. These suggestions and recommendations are not directed at any specific legislator or jurisdiction; rather, they offer overarching guidance from a supra-national perspective, which may help shape or enhance national laws or international soft law instruments, such as the UNCITRAL legislative guides on insolvency law. Through these normative aims, the book aspires to contribute to the advancement and improvement of insolvency law across different legal systems.

---

67 C. Thole and M. Dueñas, Some Observations on the New Group Coordination Procedure of the Reformed European Insolvency Regulation, International Insolvency Review, Vol. 24, 2015, pp. 214-227; A. de Soveral Martins, Groups of Companies in the Recast European Insolvency Regulation: Around and about the 'Group', International Insolvency Review, Vol. 28, 2019, pp. 354-362; T. Kostoula, Cross-Border Insolvency of Groups of Companies Under the Regulation (EU) 2015/848, European Company Law, Vol. 16, 2019, pp. 74-82; D. Zhang, Preventive Restructuring Frameworks: A Possible Solution for Financially Distressed Multinational Corporate Groups in the EU, EBOR, Vol. 20, 2019, pp. 285-318.

68 S. Smith, Contract Theory, OUP, 2004, p. 5, noting that '[b]efore attempting to reform the law, reformers must understand the law that they are planning to reform. Indeed, once the theoretical foundations of the law are understood, it is usually a short step to suggesting reforms of that law.'

1.3 ORGANISATION OF THIS BOOK

This book is divided into six parts. **1.45**

Part I. 'Introduction' comprises the present chapter. It introduces the reader to the subject, aims and scope of this book. Additionally, it sets the scene by describing three 'benchmark' insolvency cases: Lehman Brothers, Nortel Networks and Oi Brazil. These cases exemplify the problems and complexities created by intra-group financing in insolvency.

Part II. 'Enterprise groups: their life and death' introduces groups of companies. It presents a descriptive account of what defines a group, elucidates its common characteristics and various types. It shares some historical insights into the emergence of modern multinational enterprise groups. This part is integral to the book's overall thesis, setting the stage for further discussions and helping readers better understand the issues associated with group economic and legal structures. **1.46**

Part III. 'Principles of insolvency law and how to balance them' builds a theoretical foundation for analysing intra-group financial arrangements and enterprise group insolvency. It identifies legal principles that are most relevant in the context of group insolvency. It notes that in many cases, these principles conflict with each other and explores ways to resolve conflicts between legal principles. **1.47**

Part IV. 'Intra-group financing and insolvency: transactions and problems' is one of the core parts of this book. It serves a dual purpose. First, it describes the financial arrangements commonly found in corporate groups, including intercompany guarantees, co-debtorship, intra-group loans and centralised cash management. Second, it analyses the benefits of intra-group financing and underscores the problems that this financing and the applicable rules can pose for efficient group insolvency and restructuring. **1.48**

Part V. 'Group sensitive insolvency law: tools and solutions' analyses potential solutions to the problems arising from or related to intra-group financing for the efficient resolution of financial distress within enterprise groups. It explores various legal tools that have emerged in response to the economic reality of groups and their typical failure patterns. These tools include third-party releases and extended enforcement stays. The discussed tools embrace the so-called 'extension effect'. The aim of this part – and indeed the entire **1.49**

book – is to develop suggestions on how the law can address the challenges of intra-group financing and group insolvencies in a principled way.

1.50 **Part VI**. 'Conclusion' summarises the key findings of this book and offers final observations and reflections.

PART II

ENTERPRISE GROUPS: THEIR LIFE AND DEATH

2

PHENOMENON AND RISE OF MULTINATIONAL ENTERPRISE GROUPS

2.1 INTRODUCTION

2.01 This chapter introduces multinational enterprise groups – the key actors explored in this book. Various theories, such as network theory and agency theory, attempt to explain the emergence and dominance of these groups. A group structure can be viewed as a response to a negative outside environment (e.g. underdeveloped external markets) and as a driver of economic growth and wealth accumulation (e.g. improved risk management, reduced transaction costs and efficient resource allocation).[1] This chapter does not aim to address all factors contributing to the rise of enterprise groups. My focus is primarily legal, with some historical and economic insights.

2.02 Section 2.2 examines the emergence of groups of companies as a method of organising and conducting business, noting that what we now recognise as an 'enterprise group' is a relatively recent invention. It should be distinguished from other related but separate phenomena, such as: (i) legal personhood – the recognition of a legal personality separate from its shareholders; (ii) limited liability – the protection of shareholders' assets from the company's creditors;

1 For an overview of value-creation-based explanations for the existence of a group organisational form, see L. Enriques and S. Gilotta, The Case Against a Special Regime for Intragroup Transactions, ECGI Law Working Paper No. 641/2022, May 2022, pp. 11–15; G.G. Triantis, Organizations as Internal Capital Markets: The Legal Boundaries of Firms, Collateral, and Trusts in Commercial and Charitable Enterprises, Harvard Law Review, Vol. 117, 2004, p. 1112, observing that '[i]nternal capital markets play a greater role in capital reallocation when external capital markets are less developed and when significant information asymmetry impedes external finance'.

and (iii) entity shielding – the protection of the company's assets from the shareholders' creditors. Section 2.3 addresses the definition of an enterprise group and underlines its most common defining elements. Section 2.4 investigates the various characteristics and types of enterprise groups, while section 2.5 analyses possible reasons why a group structure has become one of the most prevalent forms of a business organisation. Section 2.6 concludes.

2.2 HISTORY AND LEGAL FOUNDATIONS OF ENTERPRISE GROUPS

It is difficult, and perhaps even impossible, to pinpoint the exact date when enterprise groups came into existence. Early precursors of business groups can be found in the way the Medici empire was set up in the fifteenth and sixteenth centuries. The Medici family ruled Florence from the 1430s to 1530s. Its businesses included banking, textile manufacturing and trade across Europe. The Medici empire was organised as a system of partnerships, with a senior partnership based in Florence. The senior partnership held a controlling interest in junior partnerships and entered into separate agreements with junior partners who took charge of the local operations and received a share of profits. Commenting on this structure, De Roover observed: 'There are consequently two layers: a controlling partnership – the parent – and several tributary partnerships – the subsidiaries. Only this subspecies prefigures the modern holding company.'[2] **2.03**

However, the Medici enterprise was not a corporate group with separate group companies fully protected by the entity shields. De Roover describes a lawsuit heard before the court in Bruges in 1453.[3] It was brought against the acting manager of the Medici partnership in Bruges for defective packing of nine bales of wool purchased by the plaintiff from the London branch. The plaintiff argued that 'the Medici branch in Bruges and the one in London were all one company and had the same master'.[4] The court dismissed the claim, ruling that the London partnership should first take responsibility. Yet, the plaintiff's right to sue the Bruges partnership was preserved. This case demonstrated what Hansmann et al. refer to as 'weak entity shielding'[5] and 'location-based entity shielding'.[6] Nevertheless, in many aspects (e.g. a common brand – in **2.04**

2 R. De Roover, The Rise and Decline of the Medici Bank, 1397-1494, HUP, 1963, p. 77.
3 R. De Roover, The Medici Bank: Organization and Management, The Journal of Economic History, Vol. 6, 1946, p. 31.
4 Ibid.
5 H. Hansmann, R. Kraakman and R. Squire, Law and the Rise of the Firm, Harvard Law Review, Vol. 119, 2006, p. 1366.
6 Ibid., p. 1368.

this case, the good name of the Medici, control from 'headquarters'), the partnership-based system resembles modern-day multinationals.

2.05 Some authors trace the genesis of modern multinational enterprises to the colonial trading companies of the seventeenth century – the Dutch East India Company (*Vereenigde Oostindische Compagnie* or VOC) and the English East India Company (EIC).[7] Both companies engaged in long-distance oceanic trade and combined the idea of separate legal personhood with joint-stock investment financing. Separate legal personality meant that these companies had their own distinct pools of assets and could enter into transactions on their own behalf.[8] They could own land, litigate in court and hold franchises. Additionally, these companies manifested a feature of 'shareholder lock-in', meaning that shareholders could not redeem their shares (i.e. withdraw their initial contribution) at will. This laid down 'the foundation for durable asset pools that could grow and produce wealth indefinitely …'[9] Still, shareholders could sell their shares on the vibrant secondary market that ensured liquidity for the locked-in capital. Secondary markets in shares were booming.

2.06 Notably, separate legal personality and shareholder lock-in did not signal the existence of either limited liability or a group structure. It remains debated whether early business corporations embraced the concept of limited liability. Gelderblom et al. argue that the VOC had transferable shares and limited liability for shareholders from the outset.[10] Harris, however, challenges this view and emphasises that the Dutch East India Company had two classes

---

7 A.M. Carlos and S. Nicholas, 'Giants of an Earlier Capitalism': The Chartered Trading Companies as Modern Multinationals, The Business History Review, Vol. 62, 1988, pp. 398–419.

8 The corporate form was originally, up until the sixteenth century, employed for public and semi-public purposes (e.g. municipalities, monasteries) and only a partnership served as a viable form for organising business affairs. R. Harris, Industrializing English Law: Entrepreneurship and Business Organization, 1720–1844, CUP, 2000, p. 21. See also D. Graeber, Debt: The First 5,000 Years, Melville House Publishing, 2011, p. 304, noting that the 'legal idea of a corporation as a "fictive" person … was first established in canon law by Pope Innocent IV in 1250 AD, and one of the first kinds of entities it applied to were monasteries – as also to universities, churches, municipalities, and guilds'.

9 K. Pistor, The Code of Capital: How the Law Creates Wealth and Inequality, Princeton University Press, 2019, p. 66. The lock-in capital feature was first applied in the VOC and only later in the EIC. This is believed to be one of the reasons why the VOC outperformed the EIC for a number of decades. See G. Dari-Mattiacci, O. Gelderblom, J. Jonker and E.C. Perotti, The Emergence of the Corporate Form, The Journal of Law, Economics, and Organization, Vol. 33, 2017, p. 196.

10 O. Gelderblom, A. de Jong and J. Jonker, The Formative Years of the Modern Corporation: The Dutch East India Company VOC, 1602–1623, The Journal of Economic History, Vol. 73, 2013, p. 1051; M. Prak and J.L. van Zanden, Pioneers of Capitalism, Princeton University Press, 2022, p. 122, claiming that the VOC 'exemplified the new capitalism that was taking shape around 1600 … For the first time, we see the limited liability company emerging as a new business entity, the trading of company shares, speculation in these shares on a stock exchange, conflicts between shareholders and management over the policy of the new company – all rooted in the "modern" separation between ownership and management of a company.'

of shareholders – passive shareholders (*participanten*) and active shareholders (*bewindhebbers*). According to Harris, while the liability regime of the former was not defined in the charter or elsewhere, the latter assumed personal liability.[11] There is no need to take sides in this debate. More importantly, even though the early intercontinental trading companies had complex governance structures, they were not truly groups of companies in the modern sense. Instead, most shareholders were merchants and regular citizens.[12] The recognition of a company as a legal person with transferable shares, being the foundation of 'entity law', was not necessarily the basis of 'group law'.

The emergence of webs of companies linked through control or significant ownership – enterprise groups – occurred after the recognition of legal personhood and following the crystallisation, if not the universal acceptance, of the idea of limited liability.[13] Many historians and economists consider that modern multinational enterprises developed in the mid- to late nineteenth century.[14] This period was marked by the advent of new industrial technologies, improvements in manufacturing and management processes, and the international division of production. It was also a time when corporate laws in several jurisdictions were liberalised. A key feature of this liberalisation was the right of legal persons (companies) to own shares in other legal persons, a development essential for the creation of multi-layered group structures. **2.07**

---

11 R. Harris, A new understanding of the history of limited liability: an invitation for theoretical reframing, Journal of Institutional Economics, Vol. 16, 2020, p. 646. Harris identifies three historical periods in the formation of limited liability, and states that limited liability, in its present-day sense, became a uniform attribute of corporations only in the twentieth century. He attributes this development to the establishment of corporate insolvency and liquidation procedures and the proliferation of debt finance. Interestingly, Harris notes that limited liability was not a prerequisite for economic growth or for the expansion of large businesses in the modern period of history.

12 P. Frentrop, The Dutch East India Company: the first corporate governance debacle, in T. Clarke, J. O'Brien and C.R.T. O'Kelley (eds), The Oxford Handbook of the Corporation, OUP, 2019, pp. 51–74.

13 For the history of limited liability, see S.M. Bainbridge and M.T. Henderson, Limited Liability: A Legal and Economic Analysis, Edward Elgar Publishing, 2016, observing that limited liability has ancient roots (the Roman legal device *peculium*), that it surfaced in the Middle Ages in the form of *commenda*, where passive investors enjoyed limited liability, and that it became more institutionalised in the nineteenth century (e.g. *société anonyme* under the Napoleonic *Code de Commerce* of 1807; the UK's Limited Liability Act of 1855 and the Joint Stock Companies Act of 1856; New York Act of 22 March 1811).

14 M. Wilkins, The History of the Multinational Enterprise, in A.M. Rugman (ed), The Oxford Handbook of International Business, 2nd edn, OUP, 2009, p. 16, arguing that the modern multinational firm is a 'post-industrial revolution phenomenon' and that '[o]nly with steamships, railroads, and cables was it possible for managers to exercise control over business operations across borders in a meaningful manner'. Also M. Wilkins, The Emergence of Multinational Enterprise: American Business Abroad from the Colonial Era to 1914, HUP, 1970; L. Franko, The European Multinationals: A Renewed Challenge to American and British Big Business, Harper and Row, 1976. For a comprehensive study of business groups in the developed economies of the West, see A.M. Colpan and T. Hikino (eds), Business Groups in the West: Origins, Evolution, and Resilience, OUP, 2018, p. 3, observing that '[b]usiness groups actually rose to function as a critical factor of industrial dynamics in the context of the Second Industrial Revolution in the late nineteenth century'.

2.08 For contemporary lawyers, it may seem self-evident that companies can create other companies, acquire and own shares in them. However, this has not always been the case. Describing the American experience, Blumberg observes that '[i]n the absence of an express provision in the statute or charter, it was settled that acquisition by one corporation of another corporation's shares was *ultra vires*'.[15] In the USA, New Jersey was one of the first states to amend its corporation laws in 1888–1893 to allow corporate ownership of shares. Other states followed suit, though by 1910 only thirteen of them had similar laws.[16] Gradually, intercorporate stockholding became widely recognised, giving rise to groups of companies that expanded their operations nationally and internationally.[17] Most of these groups had a pyramidal structure. The building of corporate pyramids was driven by state policies, with many states requiring local chartering of regulated industries, including insurance, banking, and utility companies. The incorporation of local subsidiaries became a pathway to circumvent the states' protectionist requirements.[18]

2.09 Corporate ownership of shares in another company was a late arrival in the UK too. Historically, it was believed that a company, as an artificial person, lacked the legal capacity to own shares. This changed in the mid-nineteenth century when the power of intercompany stock ownership was attributed to the provisions of memoranda of association, despite the lack of express recognition of such power in incorporation statutes. English courts held in the 1860s that neither common law nor the Companies Act of 1862 prohibited companies from acquiring and owning shares in other companies, provided the memorandum of association permitted it.[19] However, it was not until the 1890s that corporate groups began to take shape in the UK. This development was largely linked to merger activity aimed at reducing competition and increasing prices. Unlike their US counterparts, these early groups were 'more

---

15 P. Blumberg, Limited Liability and Corporate Groups, The Journal of Corporation Law, Vol. 11, 1986, p. 606. Note that such special legislative enactment or charter provision was virtually never granted to manufacturing companies.

16 F. Freedland, History of Holding Company Legislation in New York State: Some Doubts as to the 'New Jersey First' Tradition, Fordham Law Review, Vol. 24, 1955, pp. 369–411.

17 M.J. Roe, Corporate Strategic Reaction to Mass Tort, Virginia Law Review, Vol. 72, 1986, p. 47, arguing that '[a]uthority to own subsidiaries was a device to facilitate molding the disparate local companies into a nationwide enterprise'.

18 M. Pargendler, The Grip of Nationalism on Corporate Law, Indiana Law Journal, Vol. 95, 2020, p. 566.

19 *In re Barned's Banking Company* (1867) 3 LR Ch 105, 112–13; *Re Asiatic Banking Corporation* (1868–69) LR 4 Ch App 252 at 257; *The Gramophone and Typewriter Ltd v. Stanley* [1908] 2 KB 89, affd *The Gramophone and Typewriter Ltd v. Stanley* [1906] 2 KB 856. C. Witting, Liability of Corporate Groups and Networks, CUP, 2018, pp. 65–66.

in the nature of loose federations than integrated corporations'.[20] It was during the 1920s and 1930s that corporate groups entered 'the conscious jurisprudence of UK company law'.[21]

As for continental Europe, there seems to have been no general prohibition of intercorporate stockholding. As a result, various group structures took shape.[22] Commenting on the German experience, Van Oostrum notes that the growing economic concentration and power of group enterprises in the mid- and late nineteenth century prompted the crystallisation of group law.[23] A group structure was utilised by Siemens, Europe's leading producer of telegraphic equipment, which diversified its production by setting up subsidiaries for different lines of business (e.g. electro-chemicals, telephone equipment, fertilisers) and building joint ventures like Telefunken, created to develop wireless telegraphy.[24] However, the proliferation of group structures in Germany occurred only in the 1920s, during the period of the Weimar Republic. At that time, the number of stock corporations (AGs) rose explosively, indicating an increase in the number of corporate groups.[25] Kuntz confirms that corporations actively invested in shares, 'building groups or at least holdings of large blocks of stock'.[26] The first definition of a group in German company law appeared in 1937,[27] while the standalone regulation of groups – the well-known *Konzernrecht* – was introduced in 1965.[28] **2.10**

The industrial revolution prompted the development of enterprise groups in the Netherlands. While some business groups trace their origin to the late nineteenth century, the majority of companies at that time remained small-scale **2.11**

20 P. Lipton, The Mythology of Salomon's Case and the Law Dealing with the Tort Liabilities of Corporate Groups: An Historical Perspective, Monash University Law Review, Vol. 40, 2014, p. 475.

21 I. Mevorach, Insolvency within Multinational Enterprise Groups, OUP, 2009, p. 11, referring to T. Hadden, Inside Corporate Groups, International Journal of the Sociology of Law, Vol. 12, 1984, pp. 271-286.

22 T. Hadden, Regulating Corporate Groups: An International Perspective, in J. McCahery, S. Picciotto and C. Scott (eds), Corporate Control and Accountability, Oxford: Clarendon Press, 1993, p. 343 and pp. 350-351.

23 C.H.A. van Oostrum, Regres bij concernfinanciering (Serie Van der Heijden Instituut nr. 156) (diss. Leiden), Deventer: Wolters Kluwer, 2019, p. 232.

24 A.D. Chandler, Scale and Scope: The Dynamics of Industrial Capitalism, HUP, 1994, p. 466.

25 F. Hoffmann, Konzernhandbuch, Wiesbaden: Gabler, 1993, p. 61.

26 T. Kuntz, German Corporate law in the 20th Century, in H. Wells (ed), Research Handbook on the History of Corporate and Company Law, Edward Elgar Publishing, 2018, p. 207.

27 *Gesetz über Aktiengesellschaften und Kommanditgesellschaften auf Aktien*, 1937, § 15(1).

28 The adoption of the Stock Corporation Act (*Aktiengesetz*), dealing with stock corporations (*Aktiengesellschaft*). A. Scheuch, *Konzernrecht*: An Overview of the German Regulation of Corporate Groups and Resulting Liability Issues, European Company Law, Vol. 13, 2016, pp. 191-198.

and family-owned.[29] The early twentieth century saw a spike in merger activity, giving rise to famous names. For example, in 1929, Dutch Margarine Union merged with the British soap manufacturer Lever Company to form Unilever Group (Unilever). Until 2020, Unilever had a dual-parent holding company structure with Unilever Plc (the UK) and Unilever N.V. (the Netherlands).[30] In 1890, a number of Dutch entrepreneurs founded the Royal Dutch Petroleum Company, which focused on the sale of petroleum in East Asian markets. This company merged with British Shell Transport and Trading Company Limited in 1907 – a move dictated by competition with American Standard Oil. Until recently, Shell had a dual nationality and organisational structure. In 2005, its shareholders supported the unification of Shell's Dutch and UK parent companies under a single parent company, Royal Dutch Shell plc.

2.12 The history of enterprise groups is closely interwoven with economic and political history.[31] This is because group operations are often international and dependent on political processes. They are also affected by technological inventions and market developments. The rise of modern groups in Europe and the USA dates back to the late nineteenth and early twentieth centuries. This was the time of the expansion of foreign direct investment and the establishment of cross-border operations. Technological progress, including the invention of the telegraph and the telephone, promoted the integration and centralisation of group structures.[32] Skeel notes that America's first large-scale business enterprises, the railroads, brought many units carrying on different types of economic activities under their control and adopted hierarchical business structures, 'with a class of middle managers between the railroad's

29 For a study of Dutch business groups in 1903–2003, see F. De Goey and A. De Jong, The Netherlands: The Overlooked Variety of Big Businesses, in A.M. Colpan and T. Hikino (eds), Business Groups in the West: Origins, Evolution, and Resilience, OUP, 2018, pp. 165–192.

30 For background and reasons for the unification, see Form F-3 Registration Statement under the Securities Act of 1933 <https://www.sec.gov/Archives/edgar/data/110390/000110465920094571/tm2027199-1_f3asr.htm> (accessed 10 October 2024).

31 For a study of multinational enterprises, see P. Muchlinski, Multinational Enterprises and the Law, 2nd edn, OUP, 2007 and P. Muchlinski, Multinational Enterprises and the Law, 3d edn, OUP, 2021. Note that the term 'multinational enterprise' as used by Muchlinski, is broad and does not entail a specific form of a corporate structure or the juridical form of an enterprise. This is why it should be distinguished from an enterprise group – a term that implies a certain pattern of ownership and control.

32 Before the nineteenth century, enterprises were largely organisationally decentralised. This was the case with the EIC, whose multi-divisional nature – a separation of powers between the board of directors and relatively independent overseas managers (factors), was highlighted in a number of studies. See E. Erikson, Between Monopoly and Free Trade: The English East India Company, Princeton University Press, 2014; G.M. Anderson, R.E. McCormick and R.D. Tollison, The economic organisation of the English East India Company, Journal of Economic Behavior and Organization, Vol. 4, 1983, p. 226, noting that the 'Central Office was too far removed from the Indies to do much more than endorse decisions already made by its chief factors or to sanction decisions of which it disapproved'.

workers and its executive officers'.[33] Hadfield describes this 'old' economy as the 'economy of consolidation and vertical integration, the absorption of economic activity in entire industries within the walls of a handful of, maybe even a single, corporation'.[34] According to Hadfield, this is the 'world of General Motors, U.S. Steel, AT&T, and, eventually, IBM'.[35]

The 1990s witnessed the deepening of global production and supply chains, a shift from raw materials and manufacturing towards the service economy and the liberalisation of trade and investment regimes. Interestingly, unlike the technological advancements of the nineteenth century, the current technological progress pulls in the opposite direction by instilling decentralisation.[36] The ease with which information is accessed and disseminated across the globe simplifies access to corporate decision-making and corporate ownership. Another 'decentralising' factor arises from the operation of platform-based businesses and their asset base. Baird points out that, '[f]ew businesses today center around specialized long-lived assets. In a service-oriented economy, the assets walk out the door at 5:00 pm.'[37] One might argue that 'assets-light' and platform-based businesses have fewer incentives to adopt hierarchical or pyramidal corporate structures that prevailed over the twentieth century. Decentralisation is further promoted by the advent of distributed ledger technology, including blockchain, which empowers the creation of decentralised autonomous organisations (DAOs).[38] This may boost new models of industrial and legal organisation. 2.13

33 D.A. Skeel, Icarus in the Boardroom: The Fundamental Flaws in Corporate America and Where They Came From, OUP, 2005, p. 25.

34 G. Hadfield, Legal Infrastructure and the New Economy, I/S: A Journal of Law and Policy for the Information Society, Vol. 8, 2012, p. 12.

35 Ibid.

36 M.J. Roe, Three Ages of Bankruptcy, Harvard Business Law Review, Vol. 7, 2017, p. 215, suggesting that while collective bankruptcy proceedings are needed for industries comprised of big, vertically integrated firms, they may lose appeal in the case of decentralised organisational structures.

37 D.G. Baird, The New Face of Chapter 11, American Bankruptcy Institute Law Review, Vol. 12, 2004, p. 82.

38 See I. Kokorin, Contracting Around Insolvency Jurisdiction: Private Ordering in European Insolvency Jurisdiction Rules and Practices, in V. Lazic and S. Stuij (eds.), Recasting the Insolvency Regulation: Improvements and Missed Opportunities. Short Studies in Private International Law, Asser Press, 2020, pp. 35–40. For rather sceptical views on whether blockchain is capable of transforming the corporate form, see K.F.K. Low, E. Schuster and W.Y. Wan, The company and blockchain technology, in M. Petrin and C. Witting (eds), Research Handbook on Corporate Liability (Edward Elgar Publishing 2023). On intersection of DAOs and bankruptcy law, see R. Levin, Bankrupting the Matrix: DAOs and the Code, Emory Bankruptcy Developments Journal, Vol. 40, 2024, pp. 455–510.

2.3 DEFINING AN ENTERPRISE GROUP

2.14 Despite the proliferation of multinational enterprise groups and the significant economic power they hold today, there is no universal legal definition of an enterprise group.[39] For instance, Dutch law adopts an approach that embraces the economic reality of groups of companies. Under the Dutch Civil Code (*Burgerlijk Wetboek* or BW), a group is defined as 'an economic unit in which legal persons and partnerships are organisationally interconnected'.[40] It specifies that group entities are legal persons and partnerships connected to each other in one group.[41] From this definition, two criteria are relevant: (i) economic unity, and (ii) organisational connection.

2.15 'Economic unity' entails an economic bond between companies within the group. This may be observed in external communication, joint reporting, consolidated annual accounts, a common financial and economic policy, intra-group financing, and the dependence of group entities on each other. These characteristics serve as points of reference, and their absence does not necessarily mean that there is no economic unity.[42] 'Organisational connection' indicates a certain degree of integration within the group structure. This integration could take various forms and degrees, arising from capital participation, membership rights or an agreement that makes it possible to exercise control rights. From legislative history, the third element can be deduced – (iii) centralised management (*centrale leiding*).[43] In practice, there can be varying degrees of such centralised direction and the autonomy of individual group companies. Yet this element suggests the existence of some central decision-making on a joint strategy and hierarchy between group members, making it possible to implement a common group strategy.[44] A necessary complement of, but not the only requirement for, central management is that it must be able

---

39 On the problem of defining a corporate group, see S. Pepels, Defining Groups of Companies under the European Insolvency Regulation (recast): On the Scope of EU Group Insolvency Law, International Insolvency Review, Vol. 30, 2021, pp. 96–123.

40 Dutch Civil Code, Article 2:24b.

41 Ibid. Foreign legal entities can also form part of a group.

42 J. van der Kraan, Toepassing en rechtskarakter van de groepsvrijstelling van artikel 2:403 BW (Serie Van der Heijden Instituut nr. 171), Deventer: Wolters Kluwer, 2022, 3.3.2.

43 *Kamerstukken II* 1979/80, 16 326, nr. 3, MvT, p. 42, noting that the bond between group members would usually find expression in capital participation, 'in view of the control required to act as a unit, this participation will generally be a – direct or indirect – majority shareholding; 50% and minority shareholdings will only lead to group membership if the shareholding is reinforced with special rights, otherwise the participating company will not be able to continue its leadership with a decisive vote'. *Kamerstukken II* 1987/88 19 813, nr. 5, MvA, punt 14, zie voorts art. 2:406, aant. 2.1. Since 2005, the concept of central management can be found in a closely related provision concerning consolidated annual accounts (Article 2:406 BW).

44 Asser/Kroeze 2-I 2021/261.

to be 'imposed', if necessary, against the will of the directors of subordinate companies.[45]

There is a connection between these three criteria. After all, economic unity presupposes a certain organisational connection that is established under central leadership.[46] This is why it is argued that companies connected through a franchise agreement may not constitute a group, since both central management and economic unity could be weak or absent. In most cases, the franchisor is not responsible for and does not take a share in the business of its franchisees.[47] Equally, a pure investment company that holds shares in another company may not be associated with that company in a group, because the element of central management (planning, coordination and control of the policy of subsidiaries) might be missing.[48] **2.16**

The German Stock Corporation Act (*Aktiengesetz* or AktG) provides that 'where a controlling enterprise and one or several controlled enterprises are combined under the common management of the controlling enterprise, they form a group'.[49] The key element defining a group is therefore control, which is manifested in the ability to 'directly or indirectly exert controlling influence'.[50] Control exists if group members have entered into a control agreement (*Beherrschungsvertrag*) and is presumed if one legal entity holds the majority stake in another legal entity.[51] This is a situation of a vertical group, structured in a pyramidal hierarchical form. This group type is reflected in the definition of a corporate group given by Blumberg, according to which a group is an enterprise 'organized in the form of a dominant parent corporation with scores or hundreds of subservient sub-holding, subsidiary, and affiliated companies'.[52] The AktG also states that if 'legally separate enterprises are subject **2.17**

45 Ibid.

46 M. Olaerts, GS Rechtspersonen, commentaar op art. 2:24b BW.

47 S. Bartman, A. Dorresteijn and M. Olaerts, Van het Concern, Wolters Kluwer, 2020, 2.2.1.

48 Asser/Maeijer, Van Solinge & Nieuwe Weme 2-II* 2009/816.

49 Stock Corporation Act of 6 September 1965 (Federal Law Gazette I, p. 1089), § 18.

50 AktG, § 17(1). The Federal Court of Justice (*Bundesgerichtshof* or BGH) emphasised that 'controlling influence' should at least in part be conveyed by means of company law and not solely through economic links. BGH, Urteil vom 26-03-1984 - II ZR 171/83. On the regulation of corporate groups in German law, see A. Cahn and D.C. Donald, Comparative Company Law: Text and Cases on the Laws Governing Corporations in Germany, the UK and the USA, 2nd edn, CUP, 2018, pp. 834–840. The ability to exercise the dominant influence over another undertaking characterises a parent undertaking for the purposes of prudential supervision and accounting under EU banking legislation. See e.g. Article 4(15) of the Regulation (EU) No 575/2013 of the European Parliament and of the Council of 26 June 2013 on prudential requirements for credit institutions and investment firms (CRR).

51 AktG, § 17(2). Also, A. Scheuch, Konzernrecht: An Overview of the German Regulation of Corporate Groups and Resulting Liability Issues, European Company Law, Vol. 13, 2016, pp. 191–198.

52 P. Blumberg, The Transformation of Modern Corporation Law: The Law of Corporate Groups, Connecticut Law Review, Vol. 37, 2005, p. 606, noting that group enterprises 'typically conduct a single

to common direction, although none of such enterprises controls the other, such enterprises shall constitute a group and the individual enterprises shall constitute members of such group'.[53] This is the case of a horizontal or heterarchical group, in which legal entities could enjoy more autonomy, and the group as a whole may operate in a more decentralised fashion.[54]

2.18 The UK's Companies Act 2006 recognises two main types of corporate groups: (i) parent and subsidiary undertakings, relevant primarily for accounting purposes, and (ii) a holding company and its subsidiaries, used in other statutory contexts. For the first type, the law obliges parent companies, incorporated in the UK (with certain exceptions), to produce annual consolidated group accounts.[55] These group accounts should encompass subsidiary undertakings and give creditors and shareholders a clear picture of the group's performance. An undertaking is considered a parent undertaking if it holds a majority of voting rights in another undertaking (subsidiary), has a participating interest in that undertaking, and can appoint or remove the majority of its board members. Also, a parent and subsidiary undertaking relationship exists where a parent undertaking has the right to exercise dominant influence over the subsidiary, either by virtue of the provisions contained in the undertaking's articles or through a control contract (legal control),[56] or where it has the power to exercise or actually exercises dominant influence over a subsidiary (factual control).[57]

2.19 Outside the accounting context – for general purposes – the 'scope' of a group may often be relevant as well. For example, under English law, a subsidiary is prohibited from holding shares in its parent (holding) company.[58] The determination of a group can also be important in calculating various types of tax liability and even for commercial contractual construction.[59] The definition applicable for non-accounting purposes is largely similar (e.g. majority of voting rights, right to appoint or remove a majority of the board of directors),[60] but seems to be narrower. This is because the tests for the existence of a corporate

---

integrated enterprise under common control and often under a common public persona'.

53 AktG, § 18(2).

54 I. Mevorach, Insolvency within Multinational Enterprise Groups, OUP, 2009, p. 19.

55 Companies Act 2006, sections 399–402.

56 Companies Act 2006, section 1162(1), (2), (3). A control contract functions like German *Beherrschungsvertrag*.

57 Companies Act 2006, s. 1162(4).

58 Companies Act 2006, s. 136.

59 *Enviroco Ltd v. Farstad Supply A/S* [2011] 1 WLR 921. The case concerned interpretation of an indemnity clause, which covered 'affiliates', being defined by reference to a 'subsidiary' under the Companies Act 1985.

60 Companies Act 2006, s. 1159.

group based on legal and factual control do not apply with respect to the second type of corporate groups.[61]

So far, the overview of laws addressing the concept of a group has touched upon commercial, company or accounting legislation. The definition of an enterprise group can also be found in insolvency-specific rules, even though these rules are rare. The EIR Recast defines a 'group of companies' as a 'parent undertaking and all its subsidiary undertakings',[62] where the 'parent undertaking' means 'an undertaking which controls, either directly or indirectly, one or more subsidiary undertakings'.[63] In a similar, inclusive manner, the BRRD and the SRMR define a group as a 'parent undertaking and its subsidiaries'.[64] The MLEGI refers to 'two or more enterprises that are interconnected by control or significant ownership',[65] with control being the 'capacity to determine, directly or indirectly the operating and financial policies of an enterprise'.[66] **2.20**

In sum, a 'group' does not have a single definition and may even be defined differently in the same jurisdiction, depending on the purpose and relevant area of regulation (tax, accounting, competition, company, insolvency). That said, control and share ownership often determine the existence of a corporate group. However, the degree of autonomy within an enterprise and the strength and significance of centralised direction or a group-wide strategy may vary from one group to another. Limiting the definition of an enterprise group to a particular degree of control or stockholding, whether direct or indirect, or a specified percentage of capital or votes may be counterproductive. It inevitably creates a mismatch between legal and economic reality, allows some groups to avoid legal consequences, and deprives other groups of many benefits and tools available under insolvency law.[67] A more inclusive approach is therefore appropriate. The adoption of this approach does not mean that all groups should be treated in the same way. Quite the opposite. **2.21**

61 E. Ferran and L.C. Ho, Principles of Corporate Finance Law, 2nd edn, OUP, 2014, p. 26; R. Valsan, National Report on the United Kingdom, in R.M. Manóvil (ed), Groups of Companies: A Comparative Law Overview, Springer, 2020, p. 631.

62 EIR Recast, Article 2(13).

63 EIR Recast, Article 2(14).

64 BRRD, Article 2(26); Regulation (EU) No. 806/2014 of 15 July 2014 establishing uniform rules and a uniform procedure for the resolution of credit institutions and certain investment firms in the framework of a Single Resolution Mechanism and a Single Resolution Fund (SRMR), Article 3(23).

65 MLEGI, Article 2(b).

66 MLEGI, Article 2(c). Definitions of an 'enterprise group' and 'control' are derived from the UNCITRAL Legislative Guide, Part three.

67 Mevorach points out that 'narrowing the meaning of the term MEG *a priori* could be detrimental to a meaningful approach to [insolvencies within MEGs]'. See I. Mevorach, Insolvency within Multinational Enterprise Groups, OUP, 2009, p. 24.

2.4 CHARACTERISTICS AND TYPES OF ENTERPRISE GROUPS

2.22 Enterprise groups are distinct from each other.[68] Group structures have different shapes and sizes, ranging from colossal worldwide-operating multinationals, such as Lehman Brothers, Nortel Network, Royal Dutch Shell and Unilever, to groups consisting of a parent company and one subsidiary incorporated and operating in the same country. Enterprise groups diverge in terms of their corporate and operational structures, ways of group financing, management and ownership. They may consist of complex networks of wholly or partly owned subsidiaries, sub-subsidiaries and companies not linked by equity ownership but still closely related to or dependent on the business of an enterprise group (e.g. suppliers, distributors, franchisees).

2.23 Mevorach developed a comprehensive typology of multinational enterprise groups, depending on the degree of their integration/interdependence – to what extent the group operates as a single economic unit, and the level of control – how centralised control and decision-making are.[69] In terms of integration, a distinction is made between business integration, asset integration and no integration. As for patterns of control, group entities may be centrally controlled from a single or multiple 'heads' (centralised group),[70] enjoy certain autonomy but still be subject to direction or supervision by the parent company (decentralised group), or even lack a common head office (heterarchical group).

2.24 Some group enterprises are notable for running a single business. It is observed that a typical group 'is a single business firm organized as a collection of legal entities'.[71] The degree of integration can be determined by reference to a wide variety of factors reflecting the economic structure of the group (e.g. centralised administration of resources and intensity of intra-group transactions, handling

68 For a discussion of different types of groups (e.g. 'hierarchy type', comprising diversified business groups and pyramidal business groups vs. 'network-type' business groups, wherein individual entities maintain autonomy regarding strategic and budgetary decisions), see A.M. Colpan and T. Hikino (eds), Business Groups in the West: Origins, Evolution, and Resilience, OUP, 2018.

69 I. Mevorach, Insolvency within Multinational Enterprise Groups, OUP, 2009, pp. 135–47.

70 A good example of a corporate group with multiple parent companies was Unilever. Since its formation in 1930, Unilever was owned through two separately listed companies, Unilever Plc (UK) and Unilever NV (NL). It was agreed that the two holding companies would seek to operate as a single company, both administratively and economically. This was made possible over the years by a number of agreements entered into between the entities (Foundation Agreements) and by special provisions in their articles of association. The NV and PLC had the same directors and applied the same accounting policies. R. Abma, De mislukte unificatie van Unilever, Maandblad voor Ondernemingsrecht, n. 1–2, 2019, pp. 40–48. In 2020, Unilever unified its group legal structure under a single parent company, Unilever Plc.

71 H. Hansmann and R. Squire, External and Internal Asset Partitioning: Corporations and Their Subsidiaries, in J.N. Gordon and W-G. Ringe (eds), The Oxford Handbook of Corporate Law and Governance, OUP, 2018, p. 262.

of personnel), management of marketing (e.g. common trademarks and logos) and public image.[72] Integrated groups may have a vertical hierarchical structure, where a parent company owns, controls and directs its subsidiaries.[73] Such pyramid-like groups are typical for some European jurisdictions, such as Germany and Italy.[74] They also prevail among large US banks.[75]

Other groups consist of relatively self-sustaining, loosely connected business units, which are responsible for separate product or industry lines and can survive on their own. Some banking groups have chosen a decentralised corporate structure, organised according to a business segment, geographical presence or functions. A good example is HSBC, the largest UK bank. It is composed of separate operating banks active in different geographical markets. Notably, the critical shared infrastructure, services and systems are moved into a bankruptcy-remote group of separately capitalised non-bank service companies. This division is made to reduce operational dependencies across critical functions, jurisdictions and legal entities. **2.25**

The separability embedded within the structure of the HSBC Group corresponds to the chosen resolution strategy, the multiple point of entry (MPOE) model, which entails 'resolution of regional or national groups of affiliated companies',[76] as opposed to a resolution at a holding company level. This demonstrates how a regulatory (i.e. resolution) model could affect the way a banking group is internally organised, and the other way round (see Figure 2.1). **2.26**

While HSBC Group manifests a substantial degree of decentralisation, when it comes to global strategy, it is still centrally directed. Other enterprise groups may lack centralised control and hierarchical patterns and operate in a more heterarchical way, characterised by decentralised and flatter corporate networks with largely autonomous profit centres.[77] **2.27**

---

72 UNCITRAL Legislative Guide, Part three, Ch. I, para. 15.

73 Note that business integration and control patterns within a group do not always correlate in a specific way. Thus, centralised control does not necessarily lead to high business integration.

74 K.J. Hopt, Groups of companies: A Comparative Study of the Economics, Law, and Regulation of Corporate Groups, in J.N. Gordon and W-G. Ringe (eds), The Oxford Handbook of Corporate Law and Governance, OUP, 2018, p. 604.

75 J.N. Gordon and W-G. Ringe, Bank Resolution in the European Banking Union: A Transatlantic Perspective on What it Would Take, Columbia Law Review, Vol. 115, 2015, pp. 1297–1370.

76 HSBC Holdings Plc, SIFI Plan, Public Section, 17 December 2021, p. 2, noting that HSBC considered switching to a single point of entry (SPOE) model, but concluded that the MPOE is a preferred model, because it is 'consistent with the decentralized financial, operational and legal entity structure of the HSBC Group'. See further, Chapter 10.

77 P. Muchlinski, Multinational Enterprises and the Law, 3rd edn, OUP, 2021, p. 62, arguing that we may witness the 'gradual replacement of closely held subsidiaries with free-standing companies linked to the parent by contract'.

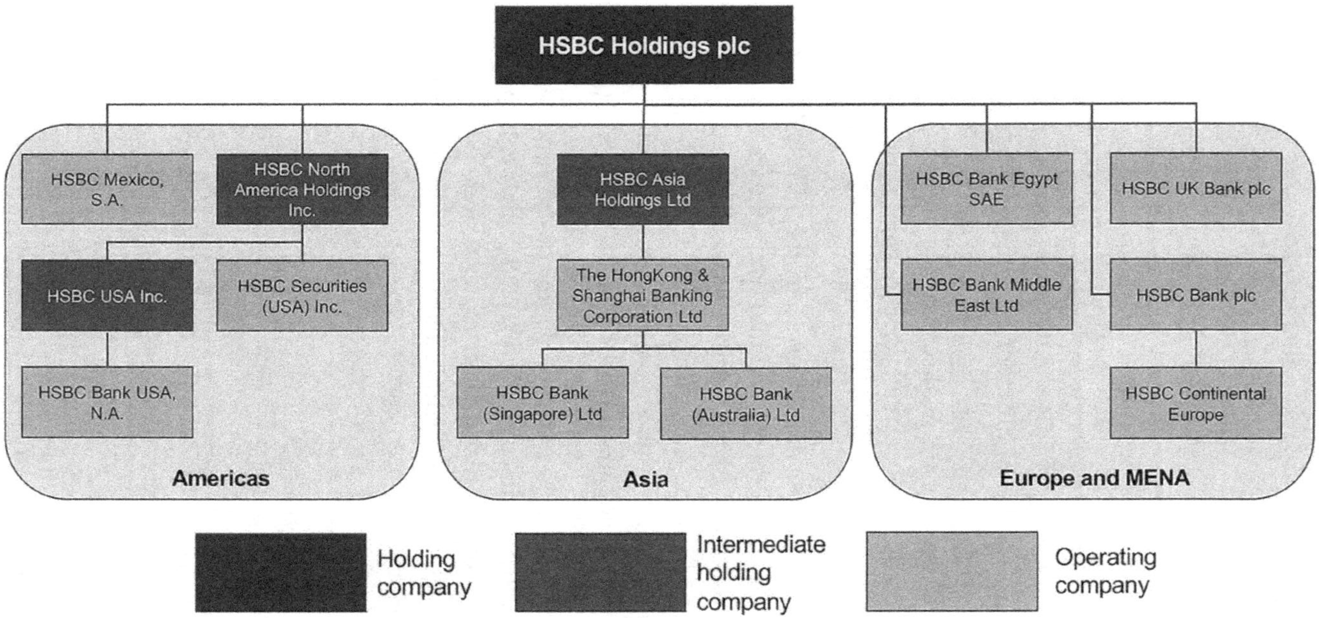

Note: This figure is based on the Simplified structure chart of the HSBC group of companies, available at <https://www.hsbc.com/investors/investing-in-hsbc/group-structure> (accessed 10 October 2024). Please note that this figure does not include all group entities and specifically excludes service companies, insurance companies and special purpose entities.

Figure 2.1 *Simplified HSBC Group structure (as of 24 April 2024)*

The diversity of corporate forms and structures complicates or makes impossible the adoption of a one-size-fits-all approach to their regulation, including regulation in situations of financial distress and insolvency. At the same time, it is important to emphasise that closely integrated groups – groups consisting of separate legal entities but operating as a single economic unit – deserve special attention in insolvency. The reason is, first, that the interests of group members may differentiate them from any legal entity that operates on its own in any market. Second, and consequently, in such groups, a failure of one group member may be triggered by the financial distress of other group members, while value can be preserved and maximised when a group is taken into account (see section 1.1.2, describing the global sale of Nortel's assets). Another reason for paying special attention to integrated groups is that the gradually emerging group-mindful insolvency law is particularly relevant to them.[78] **2.28**

2.5 RATIONALE BEHIND ENTERPRISE GROUPS

There are multiple financial, economic, operational, fiscal and other reasons for enterprises to operate through the establishment of separate legal entities. Underpinned by the principles of entity shielding and limited liability, the separation of a single enterprise into distinct legal entities can decrease exposure to risks arising from failures related to a particular geographical market (e.g. when a group is planning to enter a new untested market) or a business segment (e.g. when a certain activity can lead to significant environmental liability or is simply riskier).[79] Thus, entity separation within groups can pursue a 'protective' or risk-reduction function. **2.29**

78 EIR Recast, Articles 56(1), 57(1) and 58, mandating cooperation between IPs and courts in a group insolvency, but only 'to the extent that such cooperation is appropriate to facilitate the effective administration of those proceedings'. G. Moss, I. Fletcher and S. Isaacs (eds), Moss, Fletcher and Isaacs on the EU Regulation on Insolvency Proceedings, 3rd edn, OUP, 2016, para. 8.756, noting that '[i]n order to obtain full value of the sale of assets which span different legal entities, a co-operative approach is likely to be essential'. See also Singapore's Insolvency, Restructuring and Dissolution Act 2018 (IRDA), section 65(2), permitting the court to restrain commencement or continuation of any proceedings or enforcement actions against a related company (subsidiary or holding company), but only if such related company plays a 'necessary and integral role' in debtor's restructuring. See *Re IM Skaugen SE and other matters* [2019] 3 SLR 979; [2018] SGHC 259, at [63].

79 English courts accept that corporate risk compartmentalisation constitutes a legitimate use of the group structure. See *Adams v. Cape Industries plc* [1990] Ch 433. This, however, does not insulate parent companies from potential liability for actions of their subsidiaries on the principles of tort law. See *Lungowe v. Vedanta Resources plc* [2019] UKSC 20, and *Okpabi and others (Appellants) v. Royal Dutch Shell Plc and another (Respondents)* [2021] UKSC 3. On the advantages of group structures, see K.J. Hopt and K. Pistor, Company Groups in Transition Economies: A Case for Regulatory Intervention? European Business Law Review, Vol. 2, 2001, p. 13.

2.30 The 'protective' function is closely related to another function that can be referred to as the 'enabling' function. Bainbridge and Henderson argue that the division of an enterprise into separate entities allows businesses to 'benefit from efficiencies of specialization, avoid various market risks, and allocate and capture tax benefits such as depreciation'.[80] A layered corporate structure may enable the maximisation of financial returns. For example, a group can establish special entities responsible for raising funds on capital markets (SPVs), which can provide access to foreign investors and secure better financing terms (see section 1.1.3 regarding Oi Brazil).

2.31 The use of a group structure can also be driven by reasons of regulatory partitioning, defined by Pargendler as a 'separation between the legal spheres of the corporation and its members beyond the attribution of property rights over assets'.[81] Regulatory partitioning might be underpinned by fiscal considerations (tax allowances, tax exemptions for intra-group dividends, group relief).[82] It could also be mandated by specific regulatory requirements, such as those applicable to financial institutions.[83] Another example of regulation that prompts the creation of group structures and intra-group financial arrangements is Article 3:2 of the Dutch Act on Financial Supervision (*Wet op het financieel toezicht* or Wft). Under this article, no banking licence is required for a group finance company if, among other requirements, such a finance company on-lends or invests at least 95 per cent of its balance sheet total within the group, and its liabilities arising from bond issuance are unconditionally

80 S.M. Bainbridge and M.T. Henderson, Limited Liability: A Legal and Economic Analysis, Edward Elgar Publishing, 2016, p. 298.

81 M. Pargendler, Regulatory partitioning as a key function of corporate personality, in E. Pollman and R.B. Thompson (eds), Research Handbook on Corporate Purpose and Personhood, Edward Elgar Publishing, 2021, p. 264.

82 UNCITRAL Legislative Guide, Part three, Ch. I, para. 23; A.A. Berle Jr., The Theory of Enterprise Entity, Columbia Law Review, Vol. 47, 1947, p. 343; M. Sáez Lacave and M. Gutiérrez Urtiaga, Corporate Groups: Corporate Law, Private Contracting and Equal Ownership, ECGI Law Working Paper No. 581, 2021, p. 8, noting that the 'first reason why groups are valuable is that they offer the possibility to engage in regulatory arbitrage' and arguing that '[r]egulatory arbitrage can explain why many group structures are so complex and legally intractable'.

83 For instance, the UK's banking sector structural reform of 2019 mandated that core banking services (e.g. taking deposits, making payments and providing overdrafts for UK retail customers and small businesses) was made financially, operationally and organisationally separate from investment banking and international banking activities. Therefore, retail and investment banking should be provided by separate legal entities. For discussion and criticism of this strategy, see T. Wetzer, In Two Minds: The Governance of Ring-Fenced Banks, Journal of Corporate Law Studies, Vol. 19, 2019, pp. 197–249. In response to the GFC, the USA introduced the Volcker rule (§ 619 of the Dodd-Frank Act). It imposes the group-level restrictions on banks and prohibits groups which include FDIC-insured banks from engaging in proprietary trading. The Volcker rule is of structural nature and affects the internal structure of banking groups. See J.C. Coates IV, The Volcker Rule as structural law: implications for cost-benefit analysis and administrative law, Capital Markets Law Journal, Vol. 10, 2015, pp. 447–468.

guaranteed or otherwise secured by the parent company.[84] This is one of the reasons why, in the Lehman Brothers and Oi Brazil cases, bonds issued by Dutch SPVs were guaranteed by parent companies.

Complex group structures have also developed naturally as a result of acquisitions and joint ventures. Corporate expansions are often facilitated by the quest for monopoly gains, the search for synergies, strategies to neutralise potential competitors, and the pursuit of economies of size and scale.[85] In recent years, a prominent trend in the business world has been the surge in takeovers motivated by the pursuit of new technologies and expanded customer bases. This strategy has led to several high-profile tech acquisitions, including Microsoft's acquisitions of Skype (2011), LinkedIn (2016), GitHub (2018) and Activision Blizzard (2022); Google's acquisitions of YouTube (2006), Motorola (2012) and Fitbit (2021); and Facebook's acquisitions of Instagram (2012) and WhatsApp (2014). **2.32**

Whether driven by natural growth and expansion or by a deliberate attempt to insulate risk and gain regulatory benefits, modern enterprises predominantly exist as corporate groups. However, their existence would likely not have been feasible, or would have been significantly limited, without two fundamental doctrines: limited liability and entity shielding.[86] Limited liability insulates shareholders from the liability incurred by the company, in which they hold shares,[87] while entity shielding protects the company from personal claims against its shareholders.[88] Both doctrines are deeply ingrained in many legal traditions and corporate laws around the world.[89] Andenas and Wooldridge note that 'limited liability … has become a force driving the organization of large multi-company enterprises'.[90] That said, as noted above, limited liability does not constitute a necessary or indispensable characteristic of a legal entity or its economic prosperity. Indeed, history shows that the development **2.33**

84 W.A.K. Rank and W. van Spanje, Dutch Lehman jitters? Butterworths Journal of International Banking and Financial Law, February 2009, pp. 89–92.

85 O.E. Williamson, The Modern Corporation: Origins, Evolution, Attributes, Journal of Economic Literature, Vol. 19, 1981, pp. 1537–1568.

86 Hansmann and Kraakman refer to these doctrines as 'defensive asset partitioning' (protecting personal assets of shareholders from the company's creditors) and 'affirmative asset partitioning' (shielding the company's assets from the creditors of its shareholders and managers). See H. Hansmann and R. Kraakman, The Essential Role of Organizational Law, The Yale Law Review, Vol. 110, 2000, pp. 387–440.

87 H. Hansmann, R. Kraakman and R. Squire, Law and the Rise of the Firm, Harvard Law Review, Vol 119, 2006, p. 1333.

88 Ibid., p. 1337.

89 J. Armour, H. Hansmann and R. Kraakman, The Essential Elements of Corporate Law, ECGI Law Working Paper No. 134/2009, 2009, p. 10, observing that 'today limited liability has become a nearly universal feature of the corporate form'.

90 M. Andenas and F. Wooldridge, European Comparative Company Law, CUP, 2009, p. 829.

of limited liability and its entrenchment did not coincide with the recognition of legal personhood. Historically, early commercial firms may not have had the characteristic of limited liability. In many cases, the issue of shareholder liability did not arise at all, either due to an effective state guarantee, as in the case of the VOC, or because of the late arrival of insolvency statutes applicable to companies.[91] Without joining the ongoing discussion about the pros and cons of limited liability within enterprise groups, one explanation merits particular attention, given this book's focus on intra-group financing.

2.34 More than forty years ago, Posner suggested that the division of an enterprise into a bundle of formally separate but commonly owned and controlled entities should simplify risk assessment for creditors (i.e. evaluation of a borrower's creditworthiness), thereby reducing monitoring costs and lowering the cost of credit.[92] According to Posner, corporate division and limited liability aim to solve the problems of information and supervision. Instead of appraising the enterprise in its entirety, creditors need only assess the existing and expected assets and liabilities of a separate legal entity, which should arguably be cheaper. Paraphrasing the English poet John Donne, each group company is perceived to be 'an island entire of itself'. However, in practice, a clear-cut division of an enterprise into isolated islands of assets and liabilities does not occur and is therefore unrealistic.[93] In many groups, the internal organisation and partition are rather complex. Consequently, the monitoring costs for creditors may not be reduced, and the informational efficiency attributed to limited liability may be overstated. As will be demonstrated later in the book, various group liability arrangements (e.g. cross-guarantees, co-debtorship) exacerbate this problem by contractually perforating limited liability and creating bridges – channels for interdependence and contagion – between group 'islands'.

2.35 The principle of limited liability and the related principle of entity shielding are deeply ingrained in legal traditions, even though the degree of their assertion may vary from one jurisdiction to another[94] and from one area of law to

91 R. Harris, A new understanding of the history of limited liability: an invitation for theoretical reframing, Journal of Institutional Economics, Vol. 16, 2020, pp. 643–664; P. Wood, Corporate, Bank and Sovereign Insolvencies: Why the Difference? Business Law International, Vol. 22, 2021, p. 315, noting that '[h]istorically, the seeds of corporate bankruptcies germinated out of the bankruptcy of individuals, an area of law stretching back to the far past'.

92 R.A. Posner, The Rights of Creditors of Affiliated Corporations, University of Chicago Law Review, Vol. 43, 1975, pp. 499–526.

93 K. Ayotte and H. Hansmann, Legal Entities as Transferable Bundles of Contracts, Michigan Law Review, Vol. 111, 2013, p. 722, noting that the 'ambiguity of entity boundaries, therefore, may in fact raise creditor-monitoring costs in large corporate groups, not lower them'.

94 See with respect to Brazil, M. Pargendler, How Universal Is the Corporate Form? Reflections on the Dwindling of Corporate Attributes in Brazil, Columbia Journal of Transnational Law, Vol. 58, 2019,

another.[95] It is not our purpose to question the many benefits of limited liability, particularly for public companies with distributed shareholding[96] and for highly diversified or heterarchical groups, in which business and risk compartmentalisation develops naturally. But it is worth pointing out that for those groups operating an integrated business with 'perforating' intra-group liability arrangements, the rationale for limited liability is weaker.[97] Given that distinguishing the two situations is not easy, the policy of limited liability applies by default. Yet the strength of this policy and the policy of preserving separateness of assets and liabilities of group entities (asset partitioning) should not prevent legal responses that recognise the group reality without contravening these policies. Entity separateness does not mean entity insulation in law.

2.6 CONCLUSION

This chapter introduces the phenomenon of enterprise groups, highlighting that corporate groups arrived relatively late on the historical stage. This arrival post-dated the recognition and conceptualisation of the legal personhood attribute – a legal personality separate from its members. It also came after the idea of limited liability had crystallised, albeit not universally at the same time. The rapid rise of hierarchical groups coincided with the fast-paced industrial progress of the late nineteenth and early twentieth century, and the liberalisation of corporate laws in the UK and the USA. This liberalisation paved the way for intercorporate stockholding – a prerequisite for the emergence of a parent–subsidiary structure. Throughout the twentieth century, enterprise groups grew in size and complexity, becoming one of the predominant forms for organising business. 2.36

p. 4, pointing out that 'Brazilian law has eroded the most fundamental elements of the corporate form – namely, "capital lock-in" (or "entity shielding") and limited liability – with the effect that there is no longer a strong separation between the assets of Brazilian business corporations and their shareholders'. On the other side of the spectrum is the UK, where, since the House of Lords' decision in *Salomon v. A Salomon and Co Ltd* [1897] AC 22 (dealing with a one-man company), the 'principle of separate personality and the privilege of limited liability enjoy great force in English common law'. C. Gerner-Beuerle and M. Schillig, Comparative Company Law, OUP, 2019, p. 975.

95 K.E. Sørensen, Groups of Companies in the Case Law of the Court of Justice of the European Union, European Business Law Review, Vol. 27, 2016, pp. 393–420; M.-P. Weller, V. Habrich, L. Korn and A. Zimmermann, Liability of the Economic Unit – A General Principle of EU Law?, ECFR, Vol. 20, 2023, pp. 759–793.

96 S.M. Bainbridge and M.T. Henderson, Limited Liability: A Legal and Economic Analysis, Edward Elgar Publishing, 2016, p. 10, noting that 'the idea of limiting liability of shareholders in large public companies, especially when those shareholders are individuals with modest means, is fairly uncontroversial'.

97 H. Hansmann and R. Squire, External and Internal Asset Partitioning: Corporations and Their Subsidiaries, in J.N. Gordon and W-G. Ringe (eds), The Oxford Handbook of Corporate Law and Governance, OUP, 2018, p. 252, arguing that 'a corporate group's use of intra-group guarantees weighs in favor of disregarding the group's internal partitions'.

3

ENTERPRISE GROUPS AND INSOLVENCY LAW

3.1 INTRODUCTION

3.01 Thomas H. Jackson, the author of the well-known creditors' bargain theory, recently wrote that '[o]ne need not reinvent the wheel to recognize that bankruptcy will always be a "work in progress (a good thing for bankruptcy scholars!)"'.[1] Another expert in insolvency and financial law, Philip Wood, noted that '[e]verything in insolvency law is controversial'.[2] These insightful remarks reflect the current state of affairs in the area of enterprise group insolvency law, which has undergone significant developments over the past few decades.

3.02 The outbreak of COVID-19 and the subsequent drastic governmental measures to curb the spread of the virus had a profound impact on businesses of all sizes. Multinational companies that heavily rely on global supply chains, uninterrupted liquidity flows and free travel – such as airlines and car rentals

1 T.H. Jackson, Bankruptcy's Logic and Limits in the 21st Century: Some Thoughts on Chapter 11's Evolution and Future, in B.E. Adler (ed), Research Handbook on Corporate Bankruptcy Law, Edward Elgar Publishing, 2020, p. 7.

2 P. Wood, Corporate, Bank and Sovereign Insolvencies: Why the Difference? Business Law International, Vol. 22, 2021, p. 307.

– were particularly affected. LATAM Airlines, Norwegian Air and Hertz,[3] the early victims of the pandemic, filed for insolvency or restructuring. The economic recession has been accompanied by a surge in global debt. According to the Institute of International Finance, the total global debt reached USD 296 trillion by the end of the second quarter of 2021, up from USD 270.9 trillion a year earlier. This debt includes USD 86 trillion in government borrowing, USD 86 trillion in non-financial corporate borrowing, USD 69 trillion in the financial sector, and USD 55 trillion in household borrowing.[4] With the eventual termination of state support, along with soaring inflation rates and gas prices, the number of insolvencies is on the rise.[5]

This chapter discusses the application of insolvency law to groups of companies. Section 3.2 outlines different approaches to group insolvencies, noting that insolvency law is traditionally entity-focused (entity bias). This results in an entity-by-entity treatment of group companies in financial distress, with a focus on post-crisis liquidation of the debtor's assets and the allocation of sale proceeds among the creditors of each legal entity. However, the situation could be changing with the emergence of laws that increasingly acknowledge the unique features of groups, premised on operational and financial links and interdependencies between group companies forming a single enterprise. **3.03**

Section 3.3 introduces three restructuring procedures that occupy a prominent place in the modern restructuring law toolbox of the selected jurisdictions: (i) UK schemes of arrangement, (ii) US Chapter 11 reorganisations, and (iii) Dutch WHOA schemes. These procedures are widely used in practice to facilitate the financial and/or operational restructuring of business enterprises, including groups of companies. Section 3.4 addresses the gradual shift from a single-entity approach to a single-enterprise approach, exploring the potential triggers for this transition. Section 3.5 identifies the limits of a single enterprise approach, pointing out that it does not need to interfere with the core of entity separateness, preserving the value of limited liability and entity shielding. Section 3.6 concludes. **3.04**

---

3 For the analysis of Hertz's bankruptcy, see J.A.E. Pottow, Love *Hertz*: Corporate Groups and Insolvency Forum Selection, Texas International Law Journal, Vol. 56, 2021, pp. 155–180.

4 G. Tett, Global debt is soaring – and we need to talk about it, Financial Times, 16 September 2021.

5 UK Office for National Statistics, Rising business insolvencies and high energy prices, 7 October 2022, observing that corporate insolvencies in England and Wales in the second quarter of 2022 reached their highest quarterly level since Quarter 3 (July to September) 2009. More than one in ten UK businesses reported a moderate-to-severe risk of insolvency in August 2022. For more recent data, see Q2 2024: bankruptcies go up, registrations decrease, Eurostat, 16 August 2024 <https://ec.europa.eu/eurostat/web/products-eurostat-news/w/ddn-20240816-2> (accessed 10 October 2024).

3.2 THREE GENERATIONS OF INSOLVENCY LAW

3.05 The evolution of (international) insolvency law, with a specific focus on group insolvencies, can be categorised into distinct stages or generations.

3.06 The first generation (until the mid-1990s) – 'insolvency law 1.0' – exhibits a lack of rules for dealing with failing enterprise groups, as well as for handling cross-border insolvencies more generally. In the absence of a special legal framework, territorialist inclinations often prevailed,[6] resulting in fragmented country-by-country responses to group distress. This is not to say that there were no examples of successful administration of group cases. In practice, pragmatic solutions emerged as commercially minded IPs and courts intuitively sought to navigate the challenges posed by underdeveloped international insolvency law. One notable solution was the adoption of cross-border insolvency protocols. Early examples of these protocols were negotiated as a response to the failures of multinational enterprise groups, such as Maxwell Communication, Olympia and York, and Commodore.[7] These protocols sought to promote cooperation between courts and IPs in different jurisdictions, coordinate the administration of parallel insolvency proceedings, reduce associated costs, and avoid duplicative efforts and irreconcilable judgments.

3.07 The second generation (from the mid-1990s until the mid/late 2010s) – 'insolvency law 2.0' – coincides with the appearance of hard and soft law instruments that target international aspects of insolvency proceedings. These instruments include, inter alia, the UNCITRAL Model Law on Cross-Border Insolvency (MLCBI),[8] the EU Directive on the reorganisation and winding up of credit institutions (CIWUD),[9] and the original EU Regulation on insolvency proceedings (EIR 2000).[10]

3.08 The MLCBI addresses matters such as access to foreign courts, recognition of and relief for foreign insolvency proceedings, and cooperation in cross-border insolvency cases. It is a soft law instrument, meaning it requires transposition

6 I. Mevorach, The Future of Cross-Border Insolvency: Overcoming Biases and Closing Gaps, OUP, 2018, Chapter 2, discussing how territorialist inclinations and tendencies may be driven by different cognitive biases, including loss aversion, status quo bias, endowment effect and short termism. The debate between universalism and territorialism is well known in literature. For integrated enterprise groups, coordinated responses and centralisation promoted by universalism or modified universalism is beneficial.

7 On cross-border protocols used in group insolvency scenarios, see I. Kokorin and B. Wessels, Cross-Border Protocols in Insolvencies of Multinational Enterprise Groups, Edward Elgar Publishing, 2021.

8 UNCITRAL Model Law on Cross-Border Insolvency (1997).

9 Directive 2001/24/EC of the European Parliament and of the Council of 4 April 2001 on the reorganisation and winding up of credit institutions.

10 Council Regulation (EC) No. 1346/2000 of 29 May 2000 on insolvency proceedings.

into national law to become legally binding. Once implemented, it becomes part of the domestic legal order.[11] As of 31 October 2024, legislation based on or influenced by the MLCBI has been adopted in sixty states in a total of sixty-three jurisdictions, including the USA, the UK, Brazil, Singapore, Japan, Australia, Canada, Mexico and Israel.[12] Several other countries are considering adopting the MLCBI (the Netherlands, India) or have enacted rules that are similar to or strongly inspired by the MLCBI, including Spain, Germany and Belgium.[13] The CIWUD and the EIR 2000 are instruments of mandatory EU law that address enterprise failures but differ in their personal scope. The CIWUD applies to credit institutions,[14] while the EIR 2000 covered natural persons and non-financial entities.[15] These EU law instruments establish uniform rules on, inter alia, international jurisdiction, recognition and applicable law in insolvency matters.

A notable feature of the second generation of insolvency law instruments is that they focus on single-debtor insolvency. The MLCBI, the CIWUD and the EIR 2000 lack provisions designed for enterprise group insolvency. The explanation offered by the UNCITRAL Working Group V, which drafted the text of the MLCBI, is quite revealing. It stated that '[w]hen the text of what became the UNCITRAL Model Law on Cross-Border Insolvency (Model Law) was debated, groups were regarded as "a stage too far"'.[16] This also explains the absence of group-oriented insolvency rules at the EU level at that time.[17] Nevertheless, the emergence of instruments for cross-border insolvency, even if limited to single debtors, represented significant progress and had a spill-over effect on group insolvencies. The EIR 2000 and the MLCBI were instrumental in resolving complex insolvencies involving groups 3.09

11 Noting this transformational aspect of soft law, Pottow uses the terms 'semi-soft law' or 'contingently soft law'. He also points out the dialogue-provoking role of soft law and its influence on the evolving international norms. See J.A.E. Pottow, The Dialogic Aspect of Soft Law in International Insolvency: Discord, Digression, and Development, Michigan Journal of International Law, Vol. 40, 2019, p. 481.

12 Status: MLCBI <https://uncitral.un.org/en/texts/insolvency/modellaw/cross-border_insolvency/status> (accessed 31 October 2024).

13 S. Madaus, A.K. Wilke and P. Knauth, Bringing Non-EU Insolvencies to Germany: Really so Different from the UNCITRAL Model Law on Cross-Border Insolvency? International Corporate Rescue, Vol. 17, 2020, pp. 21–28.

14 CIWUD, Article 1.

15 EIR 2000, Article 1(2). The EIR 2000 was repealed with the entry into force of the EIR Recast on 26 June 2017.

16 UNCITRAL Working Group V, Thirty-eighth session, UNCITRAL Legislative Guide on Insolvency Law, Part three: Treatment of enterprise groups in insolvency, 11 February 2010, p. 3.

17 M. Virgós and E. Schmit, Report on the Convention on Insolvency Proceedings, 1996, para. 76, making it clear that the European Convention 1995, the never-adopted predecessor of the EIR 2000, 'offers no rules for groups of affiliated companies (parent-subsidiary schemes)'.

of companies.[18] They were used to achieve centralisation of proceedings concerning group entities in a single jurisdiction and ensured cross-border recognition of group-wide solutions.[19]

3.10 The third generation (from the mid/late 2010s) – 'insolvency law 3.0' – is distinguished by legal texts that acknowledge the need to adjust insolvency law approaches to the characteristics and business reality of groups of companies. Recent years have witnessed the emergence of initiatives and new legal instruments that modernise insolvency law to ensure the effective and efficient administration of insolvency within enterprise groups. This has occurred at the national, regional and international levels.

3.11 At the national level, group insolvency is addressed in some EU Member States. For example, Germany reformed its law in 2017 to facilitate the efficient administration of group insolvency proceedings through enhanced coordination. This is achieved by concentrating insolvency proceedings in the same court, appointing the same IP in separate proceedings, and opening special group coordination proceedings (*Koordinationsverfahren*).[20] Group-focused insolvency rules have also recently been enacted in Italy,[21] Spain[22] and France.[23] For the most part, they concentrate on procedural aspects, such

18 I. Mevorach, On the Road to Universalism: A Comparative and Empirical Study of UNCITRAL Model Law on Cross-Border Insolvency, EBOR, Vol. 12, 2011, pp. 517-557.

19 I. Mevorach, The Future of Cross-Border Insolvency: Overcoming Biases and Closing Gaps, OUP, 2018, p. 227, emphasising that '[p]ractice demonstrates that often the professionals and courts implementing the MLCBI or the EIR could achieve [group] solutions through a "pragmatic" approach, paving the way for the emergence of the modified universalist norm concerning groups by applying the jurisdiction and recognition rules expansively to accommodate these more complex structures'. This is evidenced in the group-sensitive understanding of COMI, as demonstrated by some courts. See *Re: Zetta Jet Pte Ltd and others* [2019] SGHC 53, holding that 'in ascertaining a specific company's COMI, there is no need to maintain strictly the distinction between different entities within a group. It is possible for the analysis to be made of the activities of an entire group of companies, rather than of the specific debtor company in question.'

20 *Gesetz zur Erleichterung der Bewältigung von Konzerninsolvenzen* (KonInsoErlG) (Law for the facilitation of the handling of group insolvencies), 13.04.2017, Bundesgesetzblatt Jahrgang 2017 Teil I Nr. 22, ausgegeben am 21.04.2017, p. 866. On this law, see J. Schmidt, Corporate groups, in P.J. Omar and J.L.L. Gant (eds), Research Handbook on Corporate Restructuring, Edward Elgar Publishing, 2021, pp. 214-227.

21 *Codice della crisi d'impresa e dell'insolvenza in attuazione della legge 19 ottobre 2017*, n. 155, Titolo VI. Disposizioni relative ai gruppi di imprese. D. Corapi and D. Benincasa, The Law on Groups of Companies in Italy, European Company Law, Vol. 16, 2019, pp. 121-129; A. Zorzi, The Italian Insolvency Law Reform, European Business Law Review, Vol. 32, 2021, pp. 935-964.

22 *Ley Concursal*, Artículo 25, allowing a debtor or a creditor to submit a petition for declaration of joint insolvency proceedings of several debtors if they are part of the same group of companies.

23 *Loi n° 2015-990 du 6 août 2015 pour la croissance, l'activité et l'égalité des chances économiques*, adding Article L. 721-8 to *Code de commerce*. This article specifies the jurisdiction of specialised commercial courts over certain insolvency proceedings and provides that companies facing an insolvency proceeding with subsidiaries in a similar position are subject to the same court. See also Article L. 621-2 of *Code de commerce*,

as jurisdiction, the appointment of a single IP, and communication between courts and IPs. A wave of restructuring-related reforms in the EU has led to the emergence of group-mindful substantive rules. For example, both the Dutch WHOA and the German StaRUG[24] introduced important innovations, like third-party releases.

Insolvency of groups has also attracted the attention of policymakers outside Europe. In 2019, the Insolvency and Bankruptcy Board of India created a Working Group on Group Insolvency to discuss and draft a possible group insolvency framework.[25] In Argentina, insolvency law focuses on group reorganisations and provides for the possibility of a single or joint application to include all group members.[26] This happens in cases where the insolvency of one group member may affect other group members or where companies within the group are closely integrated. Interestingly, Argentine law permits the inclusion of solvent group members in an insolvency application, so long as it is in the interest of the entire group and facilitates a group reorganisation.[27] In Brazil, group insolvency cases often result in substantive consolidation, even without direct statutory authority for such consolidation. There, a lenient approach to procedural consolidation has led to a tacit acceptance of substantive consolidation as a norm.[28] 3.12

In EU law, in the area of insolvency and bank resolution, enterprise groups have, for the first time, been directly acknowledged in the BRRD (2014) and the EIR Recast (2015). They reflect the distinct characteristics of groups, provide a definition of a group of companies and offer or mandate special mechanisms and tools to respond to the challenges of enterprise group insolvencies 3.13

---

which allows the extension of insolvency proceedings to a related company in the event of a confusion of its assets with those of the debtor or if that legal entity is deemed fictitious. See H. Bourbouloux and S. Hustaix, National Report on France, in B. Wessels and S. Madaus (eds), Rescue of Business in Europe. A European Law Institute Instrument, OUP, 2020, pp. 674–676.

24 *Gesetz über den Stabilisierungs- und Restrukturierungsrahmen für Unternehmen (Unternehmensstabilisierungs- und -restrukturierungsgesetz – StaRUG)* vom 22. Dezember 2020 (BGBl. I S. 3256), Enterprise Stabilization and Restructuring Act.

25 Report of the Working Group on Group Insolvency, 23 September 2019; Report of CBIRC-II on Group Insolvency, December 2021.

26 Argentina's Bankruptcy and Liquidation Law No. 24,552 (*Ley de Concursos y Quiebras*), Chapter VI, art. 65–68. See M.E. Uzal, National Report on Argentina, in R.M. Manóvil (ed), Groups of Companies: A Comparative Law Overview, Springer, 2020, pp. 614–616.

27 Ibid., p. 615.

28 For criticism of the Brazilian approach, see S.C. Neder Cerezetti, Reorganization of Corporate Groups in Brazil: Substantive Consolidation and the Limited Liability Tale, International Insolvency Review, Vol. 30, 2021, p. 182, noting that the current Brazilian cases of substantive consolidation treat 'an exceptional measure as a day-to-day event, dramatically altering the rights of creditors and the obligations of debtors without regard to the limitation of liability'.

(e.g. group coordination proceedings, group recovery and resolution plans, group financial support agreements).

3.14 At the global level, I should mention the MLEGI – a relatively new model law published by UNCITRAL in 2019.[29] The MLEGI seeks 'to provide effective mechanisms to address cases of insolvency affecting the members of an enterprise group'.[30] It is specifically designed for group insolvencies and aims to promote several objectives: making the administration of cross-border insolvencies of groups more efficient, ensuring the protection and maximisation of the insolvency estate value, facilitating the rescue of financially troubled groups of companies and supporting the adoption of group insolvency solutions. While it remains to be seen whether the MLEGI will repeat the success of its predecessor,[31] it might face some opposition at the national level, perhaps due to concerns about corporate separateness and state control over local companies. Equally important is the observation that the enactment of hard law does not guarantee its effectiveness; hard law does not necessarily mean widely used law. A good example is the EIR Recast's framework on group coordination. Since the EIR Recast became binding in 2017, I am not aware of a single significant case of a cross-border group insolvency that has been handled under the group coordination procedure.[32]

3.3 THREE RESTRUCTURING PROCEDURES

3.3.1 The UK: schemes of arrangement

3.15 A scheme of arrangement is a statutory procedure available under Part 26 (ss. 895–901) of the UK Companies Act 2006.[33] Section 895 of this law defines a scheme as a compromise or arrangement between a company and its creditors, or any class of them, or between a company and its members (shareholders).

29 Another instrument worth mentioning is the World Bank Principles for Effective Creditor Rights and Insolvency Regimes, 2011, which for the first time included new principles 'to reflect best international practice in the regulation of the insolvency of enterprise groups'.

30 MLEGI, Preamble.

31 As of October 2024, the MLEGI has not been transposed in national laws. In July 2022, the UK Insolvency Service launched a consultation on the implementation of MLEGI. In July 2023, the UK government announced its intention to implement the MLEGI at the earliest opportunity.

32 CERIL Statement 2021-2 on EU Group Coordination Proceedings, 29 June 2021. See also C. Thole, M. Dueñas, Some Observations on the New Group Coordination Procedure of the Reformed European Insolvency Regulation, International Insolvency Review, Vol. 24, 2015, p. 214, noting that, whereas a coordination procedure is 'a step into the right direction, the procedure has significant shortcomings such as the weak position of the coordinator, a liberal opt-in and opt-out mechanism and the problem of forum shopping'.

33 For an overview of English schemes of arrangement, see J. Payne, Schemes of Arrangement: Theory, Structure and Operation, CUP, 2021.

Companies use schemes for a wide variety of debt-reduction strategies affecting debt and/or equity. These strategies may include a debt-to-equity swap,[34] modification (e.g. extension of maturity dates),[35] or reduction (e.g. partial write-off) of creditors' claims.[36]

Schemes of arrangement have not always enjoyed the level of popularity they do today. Available under the UK Companies Act 1948, they were regarded as time-consuming, complex (requiring the involvement of experts and preparation of extensive documentation), costly and not particularly well-suited for companies on the verge of insolvency or insolvent companies.[37] Yet, since the 2000s, schemes have become a widely used mechanism for the restructuring of financially distressed or insolvent companies. Several factors contribute to this revival. It is now clear that schemes of arrangement are available to both solvent and insolvent debtors.[38] To the extent that a scheme of arrangement is open to non-insolvent debtors and is regulated by non-insolvency legislation (i.e. Companies Act 2006), it avoids insolvency-related stigma and usually does not trigger cross-default and forfeiture clauses in contracts.[39] **3.16**

The flexibility of schemes of arrangement makes them suitable for achieving a wide range of purposes. In principle, schemes can be used for any compromise or arrangement between the debtor and its creditors, as long as there is some form of 'give and take' between them.[40] The procedure for entering a scheme consists of two stages. The first involves a hearing on class composition and does not entail an assessment of the scheme's fairness or merits.[41] The second comprises a scheme meeting, where creditors vote on the proposed arrangement, and a court confirmation (sanctioning) hearing. At this hearing, the court must be satisfied, inter alia, that the scheme is fair. In this context, fairness has a specific and rather narrow meaning. The court simply has to be **3.17**

34 *Re Uniq Plc* [2011] EWHC 749 (Ch); *Re Avanti Communications Group Plc* [2018] EWHC 653 (Ch).

35 *Re Apcoa Parking Holdings GmbH et al.* [2014] EWHC 3849 (Ch).

36 *Primacom Holdings GmbH* [2012] EWHC 164 (Ch).

37 P.J. Omar and J.L.L. Gant, Corporate Rescue in the United Kingdom: Past, Present and Future Reforms, Insolvency Law Journal, Vol. 24, 2016, pp. 40–61.

38 See *Scottish Lion Insurance Co Ltd v. Goodrich Corp* [2010] CSIH 6, 2010 SC 349, confirming that '[t]here is nothing in that statute nor in its descendents … to suggest that applications for sanction of a "solvent scheme" are in principle to be dealt with differently from those where the company is insolvent or on the verge of insolvency'.

39 P. Wood, Principles of International Insolvency, 2nd edn, Sweet & Maxwell, 2007, para. 23-038.

40 Thus, where creditors or shareholders 'give up all their rights and receive no benefit, there is no compromise or arrangement'. *Re NFU Development Trust Ltd* [1972] 1 WLR 1548. In *In Re Uniq Plc* [2011] EWHC 749 (Ch), the court was satisfied that a compromise was present in a situation where the existing shareholders saw 100 per cent of their equity stake diluted to 9.8 per cent, but that dilution was an integral part of the restructuring that allowed the company to remain viable and survive.

41 *Re Telewest Communications Plc (No. 1)* [2004] EWHC 924 (Ch); [2004] BCC 342.

'satisfied that the scheme is one that an intelligent and honest man, acting in respect of his interests, might reasonably approve'.[42] This does not mean that the court should 'form a view of whether the scheme is, in some general sense, or even in the court's own opinion, the "fairest" or "best" scheme'.[43]

3.18 A scheme of arrangement offers a very practical mechanism to overcome the holdout problem without opening a cumbersome, litigation-heavy insolvency procedure. It allows the majority of creditors to bind the minority in each creditor class. A creditor class must be 'confined to those persons whose rights are not so dissimilar to make it impossible for them to consult together with a view to their common interest'.[44] For approval, a scheme requires a vote of 75 per cent by value and the majority in number of members in a class present at the meeting and voting, either in person or by proxy.[45] If the requisite majority within the class is reached, the dissenting minority of creditors, including secured creditors,[46] is bound by the majority vote. Upon the sanctioning of the scheme, it becomes effective and binding on the company, its creditors and shareholders involved in the scheme, including dissenting creditors and shareholders.

3.19 One important limitation of schemes of arrangement is that they do not permit a cram down of entire classes of creditors. Hence, unlike inter-class cram down, cross-class cram down is not available in a scheme. To overcome this limitation, a sale via pre-packaged administration is often arranged. In such cases, the business or assets are transferred to a newly incorporated entity through the administrator's power of sale. The select classes of senior creditors agree by way of a scheme to take an interest in this new entity. Junior 'out of the money' creditors and shareholders are left in the old company, which becomes an empty shell.[47] This practice has created an attractive restructuring mechanism for large companies with complex capital structures. Alternatively, a Part 26A restructuring plan may be used. Unlike schemes of arrangement, restructuring plans under Part 26A of the Companies Act 2006, recently

42 *Re KCA Deutag UK Finance Plc* [2020] EWHC 2977 (Ch), at 28.

43 Ibid.

44 *Sovereign Life Assurance Company v. Dodd* [1892] 2 QB 573. See also *Re Hawk Insurance Company Limited* [2002] BCC 300. For a useful review of the current position on class composition, including the distinction between rights and interests, see *In Re Lehman Brothers International (Europe) Ltd* [2018] EWHC 1980.

45 Companies Act 2006, s. 899.

46 In this respect, schemes of arrangement are different from company voluntary arrangements (CVAs) that cannot be used to cram down secured creditors.

47 K. van Zwieten, Goode on Principles of Corporate Insolvency Law, 5th edn, Sweet & Maxwell, 2018, para. 12-25; C. Gerner-Beuerle, M. Schillig, Comparative Company Law, OUP, 2019, p. 959; G. McCormack, The European Restructuring Directive, Edward Elgar Publishing, 2021, para. 3.27.

introduced by the Corporate Insolvency and Governance Act 2020 (CIGA), permit cross-class cram down.[48] A restructuring plan can be relied on to exclude a particular class from voting on the basis that such class is out of the money or has no genuine economic interest in the relevant alternative.[49] While offering new options and additional flexibility, Part 26A plans are only available to companies that have encountered, or are likely to encounter, financial difficulties that are affecting, or will or may affect, their ability to carry on business as a going concern.[50]

3.3.2 The USA: Chapter 11 of the US Bankruptcy Code

Chapter 11 procedure of the US Bankruptcy Code was named 'the most important insolvency procedure worldwide'.[51] It deserves a prominent place in 'the pantheon of extraordinary laws that have shaped the American economy and society and then echoed throughout the world'.[52] Introduced in 1978, Chapter 11 gained popularity and became a source of inspiration for insolvency laws in other countries.[53] There are several good reasons for this success.[54] **3.20**

Chapter 11 permits the restructuring of the debtor's obligations by means of the adoption of a reorganisation plan. It is usually commenced by the debtor on a voluntary basis. While creditor-initiated Chapter 11 filings are possible,[55] they are rare in practice. Chapter 11 does not require the material insolvency of the debtor.[56] Still, it is a matter of bankruptcy law regulated by federal **3.21**

---

48 Corporate Insolvency and Governance Act 2020, Schedule 9, part 1. See e.g. *Re DeepOcean 1 UK Ltd* [2021] EWHC 138 (Ch); *Amicus Finance Plc (In Administration)* [2021] EWHC 3036 (Ch); *Re Prezzo Investco Limited* [2023] EWHC 1679 (Ch); *In the matter of Fitness First Clubs Limited* [2023] EWHC 1699 (Ch).

49 Companies Act 2006, Part 26A, s. 901C(4). *Re Smile Telecoms Holdings Limited* [2022] EWHC 740 (Ch).

50 Companies Act 2006, Part 26A, s. 901A(2).

51 B. Wessels and R.J. de Weijs (ed), International Contributions to the Reform of Chapter 11 U.S. Bankruptcy Code, Eleven International Publishing, 2015, p. 2.

52 E. Warren and J.L. Westbrook, The Success of Chapter 11: A Challenge to the Critics, Michigan Law Review, Vol. 107, 2009, p. 604.

53 N. Martin, The Role of History and Culture in Developing Bankruptcy and Insolvency Systems: The Perils of Legal Transplantation, Boston College International and Comparative Law Review, Vol. 28, 2005, p. 4.

54 For an overview of Chapter 11 reorganisation plans, see S.J. Lubben, American Business Bankruptcy: A Primer, Edward Elgar Publishing, 2021, Part IV.

55 11 U.S. Code § 303.

56 Note that the lack of a valid reorganisational purpose may be interpreted as bad faith and could lead to dismissal or conversion under 11 U.S. Code § 1112(b). *In re SGL Carbon Corp.*, 200 F.3d 154, 166 (3d Cir. 1999), stating that courts 'have consistently dismissed Chapter 11 petitions filed by financially healthy companies with no need to reorganize under the protection of Chapter 11'. More recently, financial distress as a requirement of good faith was confirmed in *In re LTL Management, LLC*, 2023 WL 1098189, at *9 (C.A.3 (N.J.), 2023), observing that the debtor's financial distress 'must not only be apparent, but it must be immediate enough to justify a filing'. Two inquiries are particularly relevant in this regard: '(1) whether the petition serves a valid bankruptcy purpose' and '(2) whether the petition is filed merely to

statute. Madaus explains this seeming inconsistency (debtor's solvency and bankruptcy law) by referencing the specificity of the US constitutional regime and the division of powers between the federal government and the states.[57] According to this regime, non-consensual debt impairment requires a legal basis in bankruptcy law, which belongs to the exclusive federal jurisdiction,[58] regardless of the actual insolvency of the debtor.[59]

3.22 The filing of a voluntary petition automatically opens the case with important consequences. Among them is a worldwide stay or moratorium on debt-enforcement actions by all creditors, whether secured or unsecured.[60] In Chapter 11, the debtor's management continues to run the business.[61] However, in cases of fraud, dishonesty, incompetence or gross mismanagement by directors, or if it is deemed 'in the interests of creditors, any equity security holders, and other interests of the estate', the court may appoint a bankruptcy trustee.[62] This bankruptcy trustee assumes the powers of the debtor's management.

3.23 Chapter 11 is a flexible instrument that enables the debtor to preserve going concern value, while it negotiates the options for financial recovery.[63] These options should be included in the reorganisation plan, which the debtor has the exclusive right to propose within a 120-day period following the commencement of the bankruptcy proceeding.[64] A plan must designate creditor classes, specify their treatment, and provide adequate means for its implementation.[65] It may prescribe measures such as the transfer of assets to other entities, extension of maturity dates, impairment of any class of claims (including

---

obtain a tactical litigation advantage'. *In re 15375 Memorial Corp. v. Bepco, L.P.*, 589 F.3d 605, 618 (C.A.3 (Del.), 2009). A valid bankruptcy purpose includes preservation of a going concern and maximising the value of the debtor's estate.

57 S. Madaus, Leaving the Shadows of US Bankruptcy Law: A Proposal to Divide the Realms of Insolvency and Restructuring Law, European Business Organization Law Review, Vol. 19, 2018, p. 628.

58 Constitution of the United States, Article I, Section 8, Clause 4: Bankruptcy Clause: 'The Congress shall have Power to establish … uniform Laws on the subject of Bankruptcies throughout the United States'.

59 Constitution of the United States, Article I, Section 10, Clause 1: Contract Clause: 'No State shall … pass any … Law impairing the Obligation of Contracts'.

60 11 U.S. Code § 362.

61 11 U.S Code § 1107. Under § 1101, 'debtor in possession' means 'debtor except when a person that has qualified under section 322 of this title is serving as trustee in the case'.

62 11 U.S. Code § 1104.

63 On the evolving nature of Chapter 11, see M.J. Roe, Three Ages of Bankruptcy, Harvard Business Law Review, Vol. 7, 2017, p. 205, noting that instead of implementing the original idea of a deal among creditors and a debtor, Chapter 11 is now increasingly used for a market sale of distressed firms. For similar observations, see ABI Commission to Study the Reform of Chapter 11, Final Report and Recommendations, 2014, p. 15.

64 11 U.S. Code § 1121(b). *Tamir v. U.S. Trustee*, 566 B.R. 278, 283 (D. Me. 2016), observing that the primary goal of Chapter 11 is to 'formulate a comprehensive reorganization plan that will ultimately rehabilitate financially distressed debtors'.

65 11 U.S. Code § 1123(a).

those of secured creditors), assumption, rejection or assignment of executory contracts, along with other commercially driven measures. There are important statutory requirements that must be satisfied for a plan to be confirmed by the court,[66] some of which are mentioned below.

- First, a plan must comply with the applicable provisions and requirements of Title 11,[67] such as ensuring equal treatment of claims within the same creditor class.[68]
- Second, it must be proposed in good faith, which generally indicates 'a reasonable likelihood that the plan will achieve a result consistent with the objectives and purposes of the Bankruptcy Code'.[69]
- Third, the reorganisation plan should comply with the best-interest-of-creditors test.[70] This test guarantees that every dissenting creditor receives in Chapter 11 at least as much as they would have received in a Chapter 7 liquidation. Therefore, the Chapter 7 liquidation sets the baseline for distribution. The liquidation value is guaranteed to each creditor, and only the reorganisation surplus – the firm's value above the liquidation value – is subject to negotiation and voting in Chapter 11.
- Fourth, the plan should treat non-consenting classes of creditors fairly and equitably.[71] This includes compliance with the well-known absolute priority rule (APR).[72] This rule applies if a dissenting class of creditors is crammed down. The APR stipulates that no junior class can receive or retain any property under the plan unless the claims of senior interests are fully satisfied. Essentially, this rule requires the plan to adhere to the order of priority entitlements under applicable non-bankruptcy law. It should be clarified that the APR focuses on the rights of a dissenting class of creditors vis-à-vis junior or senior classes and not on the rights vis-à-vis classes of the same rank. The latter is addressed by the prohibition of unfair discrimination between different classes of the same rank.[73]

---

66 11 U.S. Code § 1129.

67 11 U.S. Code § 1129(a)(1).

68 11 U.S. Code § 1123(a)(4).

69 11 U.S. Code § 1129(a)(3). *In re Madison Hotel Associates*, 749 F.2d 410, 424-25 (7th Cir. 1984).

70 11 U.S. Code § 1129(a)(7).

71 11 U.S. Code § 1129(b)(1).

72 11 U.S. Code § 1129(b)(2)(B)(ii). The APR was characterised as the 'organizing principle of the modern law of corporate reorganizations', the 'cornerstone of reorganization practice and theory' and 'bankruptcy's most important and famous rule'. See D.G. Baird, Priority Matters: Absolute Priority, Relative Priority, and the Costs of Bankruptcy, University of Pennsylvania Law Review, Vol. 165, 2017, p. 786; B.A. Markell, Owners, Auctions, and Absolute Priority in Bankruptcy Reorganizations, Stanford Law Review, Vol. 44, 1991, p. 123; M.J. Roe, F. Tung, Breaking Bankruptcy Priority: How Rent-Seeking Upends the Creditors' Bargain, Virginia Law Review, Vol. 99, 2013, p. 1236. Yet the absolute priority rule is not always absolute. For example, Chapter 11 was recently amended to address the needs of small and medium-sized firms. Small Business Reorganization Act, 11 U.S.C. §§ 1181-1195 (2019). Among other things, the new subchapter V on small business debtor reorganisation stipulates that the rule of the APR does not apply in cases falling under its scope. See 11 U.S. Code § 1181(a).

73 11 U.S. Code § 1129(b)(1). Thus, the US Bankruptcy Code allows discrimination between classes, as long as it is not 'unfair'. Courts apply different tests to determine whether discrimination is unfair. See e.g. *In*

3.24 Like an English scheme of arrangement, a Chapter 11 plan helps resolve the holdout problem by allowing both consensual and non-consensual plan confirmation. In US terminology, the former means acceptance by a class, which is achieved if the majority of creditors in number and two-thirds in amount vote in favour of the plan (intra-class cram down).[74] Non-consensual plan confirmation allows a restructuring plan to be imposed, or crammed down, on a dissenting class of creditors (cross-class cram down) as long as at least one impaired class of creditors has approved the plan and the plan complies with other requirements, such as good faith, best interest of creditors, non-discrimination, APR, fairness and equity.[75]

3.3.3 The Netherlands: WHOA schemes

3.25 The Dutch Bankruptcy Act (*Faillissementswet* or Fw) dates back to 1896 and has been amended several times since then. Some of the most significant changes occurred in 2020 when the Act on Court Confirmation of Extrajudicial Restructuring Plans, commonly known as WHOA, was adopted. It entered into force on 1 January 2021. In the Netherlands, discussions on reforming the national insolvency law framework to promote the adoption of extrajudicial (out-of-court) restructuring plans began in 2012 as part of the Review of Bankruptcy Law Programme (*wetgevingsprogramma herijking faillissementsrecht*).[76] This Programme had three parts or pillars: (i) preventing fraud, (ii) enhancing restructuring options for companies, and (iii) modernising insolvency proceedings.[77] These pillars resulted in several legislative proposals, including the WHOA.

3.26 Before the WHOA, restructuring options under Dutch law were limited. The existing bankruptcy procedures for legal entities – bankruptcy (*faillissement*) and suspension of payments (*surseance van betaling*) – were recognised as inefficient for rescuing financially distressed companies.[78] Outside these formal

Re Aztec Co., 107 B.R. 585 (Bankr. M.D. Tenn. 1989); *In re 203 N. LaSalle St. Ltd. P'ship*, 190 B.R. 567 (Bankr. N.D. Ill. 1995).

74 11 U.S. Code § 1126(c).

75 11 U.S. Code § 1129(a)–(b).

76 *Kamerstukken II* 2012/13, 29 911, nr. 74. For an overview of the pre-reform Dutch restructuring and insolvency regime and a detailed examination of the main features of the WHOA, see G-J. Boon, R.D. Vriesendorp and H. Koster, The WHOA: the Breakthrough for a Dutch Business Rescue Culture, HERO 2022/W-008, 15 December 2022 <https://www.online-hero.nl/art/4464/special-issue-preventive-restructuring-8-the-whoa-the-breakthrough-for-a-dutch-business-rescue-culture> (accessed 10 October 2024).

77 S. Renssen, De herijking van het faillissementsrecht. De pijler modernisering (Recht en Praktijk nr. InsR12), Deventer: Wolters Kluwer, 2019.

78 R.D. Vriesendorp, R.M. Hermans and K.A.J. de Vries, Herijking faillissementsrecht en het informeel akkoord: gemiste kans of opportunity voor een Nederlandse scheme of arrangement? TvI 2013/12. The

bankruptcy proceedings, a general principle of freedom of contract applied, requiring the consent of all affected creditors for an out-of-court debt restructuring. This led to an acute holdout problem, causing many Dutch companies to turn to English schemes of arrangement or US Chapter 11 reorganisations.[79]

According to the Dutch Bankruptcy Act, a WHOA plan can be prepared and approved through a public (publicly disclosed) pre-insolvency procedure or a non-public procedure.[80] It is available to debtors in situations where it can reasonably be assumed that they will not be able to pay their debts as they fall due.[81] In terms of substantive rules, a WHOA scheme is a flexible legal instrument that allows companies in financial distress to restructure their debt in a cost-efficient way. It combines the elements of English schemes of arrangement, such as the ability to implement restructuring outside a formal, heavily supervised bankruptcy proceeding, with features characteristic of Chapter 11, including cross-class cram down,[82] a stay of individual enforcement actions (although non-automatic),[83] a possibility to terminate executory contracts at the debtor's request[84] and limitations on ipso facto clauses.[85] These tools in the WHOA toolbox can assist the debtor in its restructuring efforts. Since their introduction in 2021, WHOA schemes have demonstrated their effectiveness,[86] and have been used by large multinational businesses like Vroon, Diebold, Steinhoff and Royal IHC. 3.27

The inherent flexibility of the Dutch scheme extends to the possible contents of a restructuring plan. It may include a debt-for-equity swap, a (partial) write-off or extension of debt, a sale of debtor's assets or a combination of these and other measures. The WHOA plan can affect the rights of secured, preferential, unsecured and subordinated creditors and shareholders, but it cannot release 3.28

---

possibility to bind non-consenting creditors to an out-of-court agreement was limited to exceptional circumstances, where non-cooperative behaviour could be interpreted as an abuse of rights (Article 3:13 BW). See HR 12 August 2005, *NJ* 2006/230, m.nt. P. van Schilfgaarde (*Groenemeijer/Payroll*); HR 24 March 2017, *NJ* 2017/466, m.nt. F.M.J. Verstijlen (*Mondia/V&D*).

79 E.g. Van Gansewinkel Groep B.V., Indah Kiat International Finance Company B.V., Estro Groep B.V., Magyar Telecom B.V., Metinvest B.V., HEMA B.V.

80 Dutch Bankruptcy Act, Article 369, indicating that, aside from the jurisdictional rules, the only major distinction between a public and a non-public proceeding is that, unlike the latter, a public proceeding is publicly disclosed in insolvency and trade registers. In addition, court requests are heard in open sessions.

81 Dutch Bankruptcy Act, Articles 370(1) and 371(3).

82 Dutch Bankruptcy Act, Articles 383(1) and 384.

83 Dutch Bankruptcy Act, Article 376.

84 Dutch Bankruptcy Act, Article 373(1).

85 Dutch Bankruptcy Act, Article 373(3).

86 F.M.J.Verstijlen et al., Evaluatie Wet homologatie onderhands akkoord, 18 December 2023 <https://repository.wodc.nl/handle/20.500.12832/3338> accessed 10 October 2024.

or reduce liabilities arising from employment contracts.[87] It also cannot be used to amend commitments under loan facilities agreements that are not fully drawn, nor can it force financiers to continue financing the debtor.[88] Once approved by the requisite majorities in each class of creditors or shareholders (two-thirds in value of those who participated in the voting)[89] and subject to court confirmation,[90] the plan becomes binding on all affected creditors and shareholders.[91] Thus, like English schemes of arrangement and US Chapter 11 plans, WHOA plans may be used to overcome a holdout problem and restore financial viability through debt restructuring. Notably, all three procedures mentioned in this section contain rules that can facilitate group restructuring, which I will explore throughout this book.

3.4 FROM A SINGLE ENTITY TO A SINGLE ENTERPRISE?

3.4.1 Why recognition of enterprise groups in insolvency law took so long

3.29 An overview of major milestones in the development of insolvency law and its recognition of enterprise groups as a commercial reality that needs to be acknowledged and reckoned with reveals a modest and uneasy progression. This section explores the likely reasons behind this slow pace and discusses the probable causes or triggers for a recent shift represented by the third generation of insolvency law instruments.

3.30 There are several reasons why, for a long time (and perhaps still), insolvency law has largely remained single-entity focused, resulting in the entity-by-entity treatment of enterprise group members in financial distress (entity bias).

3.31 First, in discussing the failure of English law to devise a special group law or a comprehensive set of rules to regulate liability within groups, Davies points out that this is likely because 'group structures and relationships within groups are highly variable and the appropriate general rules are accordingly difficult to identify'.[92] Indeed, enterprise groups differ in terms of the size, legal organisation, management, financing and business integration (section 2.4). This variability complicates the adoption of general company and insolvency law on

87 Dutch Bankruptcy Act, Article 369(4).
88 HR 25 October 2024, ECLI:NL:HR:2024:1533.
89 Dutch Bankruptcy Act, Article 381(7).
90 Dutch Bankruptcy Act, Articles 383–384.
91 Dutch Bankruptcy Act, Article 385.
92 P. Davies, Introduction to Company Law, 3rd edn, OUP, 2020, p. 259.

groups that would be sufficiently certain and predictable, yet flexible enough to suit all types of groups.

Second, the entity-centric vision in insolvency law is firmly grounded in the long-established principle of company law, namely entity separateness, which in modern times is reinforced by limited liability and entity shielding. In this respect, Teichmann notes that 'company law of most jurisdictions is still focussed on the single legal entity and does not expressly acknowledge the fact that the corporate group may create legal challenges which are different from those of an independent company'.[93] Unlike a legal entity, an enterprise group does not have its own legal personality. As a result, (i) assets within a group of companies are separated along the entity lines (one entity – one insolvency estate), (ii) creditors have legal rights (recourse) only with respect to particular entities and their assets, and (iii) IPs appointed to individual companies act in the interests of those companies and their creditors. Wessels and Madaus refer to this as the 'five one's' principle, as it establishes 'one insolvent debtor, one estate, one insolvency proceeding, one court and one insolvency office holder'.[94] The fact that, prior to insolvency, a group operated as one integrated enterprise does not easily fit this atomistic vision. 3.32

Third, the very concept of a 'group of companies' has not been comprehensively developed or harmonised across jurisdictions. While some countries apply general corporate and/or civil law to corporate groups (e.g. the UK), other countries apply special rules (e.g. Germany, Portugal, Slovenia).[95] Nevertheless, there is some convergence regarding the agency problems arising in groups, including conflicts between majority and minority shareholders and between shareholders and creditors. This convergence is evident in the rules concerning related-party transactions. In most EU Member States, but also outside Europe, company and insolvency laws usually prescribe special treatment for transactions involving related parties – directors, shareholders and their affiliates. In company law, this results in additional safeguards against intra-group self-dealing, including mandatory bid rules,[96] the allocation of certain rights 3.33

93 C. Teichmann, Towards a European Framework for Cross-Border Group Management, European Company Law, Vol. 13, 2016, p. 150.

94 B. Wessels and S. Madaus, Rescue of Business in Insolvency Law. Instrument of the European Law Institute, 2017, p. 342.

95 K.J. Hopt, Groups of companies: A Comparative Study of the Economics, Law, and Regulation of Corporate Groups, in J.N. Gordon and W-G. Ringe (eds), The Oxford Handbook of Corporate Law and Governance, OUP, 2018, p. 612.

96 See e.g. Article 5, Directive 2004/25/EC of 21 April 2004 on takeover bids. L. Enriques, The Mandatory Bid Rule in the Takeover Directive: Harmonization Without Foundation? European Company and Financial Law Review, Vol. 1, 2004, pp. 440–457.

to minority shareholders (e.g. appraisal rights) and disclosure and approval requirements.[97] In insolvency law, the interests of insiders often enjoy lesser protection, and their rights may be subordinated to the rights of external creditors.

3.34 However, the recognition of corporate groups faces significant obstacles and even resistance whenever the principle of entity separateness is at stake. This is clearly exemplified by the discussions over the recognition of a 'group interest' in European company law.[98] In 2011, the Reflection Group on the Future of EU Company Law, set up by the European Commission in 2010, issued a report recommending the recognition of a group interest at the EU level.[99] The group argued that this would enhance the flexibility of group management in international business activities and facilitate legal certainty.[100] Based on this report, a public consultation was launched regarding the recognition of a group interest. It resulted in the Company Law Action Plan which included the initiative to recognise the concept of a group interest.[101] Despite the generally positive attitude of academics and the business community towards the EU-wide move for the acceptance of a group interest,[102] this initiative has not led to a concrete legislative proposal, highlighting its complex and controversial character. The idea of an EU framework covering groups of companies was also met with caution.

3.35 The entity-by-entity treatment of group companies and their insulation in insolvency is criticised for not reflecting the economic interconnectedness of

---

97 J. Dammann, Related Party Transactions and Intragroup Transactions, in L. Enriques and T.H. Tröger (eds), The Law and Finance of Related Party Transactions, CUP, 2019, pp. 218-244.

98 Forum Europaeum Corporate Group Law, Corporate Group Law for Europe, EBOR, Vol. 1, 2000, pp. 165-264, recommending the introduction of a modified *Rozenblum* doctrine at the European level. Report of the High Level Group of Company Law Experts on a Model Regulatory Framework for Company Law in Europe ('Winter Report'), 2002, noting that it is feasible to establish a framework rule that allows the adoption and implementation of a group policy, provided that the interests of creditors are sufficiently protected.

99 Report of the Reflection Group on the Future of EU Company Law, Brussels, 5 April 2011.

100 The Report did not elaborate on the application of a group interest in a group insolvency scenario, only noting that further consideration of this principle should distinguish between two situations: (i) where a subsidiary is not close to insolvency, and (ii) where a subsidiary is close to insolvency or insolvent.

101 Action Plan: European company law and corporate governance – a modern legal framework for more engaged shareholders and sustainable companies, COM/2012/0740 final.

102 P-H. Conac, Director's Duties in Groups of Companies – Legalizing the Interest of the Group at the European Level, European Company and Financial Law Review, Vol. 10, 2013, pp. 194-226; M. Winner, Group interest in European company law: an overview, Acta Univ. Sapientiae, Leg. Stud., Vol. 5, 2016, pp. 85-96; The Informal Company Law Expert Group, Report on the recognition of the interest of the group, 2016, advocating for the incorporation of a group interest with respect to wholly owned subsidiaries. It stressed that clarity regarding such interest was essential to encourage intra-group financing, ultimately contributing to the EU's Capital Markets Union objectives.

entities within the group, which is further entrenched by the widespread use of intra-group guarantees and loans.[103] As an alternative to a 'single entity approach', a 'single enterprise approach' has been suggested.[104] This approach aims to give effect to the interrelations between group members and may treat the group as a single economic unit that operates to promote the interests of the group as a whole. The appearance of group-mindful insolvency rules supports this approach. But what explains their emergence? The growing body of scholarship devoted to groups and the accumulation of practical experience in dealing with group failures might have contributed to this trend. Yet this is not sufficient to explain the recent legislative changes; after all, there should be political will to embrace new ideas. The following sections discuss two processes that could have served as a trigger for the move to the third generation.

3.4.2 The global financial crisis as an accelerator of change

Milton Friedman famously wrote: **3.36**

> Only a crisis – actual or perceived – produces real change. When that crisis occurs, the actions that are taken depend on the ideas that are lying around. That, I believe, is our basic function: to develop alternatives to existing policies, to keep them alive and available until the politically impossible becomes politically inevitable.[105]

The Global Financial Crisis (GFC) was an 'actual' crisis that triggered far-reaching reforms in the financial industry. It led to what I refer to as the 'GFC-effect'. The GFC demonstrated that the lack of a comprehensive regulatory framework applicable to banks and banking groups, covering their supervision and resolution, could lead to their disorderly collapses. In its 2010 report, the BCBS concluded that '[e]xisting national legal and regulatory arrangements are not designed to coordinate the resolution of problems in all of the significant legal entities of a financial group operating through a multiplicity of separate legal entities'.[106] This is because 'insolvency rules apply on a legal **3.37**

---

103 H. Hansmann and R. Squire, External and Internal Asset Partitioning: Corporations and Their Subsidiaries, in J.N. Gordon and W-G. Ringe (eds), The Oxford Handbook of Corporate Law and Governance, OUP, 2018, p. 259, generally noting that internal corporate partitioning does not generate the many benefits often attributed to it.

104 The dichotomy between 'single entity approach' and 'single enterprise approach' is described in the UNCITRAL Legislative Guide on Insolvency Law, Part three. Mevorach uses slightly different terms: 'entity law' and 'enterprise law'. I. Mevorach, Transaction Avoidance in Bankruptcy of Corporate Groups, European Company and Financial Law Review, Vol. 8, 2011, pp. 235–258; P. Blumberg, The Corporate Entity in an Era of Multinational Corporations, Delaware Journal of Corporate Law, Vol. 15, 1990, pp. 283–375.

105 M. Friedman, Capitalism and Freedom, The University of Chicago Press, 2020 (originally published in 1962), Preface 1982.

106 BCBS, Report and Recommendations of the Cross-Border Bank Resolution Group, March 2010, p. 25.

entity basis'.[107] This meant that the predominant approach to resolving banking crises was territorial or nation-based.

3.38 The insolvency of Icelandic banks serves as a prime example of this nation-based approach. Following the crisis of Iceland's outsized banking industry in the summer-autumn of 2008, the Icelandic government passed emergency legislation granting protection to domestic deposits. Domestic deposits were transferred to new banks, while foreign operations and deposits remained in the old banks, which were placed under administration. Baudino et al. explain that the purpose of this exclusion of foreign depositors was to 'maintain basic banking services for domestic economy by separating domestic operations from the larger foreign operations of each bank'.[108] However, this differential treatment raised concerns over equal treatment of creditors. Ultimately, foreign depositors had to be rescued by Dutch and UK governments.[109]

3.39 After Iceland declined to offer compensation to depositors in the Netherlands and the UK, a case was brought before the EFTA Court. In its judgment from 28 January 2013, the EFTA Court took the side of Iceland, ruling that the applicable law (i.e. the EU Deposit Guarantee Directive)[110] did not impose an obligation on EEA states to ensure the payment of aggregate deposits in all circumstances, including when the deposit guarantee scheme was unable to fulfil its obligations in the event of a systemic crisis. The court ruled out the existence of an 'obligation of result'. It also dismissed allegations concerning discriminatory treatment of deposit holders, holding that 'the transfer of domestic deposits – whether it leads in general to unequal treatment or not – does not fall within the scope of the non-discrimination principle'.[111] According to the EFTA Court, 'the principle of non-discrimination requires that there is no difference in the treatment of depositors by the guarantee scheme itself and the way it uses its funds'.[112] In the case at hand, the guarantee scheme was not involved in the transfer of deposits. In 2009, the Deposit Guarantee Directive was amended; it now stipulates that the Member States

---

107 Ibid.

108 P. Baudino, J.T. Sturluson and J-P. Svoronos, The Banking Crisis in Iceland, FSI Crisis Management Series No. 1, March 2020, p. 2.

109 D. Schoenmaker, Governance of International Banking: The Financial Trilemma, OUP, 2013, Chapter 4.2. See also P. Davies, Resolution of cross-border groups, in M. Haentjens and B. Wessels (eds), Research Handbook on Crisis Management in the Banking Sector, Edward Elgar Publishing, 2015, pp. 263–265.

110 Directive 94/19/EC of 30 May 1994 on deposit-guarantee schemes (now repealed by Directive 2014/49/EU of 16 April 2014 on deposit guarantee schemes (recast)).

111 Judgment of the EFTA Court, *EFTA Surveillance Authority v. Iceland*, E-16/11, 28 January 2013, para. 216 <https://eftacourt.int/download/16-11-judgment/?wpdmdl=1260> (accessed 10 October 2024).

112 Ibid., para. 210.

shall ensure a certain coverage level for deposits.[113] Yet the question of a state guarantee in a situation where there are insufficient funds in a deposit guarantee scheme to pay all depositors remains unresolved.[114]

In response to the GFC and the numerous problems it brought to light, the Financial Stability Board (FSB) – an international body responsible for monitoring and making recommendations about the global financial system – issued the influential Key Attributes of Effective Resolution Regimes for Financial Institutions (Key Attributes).[115] These are internationally recognised standards for credit institutions, aimed at facilitating an orderly resolution of banks without causing severe systemic disruption or exposing taxpayers to losses, while safeguarding critical services and functions. The Key Attributes clearly recognise the existence of banking groups and provide for rules that consider group integration and interdependence when preparing for and implementing resolution tools. These rules cover various aspects, including (i) group recovery and resolution plans (KA 11), (ii) crisis management groups (KA 8), (iii) assessment of group resolvability (KA 10),[116] and (iv) access to information and information sharing (KA 12).[117] The Key Attributes reflect the specificity of banking groups and emphasise the need to prepare for and conduct resolution with this specificity in mind. They served as a basis for the BRRD and the SRMR, which lay down several provisions relevant to banking groups. 3.40

The complexity and interconnectedness of financial institutions (e.g. arising from intra-group transactions, deposits with each other, and ownership of securities, issued by other banks[118]), coupled with the potential drastic consequences of their failure (systemic risk) were the driving force behind the legal recognition of banking groups in rules on bank resolution. The GFC-effect showcased that 'bank risk-taking has a systematic, as opposed to idiosyncratic 3.41

113 Deposit Guarantee Directive, Article 6.

114 E.G. Gunnarsson, The Icelandic Regulatory Responses to the Financial Crisis, EBOR, Vol. 12, 2011, pp. 1-39.

115 Key Attributes of Effective Resolution Regimes for Financial Institutions, 4 November 2011. The Key Attributes were revised in 2014 with additional annexes that set out implementation guidance.

116 Ibid. Group resolvability assessment should consider how 'interconnections or interdependencies between group entities through intra-group transactions … affect the implementation of the resolution strategy'.

117 According to KA 12, firms should be required to 'maintain specific information at a legal entity level, including, for example, information on intra-group guarantees and intra-group trades booked on a back-to-back basis'.

118 W-G. Ringe and J. Patel, The Dark Side of Bank Resolution: Counterparty Risk through Bail-in, EBI Working Paper Series 2019, No. 31, 2019, observing that the current regulatory framework encourages increased interconnections between banks and noting that financial institutions' investment in securities issued by other financial institutions has been on the rise since 2016 (introduction of the bail-in tool in the EU).

(firm-specific), character'.[119] It prompted regulation extending beyond a single entity. A group-mindful regulation of banks is closely tied to public interest considerations and the significant negative externalities associated with bank failures.

3.4.3 The rise of the rescue culture

3.42 The rise of the rescue culture is characterised by the proliferation of national laws seeking to promote the restructuring of viable enterprises facing financial difficulties and minimise the negative impact of their failures. Over the last decade, several countries, including Singapore,[120] the UK, the Netherlands, Spain,[121] France[122] and Germany, to name a few, have established restructuring-friendly legislation.[123]

3.43 The expansion of restructuring laws is likely to continue. In the European Union, this trend has been influenced by the Restructuring Directive, which had to be transposed into national laws of all EU Member States by 17 July 2021, with a possible extension of up to one year. Although this directive does not aim to fully harmonise substantive insolvency law, it centres around the idea of crisis prevention and early action to forestall the escalation of financial problems and avert insolvency. It rests on the premise that an early crisis response not only prevents the loss of jobs, know-how and skills, but also maximises the total value available to creditors.[124] The importance of a timely reaction to financial struggles is emphasised in the literature.[125] Janger observes that the 'concept of rescue originates in the idea that, sometimes, even insolvent

119 J. Armour and J.N. Gordon, Systemic Harms and Shareholder Value, Journal of Legal Analysis, Vol. 6, 2014, p. 38.

120 M.S. Wee, The Singapore Story of Injecting US Chapter 11 into the Commonwealth Scheme, European Company and Financial Law Review, Vol. 15, 2018, pp. 553-584; A. Gurrea-Martínez, Building a Restructuring Hub: Lessons from Singapore, SMU Yong Pung How School of Law Research Paper 16/2021, 11 October 2021 <https://ssrn.com/abstract=3940512> (accessed 10 October 2024).

121 I. Tirado, Scheming Against the Schemes: A New Framework to Deal with Business Financial Distress in Spain, European Company and Financial Law Review, Vol. 15, 2018, pp. 516-552.

122 E. Ghio, Transposing the Preventive Restructuring Directive 2019 into French Insolvency Law: Rethinking the Role of the Judge and Rebalancing Creditors, International Insolvency Review, Vol. 30, 2021, pp. 54-74.

123 D.C. Ehmke et al., The European Union Preventive Restructuring Framework: A Hole in One? International Insolvency Review, Vol. 28, 2019, p. 185, observing that the recent reforms in Europe 'were aimed at establishing a more restructuring-friendly culture in Europe, espousing a rescue culture for insolvency frameworks'.

124 Restructuring Directive, Recital 2.

125 L. Stanghellini et al. (eds), Best Practices in European Restructuring. Contractualised Distress Resolution in the Shadow of the Law, Wolters Kluwer, 2018, p. 4, noting that 'restructuring and insolvency professionals unanimously consider late reaction to a crisis to be the single most important reason for businesses becoming unsustainable and heading towards liquidation'. B. Wessels and S. Madaus, Rescue of Business in Insolvency Law. Instrument of the European Law Institute, 2017, Recommendation 1.21, stressing

businesses are worth more in operation than they are in liquidation'.[126] While in the USA, the idea of business rescue can be traced back to railroad receiverships of the early 1900s,[127] in many countries, the idea of a value-maximising rescue is relatively novel.

A successful restructuring that maintains and maximises going concern value often relies on preserving group synergies and organisational and financial links within a group of companies. This is directly acknowledged by the EIR Recast, which states that 'cooperation should be aimed at finding a solution that would leverage synergies across the group'.[128] Although the Restructuring Directive does not contain provisions specifically targeting group restructurings, it recognises that the coherence of restructuring and insolvency proceedings should promote the restructuring of groups of companies, irrespective of the location of group members within the EU.[129] It notes that Member States may decide to implement group-mindful mechanisms, such as applying a stay for the benefit of third-party security providers, including guarantors and collateral givers.[130] Thus, the introduction of group-mindful insolvency rules has coincided with the rise of rescue as one of the leading ideologies of modern corporate insolvency law.[131] While it is difficult to establish a causal link between the two, the correlation is noticeable. **3.44**

The preservation of the group's going concern value, which is critical for group restructuring, can be promoted by: **3.45**

- cooperation and communication between courts and IPs,[132]
- joint administration of insolvency proceedings,

the value of supporting 'early warning mechanisms that detect a deteriorating business development and signal the respective urgency to act'.

126 E. Janger, The idea of rescue and the Chapter 11 model, in P.J. Omar and J.L.L. Gant (eds), Research Handbook on Corporate Restructuring, Edward Elgar Publishing, 2021, p. 59.

127 D.A. Skeel, An Evolutionary Theory of Corporate Law and Corporate Bankruptcy, Vanderbilt Law Review, Vol. 51, 1998, p. 1354, explaining the context of flexible, reorganisation based corporate bankruptcy: 'Almost everyone agreed that the railroads could not be permitted to fail. Unlike most other corporations, railroads served a crucial public function that was essential to the nation's growth.'

128 EIR Recast, Recital 52.

129 Restructuring Directive, Recital 15.

130 Restructuring Directive, Recital 32.

131 The question whether the rehabilitation of a debtor's business is a legitimate objective of insolvency law on its own, or whether it only matters to the extent that it can maximise recoveries for existing entitlement holders, is beyond the scope of this book. For discussion of different positions, see K. van Zwieten, Goode on Principles of Corporate Insolvency Law, 5th edn, Sweet & Maxwell, 2019, at 2-15 to 2-19.

132 The EIR Recast and the MLEGI establish that IPs and courts *shall* cooperate and communicate with each other to the maximum extent possible. EIR Recast, Articles 56–58 and MLEGI, Articles 9 and 14.

- granting powers to IPs to intervene in proceedings concerning other group entities,[133]
- coordinated appointment of IPs,[134]
- third-party releases,
- extending an insolvency stay to group affiliates, and
- facilitating intra-group (rescue) financing.

3.46 In conclusion, the rationale and policy goals that determine or influence the development of the third generation of insolvency laws vary. After the GFC, the regulation of bank failures is built around the concept of group resolvability, primarily focusing on the preservation of banks' critical functions, protection of public funds and mitigation of systemic risk – macroprudential goals associated with wider social costs and negative externalities. It therefore does not have as its main purpose the maximisation of value.[135] By contrast, the business rescue narrative is linked to maintaining operational continuity, retaining the enterprise's human resources, and preserving business relationships to maximise the insolvency estate value of an enterprise group and its constituent members.

3.5 LIMITS OF A SINGLE ENTERPRISE APPROACH

3.5.1 Limits of group resolvability

3.47 The post-GFC bank resolution regime recognises that banks often operate as integrated cross-border groups of companies – banking groups. In view of this, it has adjusted its approach to address group financial distress through the use of special tools, such as group recovery and resolution planning,[136] group financial support arrangements, the preparation and execution of models of bank resolution, subject to ex ante pre-positioning of resources and liabilities within a group.[137]

---

133 EIR Recast, Article 60, allowing an IP to request a stay of realisation of assets in proceedings concerning another group member. Also, MLEGI, Article 20, covering relief available to a planning proceeding.

134 EIR Recast, Article 57; MLEGI, Article 17.

135 E. Martino, The Bail-in Beyond Unpredictability: Creditors' Incentives and Market Discipline, European Business Organization Law Review, Vol. 21, 2020, p. 821, arguing that 'preserving financial stability and protecting property rights clearly outweigh market discipline in terms of minimising resolution costs and avoiding the destruction of value'.

136 An obligation to prepare resolution plans or 'living wills' was introduced after the GFC both in the USA (Dodd-Frank Act, section 165(d)) and in the EU (BRRD, Article 12). These plans generally cover a banking group globally and should reflect its corporate, operational and legal interconnectedness, and contain the steps to ensure group resolvability.

137 The two main models or strategies for bank resolution are a SPOE model and a MPOE model. They should be aligned with the group's corporate, operational and financial structure and serve as a basis for an orderly resolution.

One cannot help but notice that the group-mindful regulation of banks is more comprehensive and developed compared to the rules applicable in the insolvency of non-financial enterprises, which mainly focus on enhanced cooperation, communication and coordination. This divergence may stem from the specific goals pursued by bank resolution and the underlying system of values. Bank resolution is primarily concerned with the preservation of banks' critical functions and national, regional and global financial stability. This policy mandates a departure from a narrow entity-by-entity and territorial approach. However, the extent of this departure should not be overstated. Upon closer examination, one can observe that the essence of entity separateness is diligently preserved. 3.48

First, even the BRRD, which establishes an elaborate EU-wide framework for bank resolution, does not permit the application of resolution tools to a banking group as a whole, as if it were a single legal entity. Instead, resolution tools can only be applied at the level of separate group members (parent or subsidiary companies), unless national insolvency law provides for group treatment.[138] Elke König, the former Chair of the Single Resolution Board (SRB), noted that 'in the current framework insolvency is clearly entity-specific …'[139] Under the BRRD, 'group resolution' refers to either the taking of a resolution action at the level of a parent undertaking or an institution subject to consolidated supervision (with a view to resolving the whole or a part of the group), or the coordination of the application of resolution tools and the exercise of resolution powers by resolution authorities in relation to group entities that meet the conditions for resolution.[140] In both cases, the separateness of group members is safeguarded, as resolution tools are applied on an entity ('resolution entity') basis – the only difference being the level of such an entity within the banking group structure. 3.49

Second, the well-known no-creditor-worse-off (NCWO) principle, which protects creditors' and shareholders' rights in resolution, operates at the entity level rather than at the group level. This means that a resolution tool must not worsen a creditor's position compared to what it would be in a normal insolvency proceeding, even if the resolution enhances the combined net value 3.50

138 J. Deslandes and M. Magnus, Further Harmonising EU Insolvency Law from a Banking Resolution Perspective? April 2018, p. 7.

139 E. König, Real defragmentation of the Banking Union: the way forward, Eurofi, April 2018 <https://srb.europa.eu/en/node/544> (accessed 10 October 2024).

140 BRRD, Article 2(1)(42).

of the banking group.[141] The European Banking Authority (EBA) clarifies that 'the NCWO assessment has to be performed at the level of each group entity subject to resolution measures'.[142] However, it accepts that the ultimate assessment depends on whether national insolvency law provides for special treatment of groups of companies, inter alia, by recognising group interest or mandating the subordination of intra-group claims.[143] That being said, at this moment, the vast majority of EU Member States lack specific legislation that addresses the insolvency of corporate groups or explicitly recognises group interest.

3.51 Third, a closer examination of group-specific rules reveals their limitations. Take, for instance, group financial support agreements under the BRRD. While these agreements could take into account group interest, they must not compromise the liquidity or solvency of the entity providing support to other (receiving) group entities.[144] In other words, group interest should not override or undermine the interests of individual group entities and their creditors. Besides, the BRRD does not introduce an overarching concept of group interest; group interest surfaces in a clear way only in the provisions regarding intra-group financial support.[145]

3.5.2 Limits of a group-centric vision in corporate insolvency law

3.52 While estate value preservation and maximisation may support the adoption of a group-centric vision in insolvency, creditor positions are typically assessed at the single-entity level. This is because, in the absence of substantive consolidation, the separateness of assets and liabilities is maintained. Any relationship – whether by shareholding or other means – with another legal entity within an enterprise group generally becomes irrelevant in this context.

3.53 This is why, similar to the NCWO principle, the best-interests-of-creditors test is applied with respect to each separate entity involved in a restructuring plan. This test serves as a reference point or minimum baseline, protecting individual

141 BRRD, Articles 73–75. A breach of the NCWO principle gives rise to a compensation claim by affected creditors or shareholders.

142 NCWO principle in a group resolution, Single Rulebook Q&A, Question ID 2015_2458 <https://www.eba.europa.eu/single-rule-book-qa/-/qna/view/publicId/2015_2458> (accessed 10 October 2024).

143 Ibid. See also D. Singh, European Cross-Border Banking and Banking Supervision, OUP, 2020, pp. 137–138, underscoring that the NCWO principle 'provides a balance between the competing public and private interests', but recognising that in a group 'it is likely that the [NCWO principle] will lead to different outcomes for the creditors of the different incorporated entities'.

144 BRRD, Article 23(1)(e).

145 E. Ferran and L.C. Ho, Principles of Corporate Finance Law, 2nd edn, OUP, 2014, p. 41.

creditors and shareholders and safeguarding their property rights.[146] Thus, a reorganisation plan should not be approved if it fails to meet this standard, unless the affected parties consent to it.[147] This means that a utilitarian, group-focused vision cannot override or harm the interests of individual entities and their creditors. However, this does not imply that individual interests should be isolated from group interests, as they are often aligned. The problem arises when these interests are in conflict.

The limits of a single enterprise approach are also evident in the restrictions imposed on cross-border communication and cooperation and the appointment of the same IP. For example, the EIR Recast prescribes that in a group insolvency context, courts and IPs shall communicate and cooperate only to the extent that this does not lead to a conflict of interest.[148] Such conflicts may arise in disputes between group members involving the enforcement of intra-group claims, transaction avoidance actions, and the allocation or transfer of assets within the group.[149] Moss and Smith point out that whenever there is a disputed claim between two group entities, the obligation for IPs to cooperate may 'need to be circumscribed accordingly'.[150] This is because such cooperation might lead to the exchange of information that could substantiate a claim of one group entity against another, potentially to the detriment of the latter. Schmidt provides another example where cooperation can be limited – where it entails (gratuitous) 'transmission of valuable know-how, patents, or business secrets, or making assets available to other group members which could have been disposed of with a large profit for the individual group member'.[151] Again, this is an example of conflicting interests of group members. 3.54

146 S. Madaus, Leaving the Shadows of US Bankruptcy Law: A Proposal to Divide the Realms of Insolvency and Restructuring Law, EBOR, Vol. 19, 2018, p. 638.

147 Restructuring Directive, Articles 2(1)(6), 10(2)(d).

148 EIR Recast, Articles 56-58. On conflicts of interest in group insolvencies, see I. Kokorin, Conflicts of Interest, Intra-group Financing and Procedural Coordination of Group Insolvencies, International Insolvency Review, Vol. 29, 2020, pp. 32–60.

149 Legislative Guide, Part three, Ch. II, para. 68, referring to a situation of intra-group rescue financing where a 'conflict of interest might arise, for example, in balancing the interests of the group as a whole against the potentially different interests of the lender and the receiver of post-commencement finance'. See Lehman Brothers Insolvency Protocol (2009), para. 4.6., stating that 'Each Official Representative should cooperate in the gathering and sharing of certain data and share analysis of certain transactions by … coordinating in good faith the investigations of pre-filing activities with any other Official Representative with an interest in such activities, so long as the interests of the Official Representatives coordinating such investigations do not diverge …'

150 G. Moss and T. Smith, Commentary on Regulation 1346/2000 and Recast Regulation 2015/848 on insolvency proceedings, in G. Moss, I. Fletcher and S. Isaacs (eds), Moss, Fletcher and Isaacs on the EU Regulation on insolvency proceedings, 3rd edn, OUP, 2016, para. 8.754.

151 J. Schmidt, Commentary to Article 56, in R. Bork and K. van Zwieten (eds), Commentary on the European insolvency regulation, OUP, 2016, para. 56.22.

3.55 This problem is magnified if the same IP is appointed to administer the proceedings of multiple members of an enterprise group with complex financial and business relationships and distinct creditor groups.[152] Obtaining complete information, otherwise unavailable, might compel an IP to lodge a claim on behalf of one enterprise group member against another, thus placing him in the position of representing both the claimant and the respondent. Another example relates to the extension of cross-guarantees or the provision of post-commencement financing, which may benefit one entity (e.g. the company receiving financing or a guarantee) at the expense of another (e.g. the provider of financing, guarantee or collateral). Essentially, the IP needs to negotiate with herself the appropriateness of these measures and their terms (e.g. amount, compensation, timeframe, security). This is an epitome of the 'two masters' problem.

3.6 CONCLUSION

3.56 This chapter highlights that, despite the exponential growth of multinational enterprise groups over the twentieth century, insolvency law has primarily focused on separate legal entities. This single-entity approach rests on the difficulty of defining a corporate group, the diversity of group types and structures, and the challenge of fitting any group-oriented rules into the prevailing frameworks of company and insolvency law, which are still largely dominated by the doctrines of legal separateness, limited liability and entity shielding. However, over the last few decades, insolvency law has undergone transformative developments.

3.57 These developments were accelerated by the GFC, which exposed the interconnectedness of financial institutions and the need to address the systemic risks of their failure at a group (macro) level. At the same time, for non-financial firms, the emergence of insolvency law instruments that recognise the group's economic reality is linked to the rise of laws which aim to preserve the debtors' business and going concern value through restructuring. Achieving this goal could be compromised if group operational continuity is disrupted in insolvency. In many jurisdictions, new procedures have been established to

152 Given the prominence of these conflicts, Van Galen notes that '[i]t is remarkable that there are many domestic cases in which the same liquidator is appointed in the insolvency proceedings of more than one group company'. He observes that 'conflicts of interests between individual group companies may be much more pronounced in insolvency proceedings'. R. van Galen, Insolvent Groups of Companies in Cross Border Cases and Rescue Plans, Report to the Netherlands Association for Comparative and International Insolvency Law (8 November 2012), para. 70.

help struggling debtors resolve financial issues, overcome holdouts and reduce debt burdens. In this chapter, I introduce three procedures that are frequently used to effectuate debt restructuring, including within enterprise groups: UK schemes of arrangement, US Chapter 11 reorganisations and Dutch WHOA plans.

The question is how group-sensitive insolvency law can be reconciled with the doctrine of entity separateness discussed in the previous chapter. When answering this question, it is important to recognise that law can respond to the challenges of group insolvencies in various ways. One might envision a spectrum of legal tools, ranging from complete disregard of the corporate form and limited liability (e.g. substantive consolidation) to less intrusive tools, such as third-party releases, extended enforcement stays, invalidation or approval of intra-group transactions (e.g. cross-guarantees), limited enforceability of certain contractual provisions (e.g. cross-entity ipso facto and cross-default clauses), and simple coordination of proceedings concerning group entities. Some of these tools will be discussed in the chapters that follow. For now, it suffices to emphasise that the majority of them do not impact the core of entity separateness – limited liability and entity shielding. 3.58

PART III

PRINCIPLES OF INSOLVENCY LAW AND HOW TO BALANCE THEM

4

PRINCIPLES OF INSOLVENCY LAW AND CONFLICTS BETWEEN THEM

4.1 INTRODUCTION

Commenting on the methodological foundations of modern law scholarship, Burrows observes that 'we rarely find doctrinal scholars analysing the precise methodological approach that they are adopting'.[1] When interpreting law and making normative suggestions, one can employ various methods. One method involves the use of economic arguments, examining law from both ex ante and ex post positions.[2] Another method focuses on underlying legal principles. This method is embraced by this book, in combination with comparative analysis and occasional references to pragmatic or economic arguments. **4.01**

In choosing the research methodology, I was inspired by the work of Reinhard Bork, Professor (Emeritus) at the University of Hamburg (Germany).[3] In his **4.02**

1 A. Burrows, Remedies for Torts, Breach of Contract, and Equitable Wrongs, OUP, 4th edn, 2019, p. 21.

2 R. Posner, Economic analysis of law, 8th edn, Austin, TX: Wolters Kluwer Law & Business, 2010.

3 R. Bork, Corporate Insolvency Law. A Comparative Textbook, Intersentia, 2020; R. Bork, Principles of Cross-Border Insolvency Law, Intersentia, 2017. The principle-based approach was followed in a more recent book, written by Bork together with Michael Veder, professor at Radboud University (the

publications, Bork describes the main principles of international and national insolvency law, systematises and contextualises them, highlights the benefits of using principles as a tool to examine and better understand the law and to make suggestions for its improvement. The principle-based approach boils down to a legal analysis based on a taxonomy of relevant and widely accepted standards. It entails a study of rules, their assessment through the lens of legal principles with the goal of developing optimal policy choices.

4.03 There are multiple benefits to using the principle-based approach. Legal principles represent broad standards and core values underlying practice and behaviour. A better understanding of these values is crucial for grasping the essence of law, which is key to the interpretation and application of rules. The principle-based approach can facilitate change and harmonisation efforts, as it helps to find principle-based solutions to similar problems experienced by various legal systems. Finally, the clarity of legal principles allows for a deliberate and well-informed balancing exercise to resolve conflicts between legal principles.

4.04 The choice of the principle-based methodology in this book is premised on the realisation that financial distress within international enterprise groups gives rise to complex legal and financial issues that are not always easy to conceptualise or codify into rigid rules. Returning to legal principles is one way to address this complexity. This chapter proceeds as follows. Section 4.2 identifies those legal principles most relevant to my analysis. Section 4.3 explores how these legal principles apply in a group insolvency setting. Section 4.4 discusses the issue of collision between legal principles and explores the ways to resolve it. Section 4.5 concludes.

4.2 CORE LEGAL PRINCIPLES AT PLAY IN INSOLVENCY

4.2.1 Classification of legal principles

4.05 Law is connected to fundamental societal values by way of legal principles. These principles express certain basic standards and constitute the normative core of a legal system. Bork divides the principles of insolvency law into three broad categories: (i) jurisdictional, (ii) procedural, and (iii) substantive principles.[4] Jurisdictional principles address the relationships between sovereign

Netherlands). See R. Bork and M. Veder, Harmonisation of Transactions Avoidance Laws, Intersentia, 2022.

4 R. Bork, Principles of Cross-Border Insolvency Law, Intersentia, 2017, pp. 16–17.

states and include, among others, principles of unity, universalism, mutual trust, communication and cooperation in insolvency cases. Procedural principles relate to the organisation of a procedure, which must comply with the standards of efficiency, transparency, predictability and procedural justice. The third category is substantive principles, which are often unique and reflect the influence of insolvency on the substantive rights and legal positions of different parties, including creditors, debtors and shareholders.

Among the substantive principles, Bork mentions: (i) equal treatment of unsecured creditors, (ii) the best possible realisation of the debtor's assets (insolvency estate value maximisation), and (iii) protection of legitimate expectations, also referred to as protection of trust. The latter is closely related to the principles of party autonomy and freedom of contract. As such, protection of trust and freedom of contract are not principles 'of' insolvency law, but rather principles 'relevant for' insolvency law. This book will focus on these principles, given their relevance in a group financing and insolvency context. As noted in the introductory chapter, private international law falls outside the scope, making jurisdictional principles less relevant to our discussion. The same applies to procedural principles, at least to the extent that they do not directly implicate one of the substantive principles. The selection of principles in this book does not diminish the importance of other legal principles. On the contrary, their significance must be expressly recognised. One example is the principle of social protection, which often plays a distinct role in structuring and executing corporate and financial restructuring.[5] **4.06**

4.2.2 Principles of insolvency law v. principles of restructuring law

One may wonder (and rightly so) whether the principles of insolvency law listed above should equally apply to the types of restructuring proceedings that require neither full collectivity (such as Dutch WHOA plans, English schemes of arrangement and Part 26A restructuring plans) nor a certain degree of financial distress or, indeed, insolvency (as in the case of US Chapter 11 and English schemes of arrangement). This is an important consideration that becomes more evident as I delve into the comparative analysis in the subsequent chapters of this book. **4.07**

5 A. Kastrinou and S. Vullings, 'No Evil is without Good': A Comparative Analysis of Pre-pack Sales in the UK and the Netherlands, International Insolvency Review, Vol. 27, 2018, pp. 320–339, discussing the effects of the CJEU's ruling in *Estro/Smallstep* on pre-packaged restructurings (pre-packs). Also, Article 369(4) of the Dutch Bankruptcy Act (*Faillissementswet* or Fw), stating that the provisions on WHOA schemes do not apply to rights of employees arising from employment contracts.

4.08 The type of procedure cannot be ignored because it affects the scope of available tools. For example, transaction avoidance is not available in English company voluntary arrangements or schemes of arrangement, as well as in Dutch WHOA schemes. Yet transactions can be challenged in a Chapter 11 procedure, English administration and Dutch bankruptcy procedures. Another example is third-party releases, which have a statutory basis in the rules on WHOA schemes, but not in the rules concerning bankruptcy and suspension of payments. Given how different these procedures are, can they be subject to the same set of legal principles?

4.09 Arguing that the realms of insolvency and restructuring law, as well as the legal principles underpinning them, should be separated, Madaus writes that 'a restructuring agreement would be the result of restructuring proceedings which do not respond to a common pool problem, but instead aim at facilitating the conclusion of a contract and, thus, are governed by contract (and company) law rules and principles'.[6] For Madaus, these realms are distinguished based on the problem that law aims to solve – collective action problems (insolvency law) versus anti-commons (restructuring law). Bork and Veder also observe that the principles of insolvency law are not applicable 'where the proceedings are not dependent on the debtor's insolvency and therefore not collective proceedings'.[7] For them, the realms are separated based on the requirements of 'substantive insolvency' and 'collectivity'.[8] This means that restructuring proceedings used at an early stage of financial crisis and those not entailing collectivity are not covered by insolvency law and its principles. By contrast, Mevorach and Walters state that '[i]nsolvency and restructuring law is … a unified body of law that maps onto the continuum, rather than two discrete bodies of law'.[9]

---

6 S. Madaus, Leaving the Shadows of US Bankruptcy Law: A Proposal to Divide the Realms of Insolvency and Restructuring Law, European Business Organization Law Review, Vol. 19, 2018, p. 630.

7 R. Bork and M. Veder, Harmonisation of Transactions Avoidance Laws, Intersentia, 2022, para. 3.5.

8 Ibid., para. 3.6., defining 'substantive insolvency' as 'comprising not only present but also likely and imminent inability to pay debts as they fall due …' Thus, it encompasses actual insolvency, likely insolvency (inability to pay debts in the foreseeable future with a likelihood of >50 per cent) and imminent insolvency (inability to pay debts within the next few months). Note, however, that Bork and Veder discuss substantive insolvency in the context of transaction avoidance law and argue that its application would be difficult to justify in restructuring proceedings for companies 'in the state of looming, but not likely imminent or present, inability to pay'.

9 I. Mevorach and A. Walters, The Characterization of Pre-insolvency Proceedings in Private International Law, EBOR, Vol. 21, 2021, p. 879. Insolvency as a scalar attribute has also been noted by Mokal. See R. Mokal, What is an insolvency proceeding? *Gategroup* lands in a gated community, International Insolvency Review, Vol. 31(3), 2022, pp. 418–473.

Any attempts to strictly delineate insolvency and restructuring laws are problematic for several reasons. 4.10

- First, the same procedure may be used for the collective resolution of financial distress or targeted debt restructuring (e.g. Dutch WHOA scheme). If one adopts collectivity as a distinguishing criterion, the same procedure can fall under the insolvency or restructuring realm, depending on how it is being used in a concrete case. Besides, a combination of proceedings could be used to reach the desired goal. For example, in the UK, schemes and CVAs are often combined with administration. Applying different principles to these interlinked procedures creates unnecessary rigidity.
- Second, financial distress is a fluid concept, reflecting a demise curve or a downward spiral. In practice, looming insolvency can easily turn into likely insolvency, imminent insolvency or actual insolvency. This is why it is rather difficult and perhaps arbitrary to use the degree of financial distress as a qualifying criterion to determine if we are still dealing with restructuring law principles or whether insolvency law principles have already come into play. Think of Chapter 11. Since it does not mandate any degree of financial distress, one cannot determine in the abstract whether it belongs to the realm of insolvency or restructuring law.
- Third, given that group restructuring may be realised via different procedures – whether fully collective and insolvency-driven or not, an open approach is well-justified. The framing of law as either restructuring or insolvency does not easily fit this approach.
- Fourth, and finally, the chosen principles appear to be so fundamental and transpiring that they should and, as demonstrated below, do apply in both 'traditional' insolvent liquidations and restructuring proceedings.

4.2.3 Value preservation and maximisation

The principle of value preservation and maximisation aims to 'facilitate higher distributions to creditors as a whole and reduce the burden of insolvency'.[10] Insolvency law is often viewed as a way to resolve creditors' claims in the most efficient way. In principle, this is achieved through a collective procedure that replaces individual enforcement by creditors. The court supervises the use and disposition of assets, holding them together to preserve and maximise their value. 4.11

According to Baird, we need insolvency law 'to ensure that the self-interest of individuals does not run counter to the interests of the group'.[11] Bork and Veder distinguish between the principles of the best possible realisation of 4.12

10 UNCITRAL Legislative Guide, Part one, Ch. I, para. 5. In practice, however, due to privileges granted to certain groups of creditors, it is often not creditors 'as a whole' who benefit from insolvency estate value maximisation, but privileged groups of creditors. See C.G. Paulus, Multinational Enterprises and National Insolvency Laws: Lobbying for Special Privileges, EBOR, Vol. 29, 2018, pp. 393–415.

11 D.G. Baird, A World Without Bankruptcy, Law and Contemporary Problems, Vol. 50, 1987, p. 184.

debtor's assets (optimisation) and the best possible satisfaction of creditors' claims (satisfaction).[12] The former deals with the assets comprising the insolvency estate at the time of the opening of an insolvency proceeding and strives to secure the highest price for these assets. It does so by, among other things, providing for the termination of onerous contracts and keeping the costs of the proceeding low. The latter addresses any disadvantage caused to the general body of creditors and enriches the insolvency estate by, inter alia, undoing detrimental acts and economically revoking their disadvantageous effects. For simplicity, and given how close these principles are, I will refer to the unified principle of value preservation and maximisation.

4.13 This principle is recognised as a guiding principle of insolvency law by the World Bank,[13] UNCITRAL,[14] the European Bank for Reconstruction and Development,[15] the EU instruments[16] and many national legal systems.[17] The goal of value preservation and maximisation in the insolvency context has two major aspects: procedural and substantive efficiency.

4.14 Procedural efficiency focuses on minimising the direct and indirect costs associated with insolvency proceedings. These costs include court fees and fees of IPs, as well as reputational damage, workforce attrition, reduced access to credit and the unwillingness of third parties to continue trading with a financially distressed or insolvent entity. By some estimates, the direct costs of insolvency range between 1 per cent and 10 per cent of the firm value, while indirect costs could reach up to 23 per cent.[18]

4.15 Substantive efficiency underpins a variety of mechanisms and tools used by insolvency law to preserve or maximise existing value. This can be achieved

---

12 R. Bork and M. Veder, Harmonisation of Transactions Avoidance Laws, Intersentia, 2022, paras. 2.43–2.50.

13 The World Bank, Principles for Effective Insolvency and Creditor/debtor Regimes, 2021, C1, mentioning that an effective insolvency system should aim to '[m]aximize the value of a firm's assets and recoveries by creditors'.

14 MLCBI, Preamble, listing among its objectives the protection and maximisation of the value of the debtor's assets.

15 EBRD Core Principles of an Effective Insolvency System, September 2020, Principle 2, stating that '[i]nsolvency procedures should be designed and implemented to preserve and maximise the total value ultimately available to creditors'.

16 Restructuring Directive, Recital 2, noting that, among other policy goals, restructuring frameworks should help to maximise the total value to creditors.

17 L.G.A. Janssen, EU bank resolution framework: A comparative study on the relation with national private law, E.M. Meijers Instituut, 2020, p. 190, noting that in the UK, Germany and the Netherlands, maximising the returns to creditors is regarded as the primary objective of insolvency law.

18 Z. Sautner and V. Vladimirov, Indirect Costs of Financial Distress and Bankruptcy Law: Evidence from Trade Credit and Sales, Review of Finance, Vol. 22, 2018, pp. 1667–1704, arguing that indirect costs can be reduced by increasing the likelihood of out-of-court restructuring.

through transaction avoidance, the prohibition of ipso facto clauses and the protection of rescue financing. Some of these tools primarily aim to safeguard the present value and protect it against losses. For example, a stay on individual enforcement actions, termination of disadvantageous contracts and limitations on contract clauses that could dissipate value, all seek to keep the current asset base intact. Other tools are employed to enlarge this base by, inter alia, holding debtor's directors liable for insolvency-related misconduct.[19] To facilitate the analysis in the following chapters of this book, several preliminary points should be addressed.

First, insolvency estate value can be established as either liquidation value or going concern value. The former represents the value of the debtor's assets if sold on the market on a piecemeal basis. The latter refers to the net present worth of the business as a going concern, taking into account its operational continuity and future income (the going concern surplus).[20] Westbrook stresses that the 'going concern value may be much greater than market value (and therefore, much, much greater than liquidation value) because a living business ... may well bring a higher price as a unit than would the sale of each asset separately'.[21] **4.16**

Second, restructuring is often achieved by one of the following methods: (i) postponement of liabilities to a more distant future, (ii) conversion of debt into equity, and (iii) debt reduction or write-down.[22] The UNCITRAL Legislative Guide connects the choice between liquidation and reorganisation to the objective of value maximisation.[23] Similarly, the Conference of European Restructuring and Insolvency Law concludes that the 'rules which support restructuring efforts conceivably enforce the principle of optimal realisation of the debtor's assets'.[24] Restructuring can also contribute to the accomplishment **4.17**

19 Case C-594/14 *Simona Kornhaas v. Thomas Dithmar*, 10 December 2015, para. 20, holding that director liability action in question contributed to the 'attainment of an objective which is intrinsically linked, mutatis mutandis, to all insolvency proceedings, namely the prevention of any reduction of the assets of the insolvent estate before the insolvency proceedings are opened'.

20 Black's Law Dictionary defines the 'going concern value' as the 'value of a commercial enterprise's assets or of the enterprise itself as an active business with future earning power, as opposed to the liquidation value of the business or of its assets'. Black's Law Dictionary, 8th edn, Thomson Reuters, 2004, p. 1587.

21 J.L. Westbrook, The Control of Wealth in Bankruptcy, Texas Law Review, Vol. 82, 2004, p. 811.

22 M. Crystal and R.J. Mokal, The Valuation of Distressed Companies – a Conceptual Framework, International Corporate Rescue, Issues 2 and 3, 2006 <https://ssrn.com/abstract=877155> (accessed 10 October 2024).

23 UNCITRAL Legislative Guide, Part one, Ch. I, para. 6, stating that insolvency law 'should include the possibility of reorganization of the debtor as an alternative to liquidation, where creditors would not involuntarily receive less than in liquidation and the value of the debtor to society and to creditors may be maximized by allowing it to continue'.

24 CERIL Report 2017-1, 26 September 2017, para. 35.

of other goals, such as the prevention of job losses and the facilitation of competition. Yet, whether restructuring can be considered a substantive principle in and of itself is debatable. Bork and Veder argue that restructuring 'is not a core value in itself, since goals and policies are to be distinguished from principles'.[25] I agree.

4.18 Third, when comparing the rescue of distressed companies and individuals, Judge Conner pointed out that 'a corporation is not a biological entity for which it can be presumed that any act which extends its existence is beneficial to it'.[26] To distinguish which companies could (and should) be restructured to safeguard their value, the concept of economic viability needs to be explained. Viability is a complex concept that may indicate the competitiveness of the debtor's business model and the likelihood of its survival post-restructuring. It also characterises businesses whose going concern value exceeds the hypothetical liquidation value.[27] Economic viability, as contrasted with financial viability (i.e. the ability to pay off debt obligations), is often established as an eligibility threshold or a filtering screen for restructuring proceedings.[28] This is based on the assumption that the restructuring of non-viable firms can lead to the destruction of value, instead of its preservation.[29]

---

25 R. Bork and M. Veder, Harmonisation of Transactions Avoidance Laws, Intersentia, 2022, para. 2.46.

26 *In re Investors Funding Corp. of New York Sec. Litig.*, 523 F. Supp. 533, 541 (S.D.N.Y. 1980).

27 L. Tsioli, Viability assessment in corporate debt restructuring: Optimizing the filtration effect of the European directive on restructuring and insolvency, Norton Journal of Bankruptcy Law and Practice, Vol. 30, 2021, p. 400; M. Kahl, Economic Distress, Financial Distress, and Dynamic Liquidation, The Journal of Finance, Vol. 57, 2002, p. 141, arguing that '[v]iable firms should be continued because their continuation value is higher than their liquidation value'.

28 The viability test may take different forms and can be applied at different stages of the process. For example, in the USA, viability is not assessed at the outset of Chapter 11; it surfaces in the norms on involuntary conversion and dismissal (11 U.S. Code § 1112) and relief from the stay (11 U.S. Code § 362). In the UK, as part of a new moratorium procedure, a monitor should at the outset assess and state that it is likely that the moratorium would result in the rescue of the company as a going concern. Insolvency Act 1986, Part A1, A(1)(e). See also StaRUG, § 14, stating that a 'restructuring plan is to be accompanied by a substantiated declaration concerning the prospects for eliminating the debtor's imminent illiquidity through the plan and for ensuring or restoring the debtor's viability'. For Dutch law, see Rb. Den Haag 2 March 2021, ECLI:NL:RBDHA:2021:1798, noting that the rules introduced by the WHOA primarily focus on companies in danger of becoming insolvent due to over-indebtedness but that still have viable businesses. The court accepted that it is primarily up to the creditors to form an opinion on the viability of the debtor's business. However, it found itself competent to determine that the business would not be viable post-restructuring. As a result, the WHOA plan was not approved.

29 H. Eidenmüller, Contracting for a European Insolvency Regime, EBOR, Vol. 18, 2017, p. 288, emphasising the filtering function of insolvency law, which should be available 'to restructure only viable firms and liquidate the non-viable ones'. Eidenmüller also notes that the 'economic costs resulting from this mistake [letting non-viable firms restructure] are surely not trivial'.

4.2.4 Protection of legitimate expectations, freedom of contract and party autonomy

Insolvency is a foreseeable risk, as no business is in principle immune to it.[30] Therefore, it is crucial for creditors, debtors and other stakeholders to be able to assess insolvency-related risks ex ante, particularly when engaging in transactions with financially distressed but not yet insolvent debtors. **4.19**

Virgós and Garcimartín explain that 'parties shape their relationships "in the shadow" of a specific legal environment; an environment that includes the degree of "resistance" of [their] rights in the event of the insolvency of the debtor, which is the most typical risk faced by any creditor'.[31] When parties enter into agreements, they do so with the expectation that their claims will be satisfied in full. However, in the event of insolvency, this may not be possible. The likelihood and extent of satisfaction depend on many factors, including the insolvency forum, applicable law (*lex concursus*) and its impact on contractual rights (e.g. the permissibility of set-off, termination of executory contracts, enforceability of ipso facto clauses, protection of rights *in rem*, transaction avoidance). **4.20**

The ability to assess these factors – and hence respond to them – enhances risk calculation (where risk is understood as the uncertainty of future returns), creates incentives to engage in financial relationships ex ante, and reduces the costs of insolvency ex post.[32] In contrast, breaches of trust and legitimate expectations lead to social costs in the form of foregone transactions (those that did not occur due to legal uncertainty), higher interest rates that limit access to credit due to increased costs, extended screening or due diligence expenses, and protracted litigation. **4.21**

---

30 'Insolvency-proofness' existed in France with reference to establishments of industrial and commercial character (EPICs in their French acronym), such as La Poste. In French administrative law, EPICs are legal entities governed by public law. Yet they have a legal personality distinct from the state. The status of an EPIC entailed certain legal consequences, including inapplicability of insolvency procedures. As a result, creditors of La Poste effectively had an implied and unlimited state guarantee that their unpaid claims would not be cancelled. This immunity, however, was considered to be a source of state aid, triggering specific obligations. Case C-559/12 P, *French Republic v. European Commission*, 3 April 2014. Another example comes from Russia, where the law makes certain types of legal entities completely immune from insolvency. See Russian Civil Code, Article 65.

31 M. Virgós and F. Garcimartín, The European Insolvency Regulation: Law and Practice, Kluwer Law International, 2004, p. 87.

32 J-C. Bricongne, M. Demertzis, P. Pontuch and A. Turrini, Macroeconomic Relevance of Insolvency Frameworks in a High-debt Context: An EU Perspective, European Commission Discussion Paper 32, June 2016.

4.22 Bork noted that the protection of creditors' expectations and trust 'is an important pillar of every legal order and a basic tenet to be enforced under the rule of law'.[33] There are two important aspects of this principle.

4.23 The first aspect concerns the general protection of property rights. The violation of legitimate expectations may constitute a breach of the right to property.[34] A challenging task is to evaluate which expectations are legitimate. The European Court of Human Rights (ECtHR) held that a legitimate expectation must be of 'a nature more concrete than a mere hope and be based on a legal provision or a legal act such as a judicial decision, bearing on the property interest in question'.[35] In the case of *Boyadzhieva and Gloria International Limited Eood v. Bulgaria*,[36] the court found a violation of the right to property where national law permitted the (automatic) invalidation of all transactions concluded within the so-called 'suspect period', defined as the period after the initial date of insolvency – the date when the debtor could no longer meet its obligations to creditors. Transactions concluded within the suspect period were subject to avoidance without any proof of bad faith or assessment of whether they had adversely affected the insolvency estate or the interests of creditors.[37]

4.24 The second related aspect concerns the principle of freedom of contract. According to this principle, parties should be free to choose each other as contractual partners and determine the terms of their agreement.[38] Generally, the onset of insolvency proceedings does not alter the entitlements or vested interests created before it.[39] In this respect, the World Bank stresses that the

33 R. Bork, Principles of Cross-Border Insolvency Law, Intersentia, 2018, p. 143.

34 The right to property is guaranteed by Article 1 of Protocol No. 1 to the ECHR. M. Sigron, Legitimate Expectations under Article 1 of Protocol No. 1 to the European Convention on Human Rights, Intersentia, 2014.

35 *Gratzinger and Gratzingerova v. The Czech Republic*, Appl. no. 39794/98, Decision (GC), 10 July 2002, Reports 2002-VII, 399, § 73.

36 *Boyadzhieva and Gloria International Limited Eood v. Bulgaria*, Appl. nos. 41299/09 and 11132/10, Judgment, 5 July 2018, § 44.

37 For case analysis, see I. Kokorin and B. Wessels, annotation: European Court of Human Rights 5 July 2018, no. 41299/09 & 11132/10, *JOR* 2019, 3; 778-790 (*JOR* 2019/64 *Boyadzhieva and Gloria International Limited Eood v. Bulgaria*).

38 E. McKendrick, Contract Law: Text, Cases, and Materials, 6th edn, OUP, 2014, p. 13. Freedom of contract is not absolute and there are many exceptions imposed to protect weaker parties, ensure competition and fairness. M.J. Trebilcock, The Limits of Freedom of Contract, Harvard University Press, 1997; P.S. Davies and M. Raczynska (eds), Contents of Commercial Contracts: Terms Affecting Freedoms, Hart Publishing, 2020; R.A. Epstein, Contracts Small and Contracts Large: Contract Law through the Lens of Laissez-Faire, in F.H. Buckley (ed), The Fall and Rise of Freedom of Contract, Duke University Press, 1999, p. 28, distinguishing three interrelated concepts: security of exchange, sanctity of contract and freedom of contract.

39 M. Veder, Party Autonomy and Insolvency Law, in R. Westrik and J. van der Weide (eds), Party Autonomy in International Property Law, Sellier European Law Publishers, 2011, p. 261.

'rights of creditors and the priorities of claims established prior to insolvency proceedings … should be upheld in an insolvency proceeding *to preserve the legitimate expectations of creditors and encourage greater predictability in commercial relationships*'[40] (emphasis added). However, while freedom of contract takes precedence in contract law, it faces significant limitations under insolvency law. At this point, I will make three remarks.

First, there are ways to contractually influence the insolvency process and, to one extent or another, determine its outcome. For example, secured creditors derive their priority and power from pre-insolvency contractual relationships, which guarantee them a preferential position in insolvency or the ability to exercise significant control over the insolvency process. In some jurisdictions (e.g. the Netherlands), secured creditors are essentially immune from bankruptcy proceedings. In others (e.g. in the USA), they do not enjoy such immunity but often direct bankruptcy proceedings and dictate the conditions of the business sale.[41] Another example is inter-creditor agreements or agreements between creditors and a debtor. These agreements may include claim subordination, whereby one creditor or a group of creditors agrees to subordinate their rights in insolvency, effectively contracting out of the *pari passu* distribution.[42] A new form of insolvency-related contracting is the restructuring support agreement, used primarily in the USA to secure contractual arrangements supporting a particular plan to be later implemented via a pre-packaged deal. These arrangements provide certainty and facilitate 'a clearer, quicker, and more reliable path toward exit from Chapter 11'.[43] The rise of contractual 'regulation' in insolvency led Skeel and Triantis to conclude that US bankruptcy law is considerably less mandatory than it appears and that a new contract paradigm seems to be emerging, even if somewhat inconsistently.[44] 4.25

40 The World Bank, Principles for Effective Insolvency and Creditor/debtor Regimes, 2021, C12.1.

41 It is noted that without consent from a secured creditor, it may not be possible to sell property in a 363 sale free and clear of liens. C. Mallon, S.Y. Waisman and R.C. Schrock (eds), The Law and Practice of Restructuring in the UK and US, OUP, 2011, para. 2.21.

42 R. Goode, Principles of Corporate Insolvency Law, 4th edn, Sweet and Maxwell, 2011, p. 241; V. Finch and D. Milman, Corporate Insolvency Law: Perspectives and Principles, 3rd edn, CUP, 2017, p. 530.

43 D.G. Baird, Bankruptcy's Quiet Revolution, American Bankruptcy Law Journal, Vol. 91, 2017, p. 604.

44 D.A. Skeel and G. Triantis, Bankruptcy's Uneasy Shift to a Contract Paradigm, University of Pennsylvania Law Review, Vol. 166, 2018, pp. 1777-1818. The increased ability of 'creditors in possession' to influence business conduct prior to and during Chapter 11 proceedings is noted by Rasmussen, who identifies several control mechanisms, including covenants in credit agreements, loan-to-own strategies, appointment of a chief restructuring officer, debtor-in-possession financing and plan support and restructuring support agreements. See R.K. Rasmussen, Taking Control Rights Seriously, University of Pennsylvania Law Review, Vol. 166, 2018, pp. 1749-1776.

4.26 Second, not all expectations deserve protection – only legitimate ones. Legitimate expectations and trust in the stability of legal relations are created by existing legal rules and their judicial interpretation.[45] If law restricts contractual freedom in the context of insolvency, parties should be able to consider this when entering into a transaction and calculating their risks. To protect parties' expectations, law must be predictable, foreseeable, clear and uniform. In other words, while expectations are 'fluid' and change over time under the influence of legal developments, the law itself must possess elements of stability, foreseeability and clarity.

4.27 Third, the issue of legitimate expectations and their protection should be distinguished from party autonomy – a fundamental principle of private law. Party autonomy and its operation in insolvency are subjects of spirited academic debate with no signs of emerging consensus.[46] While legal certainty relates to the foreseeability, predictability and accessibility of legal rules, autonomy concerns the boundaries of such rules in the first place. A contract is an instrument of party autonomy. However, the virtue of party autonomy, viewed as an extension of individual autonomy, does not mean that parties' bargaining ability must be unlimited. Measures to protect the public interest,[47] weaker parties (e.g. consumers) and third parties (e.g. creditors) influence the scope of party autonomy and affect ex ante choices. Yet, this does not mean that any encroachment on party autonomy is in itself desirable or justifiable, given the importance of respecting commercial bargains and ensuring freedom of contract. Unless there are negative externalities or other compelling reasons, the law should aim to interfere with parties' choices as minimally as possible. And even then, any interference must be proportionate.

---

45 R. Bork and M. Veder, Harmonisation of Transactions Avoidance Laws, Intersentia, 2022, para. 2.54, observing that 'where people trust in the stability of their legal position, they do so in the context of a wider regime of the applicable law, which can include rules weakening their legal position under certain conditions ...'

46 S.L. Schwarcz, Rethinking Freedom of Contract: A Bankruptcy Paradigm, Texas Law Review, Vol. 77, 1999, pp. 515–604, arguing that fundamental policies underlying the US Bankruptcy Code, including equality of distribution among creditors and debtor rehabilitation should in certain cases limit contractual freedom. Also, J.L. Westbrook, Commercial Law and the Public Interest, Penn State Journal of Law and International Affairs, Vol. 4, 2015, pp. 445–458, stressing the importance of protecting public interest in insolvency and concluding that the latter cannot be ensured through the reliance on creditors' contracting.

47 M. Haentjens, Party Autonomy, Public Policy and European Bank Insolvency Law, Hazelhoff Research Paper Series No. 7, 2015, p. 11, arguing that public interest and welfare maximisation should be balanced against party autonomy.

4.2.5 Equal treatment of creditors

The principle of equal treatment of creditors requires that similarly situated creditors (creditors of the same rank) be treated similarly or identically, both in terms of procedural and substantive rights.[48] This principle is known by various names, including *pari passu* (from Latin 'on equal footing') or *par est condicio omnium creditorum* (from Latin 'the condition of all creditors is equal'). Emphasis is often placed on the pro rata or rateable distribution of the realised assets among creditors within the same class.[49] On an abstract level, the principle of equal treatment of creditors is grounded in the notions of equality, fairness,[50] distributive justice and aversion to inequity – values present in many cooperative animals, most notably humans.[51] **4.28**

Equal treatment of creditors is often regarded as a 'centrepiece of insolvency law',[52] and is closely linked to the collective enforcement regime; however, the two should not be confused. Collectivism helps reduce strategic costs, preserve the status quo and facilitate proportionate distribution of value among creditors.[53] However, while collectivity aids in ensuring equality and resolving the common pool problem, it is not a prerequisite to its realisation. This is evident in laws that do not require full collectivity.[54] For example, under the Dutch WHOA, the court shall deny a plan confirmation request if 'the plan was procured by deception, by favouring one or more creditors or shareholders **4.29**

---

48 R. Bork, Corporate Insolvency Law. A Comparative Textbook, Intersentia, 2020, p. 8.

49 K. Akintola, Creditor Treatment in Corporate Insolvency Law, Edward Elgar Publishing, 2020, paras. 3.29–3.30.

50 R. Dworkin, Taking Rights Seriously, HUP, 1977, p. 180, describing a right to equality as 'a right to equal concern and respect'. A. Keay and P. Walton, The Preferential Debts' Regime in Liquidation Law: In the Public Interest? Company Financial and Insolvency Law Review, Vol. 3, 1999, pp. 93–94, observing that the 'underlying aim behind the use of the equality principle is to produce fairness, so that every creditor is treated in the same way'.

51 M. Tomasello and A. Vaish, Origins of Human Cooperation and Morality, Annual Review of Psychology, Vol. 64, 2013, p. 243, noting that children of five to six years of age show a greater sense of equality and fairness, but also that three-year-old children tend to divide rewards equitably if they obtained the rewards by working collaboratively. S.F. Brosnan and F.B.M. de Waal, Evolution of responses to (un)fairness, Science, Vol. 346, 2014, pp. 314–321, arguing that some non-human species, such as apes, not only passively or actively protest against receiving less for the same task, but also seek to equalise the outcomes to their own detriment. According to the authors, the latter most likely 'reflects an attempt to forestall partner dissatisfaction with obtained outcomes and its negative impact on future cooperation'.

52 CERIL Report 2017-1, 26 September 2017, para. 14; R. Goode, Principles of Corporate Insolvency Law, 3rd edn, Sweet & Maxwell, 2005, p. 175; R. Bork and M. Veder, Harmonisation of Transactions Avoidance Laws, Intersentia, 2022, para. 2.38.

53 T.H. Jackson, The Logic and Limits of Bankruptcy Law, Harvard University Press, 1986, pp. 16–17, viewing the role of insolvency law as one of 'ameliorating a common pool problem created by a system of individual creditor remedies'. L.C. Ho, Goode's Swan Song to Corporate Insolvency Law, European Business Law Review, Vol. 17, 2006, p. 1737, arguing that the *pari passu* principle does not underpin collectivity and that maintaining the status quo is not meant to preserve any particular level of priority.

54 See e.g. StaRUG, § 10.

with voting rights or by other unfair means'.[55] The Restructuring Directive also stipulates that one of the conditions for the approval of a restructuring plan is that creditors with sufficient commonality of interest in the same class are treated equally and proportionately to their claims.[56] The principle of equal treatment of creditors can be found in national law,[57] EU legislation[58] and soft law instruments.[59]

4.30 Bork describes the *pari passu* principle as 'equal treatment of (unsecured) creditors belonging to the same class'.[60] Mokal explains that this principle 'requires all unsecured creditors to be repaid the same proportion of their claims, with that proportion being determined by the value available in the insolvency estate'.[61] According to Mokal, the *pari passu* principle, properly understood, concerns formal equality, which is indifferent to normatively significant differences among creditors. Therefore, priority for certain groups of unsecured creditors (e.g. employees) constitutes a derogation from the principle.

4.31 UNCITRAL prescribes equal treatment of 'creditors of the same class',[62] while the World Bank promotes 'equitable treatment of similarly situated creditors'.[63] A reference to a particular class of creditors rather than to all unsecured creditors reflects the current insolvency law reality, where creditors are treated in accordance with their priority rankings.[64] The existence and expansion of priorities led some scholars to highlight the diminishing role of the principle.[65] The relativity of the *pari passu* principle is particularly

55 Dutch Bankruptcy Act, 384(2)(g).

56 Restructuring Directive, Article 10(2)(b).

57 Insolvency Act 1986, s. 107 (UK); Code de commerce, Article L643-8 (France); Federal Law 'On Insolvency (Bankruptcy)', Article 142(3) (Russia); InsO, § 1 (Germany); Bankruptcy Code, § 726(b) (USA).

58 EIR Recast, Article 23(2); BRRD, Recital 13; CIWUD, Recital 12.

59 UNCITRAL Guide on Insolvency Law, Parts one and two, 2004; Key Attributes of Effective Resolution Regimes for Financial Institutions, 2014, para. 5.1; Principles for Effective Insolvency and Creditor/debtor Regimes, 2021, C1.

60 R. Bork, Principles of Cross-Border Insolvency Law, Intersentia, 2017, p. 115.

61 R. Mokal, The Mysterious Pari Passu Principle, SSRN publication, 19 August 2024 <https://ssrn.com/abstract=4914791> (accessed 10 October 2024), describing an expansive and a narrower way of conceptualising the *pari passu* principle.

62 UNCITRAL Legislative Guide, Part two, Ch. IV, para. 26.

63 The World Bank, Principles for Effective Insolvency and Creditor/debtor Regimes, 2021, C1.

64 US Bankruptcy Code, § 1123(a)(4); InsO, § 226.

65 R.J. Mokal, Priority as Pathology: The *Pari Passu* Myth, Cambridge Law Journal, Vol. 60, 2001, p. 582, arguing that the principle is 'less important than it is sometimes made out to be, and does not fulfil any of the functions often attributed to it'. D.A. Skeel, The Empty Idea of 'Equality of Creditors', University of Pennsylvania Law Review, Vol. 166, 2018, p. 701, analysing US practice and observing that '[b]ankruptcy courts often bless arrangements that give one group of general creditors starkly different treatment than other groups'. B. Wessels, Moeten schuldeisers altijd gelijk behandeld worden? Nederlands Juristenblad, 6, 2010, p. 340, explaining that in Dutch law equality is not a hard-and-fast principle, and that exceptions

evident in cases involving financial contracts and financial institutions, especially when financial stability is at stake.[66] For example, in *Private Equity Insurance Group SIA v. Swedbank AS*, the Court of Justice of the EU (CJEU) had to decide whether granting financial collateral takers the right to enforce collateral despite the commencement of insolvency proceedings against the collateral provider violated the *pari passu* principle. The CJEU acknowledged that the EU Financial Collateral Directive conferred an advantage on financial collateral over other types of security outside its scope. However, the court deemed this different treatment permissible, as it was based on an objective criterion and legitimate aim 'to improve the legal certainty and effectiveness of financial collateral in order to provide stability in the financial system'.[67] The departure from the equal treatment of creditors can also be found in the rules governing bank resolution.[68]

Without entering the debate about the 'viability' of the principle of equal treatment of creditors in modern insolvency law theory, it suffices to say that creditor equality is relative rather than absolute. However, once the similarity of creditors' positions has been established, the principle gains strength and requires a compelling reason or competing principle to override it. **4.32**

4.3 APPLICATION OF LEGAL PRINCIPLES IN GROUP INSOLVENCIES

4.3.1 Value preservation and maximisation within enterprise groups

The previous section focused on legal principles that have, for the most part, been developed and applied in the context of a single-debtor insolvency. One may question whether the same principles remain relevant when multiple companies within an enterprise group face financial distress or insolvency. I argue that there are no compelling reasons for such principles to lose their significance. However, applying these principles may require certain adjustments to make them more group-aware or group-sensitive.[69] For example, in economically integrated and interdependent groups, where legally separate entities act **4.33**

---

to it may follow from the considerations of effectiveness (e.g. better pay-offs to creditors), reasonableness and fairness.

66 For criticism of this special treatment, see C.G. Paulus, The Wonderful World of Privileges – The Par Condicio Creditorum vs. Closeout-Netting, ECFR, Vol. 11, 2014, pp. 531–553.

67 Case C-156/15, *'Private Equity Insurance Group' SIA v 'Swedbank' AS*, 10 November 2016, para. 51.

68 See e.g. BRRD, Article 44(2); SRMR, Article 27(3).

69 I. Mevorach, Enterprise Groups in Insolvency: Recent International Developments, in J. Sarra (ed), Annual Review of Insolvency Law, Toronto: Carswell, 2013, p. 285, noting that the promotion of insolvency law goals, such as wealth maximisation and equitable treatment of creditors 'may require treating the group as the relevant body or acknowledging inter-connections among group members'.

as a single enterprise, preserving and maximising estate value may necessitate a group-wide strategy. The failure of one group member can be contagious, potentially causing a domino effect that leads to the collapse of other group members, a piecemeal sale of assets, suboptimal returns to creditors and the liquidation of a viable but distressed business.

4.34 Imagine the following (rather typical) scenario of a group consisting of legal entities that play different roles: (i) a company issuing debt instruments and lending the received funds to other group members (FinCo), (ii) a company managing and owning assets essential for the group's business, including intellectual property, licences, know-how, real estate (SPV), (iii) a company exercising managerial control over the entire group and acting as a group treasury through the operation of a centralised cash management system (HoldCo), and (iv) operational companies offering services or manufacturing products in different countries (OpCos). Administering such companies separately in insolvency might be challenging and suboptimal for maximising the insolvency estate value, as the entity-by-entity treatment could trigger a breakup of intra-group links and sever access to vital resources and lifelines.

4.35 This scenario materialised in the insolvency of Lehman Brothers (section 1.1.1). When the parent company (LBHI) filed for bankruptcy, many of its subsidiaries lost access to critical sources of finance and information.[70] The corporate legal shields separating the legal entities in the group did not prevent their failure. One reason for this was that behind these shields, the entities were interconnected through a web of debt and cross-guarantees.[71] They relied on each other for financing, debt refinancing and services. For example, information on accounts and trades related to group companies was frequently concentrated in one jurisdiction. Thus, LBHI's UK subsidiary, LBIE, recorded data on financial notes relevant to other group entities, including its Dutch subsidiary, LBT. When LBT went bankrupt in the Netherlands, the trustees needed this information to make asset distribution in the Dutch proceedings.[72] After

70 Lehman Brothers Holdings Inc. Chapter 11 Proceedings Examiner's Report (Valukas Report), 2010, p. 1550, describing the Lehman Brothers' centralised intra-group cash pooling system. O. McDonald, Lehman Brothers: A crisis of value, Manchester University Press, 2015, p. 117, explaining the practical issues as each subsidiary was cut off from the others and LBHI, so that '[i]t was not possible to generate information and liquidate assets efficiently and identify ways to maximize value'.

71 K. Pistor, The Code of Capital: How the Law Creates Wealth and Inequality, Princeton University Press, 2019, p. 51; J.A. Kirshner, International Bankruptcy: The Challenge of Insolvency in a Global Economy, University of Chicago Press, 2018, p. 5, noting that uncoordinated insolvency proceedings faced the problem of separating intercompany arrangements, representing an elaborate system of cross-collateralisation and intercompany guarantees.

72 F. Verhoeven, Lehman Brothers Treasury, in M. Haentjens and B. Wessels (eds), Research Handbook on Cross-Border Bank Resolution, Edward Elgar Publishing, 2019, p. 349.

intense negotiations, Dutch IPs obtained an important part of LBT's records from LBIE. A similar case can be imagined if in insolvency group entities lose their access to assets held by other entities in the group, including patents, licences and customer databases. As a result, operational activity could be paralysed, and the group entities might face piecemeal liquidation.

A well-known example illustrating the importance of a group-wide strategy is the insolvency of KPN Qwest. KPN Qwest was a telecom group that owned and operated rings of fibre-optic cable around Europe and the USA. Notably, parts of the cable belonged to different group entities – the French part by the French subsidiary, the German part by the German subsidiary, and so on. When the Dutch holding company, KPN Qwest N.V., collapsed, its subsidiaries were forced to file for insolvency, and their assets were sold on a country-by-country basis.[73] This outcome was suboptimal, as the value of the entire ring was much higher compared to the value of its isolated parts. The opposite result was achieved in the case of Nortel Networks (section 1.1.2). Through a commercially sensible solution to pool the group's assets and realise them on a global scale, Nortel's assets were sold for USD 7.3 billion. This amount was much larger than could have been expected from a piecemeal, local liquidation of licences and intellectual property rights. 4.36

4.3.2 Legitimate expectations and group reality

Legitimate expectations do not exist in a vacuum; they are shaped by the existing factual and legal reality. Therefore, the group reality and the rules adopted to deal with group insolvencies play a role in the formation of parties' expectations. The exact substance of these expectations may vary depending on the totality of facts and circumstances. Several relevant factors come into play, such as the group's business (operational) integration and interconnectedness, the intensity of intra-group financial arrangements and financial integration, the role of the debtor company within the group, past experiences and assurances (e.g. on continued intra-group support), as well as the type and sophistication of creditors themselves (e.g. qualified investors, credit institutions and other professional financiers, micro, small and medium-sized enterprises (MSMEs), trade creditors and tort victims). In an integrated enterprise group, adopting a group-wide insolvency or turnaround strategy – as opposed to a 'singular' entity-by-entity approach – may align with the expectations of creditors who 4.37

73 N.H. Cooper, Insolvency proceedings in case of groups of companies: prospects of harmonisation at EU level, Briefing Note, 2011, p. 7; Commission Staff Working Document, Impact Assessment accompanying the document Revision of Regulation (EC) No 1346/2000 on insolvency proceedings, SWD/2012/0416 final.

view the group as a single enterprise. This impression can be supported by the use of the same brand, endorsements of transactions by other group members, the filing of consolidated financial statements[74] and the prevalence of intra-group financing.

4.38 It may be argued that the more centralised and integrated the group is, and as long as this fact is ascertainable by relevant third parties, the stronger the argument that a group-sensitive solution should be expected in insolvency. This line of reasoning was articulated by Justice Ramesh (Supreme Court of Singapore), who observed that 'creditors' expectation that their investment will be undisturbed in a group insolvency is to some extent a mere reflection of the orthodoxy of separate legal personality'.[75] Referring to the fluidity of expectations, he stressed that more frequent incursions into the separate legal personality doctrine may weaken the argument regarding legitimate expectations when used to justify separate (atomistic) treatment of group companies in insolvency. This point refers to the development of legal doctrine and norms of insolvency law, within which expectations crystallise. If legal rules or their application and interpretation contain group-mindful solutions, creditors should be able to take them into account. When it comes to enterprise group insolvencies, such solutions may refer to issues of international insolvency jurisdiction (e.g. determination of COMI), procedures (e.g. procedural consolidation) and substance (e.g. availability of third-party releases).

4.39 The issue of protecting trust and party autonomy typically arises with respect to intra-group transactions and their assessment in the context of transaction avoidance when a party to a transaction becomes insolvent. The question is whether the group reality and indirect group-related benefits should be considered, and to what extent. If the answer is unclear, this is problematic from the perspective of legitimate expectations and legal certainty. The voidness or voidability of a transaction also affects party autonomy to the extent that a contract is one of its key instruments. At this juncture, it suffices to cite UNCITRAL, which adopts the position that '[i]n considering … intra-group transactions, it will be desirable for the court to be able to take the group

74 S. Pepels, Defining groups of companies under the European Insolvency Regulation (recast): On the scope of EU group insolvency law, International Insolvency Review, Vol. 30, 2021, p. 108, noting the inclusion of companies in consolidated financial statements creates the legitimised expectation that such companies are doing business as a group.

75 K. Ramesh, Synthesising Synthetics: Lessons learnt from Collins & Aikman, 2nd Annual GRR Live New York, 26 September 2018.

context into account ...'[76] The positions taken by UK, US and Dutch law on this issue will be discussed in Chapter 7.

4.3.3 Explicit and hidden priorities in group insolvencies

The principle of equal treatment of creditors may seem least affected by considerations related to enterprise groups. Bufford observes that the *pari passu* principle 'has a diminished role in the insolvency of an enterprise group (apart from the insolvencies of particular members thereof)'.[77] This claim is based on the idea of entity separateness, which entails a separation of insolvency estates and pools of creditors for the entities comprising the group. In the absence of substantive consolidation, equal treatment of creditors must be maintained and preserved with respect to each separate group entity. In other words, overarching intra-group creditor equality does not exist. This is why the NCWO and best-interest-of-creditors tests are applied on an entity basis (section 3.5). Nevertheless, there are a few patterns that fine-tune the operation of the *pari passu* principle in a group setting. 4.40

The first pattern concerns a special approach to 'related' creditors and transactions concluded with them. Insider creditors (e.g. shareholders and group affiliates) may enjoy less protection against transaction avoidance. Additionally, in some jurisdictions, their claims are subordinated – downgraded in the priority ladder (see Chapter 6). 4.41

The second pattern is that some creditors can have the same claim against several companies within the group. A characteristic feature of intra-group financing is the existence of various cross-entity liability arrangements. Among them are cross-guarantees, co-debtorship and collateral arrangements, where at least one other group member acts as a guarantor, co-debtor or a collateral provider for the benefit of another group member. Should the latter be in default, a guaranteed creditor can request performance from that other member or from both entities simultaneously. As a result, this creditor enjoys covert priority or structural seniority arising from a combination of entity separateness and its simultaneous perforation by cross-entity liability arrangements. This substantially alters outcomes for non-guaranteed unsecured creditors and elevates the position of the guaranteed creditor.[78] Emphasising the prob- 4.42

76 UNCITRAL Legislative Guide, Part three, Ch. II, para. 50.

77 S.L. Bufford, Coordination of Insolvency Cases for International Enterprise Groups: A Proposal, American Bankruptcy Law Journal, Vol. 86, 2012, p. 694.

78 A.L. Jonkers, Selective Perforation by Means of Guarantees: Dutch Law, in The 800-Pound Gorilla. Limits to Group Structures and Asset Partitioning in Insolvency, NACIIL 2018 report, Eleven International Publishing, 2019, pp. 81-84, offering examples of how cross-guarantees affect the distribution among

lematic nature of cross-guarantees from an equality perspective, Westbrook submits that 'guarantees within a corporate group are a central instrument of priority and obfuscation'.[79] This book has two chapters on intercompany guarantees – Chapters 5 and 8.

4.4 COLLISION OF LEGAL PRINCIPLES AND HOW TO RESOLVE IT

4.4.1 The notion of fairness in insolvency law

4.43 Often, different principles apply simultaneously. A bankruptcy stay safeguards the debtor's assets, advancing the principle of estate value preservation. But it also facilitates the equal treatment of creditors to the extent that it ensures that creditors cannot enforce their claims ahead of other similarly situated creditors. These 'symbiotic' cases, where legal principles support each other and are aligned, are not controversial. Yet, the situation gets complicated if the applicable principles are in conflict. Wood observes that insolvency is 'the point at which the law has to make difficult and unavoidable choices between colliding principles'.[80] Take, for instance, the avoidance of transactions. Unrestricted application of transaction avoidance rules can enrich the estate, but it would likely be incompatible with the protection of legitimate expectations and certainty of transactions.[81]

4.44 The difficult question is what to do when legal principles clash. How should a judge or a lawmaker balance conflicting principles? In making difficult decisions, references to the notion of fairness often appear in various instruments of insolvency law. For example, the UNCITRAL Legislative Guide states that the objectives of insolvency law are 'protecting the value of the insolvency estate against diminution … facilitating administration of those proceedings

---

unsecured creditors. See W.H. Widen, Corporate Form and Substantive Consolidation, George Washington Law Review, Vol. 75, 2007, p. 240, noting that intra-group guarantees dilute claims for those creditors without guarantees – the phenomenon referred to as the 'squeeze down effect'.

79 J.L. Westbrook, Transparency in Corporate Groups, Brooklyn Journal of Corporate, Financial & Commercial Law, Vol. 13, 2018, p. 44. Westbrook notes that, as a general rule, creditors of the parent company have only an indirect claim on the subsidiary's assets. Consequently, the position of these creditors is subordinate to that of the creditors of the subsidiary. An upstream guarantee enables a guaranteed creditor to bypass structural subordination and compete with the non-guaranteed creditors of the subsidiary.

80 P. Wood, Law and Practice of International Finance, Sweet & Maxwell, 2008, pp. 20-21.

81 R. Bork and M. Veder, Harmonisation of Transactions Avoidance Laws, Intersentia, 2022, paras. 2.106-2.107, noting that the broad application of avoidance powers 'would pose a serious threat to the general stability of markets', as it would lead to social costs arising from foregone transactions and elaborate screening. On the flipside, the authors emphasise that 'a comprehensive protection of trust is not compatible with the application of other principles', such as the principle of equal treatment of creditors and estate value maximisation.

in a fair and orderly manner'.[82] It refers to fairness in asset allocation, the treatment of creditors more generally, transaction avoidance and the continuation of contracts when the debtor is in breach. On substantive consolidation, UNCITRAL points out that such consolidation might lead to 'unfairness caused to one creditor group when forced to share *pari passu* with creditors of a less solvent group member'.[83] References to fairness can also be found in EU law instruments, such as the BRRD[84] and the Restructuring Directive,[85] and are commonly made in national law. The US Bankruptcy Code stipulates that the court shall confirm a Chapter 11 plan if the plan 'does not discriminate unfairly, and is fair and equitable'.[86] English courts examine the fairness of any scheme of arrangement at the sanction hearing.[87] Fairness has featured in judgments related to the insolvency of Lehman Brothers, Nortel Networks and Oi Brazil.[88]

While the notion of fairness seems to underlie many rules, a uniform definition of fairness is missing. Indeed, many of the above instruments are silent on the exact meaning of fairness and whether it holds the same meaning in different contexts. It appears that fairness can refer to the quality of the *procedure* – the fair administration of insolvency proceedings. It can also pertain to the *substantive treatment* of participants in insolvency proceedings. Substantive fairness addresses the fairness of outcomes – how limited resources are divided among relevant actors. Finch asserts that 'fairness considers issues of substantive justice and distribution'.[89] For Mokal, fairness is about the distribution of **4.45**

82 UNCITRAL Legislative Guide, Part two, Ch. II, para. 25. Fair administration of insolvency proceedings is mentioned in the Preambles to the MLCBI and MLEGI.

83 Ibid., para. 109.

84 BRRD, Recitals 5 ('fair and predictable' apportion of loss), 51 ('fair and realistic' valuation of assets and liabilities) and 97 (resolution of cross-border groups should follow procedures that 'allow for efficient, fair and timely solutions for the group as a whole').

85 Restructuring Directive, Recital 35 (stay should be limited in time to achieve 'a fair balance between the rights of the debtor and those of creditors'), Recital 56 (approving derogation from the APR where it is considered 'fair').

86 11 U.S. Code § 1129(b)(1). US law does not define 'unfair discrimination'. The requirement to avoid it is generally interpreted to mean that dissenting classes should receive relatively equal value under the plan as compared with similarly situated classes. R. Olivares-Caminal et al., Debt Restructuring, 2nd edn, OUP, 2016, p. 171.

87 J. Payne, Schemes of Arrangement: Theory, Structure and Operation, CUP, 2014, p. 74. Fairness in a scheme context has a specific and limited meaning. See section 3.3.1, noting that the court is not required to form a view of whether the scheme is, in some general sense, or even in the court's own opinion, the 'fairest' or 'best' scheme.

88 See e.g. *In re Nortel Networks, Inc.*, 532 B.R. 494, 549 (Bankr. D. Del. 2015), noting that '[i]n the absence of an agreement governing allocation or a preponderance of evidence showing entitlement to assets ..., the Court's task is to arrive at a fair and equitable mechanism to allocate the billions of dollars of Sales Proceeds to numerous international entities'.

89 V. Finch, Corporate Insolvency Law: Perspective and Principles, CUP, 2002, p. 50.

rights in the insolvent company's assets.[90] In a more recent paper, Mokal and other prominent scholars observe that traditional notions of 'fairness', 'equity', 'justice' essentially describe normative defensibility, which means that the distribution of the debtor's assets is 'adequately supported by appropriate reasons and that it is not marred by inappropriate reasons'.[91]

4.46 On the matter of distribution, Lixing Sun, a professor of behavioural and evolutionary biology, writes that '[t]o be fair, rewards must be proportional to the effort or investment each party contributes to the whole'.[92] According to Sun, this rule works in the same fashion for the distribution of losses, so that the 'party who gets more when things go well should also take more responsibility or punishment when the venture goes awry'.[93] Sandel illustrates this rule by describing how, during the GFC, decisions to bail out America's largest banks and other financial firms were widely perceived as unfair because 'Wall Street' enjoyed substantial profits during good times but sought taxpayer money when things turned bad.[94]

4.47 In insolvency law, the argument of fairness, or lack thereof, is often used to advocate for the subordination of shareholder loans.[95] As shareholders benefit from the upside, 'capitalizing on the upward potential' (e.g. dividend payments and potentially unlimited increase of share price) when things go well, the argument goes, they should bear the downside risks and be excluded from competing for the debtor's assets. Therefore, equal distribution of assets in insolvency among 'insiders' and 'outsiders' is portrayed as unfair in light of

---

90 R.J. Mokal, Corporate Insolvency Law: Theory and Application, OUP, 2005, p. 121. Similarly, Sen points out that fairness reflects the demand 'to avoid bias in our evaluations, taking note of the interests and concerns of others as well, and in particular the need to avoid being influenced by our respective vested interests'. A. Sen, The Idea of Justice, HUP, 2009, p. 54. This de-biasing characteristic of fairness is noteworthy.

91 R. Mokal, S. Madaus, I. Mevorach and I. Tirado, The Cramdown: A Conceptual Framework, SSRN publication, 15 October 2024 <https://ssrn.com/abstract=4990828> (accessed 1 November 2024), classifying as appropriate reasons prior entitlement, consent, desert and need, and listing as inappropriate reasons nepotism and prejudice.

92 L. Sun, The Fairness Instinct: The Robin Hood Mentality and Our Biological Nature, Prometheus Books, 2013, pp. 62–63.

93 Ibid. Sun discusses the 'fairness instinct', noting that fairness is a trait we inherit with our genes and explaining that 'our natural penchant for cooperation is so ingrained that when we share, donate, and act fairly the brain areas associated with reward and positive reinforcement learning are mobilized'.

94 M. Sandel, Justice: What's the Right Thing to Do? 1st edn, Farrar, Straus and Giroux, 2010. For discussion of fairness of bailouts, see E.A. Posner and A. Casey, A Framework for Bailout Regulation, Notre Dame Law Review, Vol. 91, 2015, pp. 479–536.

95 R.J. de Weijs, Harmonization of European Insolvency Law: Preventing Insolvency Law from Turning against Creditors by Upholding the Debt-Equity Divide, European Company and Financial Law Review, Vol. 2, 2018, pp. 421–422, arguing that it is unfair to allow shareholders to rank above creditors for shareholder loans.

the differences in their ex ante positions. The argument of fairness is also raised in discussions about the treatment of related parties in and outside of insolvency,[96] and the practice of cross-guarantees.[97]

Fairness is connected to the idea of deservingness, which relates to our understanding of contribution, expectations, risks and rewards, power and influence, as well as the capacity to bear the costs of downside or default.[98] The question is whether fairness can serve as a metric to help balance conflicting principles. Using the example of shareholder loans, one might wonder whether legal systems that subordinate such loans are inherently fairer than those that do not. Similarly, is a legal system that enforces cross-guarantees and allows strong-form double proof, typically benefiting sophisticated, strongly adjusting creditors, while trade and tort creditors cannot rely on double proof, inherently unfair? If we were to (however unlikely) arrive at definitive answers to these questions, what should we do about it and how should we respond to this alleged unfairness? **4.48**

When discussing fairness, Paterson argues that it 'is a slippery concept, which eludes a single definition applicable to all contexts and which suffers from various levels of abstraction unless it is applied to a real situation'.[99] Similarly, Mevorach observes that 'the idea of reaching a fair or just result is open ended and suffers from indeterminacy'.[100] Paterson and Mevorach seem to agree that the determination of a fair outcome can hardly be carried out in the abstract. It requires taking various factors into account. For Mevorach, these factors include a party's ability to respond to insolvency risks ex ante – when transacting with the debtor – and to bear the loss ex post, upon insolvency. For Paterson, normative concerns for fairness vary depending on the context – such as SME insolvency, large corporate debt restructuring, or the resolution of financial institutions. **4.49**

---

96 J. Dammann, Related Party Transactions and Intragroup Transactions, in L. Enriques and T.H. Tröger (eds), The Law and Finance of Related Party Transactions, CUP, 2019, pp. 218-244.

97 W.H. Widen, Corporate Form and Substantive Consolidation, George Washington Law Review, Vol. 75, 2007, pp. 237-328, discussing the double proof problem and the conflict between the interests of multi-source creditors and single-source creditors from the perspective of fairness. Widen questions the fairness of cross-guarantees and suggests that substantive consolidation may be a solution to restore fairness.

98 E. Warren, Bankruptcy Policy, The University of Chicago Law Review, Vol. 54, 1987, pp. 775-814, mentioning among the features for ordering distributional priorities: (i) relative ability to bear costs of default, (ii) incentive effects of pre-bankruptcy transactions, (iii) similarities among creditors, (iv) owners bear the loss when business fails, and (v) benefits to the bankruptcy estate.

99 S. Paterson, Debt Restructuring and Notions of Fairness, The Modern Law Review, Vol. 80, 2017, p. 600. One such situation is cross-class cram down. For insightful analysis, see S. Paterson, The Conceptual Foundation of Cross-Class Cramdown, SSRN publication, 18 September 2024 <https://ssrn.com/abstract=4959732> (accessed 10 October 2024).

100 I. Mevorach, Insolvency within Multinational Enterprise Groups, OUP, 2009, p. 118.

4.50 To conclude, fairness is context-specific. What is considered fair in one situation may be seen as manifestly unfair in another. Furthermore, once a case of perceived unfairness has been established, it is not evident how a preferred outcome should then be determined.

4.4.2 Proportionality: key tool in a balancing exercise

4.51 Proportionality is omnipresent.[101] It regulates the exercise of powers by the European Union,[102] is mandated by the EU Charter of Fundamental Rights,[103] underpins the interpretation and application of the European Convention on Human Rights (ECHR) and manifests in many national legal systems.

4.52 According to Burg, when applied to a conflict between legal principles, proportionality is achieved if the price (the non-realisation of one principle) paid for a gain (the realisation of a competing principle) is not 'out of any reasonable proportion'.[104] This could indicate a variety of reasonable options or a single outcome. Alexy further breaks down proportionality into three sub-principles: suitability (whether taking a measure furthers at least one value or legitimate aim), necessity (the use of the least intrusive means) and proportionality in the narrow sense (the balancing requirement).[105] The latter sub-principle states that '[t]he greater the degree of non-satisfaction of, or detriment to, one right or principle, the greater must be the importance of satisfying the other'.[106] Its application can be divided into three stages:

(i) determining the degree of non-satisfaction or detriment to one principle;
(ii) assessing the importance of satisfying the competing principle; and

101 For discussion of the principle of proportionality, its origins and areas of application, see B. Pirker, Proportionality Analysis and Models of Judicial Review: A Theoretical and Comparative Study, Europa Law Publishing, 2013. See also Y. Arai-Takahashi, Proportionality, in D. Shelton (ed), The Oxford Handbook of International Human Rights Law, OUP, 2013, p. 446, observing that the principle has its origin in Prussian police law of the eighteenth century, and that it flourished in Germany after World War II, turning into a shared analytical tool.

102 Treaty on European Union, Article 5: 'The use of Union competences is governed by the principles of subsidiarity and proportionality.' R. Schütze and T. Tridimas (eds), Oxford Principles of European Union Law. Volume I: The European Union Legal Order, OUP, 2018.

103 Charter of Fundamental Rights of the EU, Article 52: 'Subject to the principle of proportionality, limitations may be made only if they are necessary and genuinely meet objectives of general interest recognised by the Union or the need to protect the rights and freedoms of others'.

104 E. Burg, The Model of Principles. The quest for rationality in the implementation of conflicting principles, Universiteit van Amsterdam, Faculteit der Rechtsgeleerdheid, 2000, p. 165.

105 R. Alexy, On Balancing and Subsumption. A Structural Comparison, Ratio Juris, Vol. 16, 2003, p. 436. Some authors distinguish four proportionality rules, singling out legitimate ends (whether the act pursues a legitimate end) and suitability (whether the act is capable of achieving this aim). See M. Klatt and M. Meister, The Constitutional Structure of Proportionality, OUP, 2012, p. 8.

106 R. Alexy, A Theory of Constitutional Rights, OUP, 2010, p. 102.

(iii) establishing whether the importance of the latter outweighs the detriment or non-satisfaction of the former.

In a similar vein, but in a different (human rights) context, Barak argues that the proportionality test 'examines the proper ratio between the benefit stemming from attainment of the object and the deleterious effect upon the human right'.[107] **4.53**

The ECtHR's approach to proportionality merits closer examination, as it is used to resolve complex situations of conflicting rights and interests. As a general rule, an interference with a protected right should have a legal basis – it must be 'in accordance with law' or 'prescribed by law',[108] pursue a legitimate aim (e.g. public safety), and strike a fair balance between the competing interests. This fair balance entails the application of the prongs of suitability (the relationship between the ends and the means) and necessity (the measure should fall within the range of reasonable options available). **4.54**

The fair balance test places most of its weight on the stage of the proportionality *stricto sensu*. It represents an open-ended case-by-case weighting exercise, in which it takes into account the facts, the degree of interference and whether such interference impairs the essence of the right,[109] as well as conflicting interests and rights. For example, in *Cipolletta v. Italy*, the court ruled that the excessive duration of the Italian 'administrative liquidation' procedure (more than 25 years) amounted to a violation of the right to a fair hearing within a reasonable time.[110] In arriving at this decision, the court acknowledged the complexity of insolvency proceedings. Yet it concluded that the excessive length was not justified. Interestingly, in the concurring opinion, Judge Koskelo argued that more emphasis and attention should have been paid to the special nature of insolvency proceedings, which entail a somewhat limited role of courts, involvement of IPs, the collective resolution of complex issues arising from financial distress and the long-term character of measures necessary to achieve optimal economic results for creditors.[111] **4.55**

---

107 A. Barak, Proportional Effect: The Israeli Experience, University of Toronto Law Journal, Vol. 57, 2007, p. 374.

108 *Sunday Times v. United Kingdom*, Appl. no. 6538/74, Judgment, 26 April 1979, para. 45.

109 S. Van Drooghenbroeck and C. Rizcallah, The ECHR and the Essence of Fundamental Rights: Searching for Sugar in Hot Milk? German Law Journal, Vol. 20, 2019, p. 904–923, questioning usefulness of the concepts of the essence, substance and core of fundamental rights.

110 *Cipolletta v. Italy*, Appl. no. 38259/09, Judgment, 11 January 2019.

111 Ibid., Concurring Opinion of Judge Koskelo, para. 6.

4.56 Because of the pervasive and adaptable nature of proportionality analysis, it can be used to determine a balance in a particular case involving intra-group financing and insolvency. It will be relied upon in our analysis of various legal tools and solutions that are available or can be proposed *de lege ferenda*. Think of the extension of an enforcement stay to non-debtor group companies, acting as guarantors, co-debtors and collateral providers (see Chapter 9). First, it should be acknowledged that this extension has a legitimate goal: it promotes the principle of estate value preservation and maximisation (suitability). Second, the extension of a stay should not be automatic and is more justified in integrated groups (necessity). Third, a restraint on enforcement against a non-debtor should not unfairly prejudice the rights of affected creditors (e.g. guaranteed creditors, creditors benefiting from collateral) or cause any substantial detriment to them (proportionality in the narrow sense). Such detriment may occur when collateral held by a debtor's group affiliate significantly depreciates in value during the extended stay. I will discuss this and other examples throughout the book.

4.5 CONCLUSION

4.57 This chapter lays the theoretical foundation for the analysis presented in this book, which will examine legal principles, understood as fundamental standards, explore how they transpire in concrete rules, and analyse how such rules can be better aligned with these principles. Among the most relevant legal principles for the purposes of this book are the preservation and maximisation of estate value, the protection of legitimate expectations and party autonomy, and the equal treatment of creditors. The following chapters will illustrate that these principles often underlie insolvency law rules, reinforce and complement one another, or, at times, conflict with each other. These conflicts are inherent in the field; indeed, insolvency law primarily revolves around resolving the competing interests that arise from the financial distress of a debtor or a group of debtors. How should the law navigate these conflicts?

4.58 One approach is to embrace the notion of fairness and use it to propose outcomes that align with this notion to the greatest extent. While references to fairness may resonate with many, and we generally agree that fair results are desirable, determining what is fair and what is not can be challenging in the abstract. The answer often depends on the position taken, the specific issue at stake, the parties involved in a dispute and the quality of legal rules. Alternatively, solutions can be grounded in proportionality analysis. Proportionality occupies a central place in law and 'makes it possible to compare and evaluate interests and ideas, values and facts that are radically different in a way that is both rational and fair'.[112] While proportionality analysis is necessarily case-specific, this does not mean that any attempt to dissect general factors and fact patterns that impact the balancing exercise is futile. Yet, what are these factors and fact patterns? This question sets the stage for the journey this book invites the reader to undertake, as it goes to the core of my inquiry: When and under what circumstances are special group-sensitive tools or solutions balanced and proportionate?

112 D.M. Beatty, The Ultimate Rule of Law, OUP, 2004, p. 169.

PART IV

INTRA-GROUP FINANCING AND INSOLVENCY: TRANSACTIONS AND PROBLEMS

5

CROSS-GUARANTEES, RECOURSE CLAIMS AND 'ORPHAN RESTRUCTURINGS'

5.1 INTRODUCTION

5.01 This chapter discusses cross-guarantees, also known as intercompany guarantees or intra-group guarantees. These transactions are common in commercial practice as they aim to improve borrowing terms by providing additional security to a guaranteed creditor, who gains access to an enlarged pool or pools of assets and thereby acquires extra protection against counterparty risk.

5.02 The purpose of this chapter is to examine the operation and functions of guarantees in a group context and to explain the problems they cause in situations of financial distress. In many cases, cross-guarantees promote interdependence among group companies and weaken the protective function of corporate shields, which in theory should ensure the separateness of the legal entities comprising an enterprise group. Instead, cross-guarantees allow for simultaneous filing of claims against both the principal debtor and the guarantor, resulting in group-wide enforcement. While this chapter emphasises the problems, it does not offer solutions, leaving that to other chapters in this book (i.e. Chapters 8 and 9).

5.03 The structure of the current chapter is as follows. First, I clarify the scope of inquiry, including the types of transactions at issue (section 5.2). Second, I describe the operation of a cross-guarantee relationship (section 5.3). Third, I explain how cross-guarantees might reduce the agency cost of debt (section 5.4.1) and how they could dilute recoveries of non-guaranteed creditors (section 5.4.2). Fourth, I discuss how cross-guarantees may affect the dynamics of insolvency and restructuring, exploring the rights and obligations of the principal debtor, group guarantor and creditor – the 'triangle of rights and liabilities' (section 5.5). In this section, two questions are examined with reference to national law. The first question concerns the effects of insolvency and restructuring of the principal debtor on the rights of the guaranteed creditor against the guarantor (section 5.5.2). The second question relates to the consequences of performance by the guarantor, specifically the rights that a paying guarantor may acquire against the principal debtor and how these rights may be exercised during or after insolvency or restructuring (section 5.5.3). Section 5.6 summarises ex post effects of group guarantees. Section 5.7 concludes.

5.2 CROSS-GUARANTEES AND CO-DEBTORSHIP ARRANGEMENTS

5.04 The main focus of this chapter is on cross-guarantees – transactions that create secondary liability. Thus, it does not separately deal with cases where several group members act as co-borrowers or co-issuers (joint obligors or co-obligors), which are examples of primary liability. I accept the differences between primary and secondary liability, for instance, with respect to the scope of potential recourse rights that may belong to a guarantor and co-debtor.[1] Yet, my decision not to separately address co-debtorship is based on the similarities in the economic and legal effects of cross-guarantee and co-debtorship arrangements, the common challenges they pose in the restructuring and insolvency of

1 For example, under Dutch law, a surety has full recourse against jointly and severally liable debtors (Article 7:866 of the Dutch Civil Code (DCC)), while a co-debtor may only be entitled to compensation of an amount exceeding the proportionate share of the debt (Article 6:10 DCC).

groups of companies, and the uniformity of legal responses needed to address these challenges.

First, cross-guarantees and co-debtorship arrangements perform a similar 'security-granting' function, providing a creditor with access to the asset pools of separate entities and purporting to satisfy the creditor's interest in full performance. The insolvency of the principal debtor or co-debtor does not release the guarantor or co-debtors, respectively, from their obligations. In both situations, the risk of default (and the incentive to control it) rests with an entity whose assets may become available to the creditor. Unless otherwise agreed, such a creditor can usually choose to enforce its claim against a single debtor company or initiate group-wide enforcement by simultaneously filing claims against multiple group companies acting as co-debtors or guarantors.[2] When the creditor's interest is satisfied by one of the co-debtors or by the guarantor, the other co-debtors, guarantors or the principal debtor are discharged from their obligations to the creditor. **5.05**

Second, upon satisfaction of the creditor's claim, a joint debtor or a guarantor may be entitled to request compensation from co-debtors or, respectively, from the principal debtor and other guarantors. The existence and extent of this compensation, particularly when the underlying debt is restructured (e.g. reduced, postponed) or fully written down, may vary depending on applicable law, the type of discharge (voluntary vs. involuntary), and the nature of the debt restructuring (pre-insolvency contractual vs. insolvency court-led). The complexities created by co-debtorship and guarantee relationships are similar. **5.06**

Third, as will be examined in more detail in the following chapters, insolvency law often treats co-debtorship and cross-guarantee arrangements similarly, for example, by sanctioning third-party releases (Chapter 8) or extending an enforcement stay to group guarantors and co-debtors (Chapter 9).[3] These insolvency law tools may also be available to protect a group company acting as a provider of collateral securing the principal debtor's performance. **5.07**

2 *In re Gessin*, 668 F.2d 1105, 1107 (9th Cir. 1982), confirming that '[i]t has long been established that a creditor is entitled to pursue his claims against others liable on the same debt to the full extent of the amount owed on that debt'.

3 See e.g. Dutch Bankruptcy Act, Article 372; Singapore's Insolvency, Restructuring and Dissolution Act (IRDA), section 65; StaRUG, section 49(3).

5.3 HOW DO CROSS-GUARANTEES WORK?

5.08 Groups of companies are special in many respects, including in the ways group entities attract financing from within and outside the group. The cases of Lehman Brothers, Nortel Networks and Oi Brazil serve as excellent examples of how a corporate group can function as a single economic enterprise, tapping into foreign capital markets, efficiently allocating resources within the group, and seeking the most favourable terms for debt financing. A typical financial arrangement used in all three cases is the group guarantee. These guarantees serve as a risk-reduction tool and involve three parties: (i) the main or principal debtor, (ii) the guaranteed creditor, and (iii) the guarantor (see Figure 5.1).

5.09 In Figure 5.1, a creditor (Bank) has a claim against the principal debtor (Company A), whose performance is guaranteed by another company, the guarantor (Company B). Thus, if the principal debtor defaults (i.e. fails to perform its obligation), the creditor is entitled to request performance – usually the payment of a specified amount – from the guarantor. As a result, the Bank gains recourse for essentially the same debt from the estates of at least two parties (Companies A and B), depending on the number of co-guarantors involved.

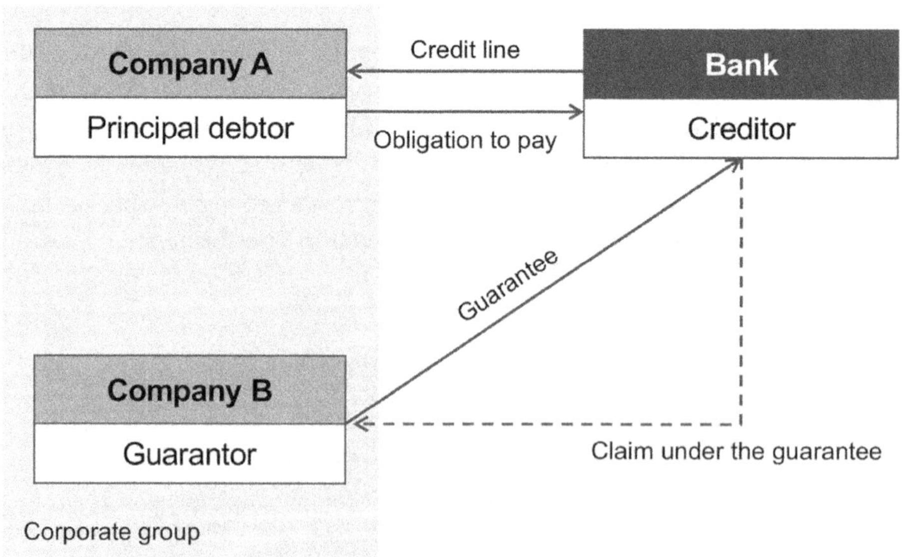

Figure 5.1 Schematic guarantee relationship

Guarantees may be personal when granted by the debtor's directors or shareholders, who are natural persons.[4] Personal guarantees often raise specific consumer protection questions and, as such, fall outside the scope of this book. The corporate guarantees discussed in this book are accessory or co-extensive and should be distinguished from an independent guarantee (in Dutch *'onafhankelijke garantie'*). Different terms may be used to refer to a type of arrangement where the guarantee is independent from an underlying obligation (e.g. demand guarantee, demand bond, letter of credit).[5] In contrast, an intercompany guarantee is typically dependent on the underlying obligation and has an accessory nature.[6] This means that the guarantor's liability is contingent upon the principal obligor's continuing liability and default. The term 'suretyship' also refers to this accessory agreement and is sometimes contrasted with a 'guarantee', where the latter is used to refer to an independent guarantee.[7] To avoid confusion that may arise from the use of different terms in different legal systems, this book will use the terms 'guarantee' and 'suretyship' interchangeably to refer to an undertaking by the surety or guarantor to be answerable for the debt or obligation of another in the event of default, where the liability of the surety or guarantor depends upon the liability of the principal or main obligor. This simplification is not intended to downplay important nuances in national law. Certain aspects and specifics of national laws will be highlighted where relevant. 5.10

Guarantees are common in groups, where the parent company guarantees the performance of its subsidiaries (downstream guarantee), a subsidiary acts as a guarantor for its parent (upstream guarantee), or one subsidiary guarantees the debt of another subsidiary (cross-stream guarantee).[8] These group guarantees, 5.11

---

4 Personal guarantees are particularly common for MSME debtors. See the World Bank Report on the Treatment of MSME Insolvency, 2017.

5 See P. Wood, International Loans, Bonds, Guarantees, Legal Opinions, Sweet & Maxwell, 2007, para. 19-016. In this case, the third party's obligation is primary and independent of that of the principal debtor. It arises regardless of whether a default has occurred and is usually not influenced by matters affecting the contract between the creditor and the main debtor.

6 S. Whittaker, Suretyship, in Chitty on Contracts, 33rd edn, Sweet & Maxwell, 2018, para. 45-009, noting that under English law 'there is a "strong presumption" that a "guarantee" concluded other than by a bank is not a demand or independent performance bond, although this presumption may be rebutted'. However, see P. Ostendorf, Demand Guarantee or Suretyship Guarantee – Have corporate guarantors lost the benefit of the doubt? OBLB, 14 September 2021, discussing recent precedents that may weaken the presumption based on the guarantor's identity.

7 For a historical overview of the appearance and usage of the terms 'guarantee' and 'suretyship', see M. Radin, Guarantee and Suretyship, California Law Review, Vol. 17, 1929, pp. 605–622. For a discussion of US law, see C. Henkel, Personal Guarantees and Sureties between Commercial Law and Consumers in the United States, The American Journal of Comparative Law, Vol. 62, 2014, pp. 333–359.

8 R. Squire, Shareholder Opportunism in a World of Risky Debt, Harvard Law Review, Vol. 123, 2010, p. 1213, noting that intra-group guarantee arrangements are extremely prevalent. See also J.F. Williams, The Fallacies of Contemporary Fraudulent Transfer Models as Applied to Intercorporate Guaranties:

along with co-debtorship and third-party (group) collateral, are examples of intra-group support transactions. They enable a group of companies to be financed as a single economic unit, securing beneficial conditions (lower interest rates and costs, and larger amounts) from outside lenders such as banks and bondholders. Yet they promote group interdependence, as the enforcement of a guarantee or the simultaneous filing of claims against multiple co-debtors may create contagion and lead to the spread of distress across the corporate boundaries of enterprise group members. These and other features and functions of cross-guarantees are discussed in the following paragraphs.

5.4 FUNCTIONS OF CROSS-GUARANTEES

5.4.1 'Protective' function of cross-guarantees

5.12 Cross-liability arrangements, such as intercompany guarantees, serve an important 'protective function'.[9] They provide additional security to a guaranteed creditor by granting access to and recourse against the asset pools of two or more companies. The laws of many jurisdictions, including the UK, the US and the Netherlands, allow a guaranteed creditor to claim full performance from both the principal debtor and the guarantor upon the default of the former.[10] In this way, the guaranteed creditor acquires protection against idiosyncratic shocks affecting the borrower.

Fraudulent Transfer Law as a Fuzzy System, Cardozo Law Review, Vol. 15, 1994, p. 1404, observing that guarantees by companies related to a corporate borrower constitute 'a common element of many financial transactions'.

9 R. Squire, Limits to Group Structures and Asset Partitioning in Insolvency: Suppressing Value and Selective Perforation by Means of Guarantees, in The 800-Pound Gorilla. Limits to Group Structures and Asset Partitioning in Insolvency, NACIIL 2018 report, Eleven International Publishing, 2019, p. 13.

10 Dutch Bankruptcy Act, Article 136; InsO § 43; Italian Bankruptcy Act, Article 61. The same holds true for US and English law. See R. Squire, Limits to Group Structures and Asset Partitioning in Insolvency: Suppressing Value and Selective Perforation by Means of Guarantees, in The 800-Pound Gorilla. Limits to Group Structures and Asset Partitioning in Insolvency, NACIIL 2018 report, Eleven International Publishing, 2019, p. 12, explaining that the 'standard American rule is that a lender holding a guarantee can "prove" the full amount of his claim against both the borrower and the guarantor'. *Ivanhoe Building & Loan Association v. Orr*, 295 US 243, 245 (1935), where the US Supreme Court held that a creditor did not need to deduct from his claim in bankruptcy an amount received from a non-debtor third party in partial satisfaction of an obligation. Also, *In re National Energy & Gas Transmission, Inc*, 492 F3d 297, 301 (4th Cir. 2007); *In re F.W.D.C., Inc.*, 158 B.R. 523 (Bankr. S.D. Fla. 1993); *In re Johnson*, 477 B.R. 879 (M.D. Fla. 2012), confirming this approach. In English law, a guaranteed creditor is entitled to claim the full amount of outstanding debt from both the primary debtor and the guarantor. G. Andrews and R. Millett, Law of Guarantees, 4th edn, Sweet & Maxwell, 2005, p. 473, noting that the 'creditor can maintain [proof in the insolvency of the surety] at the same time as a proof for the full amount from the principal and any co-sureties, provided that they are each liable for the whole debt and the creditor does not receive more than 100 pence in the pound'.

Furthermore, a guaranteed creditor can benefit when the main debtor (e.g. the issuer of bonds) lends money (e.g. proceeds of bond issuance) to another group entity acting as a guarantor. Both the main debtor and the guaranteed creditor have separate claims against the guarantor – one under the intra-group loan and the other under the guarantee. As a result, the guaranteed creditor benefits not only from the direct claim against the guarantor but also from the payments the guarantor makes to the main debtor on the intercompany loan. This 'double-dip' structure was established in the Oi Brazil case (and in the case of Lehman Brothers), where the bondholders had claims against the Dutch SPVs, which acted as the issuers of the bonds. They could also exercise their claims directly against the Brazilian parent company, acting as a guarantor, and indirectly via the claim on the intra-group loans (see Figure 5.2). 5.13

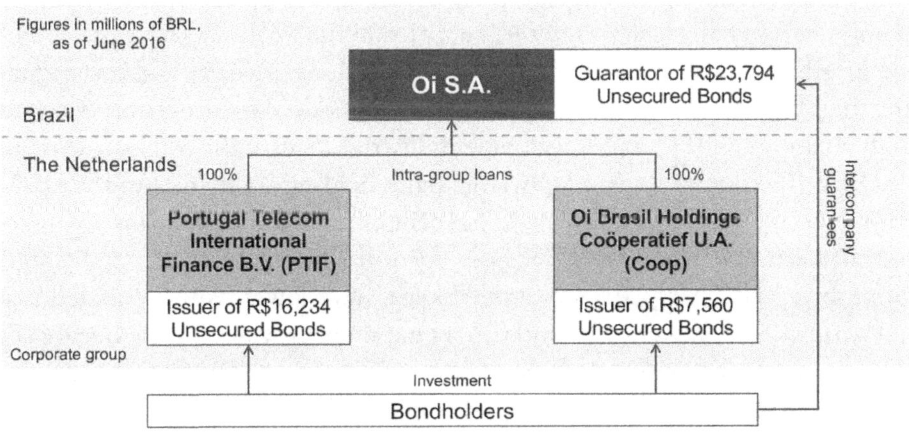

Note: This figure is based on R.J. Cooper, F.L. Cestero and J.W. Mosier, Oi S.A.: The Saga of Latin America's Largest Private Sector In-court Restructuring, Pratt's Journal of Bankruptcy Law, Vol. 14, 2018, p. 210.

Figure 5.2 Oi Brazil's intra-group financing

In addition to the described 'double dip', a guaranteed creditor receives some protection from intra-group asset shifting or asset stripping – the transfer or removal of key assets from one group entity to another, which can enrich shareholders but could be detrimental to the general body of creditors.[11] Asset stripping is a type of activity that creates what Jensen and Meckling refer to 5.14

11 A.W. Katz, An Economic Analysis of the Guarantee Contract, The University of Chicago Law Review, Vol. 66, 1999, pp. 73–74; H. Hansmann and R. Squire, External and Internal Asset Partitioning: Corporations and Their Subsidiaries, in J.N. Gordon and W-G. Ringe (eds), The Oxford Handbook of Corporate Law and Governance, OUP, 2018, p. 264.

as the 'agency cost of debt'.[12] The agency cost of debt comprises: (i) monitoring costs, incurred by creditors to limit managerial misbehaviour (e.g. through covenants, their monitoring and enforcement), (ii) bonding costs, incurred by the debtor to reassure creditors that it will not engage in value-destroying intra-group transfers, and (iii) costs of undeterred misconduct, arising in situations where the expected losses are borne by third parties, which may induce the debtor to overinvest.

5.15 Cross-guarantees reduce uncertainty for debtholders and, therefore, decrease the agency cost of debt. This reduction is attributed to their ability to curtail the negative effects of intra-group asset shifting, thereby lowering information and monitoring costs. The guaranteed creditor no longer needs to actively monitor the debtor and the transactions it enters into with its affiliate-guarantors – related-party transactions, which are often particularly difficult to monitor.[13] After all, such a creditor is entitled to file a claim against the debtor and its affiliates, acting as guarantors. This additional security and cost reduction might offset anticipatory losses and lead to reduced costs of debt. A recent study analysed USD commercial and industrial loans with commitments of USD 1 million or more, issued by large bank holding companies in the USA. The study concluded that (i) over 42 per cent of such corporate loans are guaranteed, meaning that there is recourse for full repayment of the credit obligation by a third party, (ii) guaranteed loans have lower bank estimated risk and perform better over time, and (iii) a guarantee provided by the borrower's parent or another group member generates a discount of about 9 per cent of the cost of debt for an average borrowing company.[14]

5.16 In sum, intercompany guarantees can facilitate access to finance, improve credit supply, and be ex ante efficient for the debtor,[15] its shareholders and guaranteed creditors – typically banks and other fully or strongly adjusting

---

12 M.C. Jensen and W.H. Meckling, Theory of the Firm: Managerial Behavior, Agency Costs and Ownership Structure, Journal of Financial Economics, Vol. 3, 1976, p. 305.

13 J. Dammann, Related Party Transactions and Intragroup Transactions, in L. Enriques and T.H. Tröger (eds), The Law and Finance of Related Party Transactions, CUP, 2019, p. 218, noting that 'intragroup transactions frequently serve legitimate purposes. On the other hand, the frequency, volume, and depth of such transactions can make them particularly difficult to police'.

14 M. Beyhaghi, Third-Party Credit Guarantees and the Cost of Debt: Evidence from Corporate Loans, Review of Finance, Vol. 26, 2022, pp. 287–317.

15 J. Armour et al., How do Creditor Rights Matter for Debt Finance? A Review of Empirical Evidence, in F. Dahan (ed), Research Handbook on Secured Financing of Commercial Transactions, Edward Elgar Publishing, 2015, pp. 3–25, more generally confirming that from an ex ante perspective, better protection of creditors' rights is associated with lower cost of credit and improved recoveries.

creditors. However, the overall economic efficiency of intra-group guarantees is disputed.[16]

5.4.2 'Opportunistic' function of cross-guarantees

While intercompany guarantees protect guaranteed creditors, they dilute the recoveries of non-guaranteed unsecured creditors.[17] This occurs because of the ability of a guaranteed creditor to submit its claim, often in full, against the estates of multiple entities. These claims 'compete' with the claims of creditors of those entities. Functionally, the guarantee selectively perforates the entity shields separating legal entities, effectively implementing contractual substantive consolidation for the sole benefit of the guaranteed creditor.[18] The ability of cross-guarantees to transfer value from the guarantor's pre-existing unsecured (non-guaranteed) creditors was termed by Squire as the 'opportunistic' function of intra-group guarantees.[19] He argues that the perforation of the enterprise group's internal structure constitutes shareholder opportunism termed 'correlation-seeking'. In interconnected groups, the insolvency risks of group entities are highly correlated – they tend to thrive and fail together. Thus, in good times, cross-guarantees benefit shareholders by allowing their companies to borrow at lower interest rates, while in insolvency, the triggering of guarantees may have no impact on shareholders because their equity stake in guarantors is wiped out anyway.[20] 5.17

A part of the problem is that guarantees are opaque. Unlike some *in rem* security interests, *in personam* security rights are not subject to public registration as a precondition for their validity and effectiveness against third parties. This problem of opacity has been noted in academic literature,[21] but there are no generally accepted solutions to it. Usually, a creditor is unaware of the web of 5.18

---

16 R. Squire, Strategic Liability in Corporate Groups, The University of Chicago Law Review, Vol. 78, 2011, p. 618.

17 Ibid., p. 608.

18 W.H. Widen, Corporate Form and Substantive Consolidation, George Washington Law Review, Vol. 75, 2007, p. 265, noting that 'intercompany guarantees create a type of substantive consolidation by contract'. Arguably, as 'contractual substantive consolidation' benefits only a guaranteed creditor, it is closer to a veil piercing.

19 R. Squire, Limits to Group Structures and Asset Partitioning in Insolvency: Suppressing Value and Selective Perforation by Means of Guarantees, in The 800-Pound Gorilla. Limits to Group Structures and Asset Partitioning in Insolvency, NACIIL 2018 report, Eleven International Publishing, 2019, p. 14.

20 R. Squire, Strategic Liability in the Corporate Group, The University of Chicago Law Review, Vol. 78, 2011, p. 607.

21 Ibid., p. 605, pointing out that the creation of subsidiaries and overuse of guarantees undermines transparency, complicates bankruptcy proceedings and introduces other distortions. See also J.L. Westbrook, Transparency in Corporate Groups, Brooklyn Journal of Corporate, Financial & Commercial Law, Vol. 13, 2018, p. 35, arguing for a regime 'in which transparency is required with regard to the structure of a corporate group and the activities of each of its members' and suggesting the disclosure of intercompany

contractual arrangements in which a debtor is involved. Even if it is, and even if the debtor agrees not to enter into any cross-liability arrangements (thus incurring bonding costs), creditor control over future transactions is problematic, and the monitoring costs might be excessively high, especially for unsophisticated creditors who lack the skills and incentives (e.g. due to the costs being higher than the expected benefits) to engage in it. In the end, these creditors are left in the dark and face the difficult task of calculating the risk of loss from the debtor's insolvency. Given the dilution of potential returns in insolvency, a creditor can either ask for *in rem* security or charge higher interest rates, ultimately increasing the agency cost of debt. However, these adjustments are unavailable if all or most of the debtor's assets are pledged or if the creditor cannot effectively negotiate the terms. This applies first and foremost to involuntary and poorly adjusting creditors.[22]

5.19 Another ex ante effect attributed to cross-guarantees relates to the incentives of creditors to screen and monitor the debtor. Sophisticated lenders, who would otherwise keep track of the debtor's recordkeeping and major transactions, arguably lose impetus to do so because intra-group guarantees make them indifferent or less attentive to the issue of value allocation within the group.[23] Certainly, a guarantee does not make credit risk disappear; it simply shifts risk monitoring to the guarantor.[24] This risk-shifting is efficient if the guarantor is a better risk bearer. This is likely not the case for group guarantors, as their ability to efficiently monitor the principal debtor is questionable due to the close bonds between the debtor and the guarantor in the group context. This is especially true for upstream guarantees, provided by subsidiaries with

---

guarantees, similar to that applicable to *in rem* security rights under Article 9 of the Uniform Commercial Code (UCC).

22 Non-adjusting creditors are those creditors who do not adjust the size and terms of their claims to anticipate future developments and security interests encumbering the borrower's assets. Among such creditors are tort creditors, tax and regulatory claims. Poorly adjusting creditors are voluntary creditors with few incentives or possibilities to bargain for security, e.g. due to a small size of a claim or high transaction costs of negotiations. See L.A. Bebchuk and J.M. Fried, The Uneasy Case for the Priority of Secured Claims in Bankruptcy, The Yale Law Journal, Vol. 105, 1996, p. 864; L. Enriques and M. Gelter, How the Old World Encountered the New One: Regulatory Competition and Cooperation in European Corporate and Bankruptcy Law, Tulane Law Review, Vol. 81, 2007, p. 583.

23 H. Hansmann and R. Squire, External and Internal Asset Partitioning: Corporations and Their Subsidiaries, in J.N. Gordon and W-G. Ringe (eds), The Oxford Handbook of Corporate Law and Governance, OUP, 2018, p. 264, noting that a group guarantee leaves a guaranteed creditor largely indifferent to the division of assets between group entities. See also R. Squire, Strategic Liability in the Corporate Group, The University of Chicago Law Review, Vol. 78, 2011, p. 617, arguing that without intra-group guarantees 'major lenders would pressure group managers to keep better records for each constituent entity, or to pare away extraneous subsidiary boundaries'.

24 A.W. Katz, An Economic Analysis of the Guarantee Contract, The University of Chicago Law Review, Vol. 66, 1999, p. 59, observing that guarantees 'help protect creditors against some of the risks of debtor misbehavior or insolvency by shifting those risks to guarantors'.

insufficient information on group performance (information asymmetry) or the ability to monitor and influence the parent company.[25] The resulting lack of efficient creditor oversight might contribute to managerial insulation. This is particularly problematic for enterprise groups with concentrated ownership, which might correlate with a higher risk of opportunistic behaviour by shareholders vis-à-vis creditors.[26]

In sum, the economic rationale of intercompany guarantees relates to risk mitigation. However, their ex ante effects on access to finance and corporate governance are not straightforward. It can be argued that they have a positive function, leading to the reduced agency cost of debt, lower interest rates and generally advancing the group's ability to raise capital. That being said, the cost reduction is selective and concerns only guaranteed creditors, while the outcome for non-guaranteed unsecured creditors can be the opposite. This is because non-guaranteed creditors may have to incur monitoring costs and sustain potential dilution of recoveries in insolvency. Group guarantees could also influence the degree of creditor oversight, since the guaranteed creditor may be indifferent to intra-group transfers of assets, knowing that it has recourse against several or all group entities. This can worsen the moral hazard problem. **5.20**

5.5 INSOLVENCY AND TRIANGLE OF RIGHTS AND LIABILITIES

5.5.1 Cross-guarantees and insolvency: important questions

Imagine the following scenario: a group of companies consists of Company A (the principal debtor and borrower) and Company B (guarantor). The creditor is the Bank that extends a credit line to Company A, with Company B guaranteeing its repayment (see Figure 5.3). **5.21**

Company A experiences financial distress and becomes insolvent or enters a restructuring proceeding, in which the claim of the Bank is significantly curtailed or is fully written down. In the triangle of rights and liabilities between **5.22**

25 A. Jonkers, Insider guarantees in corporate finance: An economic analysis of Dutch, US and German law, PhD thesis, 2020, p. 267, noting that guarantees in corporate finance typically shift the risk 'to inferior risk-bearers and inferior monitors, whereas the guaranteed creditors are often expert risk bearers and expert monitors'. A similar problem of the reduced incentives to monitor the debtor by sophisticated lenders has been emphasised with respect to the provision of collateral. See M. Manove, A.J. Padilla and M. Pagano, Collateral versus Project Screening: A Model of Lazy Banks, The RAND Journal of Economics, Vol. 32, 2001, pp. 726–744.

26 A. Gurrea-Martínez, Reinventing Insolvency Law in Emerging Economies, CUP, 2024.

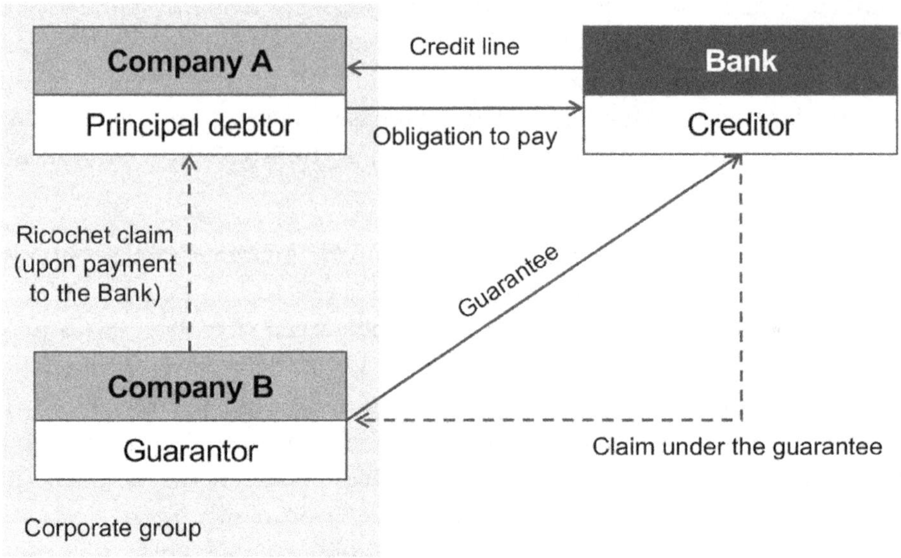

Figure 5.3 Triangle of rights and liabilities in group financing

the principal debtor, the guarantor, and the creditor, the following questions arise:

(i) Does the insolvency of Company A impact the claim of the Bank against Company B? Does the restructuring of the Bank's claim against Company A impact the claim of the Bank against Company B? In other words, can the Bank, despite Company A's insolvency or alteration or discharge of the Bank's claim against Company A in the restructuring proceedings, require performance from the guarantor and in what amount?

(ii) Can Company B, having performed its obligation to the Bank under the guarantee, file a 'ricochet' (recourse) claim against Company A and in what amount? Here, the use of the terms 'ricochet' and 'recourse' is not meant to describe a particular legal qualification or relationship under which the claim arises (e.g. subrogation, indemnity). Instead, it describes a three-party situation in which there is liability for the same debt resting on two parties, and one of them (e.g. surety) has been legally compelled to pay. In these circumstances, upon payment to the third party, the paying party may become entitled to recover from another party whose debt to the third party is discharged.[27]

5.23 The following sections explore these questions with reference to the rules of national law, as the answers may differ depending on the law that governs the relations between the parties. As I dive into the specifics of national law

27 On this three-party relationship, see C. Mitchell, The Law of Contribution and Reimbursement, OUP, 2013.

and guarantee relationships, it will become clear that cross-guarantees could complicate group restructuring and impact the long-term effectiveness of a restructuring plan.

5.5.2 Insolvency of the principal debtor and claim against a guarantor

5.5.2.1 The UK: co-extensiveness and discharge of guarantor's liability

There is a consensus among all three jurisdictions studied in this book that financial distress or insolvency of the principal debtor per se does not affect the creditor's rights against a guarantor. Thus, a creditor may lodge a proof of claim in the debtor's insolvency proceedings for the full outstanding balance and simultaneously sue the guarantor and enforce its claim against it to the extent that the creditor has not received payment from the debtor's estate and up to the limit for which the guarantor has engaged itself. This approach is taken in English law.[28] It is premised on the very purpose of a personal security right. It is precisely the insolvency of the principal debtor – a counterparty risk – that the guarantee seeks to provide a safety net against. Any other interpretation would undermine the protective function of the guarantee. 5.24

The insolvency of the principal debtor does not affect the liability of the guarantor. The question remains whether the discharge or alteration of debt in the proceedings concerning the principal debtor has any impact on the guarantor's liability. Under English law, generally, a discharge in bankruptcy of a debtor-individual does not affect the guarantor's liability. This expressly follows from the Insolvency Act 1986.[29] The same applies if the principal debtor-legal entity is liquidated by reason of insolvency.[30] The rationale behind this position is that 'the surety cannot complain of what is not the act of the creditor but [...] an act arising by operation of law'.[31] The insolvency of the principal debtor, therefore, falls within the risk assumed by the guarantor, unless otherwise agreed by the creditor and the guarantor. 5.25

However, what happens if the principal debtor enters into a company voluntary arrangement, a scheme of arrangement under Part 26 or a restructuring plan under Part 26A of the Companies Act? Goode points out that 'it 5.26

---

28 R. Goode and L. Gullifer, Goode and Gullifer on Legal Problems of Credit and Security, 6th edn, Sweet & Maxwell, 2017, para. 8-27. Note that lodging a proof of claim in insolvency proceedings may not always be needed, see e.g. Article 57 Fw.

29 Insolvency Act 1986, s. 281(7).

30 G. Moss and D. Marks, Rowlatt on Principal and Surety, 6th edn, Sweet & Maxwell, 2011, para. 12-05, clarifying that '[a]s in the case of bankruptcy, the liquidation or administration of a company will not release the surety for a company's obligations'.

31 Ibid., para. 8-22.

is a well-established principle of suretyship law that release of the principal debtor, an agreement not to sue him or a variation of the terms of the principal obligation discharges a surety unless the creditor reserves his rights against the surety either as a term of the guarantee or as a term of the release or other arrangement with the debtor'.[32] This follows from the principle of co-extensiveness of the guarantor's liability.[33] The basis for the general rule that the release of the principal debtor, without more, discharges the guarantor is that the release of the principal debtor may interfere with the guarantor's right to sue the principal debtor for compensation.

5.27 The creditor and debtor should not be able to put the rights of the surety in danger. This is why it was held that, in accepting the release subject to the reservation by the creditor of his rights against the surety, the principal debtor impliedly consents to the preservation of the surety's rights against the debtor, notwithstanding the release, so that the surety is not prejudiced.[34] Other arguments which support the discharge of the guarantor relate to the fact that: (i) the guarantor has agreed to be liable for a specific debt, and if that debt is released without the guarantor's consent, the justification for holding it liable for that same debt no longer holds; (ii) the function of a guarantee is usually to ensure the payment of a sum of money, but if that sum is no longer due, the basis of the surety's liability becomes unclear.

5.28 The release by a creditor of a surety who is jointly or jointly and severally liable can also lead to a discharge of co-sureties, unless remedies have been reserved against them.[35] The reason for this is that the release of a surety might prejudice the rights of contribution to which co-sureties may be entitled if the release were effective against co-sureties. In English law, the right of contribution is an independent right of a surety, based on the understanding that co-sureties

---

32 K. van Zwieten, Goode on Principles of Corporate Insolvency Law, 5th edn, Sweet & Maxwell, 2018, para. 12-26. *Mahant Singh v. U Ba Yi* [1939] AC 601; *Perry v. National Provincial Bank of England* [1910] 1 Ch. 464, observing that 'it is perfectly possible for a surety to contract with a creditor in the suretyship instrument that notwithstanding any composition, release, or arrangement the surety shall remain liable although the principal does not'.

33 L. Smith, Security, in A. Burrows (ed), Principles of English Commercial Law, OUP, 2015, para. 8.174, noting that 'the guarantor cannot be liable except to the extent that the primary debtor is liable'. G. Andrews and R. Millett, Law of Guarantees, 6th edn, Sweet & Maxwell, 2011, para. 6-002, explaining that the co-extensiveness principle means that 'as a general rule, the surety's liability is no greater and no less than that of the principal, in terms of amount, time for payment and the conditions under which the principal is liable'.

34 *Greene King Plc v. Stanley* [2002] B.P.I.R. 491, at 80.

35 S. Whittaker, Suretyship, in Chitty on Contracts, 34th edn, Sweet & Maxwell, 2021, para. 47-122. If co-guarantors are only severally liable, the release of one of them does not discharge others fully, but only to the extent that they are prejudiced by such a release.

have a common interest and common burden.[36] Therefore, if the surety pays the principal debt, it should be able to claim contribution from co-sureties because it discharged their obligations (common liability) to the creditor.[37] The idea is that since the suretyship creates a common burden that should be borne equitably by all co-sureties, no surety can be required, as between himself and co-sureties, to pay more than his due share.[38] In this regard, it is pointed out that 'it is immaterial that the sureties are jointly, severally or jointly or severally liable, that they are bound by different instruments, or at different times, or that they know nothing of each other's existence as such, or that the first surety agreed to be bound before the co-surety was approached'.[39]

Crucially, as the burden of paying a creditor should ultimately be borne by the principal debtor rather than (co-)sureties, 'a surety who wishes to recover a contribution from a co-surety must join the principal debtor to his proceedings, or else prove that he is insolvent'.[40] The purpose of this rule is to reduce the risk of the multiplication of suits filed by co-sureties against the principal debtor – each for an indemnity for their rateable share. **5.29**

If the creditor agrees to release the principal debtor from any liability by a valid agreement, the guarantor is discharged,[41] unless the guarantor agrees upfront that the primary obligation – or certain aspects of it – may be changed as between the principal debtor and the creditor without affecting the creditor's rights against the guarantor. Since a variation or release under a CVA is treated as consensual, it discharges the guarantor unless the guarantee provides otherwise (i.e. retaining the liability of the guarantor notwithstanding dealings between the creditor and the principal debtor).[42] In other words, a CVA is considered equivalent to a consensual arrangement outside insolvency **5.30**

---

36 G. Andrews and R. Millett, Law of Guarantees, 4th edn, Sweet & Maxwell, 2011, para. 12-001; *Dering v. Winchelsea (Earl)* (1787) 1 Cox. Eq. Cas. 318.

37 *Ellesmere Brewery Co v. Cooper* [1896] 1 QB 75. J.D. Heydon, M.J. Leeming and P.G. Turner (eds), Meagher, Gummow and Lehane's Equity Doctrines and Remedies, 5th edn, Chatswood: LexisNexis, 2015, paras. 10-040 to 10-045.

38 *Dering v. Winchelsea (Earl)* (1787) 1 Cox 318; 29 E.R. 1184; *Craythorne v. Swinburne* (1807) 14 Ves. Jun. 160 at 165; *Mahoney v. McManus* (1981) 180 C.L.R. 370 at 376; *Lavin v. Toppi* [2015] HCA 4; (2015) 254 CLR 459 at 32–34.

39 G. Andrews and R. Millett, Law of Guarantees, 4th edn, Sweet & Maxwell, 2011, para. 12-001.

40 C. Mitchell, The Law of Contribution and Reimbursement, OUP, 2013, para. 5.29; *Hay v. Carter* [1935] Ch. 397, CA.

41 G. Andrews and R. Millett, Law of Guarantees, 7th edn, Sweet & Maxwell, 2015, para. 9-010.

42 *Johnson v. Davies* [1999] Ch. 117, considering the effects of an individual voluntary arrangement (IVA), made under Part VIII of the Insolvency Act 1986 and expressing the view that the general law, by which a composition or arrangement between a debtor and his creditors releases sureties, applies to an IVA. *Lombard Natwest Factors Limited v. Koutrouzas* [2002] EWHC 1084 (QB), [2003] BPIR 444 (surety was not released by an IVA of a co-surety when a guarantee expressly provided that it would not be affected by indulgence granted to a co-surety).

proceedings (workout). The case of schemes of arrangement under Part 26 and restructuring plans under Part 26A of the Companies Act 2006 is treated differently. For example, unlike CVAs, schemes of arrangement and Part 26A restructuring plans require court sanction.[43] English courts confirm that schemes of arrangement operate to produce a discharge or variation of the debtor's obligations *by operation of law* and not by virtue of an agreement between the parties, whether actual or deemed.[44] Therefore, a scheme does not discharge a guarantor or joint debtor.[45] The same applies to a Part 26A restructuring plan, as this procedure is intended to draw on practice and principles applied by courts in sanctioning schemes of arrangement.[46]

5.31 The fact that schemes of arrangement (and by analogy, Part 26A plans) do not discharge the guarantor is also supported by cases in which courts approved schemes of arrangement with a third-party release, noting that, in the absence of such a release, the pursuit of the guarantor by a creditor will undermine the compromise between the creditor and the debtor.[47] The same approach was taken where two companies were jointly liable as co-obligors for the same debt. Specifically, it was noted that without the release of co-obligors, they would be liable for the entire debt and may be entitled to claim a contribution from the scheme company, a form of ricochet claim discussed in the following sections of this chapter.[48] If there were a discharge of guarantors or co-debtors by operation of law, the inclusion of a third-party release in schemes of arrangement would be superfluous.

43 Companies Act 2006, Part 26, s. 899 and Part 26A, s. 901F.

44 *Oceanfill Ltd v. Nuffield Health Wellbeing Ltd & Anor* [2022] EWHC 2178 (Ch), at 25ff.

45 G. Moss and D. Marks, Rowlatt on Principal and Surety, 6th edn, Sweet & Maxwell, 2011, para. 8-22; K. van Zwieten, Goode on Principles of Corporate Insolvency Law, 5th edn, Sweet & Maxwell, 2018, para. 12-26. For authorities on the predecessors of section 899 of the Companies Act, see *Re London Chartered Bank of Australia* [1893] 3 Ch. 540; *Dane v. Mortgage Insurance Corp Ltd* [1894] 1 QB 54; *Re Garner's Motors Ltd* [1937] Ch. 594, at 599, observing that the 'scheme when sanctioned by the court becomes something quite different from a mere agreement signed by the parties. It becomes a statutory scheme'.

46 *Re Virgin Atlantic Airways Ltd* [2020] EWHC 2191 (Ch), at 17-18. Restructuring plans have not been widely used. Between 26 June 2020 and 30 June 2023, in England and Wales, twenty-one companies had a restructuring plan registered at Companies House. See Official Statistics. Monthly Insolvency Statistics, June 2023, released 18 July 2023.

47 *In the Matter of Swissport Fuelling Ltd* [2020] EWHC 1499 (Ch), at 44, pointing out that a 'scheme may operate to release or modify the obligations of guarantors, as otherwise the creditors could claim against the guarantors, which would, in turn, be able to make what is called a ricochet claim against the borrower, thereby defeating the purpose of the scheme'. That the scheme may be utilised to effect releases of guarantees is shown by cases such as *Re Noble Group Ltd* [2019] BCC 34 and *Re APCOA Parking Holdings GmbH* [2015] Bus LR 374.

48 *Re Lecta Paper UK Ltd* [2020] EWHC 382 (Ch).

5.5.2.2 The USA: modification or release of primary obligation in and outside bankruptcy

5.32 In the USA, regulation of guarantees and suretyships has primarily evolved from common law. Additionally, all US states have enacted statutes that regulate this three-way contractual relationship, wherein one party (secondary obligor) agrees to be responsible to the creditor for an underlying obligation of another party (principal obligor).[49] While some of these statutes distinguish between suretyships and guarantees, others do not. The Uniform Commercial Code states that 'surety' includes 'a guarantor or other secondary obligor'.[50] The Restatement of the Law (3rd) Suretyship and Guaranty (Restatement), an influential authority in this area, observes that '[d]ifferences between these two mechanisms have been the subject of extended debate, not all of which is illuminating. A "surety" is typically jointly and severally liable with the principal obligor on an obligation to which they are both bound, while a "guarantor" typically contracts to fulfill an obligation upon the default of the principal obligor.'[51] Given the lack of a uniform body of law on suretyships and guarantees, and the fact that the same rules will often apply, whether a transaction is treated as a suretyship or a guarantee, technical differences are left out.[52] Instead, as before, I focus on the interplay between a guarantee and bankruptcy. The latter is regulated at the federal level.

5.33 Most US states follow the common law approach, allowing the creditor to choose whether to first sue the principal debtor, the surety or both simultaneously.[53] In other words, upon the default of the principal debtor, the creditor does not have to file a claim against the debtor before turning to the surety. This rule applies to both suretyship and 'guarantee of payment'. Yet if the guarantee is a 'guarantee of collection', the guarantor only incurs liability if the creditor has been unable to collect from the principal debtor using reasonable diligence.[54] In practice, guarantees of collection are rarely used, and group

49 C. Henkel, Personal Guarantees and Sureties between Commercial Law and Consumers in the United States, American Journal of Comparative Law, Vol. 62, 2014, p. 334.

50 UCC, § 1-201(b)(39).

51 Restatement 3d, Suretyship and Guaranty, § 1; F.S.H. Bae and M.E. McGrath, Rights of a Surety (or Secondary Obligor) under the Restatement of the Law, Third, Suretyship and Guaranty, Banking Law Journal, Vol. 122, 2005, p. 786, noting that 'there is considerable dispute about the distinction between a surety and a guaranty' and pointing out that 'the variations of statutory definitions among the jurisdictions do not generally affect the substantive law or the outcome of cases'.

52 For discussion of differences and similarities between a guarantee and suretyship, see T. Eisenberg (ed), Debtor-Creditor Law, Matthew Bender & Company, Inc., 2022, § 44.03.

53 Ibid., § 45.07.

54 See *Chahadeh v. Jacinto Med. Group, P.A.*, 519 S.W.3d 242, 246 (Tex. App. 2017), noting that a 'guaranty of collection is an undertaking of the guarantor to pay if the debt cannot be collected from the primary

guarantees are almost always unconditional 'guarantees of payment'.[55] If the performance of an underlying obligation is secured by collateral, the creditor may be required to proceed against the collateral first, provided that doing so does not cause substantial injury.[56] However, if there are several secondary obligors, such as co-sureties, a creditor may proceed against any of them regardless of their relative rights, as long as the creditor does not receive double recovery.[57]

5.34 It is not uncommon for a principal debtor to enter into a settlement with a creditor. Sections 39–41 of the Restatement address the effects of a release, extension and modification of an underlying obligation.[58] As a general rule, the 'release, extension, or modification discharges the secondary obligor from its duties pursuant to the secondary obligation either completely or to the extent that the obligee's [creditor's] act would otherwise cause the secondary obligor a loss'.[59] If the *modification* of an underlying obligation is material, affecting the nature, meaning or legal effect of this obligation, and if it prejudices the surety, the surety is discharged, unless it consents to the material change.[60] The material change should impose risks on the surety fundamentally different from those imposed prior to it. If the change is not material, the surety is not discharged, but its obligation is reduced to the extent of loss due to the modification (*pro tanto*).[61] It is observed that 'whether a change has been made that will discharge a surety is a question of fact, and subtle factual distinctions can lead to apparently inconsistent results'.[62]

5.35 The preceding paragraph addresses the modification of an underlying obligation. Let me now turn to a *voluntary release.* Whenever a creditor releases a principal debtor, a surety is discharged. As in English law, this is based on

obligor by the use of reasonable diligence, and requires the lender to pursue the principal debtor before collecting'.

55 A.J. Casey, The New Corporate Web: Tailored Entity Partitions and Creditors' Selective Enforcement, The Yale Law Journal, Vol. 124, 2015, p. 2680.

56 C. Henkel, Personal Guarantees and Sureties between Commercial Law and Consumers in the United States, American Journal of Comparative Law, Vol. 62, 2014, p. 352.

57 P.A. Alces, The Law of Suretyship and Guarantee, Thomson Reuters, 2021, § 5:4; Restatement 3d, Suretyship and Guaranty, § 53, comment a.

58 Restatement 3d, Suretyship and Guaranty, §§ 39–41.

59 Restatement 3d, Suretyship and Guaranty, Introductory Note to §§ 39–41. For a similar rule, see UCC, § 3-605(c).

60 *Autumn Manor, Inc. v. Jones*, No. 03-4083-SAC (D. Kan. Aug. 19, 2003); *Frost Nat'l Bank v. Burge*, 29 S.W.3d 580 (Tex. App. 2000). Note that in some US states, absent consent of a surety, any change in the principal's duties that increases such duties will discharge the surety. See e.g. Cal. Civ. Code § 2819; Ga, Code § 10-7-21.

61 *National Sur. Corp. v. United States*, 118 F.3d 1542 (Fed. Cir. 1997). The rule of *pro tanto* discharge is followed in § 3-606 UCC.

62 T. Eisenberg (ed), Debtor-Creditor Law, Matthew Bender & Company, Inc., 2022, § 45.06.

the co-extensive or accessory nature of the surety's obligation.[63] The discharge occurs unless either of the following conditions is met. First, the terms of the release preserve the surety's right of recourse against the principal debtor. If this is the case, the release does not prejudice the surety because it maintains the reimbursement right. Second, the language or circumstances of the release confirm the creditor's intent to retain the claim against the surety.[64] 'Reservation of rights' clauses are common in practice. However, a surety is nevertheless discharged to the extent that it would otherwise suffer a loss due to the release.[65]

A guarantor who performs after the release of an underlying obligation generally has no recourse against the principal debtor. This is because the release of an underlying obligation discharges not only the duty of the principal debtor to the guaranteed creditor but also the duties of performance and reimbursement owed to the guarantor. Notably, the guarantor also does not acquire subrogation rights. As a consequence of this lack of recourse, the guarantor could suffer a loss to the extent that, in the absence of the release, there would have been a recovery from the principal debtor. To prevent unfair outcomes, the guarantor is discharged to the extent necessary to avoid such a loss.[66] **5.36**

The same logic applies to the release of a co-surety or co-guarantor. State law typically provides for a right of contribution between co-sureties or co-guarantors based on a theory of implied contract. Hence, when two or more persons guarantee the debt of another, they simultaneously enter into 'an implied promise on the part of each to contribute his share if necessary to meet the common obligation'.[67] Co-sureties are treated as though they have agreed among themselves to share the cost of their performance. Pursuant to the Restatement, a co-surety is entitled to a contribution if he pays more than his contributive share, since as 'between cosureties for the same underlying obligation, each cosurety is a principal obligor to the extent of its contributive share … and a secondary obligor as to the remainder of its duty pursuant to **5.37**

63 On this point, suretyship should be distinguished from a standby letter of credit, which creates an independent, primary obligation. P.A. Alces, The Law of Suretyship and Guarantee, Thomson Reuters, 2021, § 2.8, observing that 'assurance of payment on demand, without condition, is the distinguishing feature of the standby credit'. J.F. Dolan, Standby Letters of Credit and Fraud (Is the Standby Only Another Invention of the Goldsmiths in Lombard Street?), Cardozo Law Review, Vol. 7, 1985, pp. 1-45.

64 Restatement 3d, Suretyship and Guaranty, § 39(b).

65 Ibid., § 39(c)(ii).

66 Ibid., § 39, comm. f. Arguably, if the principal debtor has no assets and the recovery on the recourse claim would not lead to any payment to the guarantor, there is no loss and no discharge.

67 *Waters v. Waters*, 148 A. 326, 327 (Conn. 1930); *Lestorti v. DeLeo*, 4 A.3d 269, 275, 298 Conn. 466, 473 (Conn., 2010).

its secondary obligation'.[68] A right of contribution therefore arises if a surety pays in excess of the share which, as between itself and co-sureties, it ought to bear.[69] In principle, if a surety is released by an act of a creditor from its obligation, which affects the right of contribution of a co-surety, this co-surety is discharged.[70]

5.38 In sum, applying US law may lead to a similar outcome as achieved under English law. Both legal systems aim to protect the surety with the understanding that the creditor and principal debtor should not be able to put the rights of a surety in danger or to place the ultimate burden solely on the surety or one of the co-sureties. It is important to stress that in practice, the effect in the form of a discharge is often prevented or waived in a guarantee agreement.[71]

5.39 This brings us to the bankruptcy scenario. As previously noted, US law permits a guaranteed creditor to sue the principal debtor and guarantor(s) simultaneously. If they are insolvent, the creditor can assert the entire claim (as it existed on the petition date) against the estates of each obligor and recover in each proceeding on the basis of the entire amount, provided that this creditor does not collect more, in total, than the amount owed to him. Until the creditor's claim has been fully satisfied, it does not need to be reduced to reflect any partial distributions in the insolvency proceedings.[72]

5.40 The question remains whether the bankruptcy discharge of the principal debtor also discharges the surety. When answering this question, it is important to keep in mind that one of the primary reasons for a creditor to seek a personal

---

68 Restatement 3d, Suretyship and Guaranty, § 55.

69 Restatement 3d, Suretyship and Guaranty, § 57(1) ('Subject to subsection (2) and to any express or implied agreement between or among the cosureties, a cosurety's contributive share is the aggregate liability of the cosureties to the obligee divided by the number of cosureties').

70 See Restatement 3d, Suretyship and Guaranty, § 54, providing the following illustration: 'To induce C to lend D $ 10,000, S[1] and S[2] guarantee D's obligation to repay the loan under circumstances such that S[1] and S[2] are cosureties with equal contributive shares. D defaults on the loan and has no assets. In exchange for $ 500, C releases S[1], who is solvent, from its guaranty and pursues S[2]. Pursuant to § 39, the release of S[1]'s duty to C also releases S[1]'s corresponding duty to S[2] and, accordingly, reduces the amount S[2] could recover from S[1] from $ 4,500 (the remainder of S[1]'s contributive share) to $ 0. Therefore, S[2] is discharged to the extent of $ 4,500 from the remaining $ 9,500 owed to C.'

71 B.D. Hulse, After the Guarantor Pays: The Uncertain Equitable Doctrines of Reimbursement, Contribution, and Subrogation, Real Property, Trust and Estate Law Journal, Vol. 51, 2016, p. 51; F.S.H. Bae and M.E. McGrath, Rights of a Surety (or Secondary Obligor) under the Restatement of the Law, Third, Suretyship and Guaranty, Banking Law Journal, Vol. 122, 2005, p. 807, observing that it is common practice for a contract between a surety and a creditor 'to be chock full of waivers inserted by the obligee's [creditor's] attorney'.

72 B.E. Greer, J.S. Moss and N.B. Herther-Spiro, Guarantees in Bankruptcy: A Primer II, Norton Annual Survey of Bankruptcy Law, 2014 edn, p. 180. *Bd. of Comm'rs v. Hurley*, 169 F. 92, 97 (8th Cir. 1909); *Reconstruction Fin. Corp. v. Denver & Rio Grande W. R.R. Co.*, 328 U.S. 495, 529 (1946); *In re Nat'l Energy & Gas Transmission, Inc.*, 492 F.3d 297, 301 (4th Cir. 2007).

security right, such as a guarantee, is to protect itself in case the principal debtor becomes bankrupt and receives a discharge in a bankruptcy proceeding.[73] The US Bankruptcy Code stipulates that the discharge of the debtor's debt does not affect the liability of any other entity on, or the property of any other entity for, such debt.[74] This is logical, as the bankruptcy discharge does not extinguish or cancel the debt but merely releases the debtor from personal liability.[75] Therefore, a bankruptcy discharge, including a Chapter 11 discharge, does not affect the liability of a co-debtor or surety for the discharged debt unless the plan provides for a release of third parties. Consequently, a surety remains liable for the original debt and not for the partly discharged debt; and Chapter 11 confirmation does not bar litigation against third parties for the remaining amount. One court has explicitly stated that extending 'the rule of equivalent liability [liability of a surety equals liability of the bankrupt principal debtor] into the bankruptcy context would destroy the value of a guarantee'.[76]

To conclude, the discharge of debt through a bankruptcy route, as opposed to a settlement outside bankruptcy (i.e. workout), does not impact the obligations of persons secondarily liable inasmuch as such a discharge is effected by operation of law.[77] This argument should be familiar to the reader, as it was previously mentioned in relation to English schemes of arrangement and restructuring plans. **5.41**

5.5.2.3 The Netherlands: suretyship, draagplicht and 403-statements

5.5.2.3.1 Insolvency and rights against third parties

The insolvency of the principal debtor or the adoption of a restructuring plan (*dwangakkoord*) in bankruptcy under the Dutch Bankruptcy Act does not **5.42**

73 Restatement 3d, Suretyship and Guaranty, § 34, comm. b. The term 'personal security right' is not common in the USA. The terms 'guarantee' and 'suretyship' are used instead. In the USA, 'security interest' usually refers to a form of collateral (i.e. *in rem* security right). In the UK, the term 'security' has traditionally been used to describe rights over assets. Yet these days it can refer to both 'proprietary' or 'real' security and 'personal' security. See R. Goode and L. Gullifer, Goode and Gullifer on Legal Problems of Credit and Security, 6th edn, Sweet & Maxwell, 2017, para. 1-06, noting that real security means 'security in an asset, whether of the debtor or of a third party' and that real security 'is to be contrasted with personal security, that is, security in the form of a personal undertaking which reinforces the debtor's primary undertaking to give payment or other performance'.

74 11 US Code § 524(e).

75 *In re Hepburn*, 27 B.R. 135 (Bankr. E.D.N.Y. 1983); *In re Lembke*, 93 B.R. 701, 702 (Bankr. D.N.D. 1988).

76 *In re Gentry*, 807 F.3d 1222, 1227 (10th Cir. 2015).

77 *NCNB Texas Nat. Bank v. Johnson*, 11 F.3d 1260, 1266 (5th Cir. 1994), noting that '[r]eorganization proceedings are judicial, not contractual, even where a secured creditor voluntarily participates'. *Citizens Bank of Pennsylvania v. Fine Cap. Assocs.*, 2014 WL 10558250 (Pa. Super. Ct. 2014); *In re Arrowmill Dev. Corp.*, 211 B.R. 497, 506 (Bankr. D.N.J. 1997).

affect creditor rights against third parties, such as sureties.[78] Furthermore, if the creditor is protected by both *in rem* (e.g. mortgage, pledge) and a personal security right (i.e. suretyship), it is generally up to the creditor to choose whether to enforce his right of pledge or mortgage or to call upon the surety.[79]

5.43 First, the above rules reflect the nature and economic function of suretyship and solidarity relationships, which serve to safeguard a creditor against the consequences of insolvency or default by the principal debtor or one of the co-debtors. Should the liberating effect of insolvency be extended to a surety, suretyship (being a personal security right) would lose its protective function at the time when it is most needed.[80] Second, Dutch law is based on the recognition that a plan (*dwangakkoord*) adopted under the Dutch Bankruptcy Act is accepted by creditors not to relinquish their rights or to make a gift, but to obtain as much as possible under the given circumstances.[81] For this reason too, sureties and co-debtors cannot invoke the plan for their release. The same rule applies, in principle, to WHOA schemes.[82] Therefore, sureties and co-debtors cannot invoke a WHOA scheme as a ground for the discharge of their obligations,[83] unless the scheme includes a third-party release. The general rule is that a surety remains liable for the payment of the original claim, in the manner stipulated and at the time agreed before the WHOA scheme has been confirmed. This outcome is not contrary to the accessory character of the surety's liability (similar to the English law principle of co-extensiveness). The principal debtor remains liable notwithstanding the plan or scheme. Only the

78 Dutch Bankruptcy Act, Article 160. A surety is a party that has committed itself to one or more creditors to fulfil the obligations of the principal debtor towards such creditors. See Article 7:850 BW. Suretyship is a form of joint and several liability. For this reason, Article 7:850(3) BW stipulates that the provisions regarding joint and several liability apply to suretyship, insofar as this title (that is, Title 14 of Book 7 BW) does not deviate from them.

79 HR 24 April 1992, *NJ* 1992/463 (*Heidenreich/Alcredis Bank NV*) and Conclusie AG Hartkamp, nr. 6. However, if a creditor's claim is secured, it may be contrary to the standards of reasonableness and fairness if the creditor first sues the surety before attempting to enforce security rights. Therefore, in certain circumstances, a creditor may be required to first enforce his other security rights before calling on the surety. Asser/Van Schaick 7-VIII 2018/84. Also under Article 3:234(1) BW, '[i]f both the debtor's and third party's property has been pledged or mortgaged for the same claim, the third party may, when the creditor proceeds to foreclosure, demand that the debtor's assets be included in the sale and that they be sold first'. A surety lacks such legal privilege of enforcement. G.J.L. Bergervoet, Borgtocht (O&R nr. 84) 2014, 6.2.2.

80 MvT, Bijlagen Handelingen II 1890/91, 100, 3, p. 61; Kortmann/Faber, Geschiedenis van de Faillissementswet, heruitgave Van der Feltz, II, Wolters Kluwer, 2016, p. 189.

81 Ibid. Note that the adoption of plans (*dwangakkoord*) in bankruptcy is rather rare in practice. In 2015, only 1.7 per cent of declared bankruptcy cases ended by means of a plan. CBS, Faillissementen, oorzaken en schulden 2015, p. 18.

82 Dutch Bankruptcy Act, Article 370(2), stating that Article 160 applies *mutatis mutandis*, unless a plan restructures group guarantees under Article 372(1). The provision prevents guarantees from being discharged after the plan has been approved. MvT, *Kamerstukken II* 2018/19, 35249, 3, p. 35.

83 Asser/Van Schaick 7-VIII 2018/93.

enforceability of his obligations is affected. The residual claim continues to exist in the form of a natural obligation, regardless of whether this is stipulated in a plan or whether the debtor can pay the residual claim.[84]

However, similar to the approach of US law to non-bankruptcy settlements and English law to the effects of company and individual voluntary arrangements (CVAs and IVAs), under Dutch law, the outcome is different for out-of-court agreements or workouts. Pursuant to Article 6:160 BW, an obligation ceases to exist when the debtor and creditor enter into an agreement with each other in which the creditor waives his right to performance. In view of the dependent, accessory nature of suretyship, the cancellation or release of the main obligation, in principle, leads to the cancellation or discharge of the secondary obligation under the guarantee. This follows directly from Articles 6:160, 3:82 and 3:7 BW. In workouts, to which the ordinary rules of contract law apply, a creditor is free to accept the composition offered by the debtor. This is why a voluntary out-of-court agreement releasing the principal debtor, discharges the surety.[85] **5.44**

5.5.2.3.2 Liability and contribution claims of co-sureties

As opposed to English and US law, under Dutch law, the release of one of the sureties by the creditor may have no effect on the liability of co-sureties. The reason for this is quite complicated and specific to Dutch law. It has to do with the fact that under Dutch law, the obligations of co-debtors (including co-sureties), while being joint and several to the creditor, are not necessarily interdependent (*afhankelijk*) as between each other.[86] **5.45**

Let us first consider the case where the principal debtor is not insolvent, as insolvency affects and creates rights of a surety against other co-sureties (see below). The difference with English and US law arises from the fact that under Dutch law, sureties may have no claim for contribution from co-sureties. This follows from the construction of Articles 6:10 and 6:12 BW, which provide for a right to contribution (*bijdragen*) only from co-debtors that are *draagplichtig*, which is the case where the debt concerns co-debtors (co-sureties) internally. One example of this is when two persons, acting as co-obligors, buy a car for **5.46**

84 HR 31 January 1992, ECLI:NL:HR:1992:ZC0492, *NJ* 1992/686, m.nt. P. van Schilfgaarde (*Van der Hoeven/Comtu*).

85 Hof Leeuwarden 7 April 2009, ECLI:NL:GHLEE:2009:BI2399, *JOR* 2009/302, refusing to apply Article 160 Fw *mutatis mutandis* to an out-of-court agreement. The court noted that for a judicial composition (*akkoord*), the unpaid part of a claim is usually treated as a natural obligation (HR 31 January 1992, *NJ* 1992/686), whereas in the event of an out-of-court agreement, this is not the case.

86 W.H. van Boom, Hoofdelijke verbintenissen. W.E.J. Tjeenk Willink, 1999, p. 133.

their common use (i.e. common benefit).[87] If the co-debtors are *draagplichtig*, a contribution claim of each individual debtor is limited to the amount that they owe in their internal relationship, their internal share.[88] This can be compared to a 'contributive share' mentioned in the previous section on US law. In other words, the paying debtor can only sue other debtors for the amount for which the debt concerns each of them internally. Whether and to what extent there is a right to contribution from co-debtors thus depends on their internal burden-sharing, a mutual internal relationship, as distinguished from an external relationship, i.e. a relationship with the creditor.[89] If such an internal relationship is not present (and there is no general presumption of its existence in law), no right to contribution arises. This is the key difference with English and US law.

5.47 In a standard (non-group) situation, co-sureties are not considered *draagplichtig* because the debt does not concern them internally.[90] As a result, Articles 6:10 and 6:12 BW would not entitle them to claim contribution from one another. In practice, however, it might be difficult to ascertain whether there is an internal relationship that gives rise to a contribution claim between co-sureties. The first step is to check whether the parties may have expressly agreed on an internal obligation to contribute (*draagplichtovereenkomst*).[91]

5.48 Particular problems arise in a group financing context, where several group members benefit, directly or indirectly, in their internal relationships.

5.49 Imagine a typical case where one entity within the group acts as a borrower and other group entities provide guarantees, subsequently benefiting from the loan via intra-group loans (e.g. the cases of Lehman Brothers and Oi Brazil). Based on the facts of the case, it is possible to argue that there is an obligation to contribute between group entities acting as joint and severally liable debtors to the extent or in the share that each of them benefited from group financing. For example, this could be determined by looking at which group entity used the borrowed money or at whose disposal the loan was made – a cash-flow based test. This conclusion follows from *Janssen/JVS Beheer*.[92] Arguably, in an

87 Asser/Sieburgh 6-I 2020/122.

88 Dutch Civil Code, Article 6:10(2). G.J.L. Bergervoet, Borgtocht (Onderneming en recht nr. 84), Deventer: Kluwer 2014, 3.2.6.

89 J. den Hoed, GS Verbintenissenrecht, commentaar op art. 6:10 BW.

90 Asser/Sieburgh 6-I 2020/122.

91 C.H.A. van Oostrum, Regres bij concernfinanciering (Serie Van der Heijden Instituut nr. 156) (diss. Leiden), Deventer: Wolters Kluwer 2019, 7.2.1.0, noting that these agreements are uncommon and arguing that even when they exist, they may not necessarily reflect the actual relations between the parties at the relevant time.

92 HR 13 July 2012, ECLI:NL:HR:2012:BW4206, *NJ* 2012/447 (*Janssen q.q./JVS Beheer*). The alternative approach argues that, in the absence of a *draagplichtovereenkomst*, the starting point should be that

integrated corporate group, it is difficult to unravel financial flows between group entities to determine which specific entity derived profit and in what amount – an important step that needs to be undertaken to calculate an internal share.[93] Therefore, the existence and scope of contribution claims between group companies may be somewhat uncertain. In a more recent decision, the Dutch Supreme Court clarified that in a group context, when deciding on the internal obligation to contribute between group members, the court may also consider direct and indirect benefits of financing for the group members.[94] Hence, indirect benefits and other relevant circumstances can be part of judicial assessment. This is a step forward in the legal development. Yet it does not offer much guidance to courts regarding specific facts or patterns which can assist them in carrying out such an assessment.

Outside insolvency, co-sureties and other jointly and severally liable debtors **5.50** who are not liable in their internal relationship (*niet draagplichtig*), do not have to share their burden with each other.[95] This is different from English law, where co-suretyship creates a common burden that needs to be borne equitably by all co-sureties.

The situation is very different when the joint and several debtor, not liable in **5.51** its internal relationship with other co-debtors, cannot recover from the principal debtor or from co-debtors with an internal obligation to contribute. This situation arises if the principal debtor is insolvent and cannot fully satisfy the surety's claim.[96] In a situation like this, Dutch law confers the right to contribution on a paying debtor against its co-debtors (Article 6:13(2) BW), and on a paying surety against co-sureties (Article 7:869 BW), even if these co-debtors and co-sureties are not internally liable.[97] The loss is shared among them in proportion to the amounts for which they could have been held liable

group entities are internally liable in equal parts, under the principle of *solidariteit*. See H.P.J. Ophof, Hoofdelijke aansprakelijkheid: solidariteit of apartheid? (Inaugurele rede Vrije Universiteit Amsterdam), Deventer: Kluwer 1987, pp. 10–13. However, following *Janssen q.q./JVS Beheer*, the point of departure is different, namely the determination of which entity has used or had access to the line of credit.

93 S.M. Bartman, annotatie bij HR 13 juli 2012, ECLI:NL:HR:2012:BW4206, Ars Aequi 2012, p. 833 (*Janssen q.q./JVS Beheer*).

94 HR 24 February 2023, ECLI:NL:HR:2023:295, r.o. 3.5.

95 Asser/Sieburgh 6-I 2020/122.

96 If there are two or more joint and several debtors (co-debtors), and if the suretyship covers both their debts, the surety can claim contribution from each of them in full, and not only the part of the debt that concerns each debtor, irrespective of debtors' internal relationships (Article 7:866(3) BW). This is an explicit derogation from Article 6:10 BW, pursuant to which a joint and several debtor can only hold other debtors liable for the part of the debt that each debtor had to bear in their internal relationship.

97 For the analysis of the rules on joint and several liability and rules applicable to suretyship, see C.J.M. Klaassen, Hoofdelijkheid ofborgtocht, wat zal het wezen? WPNR 1998/6316, pp. 347–351.

by the creditor.[98] The right of contribution under Articles 6:13(2) and 7:869 BW is subsidiary in nature.[99] As a result, in practice, if the principal debtor is insolvent, cannot be traced, or if his assets cannot be recovered to satisfy the recourse claim for any other reason, Dutch law might not be that different from English or US law. As the right of contribution arises only if the debt cannot be recovered from *draagplichtige* debtor(s), a surety can effectively be forced to first go against this debtor(s), and only then seek recovery from non-*draagplichtige* co-sureties. To conclude this section, ultimately, each surety bears the risk of the principal debtor's insolvency, although the risk exposure may be limited by the scope or amount for which the surety has been provided.

5.5.2.3.3 Intra-group liability and 403-statements

5.52 The discussion of intra-group liability arrangements in Dutch law would be incomplete without covering intra-group liability arising from a 403-statement (*403-verklaring*). Pursuant to Article 2:403 BW,[100] a group entity may be exempt from an obligation to prepare and publish annual accounts. There may be various reasons to opt for this special regime. It reduces the regulatory burden within the group and prevents competitors from becoming aware of the financial results and capital positions of individual group entities.[101]

5.53 However, there are a number of requirements. For example, information normally included in annual accounts (e.g. assets, liabilities, income, expenses) must be consolidated in the annual accounts of the group company, typically a parent company.[102] Crucially, this company shall declare in writing that it makes itself jointly and severally liable for debts arising from legal acts of other group entities, typically subsidiaries, whose accounts are being consolidated.[103] The statement to this effect, a 403-statement, should be deposited at the Chamber of Commerce (*handelsregister*).[104] The joint and several liability is solely based on the 403-statement.[105] The purpose of this statement is

98 Asser/Sieburgh 6-II 2021/287.

99 Asser/Van Schaick 7-VIII 2018/124.

100 This arrangement follows the Fourth Council Directive 78/660/EEC of 25 July 1978 based on Article 54(3)(g) of the Treaty on the annual accounts of certain types of companies (Article 57), repealed by the Directive 2013/34/EU of 26 June 2013 on the annual financial statements, consolidated financial statements and related reports of certain types of undertakings (Article 37).

101 Asser/Maeijer & Kroeze 2-I* 2015/581; J. van der Kraan, Toepassing en rechtskarakter van de groepsvrijstelling van artikel 2:403 BW (Serie Van der Heijden Instituut nr. 171), Deventer: Wolters Kluwer, 2022.

102 Dutch Civil Code, Article 2:403(1)(c).

103 Dutch Civil Code, Article 2:403(1)(f). The requirement that liability must arise from legal acts (*rechtshandelingen*) excludes from the scope of 403-statement liability in tort. E.D.G. Kiersch, in: T&C Burgerlijk Wetboek, commentaar op art. 2:403 BW.

104 Dutch Civil Code, Article 2:403(1)(g).

105 HR 28 June 2002, ECLI:NL:HR:2002:AE4663, *NJ* 2002/447, m.nt. J.M.M. Maeijer; *JOR* 2002/136, m.nt. S.M. Bartman (*Akzo Nobel/ING*).

to give protection to creditors of a group entity (e.g. a subsidiary) since such creditors – as a result of the exemption under Article 2:403 BW – cannot base their decision on whether or not to contract with the subsidiary on its annual accounts. The economic effect of a 403-statement is similar to a parent company guaranteeing the debts of its subsidiaries. If the subsidiary does not pay, its creditors can go against the parent company. However, while a guarantee is commonly addressed to a specific creditor, a 403-statement is a unilateral legal act (not a contractual relationship), not addressed to any specific party, on the basis of which direct liability of the (parent) company arises.[106]

The BW does not establish the specific content or consequences of a 403-claim. For example, if the claim of the creditor against the subsidiary is privileged, should it also have priority when filed against the parent? The Dutch Supreme Court clarified in this respect that any privileges attached to the original claim do not pass to the claim based on a 403-statement.[107] The court reasoned that the privileges could only arise from the law (Article 3:278(2) BW) and that neither Article 2:403 nor any other statutory provision attached a privilege to the claim based on a 403-statement. In another case, the court ruled that the subordinated status of a claim against the subsidiary did not lead to the subordination of a 403-statement-based claim against the parent company.[108] It stated that contractual subordination (Article 3:277(2) BW) was not a property of the obligation itself but constituted a deviation from the main (*pari passu*) rule, as applied to recovery from assets of a debtor that agreed to such subordination.[109] Thus, a subordination clause in the agreement between a creditor and a subsidiary has no influence on that creditor's recovery from assets of a third party (parent) that is jointly and severally liable for the obligation by virtue of a 403-statement and that is not a party to the subordination clause. 5.54

Liability under a 403-statement is different from a suretyship agreement when it comes to its withdrawal. The law provides that a 403-statement can 5.55

106 There are other key differences between joint and several liability arising from a guarantee and a 403-statement, inter alia, regarding the consequences of a voluntary release. As noted above, a voluntary release of the principal debtor typically discharges the surety. In contrast, the release by the creditor of the subsidiary does not necessarily lead to a discharge of the parent company, liable under a 403-statement. This follows from the fact that a unilateral declaration of joint and several liability under a 403-statement does not create a dependent right in the sense of Articles 3:7 and 3:82 BW. HR 28 June 2002, ECLI:NL:HR:2002:AE4663, *NJ* 2002/447, m.nt. J.M.M. Maeijer (*Akzo Nobel/ING*).

107 HR 11 April 2014, ECLI:NL:HR:2014:898 (*X/Curatoren Econcern N.V.*) and ECLI:NL:HR:HR:2014:904 (*UWV/Curatoren Econcern N.V.*).

108 HR 20 March 2015, ECLI:NL:HR:2015:661, *NJ* 2015/361, m.nt. J.W. Winter en P. van Schilfgaarde (*Minister van Financiën/Vereniging VEB NCVB, Stichting Beheer SNS Reaal e.a.*).

109 Ibid., r.o. 4.34.4.

be withdrawn by filing a statement to that effect with the *handelsregister*.[110] No liability can arise for legal acts after the day on which the revocation statement is filed, or from a later date if specified in the revocation statement. Nevertheless, the parent company remains liable for debts derived from legal acts predating the revocation.[111] This residual liability can be terminated if the subsidiary leaves the group, for example, as a result of a sale or because there is no longer a group in the sense of Article 2:24(b) BW.[112] When this occurs, a creditor has a two-month period to oppose the termination of the residual liability. The creditor can demand from the parent company that, 'in exchange' for termination of residual liability, it is given a personal or *in rem* security.[113] Yet the creditor is not entitled to such security if his position is sufficiently protected considering the financial strength of the subsidiary.

5.5.3 Performance by a guarantor and its rights against the principal debtor

5.5.3.1 The UK: subrogation and indemnification claims in insolvency proceedings and in schemes of arrangement

5.56 Under English law, if the guarantee is provided at the request of the principal debtor, whether express or implied, the guarantor acquires the right to be indemnified by such a debtor for payments made under the guarantee.[114] The *indemnification claim* – a claim for the payment of debt – is 'distinct from any of the creditor's rights against the debtor that it may exercise by subrogation'.[115] The right to indemnity is an independent right of the guarantor, separate from the right arising from subrogation (see below). As a result of this independent nature of the indemnity claim, any action taken by the creditor without the cooperation of the guarantor (e.g. an agreement not to sue the debtor or a compromise with the debtor) cannot prejudice the guarantor.[116] The independent nature of the right to indemnity also means that, in the absence of an agreement to the contrary, a limitation period does not start to run against the guarantor until it has paid the creditor.[117]

110 Dutch Civil Code, Article 2:404(1).

111 Dutch Civil Code, Article 2:404(2).

112 E. Nass, GS Rechtspersonen, commentaar op art. 2:403 BW. The rules on termination of residual liability can be found in Article 2:404(3)–(6) BW.

113 E.A. van Dooren, De aansprakelijkheid op grond van een 403-verklaring (diss.), Uitgaven vanwege het instituut voor Ondernemingsrecht nr. 122, Deventer: Wolters Kluwer, 2021, 8.9ff.

114 R. Goode and L. Gullifer, Goode and Gullifer on Legal Problems of Credit and Security, 6th edn, Sweet & Maxwell, 2017, para. 8-11.

115 J. Phillips, J. O'Donovan and W. Courtney, Philips and O'Donovan: Modern Contract of Guarantee, 4th edn, Sweet & Maxwell, 2020, para. 12-031.

116 G. Andrews and R. Millett, Law of Guarantees, 7th edn, Sweet & Maxwell, 2015, para. 10-001.

117 *Collinge v Heywood* (1839) 9 Ad. & El. 633; *Re Mitchell* [1913] 1 Ch. 201; *Re A Debtor* [1937] Ch. 156.

Alongside the right of indemnity, there exists the equitable remedy of *subrogation*, a remedy against the party who would otherwise be unjustly enriched.[118] Subrogation arises from the relationship between a guarantor and creditor. When a guarantor pays the guaranteed debt in full, it becomes subrogated to the rights of the creditor, both in equity and under section 5 of the Mercantile Law Amendment Act 1856.[119] In other words, the guarantor steps into the shoes of the creditor and assumes the latter's legal position and rights against another person, such as the principal debtor.[120] This means that: (i) the creditor is accountable to the guarantor for any further payments received from the debtor; (ii) the guarantor succeeds to the security rights held by the creditor; and (iii) to the extent that the creditor was a preferential creditor, the guarantor becomes a preferential creditor as well.[121] Additionally, unlike an indemnity claim, the enforceability of subrogation rights is governed by the limitation rules that apply to the creditor's right of action.[122] 5.57

In English law, there is a long-standing rule against double proof for the same debt.[123] The essence of this rule is that 'the insolvent estate should not be compelled to entertain more than one proof in respect of the same debt, for to do so would unfairly distort the *pari passu* principle of distribution in insolvency'.[124] This means that the surety cannot prove its right against the principal debtor (whether on the basis of indemnity or subrogation) until the creditor has received full payment, unless the guarantor is responsible for a specified part of the debt, in which case upon payment of that part, the guarantor becomes 5.58

---

118 *Banque Financière De La Cité v Parc (Battersea) Ltd* [1999] 1 A.C. 221, 236.

119 The exclusion in common law of subrogation for partial performance aims to protect the creditor (*nemo subrogat contra se*). See S. Meier, Recourse between Solidary Debtors, in N. Jansen and R. Zimmermann (eds), Commentaries on European Contract Laws, OUP, 2018, p. 1585, observing that while some civil law jurisdictions allow a partial subrogation, they provide for creditor preference. Notably, before 1992, Dutch law provided for the subordination of a subrogated party outside insolvency. However, this rule was subsequently dropped. See HR 1 February 2008, *JOR* 2008/115 (*ING/Provincie Utrecht*). Thus, the current law prescribes the subordination of a subrogated party in insolvency, whereas subordination outside insolvency was abandoned by the legislator.

120 See, however, C. Mitchell and S. Watterson, Subrogation: Law and Practice, OUP, 2007, para. 3.15, noting that under subrogation, 'the claimant is given new rights which replicate the creditor's extinguished rights'.

121 R. Goode and L. Gullifer, Goode and Gullifer on Legal Problems of Credit and Security, 6th edn, Sweet & Maxwell, 2017, para. 8-25; J. Phillips, J. O'Donovan and W. Courtney, Philips and O'Donovan: Modern Contract of Guarantee, 4th edn, Sweet & Maxwell, 2020, para. 12-254.

122 J. Phillips, J. O'Donovan and W. Courtney, Philips and O'Donovan: Modern Contract of Guarantee, 4th edn, Sweet & Maxwell, 2020, para. 12-280. See, however, C. Mitchell and S. Watterson, Subrogation: Law and Practice, OUP, 2007, paras 7.137–7.162, calling this approach 'parasitic', criticising it, and proposing an alternative, 'autonomous' approach.

123 *Re Fenton* [1931] 1 Ch. 85; *Re Polly Peck International Plc, In administration (No. 3)* [1996] 1 BCLC 428; *Re Kaupthing, Singer & Friedlander* [2012] 1 AC 804, at 11; *Re MF Global UK Ltd (In Special Administration), Heis v. Attestor Master Fund LP* [2014] 1 WLR 1558, at 72–78.

124 G. Andrews and R. Millett, Law of Guarantees, 7th edn, Sweet & Maxwell, 2015, para. 13-002.

entitled to lodge a proof for the sum paid.[125] The creditor's priority under the rule against double proof is often reinforced by a non-competition clause, excluding the guarantor's right to claim, prove or rank together or in competition with the creditor.[126] If the principal debtor is discharged upon the completion of the insolvency proceedings, and the creditor's claim has not been satisfied in full, the guarantor's claim against the principal debtor remains unenforceable.[127] Importantly, the sums received from the guarantor, before or after the debtor's insolvency, do not have to be deducted from the amount claimed by the creditor in the insolvency of the principal debtor, as long as the creditor does not receive more than the total amount of its claim (hotchpot rule).[128] The rule against double proof does not prevent a double proof of the same debt against separate estates, when the creditor sues simultaneously the principal debtor and the guarantor, co-debtors or co-surety.

5.59 As mentioned earlier, the restructuring of the principal debt through a scheme of arrangement or a Part 26A plan does not discharge the guarantor. The creditor can successfully proceed against the guarantor, and unless the guarantor's rights of indemnity and subrogation are expressly limited or excluded by agreement,[129] the guarantor can then recover from the principal debtor any amount the guarantor paid to the creditor. This right rests on the surety's equity not to have the whole burden of debt thrown upon it. Thus, it is in the interests of the principal debtor to propose a scheme of arrangement or a restructuring plan that provides a complete release of liabilities, including those based on indemnity or contribution rights of a guarantor or co-debtor. Payne observes that releasing the creditor's rights against third parties (e.g. guarantors) via a scheme is 'entirely sensible'. She explains that if a claim is pursued under a guarantee, it would lead to a subrogation claim by the guarantor against the company as the principal debtor, thereby defeating the purpose of the compromise between the company and the creditor.[130] Yet the indemnity claim may be more problematic, because subrogation only places the guarantor in the position of the creditor. By contrast, upon payment to the creditor, the guarantor might be entitled to claim the entire amount from the principal debtor under its right of indemnity, as if no compromise of the creditor's claim

125 *Cattles Plc v. Welcome Financial Services Ltd* [2010] 2 Lloyd's Rep. 514 per Lloyd LJ at 25.

126 Ibid., where the clause also protected the principal lender from competition from intercompany debts.

127 G. Andrews and R. Millett, Law of Guarantees, 7th edn, Sweet & Maxwell, 2015, para. 13-007.

128 R. Goode and L. Gullifer, Goode and Gullifer on Legal Problems of Credit and Security, 6th edn, Sweet & Maxwell, 2017, para. 8-18; I. Fletcher, Law of Insolvency, Sweet & Maxwell, 2017, para. 9-042.

129 J. Phillips, J. O'Donovan and W. Courtney, Philips and O'Donovan: Modern Contract of Guarantee, 4th edn, Sweet & Maxwell, 2020, paras. 12-017 and 12-260. *Highbury Pension Fund Management Co v. Zirfin Investments Ltd* [2013] EWCA Civ 1283; [2014] Ch. 359 at 5-6.

130 J. Payne, Schemes of Arrangement: Theory, Structure and Operation, CUP, 2014, p. 24.

was effected via the scheme.[131] This could render the success of the scheme illusory from the principal debtor's perspective.

5.5.3.2 The USA: reimbursement, subrogation and bankruptcy subordination

US law contains a number of remedies available to a surety in its relations with the principal debtor. They include exoneration, reimbursement and subrogation. While these remedies are grounded in equity, certain US states also regulate them through statutes.[132] Additionally, it is common for a surety to require the principal debtor to agree to an indemnity, whereby the debtor commits to indemnify the surety for any losses arising from the principal debtor's failure to fulfil underlying obligations.[133] **5.60**

The *right of exoneration* is the right of a surety to demand performance from the principal debtor, as long as doing so does not prejudice the creditor. It is based on the belief that it is the principal obligor who should perform and bear the cost of performance.[134] For the right of exoneration to arise, the principal obligor needs to be aware of the secondary obligor's identity or existence. Without such notice, a surety does not have the right to insist on performance by the principal debtor.[135] If proper notice is given, the surety may ask the court to compel the principal debtor to perform when due, so that it does not have to perform and seek reimbursement afterwards. In equity, a surety can also file a bill of *quia timet* (from Latin 'because he fears') to compel its principal to perform when it fears that the principal is going to dissipate assets that could be used to pay the creditor.[136] **5.61**

A surety has the *right to reimbursement* from the principal debtor upon satisfying an underlying obligation, either in part or in full. This equitable remedy arises from an implied contract and has been incorporated into the statutes of several US states.[137] This right arises when the surety makes partial or complete payment and can only be enforced after the underlying obligation becomes due.[138] Just like the right of exoneration, the right to reimbursement requires a notice of the secondary obligation. Without such notice, there is **5.62**

---

131 *Colouroz Investment 2 LLC & Ors, Re* [2020] EWHC 1864 (Ch), 2020 WL 03964188, at 72.

132 See Cal. Civ. Code § 2846, under which a 'surety may compel his principal to perform the obligation when due'. See also Ohio Rev. Code § 1341.19.

133 T. Eisenberg (ed.), Debtor-Creditor Law, Matthew Bender & Company, Inc., 2022, § 45.03.

134 Restatement 3d, Suretyship and Guaranty, § 21, comm. a.

135 P.A. Alces, The Law of Suretyship and Guarantee, Thomson Reuters, 2021, § 6.5.

136 T. Eisenberg (ed), Debtor-Creditor Law, Matthew Bender & Company, Inc., 2022, § 45.07.

137 See e.g. La. Civ Code, Art. 3049; Ga. Code § 10-7-41; Rev. Stat. Mo. § 433.070; N.D. Cent. Code, § 22-03-10.

138 P.A. Alces, The Law of Suretyship and Guarantee, Thomson Reuters, 2021, § 6.13. La. Civ. Code, Art. 3049; Restatement 3d, Suretyship and Guaranty, § 22, comm. d.

no implied contract. This does not mean that the paying surety is left without any means to protect itself. After paying the creditor, the surety is entitled to claim restitution from the principal debtor to the extent of the latter's unjust enrichment.[139] It is important to emphasise that the right to reimbursement is based on the (implied) promise by the principal debtor. When the surety pays the debt of the principal debtor, an entirely new obligation of that debtor to reimburse the surety arises.[140] This distinguishes the right to reimbursement from that of subrogation, just as English law distinguishes between indemnity and subrogation.

5.63 Once a surety has completely fulfilled the secondary obligation, it is subrogated to the rights that the creditor had pursuant to the underlying obligation. *Subrogation* is broadly defined as 'the substitution of another person in the place of the creditor to whose rights he succeeds in relation to the debt'.[141] US law recognises two types of subrogation: (i) conventional subrogation, which is based on an agreement, and (ii) equitable subrogation, which arises as a matter of equity and is not dependent on a contractual relationship.[142] There are several features that distinguish subrogation from reimbursement.

5.64 First, the right of equitable subrogation exists as a matter of law rather than by an (implied) consent of the parties.[143] Some US states provide for the right of subrogation by statute.[144] Second, for the right to subrogation to arise, an underlying obligation must be satisfied in full,[145] whereas the right to reimbursement can arise from partial performance. Third, as a result of subrogation, a surety succeeds to the rights of the creditor in relation to the debt or claim, and its rights, remedies or securities.[146] Since the underlying obligation has been fully satisfied, allowing the surety to enforce the creditor's rights does not harm the interests of the creditor.[147] By contrast, the right to reimbursement

---

139 Restatement 3d, Suretyship and Guaranty, § 22, comm. a, and § 26.

140 T. Eisenberg (ed), Debtor-Creditor Law, Matthew Bender & Company, Inc., 2022, § 45.07.

141 *Hanover Ins. Co. v. Corrpro Cos., Inc.*, 312 F. Supp. 2d 816, 818 (E.D. Va. 2004).

142 T. Eisenberg (ed), Debtor-Creditor Law, Matthew Bender & Company, Inc., 2022, § 45.07.

143 *In re Cone Constructors, Inc.*, 265 B.R. 302, 303 (Bankr. Ct. M.D. Fla. 2001), holding that 'equitable subrogation is a legal fiction which arises by operation of law'.

144 See e.g. Cal. Civ. Code § 2848; La. Civ. Code, Art. 3048 ('The surety who pays the principal obligation is subrogated by operation of law to the rights of the creditor'); Ala. Code § 8-3-11; Va. Code § 49-27; Ga. Code § 10-7-56; Minn. Stat. § 574.16.

145 Restatement 3d, Suretyship and Guaranty, § 27. *Nova Info. Sys., Inc. v. Greenwich Ins. Co.*, 365 F.3d 996 (11th Cir. 2004).

146 Restatement 3d, Suretyship and Guaranty, § 28, comm. a, explaining that 'by giving the secondary obligor the equivalent of an assignment of the [creditor's] rights, the law … effectuates the goal of causing the principal obligor to bear the cost of performance'.

147 Restatement 3d, Suretyship and Guaranty, § 27, comm. a. P.A. Alces, The Law of Suretyship and Guarantee, Thomson Reuters, 2021, § 6.28.

– which, as noted above, may arise from partial satisfaction – does not provide the surety with the creditor's rights concerning the underlying obligation. In other words, the right to reimbursement is a general claim with no priority over other claims except by agreement. Fourth, when enforcing the creditor's right by subrogation, the surety is subject to the statute of limitations that applies to the creditor's claim. Conversely, since the right to reimbursement is an independent cause of action, it is subject to a different statute of limitations that starts running upon the performance of the secondary obligation.[148]

The preceding paragraphs described the rights of parties outside insolvency. Reflecting on the rights and remedies of a surety in a situation where the principal debtor is insolvent, Downs observed that '[a]ny surety who has had an occasion to attempt to enforce the Bankruptcy Act [now the Bankruptcy Code] will realize why a citation of authorities would be the equivalent of entering battle with a belt filled with blank cartridges'.[149] Bankruptcy law interferes with parties' contractual or equitable rights. Two sections of the US Bankruptcy Code are of relevance here, namely sections 502 and 509. 5.65

Section 502(e), in certain circumstances, requires the disallowance of indemnity, reimbursement and contribution claims 'of an entity that is liable with the debtor on or has secured the claim of a creditor'. As in English law, the general idea is that the claims of a guarantor, surety or co-debtor should not be allowed to compete with the creditor's claim on the 'limited proceeds in the estate'.[150] There should only be one recovery on the basis of the same debt. Therefore, if the claim for reimbursement or contribution is contingent, it will be disallowed.[151] Collier on Bankruptcy further explains that by 'disallowing the guarantor's contingent claim for reimbursement or contribution, [the law] ensures that the estate will not at the same time be liable to the primary obligor and the guarantor for the same debt'.[152] However, if a surety pays a portion of a claim during the case, that portion of the claim for reimbursement is no longer contingent (i.e. it becomes fixed) and may not be disallowed. In this respect, the approach of US law seems to be different from English law and its strong stance against double proof. As noted earlier, English law does not allow the surety to prove for its claim against the principal debtor until the creditor has been paid in full. The practical effect of this difference, however, should not be overstated, because the US Bankruptcy Code contains a rule that *subordinates* 5.66

148 Restatement 3d, Suretyship and Guaranty, § 28, comm. c.
149 W. Downs, A Surety's Basic Rights and Remedies, Defense Lawyers Journal, Vol. 15, 1966, p. 172.
150 S. Rep. No. 95-989; H.R. Rep. No. 95-595, at 354.
151 11 U.S. Code § 502(e)(1)(B).
152 Collier on Bankruptcy, 16th edn, 2022, Vol. 4, ¶ 502.06[2][d].

the surety's claim to the claim of the creditor for the underlying obligation, until the surety fully satisfies such creditor's claim. This rule effectively grants priority to the creditor over the surety.

5.67 Section 509 provides that a surety who pays all or part of the claim post-petition is subrogated to the rights of the creditor to the extent of such payment.[153] While subrogation in common law and under state law typically requires the surety to have paid the underlying claim in full before asserting any rights, US bankruptcy law allows for subrogation to arise from partial payment of the creditor's claim.[154] Essentially, the surety steps into the creditor's shoes when the creditor is still wearing them! This peculiarity, however, is unlikely to have a significant effect on the outcome of the case, as, similar to claims for reimbursement or contribution, the subrogation claim is *subordinated* to the creditor's claim until the creditor is fully paid.

5.68 Section 509 also establishes that if the surety asserts its right of subrogation, the claims for reimbursement or contribution shall not be allowed.[155] The requirement for a surety to make a choice between these remedies seeks to avoid double recovery, one based on its own right and another by way of subrogation.[156] Logically, subrogation may be the preferred option if the creditor's claim is secured,[157] or if the payment under the guarantee is triggered by a post-petition breach of the principal debtor, giving rise to an administrative expense priority claim of the creditor.[158]

5.69 In sum, US law aims to achieve a fair allocation of the debtor's assets among various groups of competing claims in bankruptcy. Although a surety's claim for contribution, reimbursement or subrogation (provided it is not contingent) may be allowed, the surety cannot partake in the distribution of the debtor's

---

153 11 U.S. Code § 509(a). Note that US courts refuse to extend § 509 and to grant subrogation rights to a party who is itself primarily liable on the creditor's claim. Collier on Bankruptcy, 16th edn, 2022, Vol. 4, ¶ 509.02.

154 *In re Cornmesser's Inc.*, 264 B.R. 159, 163 (Bankr. W.D. Pa. 2001); *In re LTC Holdings, Inc.*, 597 B.R. 565, 567 (Bankr. D. Del. 2019), noting that '[i]n a departure from common law, 11 U.S.C. § 509 permitted partial subrogation'.

155 11 U.S. Code § 509(b)(1). *In re Fiesole Trading Corp.*, 315 B.R. 198 (Bankr. Ct. D. Mass. 2004); *In re Celotex Corp.*, 289 B.R. 460 (Bankr. M.D. Fla. 2003).

156 C.J. Tabb, Law of Bankruptcy, 4th edn, West Academic Publishing, 2016, p. 664.

157 *In re The Medicine Shoppe*, 210 B.R. 310, 313 (Bankr. N.D. Ill. 1997), holding that 'Subrogation under § 509(a) allows a guarantor, who pays a debt for which a debtor is primarily liable, to assume the creditor's rights. These rights include any rights to priority distribution or secured status to which the subrogor's claim was entitled.'

158 *In re Wingspread Corp.*, 116 B.R. 915 (Bankr. S.D.N.Y. 1990). B.E. Greer, J.S. Moss and N.B. Herther-Spiro, Guarantees in Bankruptcy: A Primer II, Norton Annual Survey of Bankruptcy Law, 2014 edn, p. 171. Other types of priority may not be 'assignable' to the surety's subrogation claim. See 11 U.S. Code § 507(d).

assets until the creditor's claim has been fully paid. This outcome is supported by specific rules on subordination, found in the US Bankruptcy Code. The practical effect of these rules is similar to what is accomplished under English law – the creditor goes first, without having to compete with a surety.

5.5.3.3 The Netherlands: contribution, subrogation and restructuring plans

A guarantor who has paid the creditor has a right of recourse against the principal debtor. This right can take the form of a right of contribution (*regresrecht*)[159] and a right of subrogation (*recht krachtens subrogatie*).[160] **5.70**

The *right of contribution* is an independent right that is not derived from the creditor's position. It co-exists with subrogation, discussed below.[161] It aims to prevent the principal debtor from being unjustly enriched at the expense of the guarantor because the guarantor has paid the debt owed by the principal debtor to the creditor.[162] Due to the independent nature of the right to contribution, the paying guarantor does not succeed in the security and priority rights that may have been attached to the creditor's claim. This is different in the case of subrogation, where – as in English and US law – a third party, such as a guarantor, takes the place of the creditor and therefore benefits from the associated security and other ancillary rights and privileges.[163] **5.71**

Another significant difference between a right of contribution and a right of subrogation concerns the application of the statute of limitations (*verjaring*) and, specifically, the time when it starts to run. The right of contribution is an *independent* right that only arises when a joint and several debtor makes a payment exceeding its share.[164] By contrast, a person with a right of *subrogation* 'inherits' the rights of the creditor. Consequently, the debtor is able to raise all the defences against the subrogated party that it could have raised against **5.72**

159 Dutch Civil Code, Articles 7:866 and 6:10. On *regresrechten* in general, see H.G.F.M. de Kok, Het regres (diss. Nijmegen), Deventer: Kluwer, 1965.

160 Dutch Civil Code, Article 6:12.

161 J. den Hoed, GS Verbintenissenrecht, commentaar op art. 6:10 BW; Asser/Sieburgh 6-I 2020/132.

162 Castermans & Krans, in: T&C Burgerlijk Wetboek, commentaar op art. 7:866 BW.

163 Dutch Civil Code, Articles 3:7, 3:82, 6:142. Asser/Sieburgh 6-I 2020/133.

164 HR 6 April 2012, ECLI:NL:HR:2012:BU3784, *NJ* 2016/196, m.nt. C.E. du Perron; *JOR* 2014/172, m.nt. N.E.D. Faber & N.S.G.J. Vermunt (*ASR/Achmea*). R.J. van der Weijden, GS Verbintenissenrecht, commentaar op art. 6:150 BW, noting that before *ASR/Achmea*, some authors argued that the right of contribution existed conditionally at the time when joint and several liability was assumed. The Supreme Court in *ASR/Achmea* made it clear that this was not the case and that the right of contribution could only arise at the moment the guarantor or co-debtor paid the claim for more than the part that concerns it internally. Read further, W.H. van Boom, Het ontstaansmoment en de verjaring van de regresvordering, *Ars Aequi* 2013, pp. 36–43; D.F.H. Stein, V. Tweehuysen and S.E. Bartels (red.), Verjaring, Deventer: Wolters Kluwer, 2020; D.F.H. Stein, Verjaring van wettelijke regresvorderingen en de 'afzonderlijke elemententeer', AV&S 2020/26.

the original creditor (Art. 6:145 BW), including the defence that the claim is time-barred.[165] This is also why the limitation period of the claim transferred by subrogation commences at the time the claim arose for the original creditor.[166]

5.73 In Dutch law, subrogation is understood to mean the transfer by operation of law of a claim to a person at whose expense the creditor has been paid.[167] This claim can be enforced against the debtor or several jointly and severally liable debtors.[168] A surety who pays the debt acquires a subrogation claim that can be exercised jointly and severally against co-debtors, regardless of whether such co-debtors are internally liable.[169] Subrogation is a consequence of payment. As noted above, subrogation and contribution claims are available to the paying guarantor concurrently. This means that a guarantor who has extinguished the debt is free to choose the grounds for recourse or rely on both grounds at the same time (note the difference with the US approach). At the same time, it should be noted that the guarantor's rights to contribution and subrogation are often excluded in a contract, preventing the paying guarantor from seeking recourse against the principal debtor. Such a waiver ensures that the creditor does not face competition from the guarantor's recourse claim.[170]

5.74 What happens in insolvency? Under Dutch law, the guaranteed creditor can sue both the insolvent principal debtor and the guarantor for the full amount of the debt.[171] In insolvency proceedings, distributions are calculated based on the entire claim, though the creditor can never receive more than 100 per cent of the claim. The amount of a claim is determined at the time of the insolvency order. Therefore, only payments received by the creditor prior to this point are deducted from the claim. If partial satisfaction of a claim occurs after the initiation of insolvency proceedings (e.g. partial payment by a guarantor or co-debtor), no such deduction is made.[172] On this latter point, Dutch law is similar to English and US law.

---

165 A.C. van Schaick, Het glibberige pad van de verjaring van de regresvordering, *NTBR* 2012/55, explaining that the subrogated party under the suretyship agreement exercises the creditor's claim and that this claim continues to be subject to the limitation period already applicable.

166 R.J. van der Weijden, GS Verbintenissenrecht, commentaar op art. 6:150 BW.

167 Asser/Sieburgh 6-I 2020/132; Asser/Sieburgh 6-II 2021/269.

168 Asser/Sieburgh 6-II 2021/284.

169 Dutch Civil Code, Article 7:866(3).

170 G.J.L. Bergervoet, Borgtocht (O&R nr. 84), Deventer: Kluwer, 2014, 8.3.6. and 8.4.5. A surety can waive his right of recourse even if he is a consumer under Article 7:857 BW (*borgtocht, aangegaan buiten beroep of bedrijf*). See Article 7:866 BW.

171 Dutch Bankruptcy Act, Article 136.

172 Article 136 Fw constitutes an exception to the basic principle of Article 6:7(2) BW, according to which a fulfilment of the joint obligation by one of the co-debtors discharges other co-debtors. See A. Jonkers,

Dutch insolvency law adopts a position similar to English law regarding a guarantor's right of recourse. As mentioned earlier, English law does not allow double proof – a situation where two or more persons (e.g. a creditor and a guarantor) file claims in the principal debtor's insolvency proceedings for the same debt. As a general rule, a guarantor can only claim in the insolvency of the principal debtor after satisfying the creditor's claim. The same outcome is achieved in the USA, where, instead of disallowing recourse claims, bankruptcy law imposes special subordination rules (see section above). 5.75

Yet, as an exception to this general rule, according to Article 136(2) Fw, a recourse claim (i.e. contribution or subrogation) of the joint and several debtor (*hoofdelijke schuldenaar*), such as a guarantor, for amounts for which it has acquired or will acquire a claim against the principal debtor, may be – if necessary, conditionally[173] – admitted in the insolvency proceedings of the principal debtor, but only in three specific circumstances. These include cases where: (i) the creditor itself may not submit a claim or, although entitled to do so, does not submit a claim in the insolvency proceedings of the principal debtor;[174] (ii) the creditor receives full payment of its claim in the insolvency proceedings;[175] or (iii) such an admission does not adversely affect unsecured creditors by introducing a competing claim.[176] 5.76

As previously noted, if a creditor is involved in a restructuring plan (*dwangakkoord*) under the Dutch Bankruptcy Act, and if its rights against the principal debtor are affected by such a plan – meaning the enforceability of its claim is limited by the plan – as a general rule, the creditor retains the right to sue the guarantor for the amount of the original claim (Article 160 Fw). The question remains whether a guarantor is allowed to recover from the principal 5.77

Insider guarantees in corporate finance: An economic analysis of Dutch, US and German law, PhD thesis, 2020, p. 156, explaining that the reason for this exception is simplicity. Without it, any payments on the guaranteed debt made after the date of insolvency would have to be taken into account.

173 Conditional admission appears to apply to both the claim itself and the conditions of Article 136(2)(a–c) Fw.

174 This section of the article may apply if the creditor has been paid in full before insolvency or where it has waived its claim against the insolvent debtor. J.M. Hummelen, GS Faillissementswet, commentaar op art. 136 Fw, aant. 5. Such a waiver does not preclude recourse against the insolvent principal debtor (Article 6:14 BW). The creditor can also decide not to bother filing its claim against the debtor, as it can claim the full payment from the guarantor.

175 F.M.J. Verstijlen, in: T&C Insolventierecht, commentaar op art. 136 Fw, providing an example where the creditor, who has already had a part of its claim paid by the co-debtor, would receive such a high percentage in the bankruptcy from the insolvent joint and several debtor that it would receive more than 100 per cent of its claim.

176 J.M. Hummelen, GS Faillissementswet, commentaar op art. 136 Fw, offering an example where the recovery of the guarantor is on the basis of a security right not vested in the creditor. Under Dutch law, insolvency does not preclude the enforcement of an *in rem* security right by a secured creditor.

debtor the sums that it has paid to the guaranteed creditor after the WHOA plan has been approved. With respect to WHOA plans, the answer can be found in Article 370(2) Fw, under which, if the creditor's claim is restructured via the WHOA plan, the guarantor cannot take recourse against the principal debtor to enforce payment of the original debt in full. This provision is intended to prevent the debtor, after the plan has been homologated and the debtor has restructured its debts, from becoming insolvent due to an inability to pay recourse claims that arise after the plan confirmation.[177] The question is whether the outcome would be different if a recourse claim was secured. In a recent case, the court ruled that a secured creditor cannot claim recourse against the scheme debtor after the confirmation of the WHOA plan. It pointed out that the 'fact that the bank [guarantor] has security for this recourse claim does not alter this. It does not matter in what way the redress is sought against the estate, the nature of the claim precludes it'.[178]

5.78 That said, if the payment by the guarantor results in the creditor receiving the full satisfaction of its original claim, the rights granted to the creditor in the plan are transferred by operation of law (subrogation) to the guarantor.[179] This is in line with the rule that a creditor should not receive more than 100 per cent of its claim. For example, if pursuant to the WHOA plan, the creditor can only enforce its claim against the principal debtor for 40 per cent of the original claim, and before such a claim for 40 per cent has been enforced, the creditor can still claim 100 per cent from the guarantor. If the guarantor pays the entire claim (100 per cent), the creditor's rights under the WHOA plan (i.e. a claim enforceable only for 40 per cent) are automatically transferred to the guarantor.

---

177 R. van den Sigtenhorst, in: T&C Insolventierecht, commentaar op art. 370 Fw. A similar position is taken in German insolvency law, which recognises that an insolvency plan can be jeopardised if a third party (e.g. guarantor) could take recourse against the principal debtor. This is why German law provides that the transformation of the substantive relationship between the principal debtor and its creditor under a restructuring plan also applies to the right of recourse against the principal debtor. See § 254(2) InsO. This means that the recourse claim follows the original claim in its reduced or extinguished scope.

178 Rb. Amsterdam 1 February 2023, ECLI:NL:RBAMS:2023:569, *JOR* 2023/83, m.nt. V.G. Koolen. The court addressed the bank's (guarantor's) argument that the refusal to allow the recourse claim constituted a violation of Art. 1 Protocol 1 of the ECHR (protection of property). The court observed that the Dutch legislator had deemed the infringement of the right of (in this case) the bank, as laid down in Art. 370(2) Fw, necessary for the public interest, to prevent the debtor from becoming insolvent after the homologation due to the enforcement of a recourse claim. It noted that it is up to the bank to demonstrate that, due to the concrete circumstances of this specific case, an infringement of property rights is disproportionate. In the court's view, such concrete circumstances have not been established, nor have they become apparent. Hence, the appeal to Art. 1 Protocol 1 of the ECHR fails. However, in my opinion, it may be disputed whether the differences in the outcomes for a guaranteed creditor in a bankruptcy proceeding and in a WHOA scheme are justified.

179 Dutch Bankruptcy Act, Article 370(2). MvT, *Kamerstukken II* 2018/19, 35249, 3, p. 10.

The rule in Article 370(2) Fw establishes a special regulation that deviates from the general rule by prescribing (limiting) the circumstances in which a right of recourse can be exercised and determining the value that can be claimed. Whereas this special regulation applies to WHOA plans, it does not necessarily follow that the same approach is or should be taken in law with respect to a *dwangakkoord* (plan or composition) adopted in other procedures, namely in bankruptcy (*faillissement*) and suspension of payments (*surseance van betaling*). According to Article 160 Fw, despite such a plan, a guarantor remains liable for the full amount. With this in mind, the question arises whether it is possible for the guarantor to claim a contribution from the principal debtor in an amount that exceeds what the creditor is entitled to under the approved *dwangakkoord*. **5.79**

No problem arises regarding the right of subrogation, as the paying guarantor steps into the creditor's shoes, meaning its claim can only be enforced to the same extent as the creditor's claim is enforceable under the *dwangakkoord*. The right of contribution (*regres*) is different. Since the right of contribution is an independent right, not derived from the position of the creditor, it cannot be affected by the *dwangakkoord* concluded before the contribution claim arises in the first place.[180] In the absence of a special rule to the contrary, it does not follow from Dutch law that any future contribution rights are affected by the *dwangakkoord* concluded in bankruptcy or suspension of payments. Thus, building on the hypothetical example above, if the *dwangakkoord* concluded in bankruptcy reduces the creditor's claim to 40 per cent of the original claim, the creditor can claim 100 per cent from the guarantor. If the guarantor satisfies the creditor's claim in full, it acquires the right to claim the full amount (100 per cent) from the principal debtor via a contribution claim. **5.80**

5.6 INSOLVENCY AND EX POST EFFECTS OF CROSS-GUARANTEES

This section summarises the effects of cross-guarantees on debtors' and creditors' behaviour in situations of financial distress or insolvency (ex post effects). It appears that intercompany guarantees have certain features that may **5.81**

180 R. van den Sigtenhorst, Herstructurering van groepen onder de WHOA, in C.M. Harmsen and M.L.H. Reumers (red.), De WHOA van wet naar recht (Recht & Praktijk, nr. InsR18), Deventer: Wolters Kluwer, 2021, 8.3.4., noting that 'De WHOA-regeling is bijzonder, vanwege de uitsluiting van verhaal door garantiegevers op de WHOA-schuldenaar na eventueel verhaal op hen door schuldeisers die door het akkoord zijn geraakt: dit bestaat niet in faillissement en surseance' ('the WHOA scheme is special, because it excludes recourse by guarantors from the WHOA debtor after possible recovery from them by creditors who have been affected by the plan: the same does not apply in bankruptcy and suspension of payments') (translated by the author).

contribute to debtor and creditor opportunism, potentially undermining efficient group restructuring. Here, creditor opportunism is broadly understood as the pursuit of economic self-interest by a creditor, even if such behaviour leads to negative side effects on third parties and is therefore Pareto-inefficient.[181] These features are observed and explored through the lens of the relationships between group members and between non-guaranteed unsecured creditors and guaranteed creditors.

5.82 First, cross-guarantees intensify the interdependence between group entities. In a crisis, they enable group-wide enforcement action, allowing the guaranteed creditor to foreclose on the assets of both the principal debtor and the guarantor(s) or to push them into insolvency. The study of English, US and Dutch law shows that a guaranteed creditor has considerable discretion in pursuing its claim against the principal debtor, guarantor or both at the same time. This approach results in group-wide enforcement, where the full amount of the debt is claimed from several group companies. The threat of such enforcement may pressure the debtor's management to make selective payments in favour of the guaranteed creditor.[182] An insider-guarantor might also pressure the principal debtor to pay the guaranteed creditor first, indirectly benefiting from a reduced exposure under the guarantee. However, this benefit is indirect, as the payment goes to a non-insider creditor rather than to the guarantor.[183] If these payments are made close to insolvency, they may constitute preferential treatment, violating the principle of equal treatment of creditors.

5.83 Second, cross-guarantees strengthen the position of a guaranteed creditor relative to other (unsecured) creditors, creating a particular form of creditor governance and control.[184] In this context, an analogy can be drawn with the interests and incentives of creditors whose claims are secured by rights *in rem*. The literature suggests that secured creditors may prefer immediate debt enforcement over restructuring, since the latter is naturally more unpredictable

181 For discussion of the negative effects of creditor opportunism on economically efficient restructurings, see D. Ehmke, Publicly Offered Debt in the Shadow of Insolvency, EBOR, Vol. 16, 2015, pp. 63-96.

182 A. Jonkers, Selective Perforation by Means of Guarantees: Dutch Law, in The 800-Pound Gorilla. Limits to Group Structures and Asset Partitioning in Insolvency, NACIIL 2018 report, Eleven International Publishing, 2019, p. 75, noting that 'intergroup guarantees can be seen as promises to the lender to make preferential payments, especially on the eve of bankruptcy'.

183 J. Gordon and R.J. Landry III, The Risk-Shifting Effect of Business Bankruptcy: A Statutory Solution to Provide Additional Protections for Personal Guarantors of Debts by Closely-Held Business Ventures, Emory Bankruptcy Development Journal, Vol. 32, 2015, p. 76, whereby the benefit of the guarantor is termed a 'phantom benefit'.

184 K.M. Ayotte and E.R. Morrison, Creditor Control and Conflict in Chapter 11, Journal of Legal Analysis, Vol. 1, 2009, pp. 511-551; J.L. Westbrook, The Control of Wealth in Bankruptcy, Texas Law Review, Vol. 82, 2004, pp. 795-862.

and riskier.[185] Garcimartín and Bermejo observe that secured creditors may be more interested in foreclosing the collateral and getting paid as soon as possible, even if this entails a fire sale that frustrates other options potentially more advantageous for unsecured creditors. They also argue that a secured creditor can be more focused on maximising the value of the collateral than on the overall value of the firm.[186]

Similarly, in a situation where, because of a cross-guarantee, the lender is interested in a quick 'mass enforcement' against the estates of several group entities without bearing the downside risk of reorganisation, its position becomes analogous to that of a creditor over-insured on its loan. Just as the lender protected by collateral can exert significant influence in insolvency proceedings,[187] a guaranteed creditor might drive group-wide (pre-)insolvency dynamics. For this creditor, group-wide enforcement may serve as a means to recoup the investment with minimal or no loss. For unsecured creditors, however, such enforcement could entail large costs, especially if it leads to the group's disintegration. **5.84**

Third, cross-guarantees complicate group restructurings. As discussed in previous sections dealing with national law, the insolvency of the principal debtor typically has no effect on the creditor's rights against guarantors or co-debtors. Any other interpretation would effectively undermine the essence and protective function of the guarantee relationship. The ability of a guaranteed creditor to pursue the group guarantor can lead to two problems: **5.85**

---

185 C. Bergström, T. Eisenberg and S. Sundgren, Secured Debt and the Likelihood of Reorganization, International Review of Law and Economics, Vol. 21, 2002, p. 360, noting that '[s]ecured creditors receive only part of the gain if the value of the reorganized firm increases, but bear all of the costs if the value decreases'. E.J. Janger, The Logic and Limits of Liens, University of Illinois Law Review, Vol. 2015, 2015, p. 592, stressing that the secured creditor control over governance in insolvency may 'allow the secured creditor to capture a disproportionate share of bankruptcy-created value, or even prevent value maximizing reorganizations'.

186 F. Garcimartín and N. Bermejo, Involving secured creditors in restructuring proceedings, in P.J. Omar and J.L.L. Gant (eds), Research Handbook on Corporate Restructuring, Edward Elgar Publishing, 2021, p. 122.

187 The ever-increasing control by secured creditors over the insolvency process has been particularly emphasised in US literature. See D.G. Baird and R.K. Rasmussen, The End of Bankruptcy, Stanford Law Review, Vol. 55, 2002, pp. 751–789; D.A. Skeel, Creditors' Ball: The New Corporate Governance in Chapter 11, University of Pennsylvania Law Review, Vol. 152, 2003, p. 918, noting that '[w]hereas the debtor and its managers seemed to dominate bankruptcy only a few decades ago, Chapter 11 now has a distinctly creditor-oriented cast'; R.K. Rasmussen, The end of bankruptcy revisited, in B.A. Adler (ed), Research Handbook on Corporate Bankruptcy Law, Edward Elgar Publishing, 2020, p. 42, listing among factors strengthening the position of secured creditors in insolvency: 1998 amendments to Article 9 UCC, making it easier to obtain a blanket security interest in all debtor's assets; debtor-in-possession financing and the use of far-reaching lending covenants, giving a senior lender control over the debtor's access to cash in his accounts.

- **Ricochet problem**. Under national law, a guarantor might be entitled to recover from the principal debtor the sums that he has paid to the creditor. This recovery right could 'survive' the approval of a restructuring plan, which affects the creditor's claim. If the guarantor is allowed to file a ricochet claim for the full amount against the restructured principal debtor, it could undermine the effectiveness of the restructuring.
- **Orphan restructuring problem**. The principal debtor may require the guarantor's assistance to implement the restructuring and sustain its business post-restructuring. However, if the guarantor remains exposed to claims from the debtor's creditors, it may be reluctant to contribute to the restructuring or provide continued support. The guarantor might even face insolvency or be sold to a competitor. Consequently, given the group's interdependence, the restructured principal debtor risks becoming an 'orphan' with remote chances for long-term survival.

5.86 Summarising the ex post effects of cross-guarantees, it should be emphasised that they raise a number of red flags. They perforate limited liability, increase the correlation between different group entities, and can facilitate a misalignment of creditors' interests, complicating the adoption of a group solution. The default of the principal debtor may cause a guaranteed creditor to launch group-wide enforcement by filing the same claim against separate companies. As a result, the effectiveness of the debtor's restructuring may be threatened, especially in integrated groups where group entities depend on each other and the failure of a single entity leads to a domino-like collapse of other group entities.

5.7 CONCLUSION

5.87 This chapter discusses cross-guarantees – one of the most common contractual arrangements accompanying the attraction of funds from external lenders. It examines both the ex ante and ex post effects of group guarantees, exploring their economic rationale and impact on the agency cost of debt, access to finance, managerial behaviour, as well as the position and rights of guaranteed and non-guaranteed unsecured creditors.

5.88 A guarantee relationship serves an important protective and risk-reduction function. As neatly pointed out by Wood, '[g]uarantees are usually taken to provide a second pocket to pay if the first should be empty'.[188] In addition, the existence of a claim against several or all group entities makes the lender

188 P. Wood, International Loans, Bonds, Guarantees, Legal Opinions, Sweet & Maxwell, 2007, para. 18-002.

less exposed to risks arising from intra-group asset transfers. This additional security means that the borrower and the entire group may be financed on more advantageous terms. There are other valid reasons for entering into cross-guarantees from both the creditor's and debtor's perspectives, including those related to the value and marketability of corporate bonds, the exercise of set-off rights by a creditor, tax optimisation, etc. These reasons can be termed as reasons of (economic) ex ante efficiency.

Yet the web of cross-guarantees, often combined with intra-group loans, can cause significant problems in insolvency (ex post). Intercompany guarantees weaken the protections granted by the doctrines of limited liability and entity shielding. These protections are traded for ex ante efficiency, as noted above. In a situation of insolvency, cross-guarantees may prompt the destruction of value as a result of the simultaneous group-wide enforcement of the same debt. This might complicate group restructuring and lead to the collapse of the enterprise. **5.89**

This chapter examined the complex relationships between the various parties involved in a typical group financing arrangement – 'triangle of rights and liabilities': a principal debtor-borrower, a group guarantor (or co-guarantor) and a creditor-lender (guaranteed creditor). In all three jurisdictions studied in this book – the UK, the USA and the Netherlands – insolvency of the principal debtor per se does not affect the creditor's claim against the guarantor.[189] After all, it is the very purpose of the guarantee to protect the creditor against the insolvency of the debtor. However, should the guarantor play a key role within the group and be forced into insolvency itself, the efficiency of the principal debtor's restructuring and its long-term survival might be at risk – a problem coined as the 'orphan restructuring problem'. But this is not the only problem. Upon payment to the creditor, the guarantor may be entitled to file a claim against the principal debtor – a recourse claim. The legal basis (e.g. subrogation, contribution), availability, and amount of this claim depend on the applicable law and the type of proceeding in which the creditor's original claim is affected. For example, the sanctioning of an English scheme of arrangement with respect to the principal debtor as such does not deprive the paying guarantor of its right to be compensated (indemnified) by the debtor for **5.90**

189 The case of restructuring is less straightforward. In some cases, a semi-voluntary or purely voluntary alteration of the terms of the underlying agreement between the principal debtor and a creditor may affect the guarantor's obligations. Thus, unless the guarantor consents to be bound by the amended terms of the underlying obligation, a CVA or IVA under English law or an out-of-court agreement or workout under Dutch and US law might result in a complete or partial discharge of the guarantor.

the payments made pursuant to the guarantee.[190] Enforcement of this recourse claim can undermine the efficiency of restructuring proceedings – the 'ricochet problem'.

5.91 Both the ricochet problem and the orphan restructuring problem have led to the emergence of practices and rules that permit group debt deleveraging or group debt adjustment through so-called third-party releases. Third-party releases are discussed in Chapter 8.

190 By contrast, in the Netherlands, following the explicit statutory language, if the creditor's claim is restructured in the WHOA scheme of the principal debtor, the guarantor is prevented from taking a recourse against the principal debtor to force him to pay the original debt in full. The same result is achieved under US Chapter 11.

6

INTRA-GROUP LOANS AND STATUTORY SUBORDINATION

6.1 INTRODUCTION

6.01 The previous chapter discussed intra-group guarantees, which are used to attract financing from external investors and financiers, or to secure better terms for such financing. However, this is only part of the picture. A review of intra-group financing would be incomplete without analysing ways to reallocate funds within an enterprise group. This reallocation typically takes the form of a single loan transaction or a series of transactions within a centralised cash management or cash-pooling system. Both forms are prevalent in intra-group financing, as exemplified by the cases of Lehman Brothers, Nortel Networks and Oi Brazil.

6.02 The purpose of this chapter is to discuss intra-group loans – a common way to reallocate money within an enterprise group. UNCITRAL notes that '[g]roup financing might involve intra-group lending between the parent and other group members, involving loans both from and to the parent and the granting of cross-guarantees'.[1] In large groups, such as the Lehman Brothers group, intra-group lending is often arranged through an 'internal bank' which manages the allocation of liquidity across the group. If we imagine a group as a human body, intra-group loans can be compared to blood circulating throughout the body, supporting its various organs. When one group member is in need of liquidity, other group members have a strong incentive to provide this liquidity.[2] Continuing with the human body analogy, this financing resembles a targeted transfer of resources from one organ to another to preserve its functions and possibly save the entire body. Yet, a different scenario – where funding is withdrawn, and 'selective' insolvency is used – is also possible. In this scenario, one group member may be placed into insolvency to prevent financial contagion from spreading across the entire group. The 'selective' insolvency strategy may result in the removal of assets (i.e. asset stripping) from a group entity placed in insolvency for the benefit of its affiliates and ultimately, shareholders.[3] These value extraction patterns can be challenged using transaction avoidance rules, touched upon in Chapter 7.

6.03 This chapter focuses on a situation where the value is infused rather than taken out of a group company. It proceeds as follows. Section 6.2 mentions some of the reasons why enterprise groups engage in intra-group loans and centralised cash management. Section 6.3 examines the specificity of 'insider' or 'internal' creditors, as the divide between internal and external creditors often underlies different treatment in insolvency. This different treatment primarily manifests in the subordination of intra-group (shareholder) loans in insolvency (section 6.4).

6.04 The treatment of shareholder loans and, more generally, intra-group claims is a contentious topic, on which positions vary considerably among jurisdictions and among scholars. In countries like Germany, Austria, Sweden, Portugal,

1 UNCITRAL Legislative Guide, Part three, Ch. I, para. 10.

2 R. Squire, Limits to Group Structures and Asset Partitioning in Insolvency: Suppressing Value and Selective Perforation by Means of Guarantees, in The 800-Pound Gorilla. Limits to Group Structures and Asset Partitioning in Insolvency, NACIIL 2018 report, Eleven International Publishing, 2019, p. 1.

3 See Final Report of Examiner Richard J. Davis, 15 March 2016, *In re Caesars Entertainment Operating Company Inc.*, Case No. 15-01145 (ABG) (Bankr. N.D. Ill.). The examiner concluded that in the period preceding the debtor's bankruptcy, as a result of a number of transactions, assets were removed from the debtor to its own detriment and to the detriment of its creditors. The damage was estimated to range from USD 3.6 to USD 5.1 billion. The examiner pointed out that 'in those transactions no one was focused on CEOC's [debtor's] interest alone as opposed to how transactions impacted Caesars as a whole'. See C. Gerner-Beuerle and M. Schillig, Comparative Company Law, OUP, 2019, p. 826, noting that the withdrawal of the company's assets may take the form of loans advanced by the debtor companies to the parent or other group companies.

Italy, Spain, Brazil, Slovenia, Poland and Russia,[4] claims from shareholder loans may be subject to statutory subordination rules that re-prioritise or downgrade insider claims in the creditor ranking. In other countries, such as the UK and the Netherlands, no general doctrine of subordination has been developed. In the USA, claims of insiders can be subordinated under the doctrine of equitable subordination or recharacterised as equity contributions.

There are different opinions on whether claims of shareholders should rank **6.05** *pari passu* with those of external creditors or whether they should be placed in a lower rank or treated as equity contributions. The complexity arises from the dual role of a party that holds an equity stake in the debtor or is otherwise connected to it by way of control or corporate ties, while also acting as a lender (the 'double hat' problem). The question is whether the disparities in the nature, incentives and risks of internal and external creditors justify the different (unequal) treatment of creditors in insolvency. No signs of consensus seem to have appeared on this issue, either in academic literature or in law. This chapter summarises arguments for and against the subordination of insider (intra-group) loans and highlights the most serious critique of such subordination – the problem of underinvestment (section 6.5). Section 6.6 concludes.

6.2 INTRA-GROUP LOANS AND CENTRALISED CASH MANAGEMENT

There are various reasons why enterprise groups use intra-group loans and cen- **6.06** tralised cash management. An intra-group loan offers a relatively easy and quick way to put the funds available within the group to the best use. It provides flexibility, convenience and confidentiality compared to equity finance, which often requires complying with various formalities.

Within a corporate group, one member may be able to secure better credit **6.07** terms due to its credit history or asset and liability levels. This is why the borrower or issuer of corporate bonds is frequently established as a special purpose financing company, acting for the benefit of other group companies or the entire group. For instance, an SPV arrangement was used by the Parmalat group, a dairy and food enterprise, whose failure produced one of the most important cases on the interpretation of the EIR 2000.[5] Parmalat established the Irish subsidiary Eurofood IFSC Ltd (Eurofood) with the primary objective

4 For analysis of the subordination doctrine in insolvency law, see A. Shaydullin, Subordination of shareholder claims in insolvency law, PhD dissertation, 2022 (in Russian) <https://izak.ru/upload/iblock/151/SHaydullin-A.I._Kandidatskaya_dissertatsiya_final_pdf.pdf> (accessed 10 October 2024).

5 Case C-341/04, *Eurofood IFSC Ltd*, 2 May 2006.

of providing financing facilities to other entities in the group. Its main purpose was to serve the interests of the group by engaging in the issuance of bonds, which were guaranteed by the Italian holding company Parmalat SpA.[6] Similar financial arrangements were adopted by Lehman Brothers and Oi Brazil. In the Oi group, the operations of Dutch-incorporated SPVs were limited to issuing notes and on-lending the received funds to other group entities.[7] The notes documentation highlights the Dutch companies' conduit role and their complete reliance on the group's performance:

> [Coop, a Dutch SPV] has no operations other than the issuing and making payments on the Notes ... and using the proceeds therefrom [to effectuate] lending the net proceeds of the Notes ... to Oi and subsidiaries of Oi. Accordingly, the ability of [Coop] to pay principal, interest and other amounts due on the Notes and other indebtedness will depend upon the financial condition and results of operations of Oi and its subsidiaries that are creditors of [Coop].[8]

6.08 One should also keep in mind tax considerations, which often play a large role in determining the way intra-group transactions are structured.[9] For all these reasons, it may be more cost-effective for a corporate group to use an SPV to attract financing, irrespective of whether this entity will use the funds on its own or transfer them through a chain of other group members.

6.09 Centralised cash management or cash pooling facilitates economic and operational efficiency and contributes to increased profitability. Cash pooling can be divided into 'notional pooling' (also referred to as 'virtual cash pooling') and 'physical pooling' (or 'cash sweeping' or 'cash balancing'). In notional pooling, no physical transfer of funds takes place; instead, it involves the purely arithmetic consolidation of balances from different accounts. In physical pooling, balances of different accounts are physically consolidated into a single balance in a designated master account.

6.10 Cash pooling is popular among corporate groups as it allows a parent company or a financing SPV to manage intra-group cash balances of group companies, transferring liquidity from entities with a surplus to those with a shortfall, without needing to secure funds externally. The latter option may be more costly, considering the financial standing and availability of unencumbered assets of the entity seeking financing. However, the centralisation of funds

---

6 These financial arrangements have been described in the Opinion of Advocate General Jacobs, delivered on 27 September 2005 in *Eurofood IFSC Ltd*, Case C-341/04, ECLI:EU:C:2005:579.

7 See *In re Oi Brasil Holdings Coöperatief U.A.*, 578 B.R. 169 (Bankr. S.D.N.Y. 2017).

8 Ibid.

9 On the use of tax havens by multinational enterprises, see P. Muchlinski, Multinational Enterprises and the Law, 3rd edn, OUP, 2021. Tax law aspects of intra-group financing fall outside the scope of this book.

creates its own problems, particularly when a company holding subsidiaries' cash in the master account becomes insolvent, as happened with LBHI (see Figure 1.1 for an illustration of Lehman Brothers' cash management system).

Finch and Milman point out that the 'arrangements that best meet the needs of healthy, trading companies ... are not those that necessarily produce the smoothest-operating insolvency regimes'.[10] This is certainly true for centralised cash management. This group-level liquidity-allocation tool is unique (e.g. participating entities may agree to joint and several liability for deficits in the top account, potentially affecting the position of creditors), presents notable challenges for group restructurings (e.g. access to funds in a master account might be cut off if the company holding a master account becomes insolvent), and may require tailored solutions to preserve the continued operation of a cash pool (e.g. first-day orders in US bankruptcy cases on cash management). Legally, however, transfers of funds between participants in a physical cash pool can be classified as up-, cross- or downstream loans.[11] This is why the issues addressed below, including subordination, are equally relevant for transfers in a cash management system.[12] 6.11

6.3 INTERNAL V. EXTERNAL CREDITOR DIVIDE

6.3.1 Information asymmetry

Despite the proclaimed principle of equal treatment of creditors, the reality is more complex. To paraphrase George Orwell, all creditors are equal, but some creditors are more equal than others.[13] In many countries, insolvency law provides special treatment for transactions involving related parties, such as directors, shareholders and their affiliates, sometimes referred to as 'insiders'. 6.12

10 V. Finch and D. Milman, Corporate Insolvency Law: Perspectives and Principles, 3rd edn, CUP, 2017, p. 55.

11 J. Jansen (ed), International Cash Pooling: Cross-border Cash Management Systems and Intra-group Financing, Sellier European Law Publishers, 2011, p. 6, emphasising that the 'purpose of a cash management system is to grant financial assistance between companies within a corporation on a constant basis'. P. Mäntysaari, The Law of Corporate Finance: General Principles and EU Law. Volume III: Funding, Exit, Takeovers, Springer, 2010, p. 72, noting that cash concentration creates loans and debts between participating companies. See also W.A.K. Rank, Van saldocompensatie naar saldoconcentratie? MvV, nummer 11, 2018, p. 333, stating that from a legal standpoint, surplus transfers from group companies to the holding or financing company can be regarded as cash loans.

12 For a country-by-country overview of national law approaches to cash pooling and the implications of insolvency for parties involved in it, see M. Willems (ed), Cash Pooling and Insolvency: A Practical Global Handbook, Globe Business Publishing, 2012.

13 G. Orwell, Animal Farm, 1984. The original quote reads as follows: 'All animals are equal. But some animals are more equal than others.' This quote was of course made in a very different setting and with a different message.

Related parties typically enjoy reduced protection against transaction avoidance.[14] This materialises in extended suspect periods,[15] the acceptance of certain mental elements (e.g. knowledge or intent to prefer or defraud),[16] or a rebuttable presumption of harm caused to creditors.[17] The distinct treatment of related parties manifests in other rules of insolvency law. For example, US bankruptcy law requires that at least one class of impaired creditors accepts a reorganisation plan, excluding the votes of insiders.[18]

6.13 Several key characteristics distinguish internal (related) creditors from external (non-related) creditors. One of them has to do with information asymmetry. Internal parties, like shareholders and directors, may have access to internal, non-public information concerning the debtor, including its financial situation and likely prospects of survival. They 'tend to have the earliest knowledge of when the debtor is, in fact, in financial difficulty'.[19] Conversely, external creditors, outside formal insolvency proceedings, usually lack up-to-date and full information about the debtor and must rely on either publicly available sources or data shared by the debtor.[20] The problem of information asymmetry is even more pronounced in corporate groups because the financial health of the entire group may need to be assessed to make risk calculations. External creditors could be unaware of the true state of affairs of the distressed debtor, given its position within the group.

---

14 In many cases, related parties include members of the same group of companies. For an overview, see Clash of Principles: Equal Treatment of Creditors vs. Protection of Trust in European Transaction Avoidance Laws, CERIL Report 2017/1, 26 September 2017; G. McCormack et al., Study on a new approach to business failure and insolvency, 2016, pp. 142–143.

15 E.g. in the UK, the suspect period for preference transactions is two years for connected persons, compared to the otherwise applicable six-month period (see Insolvency Act 1986, section 240). In the USA, the preference period is extended from the usual ninety days to one year in the case of an insider (11 U.S. Code § 547).

16 Under InsO, § 131(2), a person with a close relationship to the debtor on the date of a [preferential] transaction (§ 138) shall be presumed to have been aware of the disadvantage to creditors in insolvency proceedings. Under Insolvency Act 1986, s. 239(6), a company that gave a preference to a person connected with it 'is presumed … to have been influenced in deciding to give it by such a desire as is mentioned in subsection (5)' (desire to create advantage to a counterparty). The knowledge of prejudice in related-party transactions is codified in Article 43(1) Fw.

17 See e.g. Spanish Insolvency Act (*Ley Concursal*), Article 228(1).

18 11 U.S. Code § 1129(a)(10).

19 UNCITRAL Legislative Guide, Part two, Ch. II, para. 182. D.A. Skeel and G. Krause-Vilmar, Recharacterization and the Nonhindrance of Creditors, EBOR, Vol. 7, 2006, p. 268, observing that shareholders 'see the problems first, and they may conclude that arranging an outside loan would be too time-consuming and uncertain'.

20 Information asymmetry may be mitigated (but not fully solved) through the inclusion of information covenants. R. Carrizosa and S. Ryan, Borrower Private Information Covenants and Loan Contract Monitoring, Journal of Accounting and Economics, Vol. 64, 2017, pp. 313-339.

6.3.2 Power and control

Shareholders can exercise control over the debtor. In the absence of insolvency proceedings, and in some cases even during such proceedings, they retain decision-making rights, including the right to appoint and remove directors. Due to this advantage in knowledge and control, they might be able to 'prepare' for insolvency by transferring, or pressuring the debtor's directors to transfer, assets or value from the debtor to another group member in the vicinity of insolvency (asset dilution), ultimately to the detriment of the transferring company and its creditors. They may also choose to increase the riskiness of the debtor's business (asset substitution) or its borrowing (debt dilution). These are examples of opportunistic behaviour, which should be controlled ex ante and remedied ex post.[21] **6.14**

Adopting the agency-costs-of-debt language from Jensen and Meckling, a threat of opportunistic actions by shareholders induces lenders to engage in additional monitoring efforts, producing monitoring costs. In return, shareholders incur bonding costs to reassure creditors that no such actions will occur. **6.15**

6.3.3 Risk appetite and misalignment of incentives

The risk appetite of shareholders is often higher compared to external creditors because, in insolvency, shareholders' equity stake is wiped out. Shareholders of an insolvent company are last in line and give way to creditors as new residual claimants. At the same time, the limited liability shield protects shareholders from the claims of the debtor's creditors. The combination of these features provides economic incentives for shareholders to pressure the debtor's management to pursue high-risk, high-reward strategies, including projects with negative net present value (NPV), to avoid liquidation, retain their equity and create potential upside.[22] **6.16**

---

21 J. Armour, G. Hertig and H. Kanda, Transactions with creditors, in R. Kraakman et al. (eds), The Anatomy of Corporate Law: A Comparative and Functional Approach, 3rd edn, OUP, 2017, pp. 111-112.

22 D. Scarlino, Zone of Insolvency, Directors' Duties and Creditors' Protection in U.S., European Business Law Review, Vol. 29, 2018, p. 7. On misalignment of incentives in insolvency, see H. Eidenmüller, Trading in Times of Crisis: Formal Insolvency Proceedings, Workouts, EBOR, Vol. 7, 2006, pp. 239–258; P. Davies, Directors' Creditor-Regarding Duties in Respect of Trading Decisions Taken in the Vicinity of Insolvency, EBOR, Vol. 7, 2006, p. 306, stating that in the vicinity of insolvency, directors may focus solely on the upside, however remote the probability of success is. Empirical evidence of insolvency-related risk shifting is inconclusive. A. Eisdorfer, Empirical Evidence of Risk Shifting in Financially Distressed Firms, The Journal of Finance, Vol. 63, 2008, pp. 609–637, supporting the risk-shifting hypothesis. However, see E. Gilje, Do Firms Engage in Risk-Shifting? Empirical Evidence, The Review of Financial Studies, Vol. 29, 2016, pp. 2925–2954, finding that companies in distress reduce investment risk.

6.17 The risk-shifting incentives of shareholders and managers can lead to what is known as the 'gamble for resurrection', further diluting the value available to external creditors. This occurs when the life of an economically unviable business – a business whose going concern value is lower than its liquidation value – is artificially prolonged, to the detriment of outside financiers. It is important to note that this behaviour is not necessarily rational or intentional. Shareholders and managers may genuinely believe in their company's viability, a belief influenced by various cognitive biases, such as self-serving bias, optimism bias and the illusion of control.[23]

6.18 Unlike shareholders, external creditors may prefer risk-averse behaviour or immediate liquidation of the debtor. The reason for this is that they do not share in the potential upside of high-risk, high-reward strategies; they are entitled only to the principal (the original amount borrowed) plus interest. However, they are among the most affected parties if a risky or life-extending strategy fails, pushing the debtor into insolvency.

6.3.4 Minimum capital requirements and capital maintenance

6.19 Companies may be financed through debt or equity. The return on debt usually includes the payment of fixed interest, while the return on equity depends on the success of the company and is distributed in the form of dividends or reflected in an increase in share value. Unlike the return on debt, the return on equity investment is, in principle, unlimited but can be subject to specific company law rules. These rules provide creditors with a guaranteed equity cushion by means of minimum capital requirements and capital maintenance.

6.20 In recent decades, many jurisdictions have either eliminated or significantly reduced the need for private companies to maintain minimum capital levels. This trend has been instigated by regulatory competition and the positions of standard-setting organisations, such as the World Bank.[24] The abolition of minimum capital requirements has simplified the partition of a single

23 On cognitive biases in vicinity-of-insolvency decision-making, see M-W. Hung and W-H. Tsai, Managerial optimism, CEO retention, and corporate performance: evidence from bankruptcy-filing firms, Journal of Economics and Finance, Vol. 44, 2020, pp. 506–526, analysing data on bankruptcy-filing companies in the USA and concluding that managerial optimism is detrimental to operating performance at filing and survival probability. See also F. Drescher, Insolvency Timing and Managerial Decision-Making, Springer Gabler, 2014, p. 84, noting that 'context factors of the insolvency timing decisions are very likely to aggravate the manager's cognitive limitations'.

24 M. Becht, C. Mayer and H. Wagner, Where do Firms Incorporate? Deregulation and the Cost of Entry, Journal of Corporate Finance, Vol. 14, 2008, pp. 241–256, concluding that incorporations are primarily driven by minimum capital requirements. V. Saltane and P.G. Serna, Why are Minimum Capital Requirements a Concern for Entrepreneurs? World Bank Doing Business, 2014, pp. 41–45, arguing that such requirements significantly slow entrepreneurship and fail to serve the purpose of protecting creditors.

enterprise into a myriad of legal entities. In any event, the efficiency of minimum capital requirements is doubtful, as they do not reflect the riskiness of the business nor account for the potential size of the debtor or its debts.

Capital maintenance rules curb the distribution of corporate assets to shareholders (e.g. through the payment of dividends or the redemption or repurchase of the company's own shares) in situations where there are no distributable profits.[25] It is important to note that capital maintenance is not about avoiding insolvency but about giving effect 'to the rule that creditors' claims take priority over those of shareholders' and ensuring that distributions to shareholders do not compromise creditors' interests.[26] In other words, capital maintenance rules impose a negative obligation not to make distributions. They do not translate into any positive obligation for shareholders to make new equity contributions or refrain from intra-group lending. **6.21**

To conclude, the disparities in the nature, risk appetite and incentives between external and internal creditors are worth keeping in mind. They could be relied on to justify special treatment, consistent with the idea of formal (as opposed to universal) equality, pursuant to which different situations should not be treated in the same way. One may even argue that, since shareholders differ from outside creditors, it is fair to treat them differently. However, this simple conclusion does not solve the problem or provide an answer to the question of whether financial support provided by one group member to another should be subordinated in insolvency. For now, it suffices to stress that the distinct traits of internal creditors are at the heart of the subordination debate. **6.22**

6.4 SUBORDINATION OF SHAREHOLDER LOANS: NATIONAL PERSPECTIVES

6.4.1 Contractual v. statutory subordination

Subordination can be achieved through a contract – contractual subordination. Inter-creditor agreements that establish the ranking of creditors are common in syndicated loan transactions.[27] It is also common for a parent company **6.23**

25 See Companies Act 2006, s. 830(2), according to which 'company's profits available for distribution are its accumulated, realised profits … less its accumulated, realised losses'. See also Article 56 of the Directive (EU) 2017/1132 of the European Parliament and of the Council of 14 June 2017 relating to certain aspects of company law.

26 A. Cahn and D.C. Donald, Comparative Company Law: Text and Cases on the Laws Governing Corporations in Germany, the UK and the USA, 2nd edn, CUP, 2018, p. 257.

27 L. Gullifer and J. Payne, Corporate Finance Law: Principles and Policy, 3rd edn, Hart Publishing, 2020, p. 265.

to agree to subordinate its loan to a subsidiary in favour of an outside lender, such as a bank. Such subordination can be a precondition for securing external financing, as it provides an outside financier with additional protection in case the debtor cannot overcome financial difficulties and becomes insolvent. This protection comes from the fact that the outside financier is paid in priority to, and without competition from, the parent company, whose claim is contractually subordinated.[28]

6.24 In the context of group financing, subordination can also attach to recourse claims.[29] The main question is whether contractual subordination remains effective in the event of the borrower's insolvency, considering that the ranking of creditors' claims is prescribed by mandatory rules of insolvency law. The default rule for insolvency distribution is that creditors are to be treated equally, which may raise doubts about whether creditors can opt out of equal treatment through a subordination agreement.

6.25 Contractual subordination is generally allowed and effective in insolvency proceedings in the three jurisdictions discussed in this book. Burrows emphasises that the *pari passu* principle 'prevents a creditor from bargaining for an advantage on the distribution of an insolvent's assets, which is not the case with a subordination agreement of this kind [subordination to all other creditors]'.[30] He further observes that prohibiting such subordination agreements would have a prejudicial effect on companies that depend on the infusion of funds from parent and sister companies willing to accept subordination.[31]

---

28 *Lehman Brothers International (Europe) (In Administration), Re* [2017] UKSC 38, [2018] AC 465, [2017] 5 WLUK 397, addressing the issue of contractual subordination as applied to loans extended by LBIE's immediate holding company and noting that 'the perception of the reasonable reader would be that the holders of the subordinated debt were to be at the end of the queue – and, in the event of an Insolvency, at the bottom of the waterfall'.

29 See LMA Multicurrency Term and Revolving Facilities Agreement, sec. 18.7 (Deferral of Guarantors' Rights).

30 A. Burrows, English Private Law, 3rd edn, OUP, 2013, para. 19-130.

31 Ibid. See also P. Wood, Project Finance, Securitisations, Subordinated Debt, 2nd edn, Sweet & Maxwell, 2007, para. 11-025, noting that '[n]o policy of the insolvency laws is offended if one creditor voluntarily agrees to postpone himself to the others, but only if he seeks to put himself ahead of other unsecured creditors'.

The validity and effectiveness of subordination agreements are recognised and upheld by courts in the UK,[32] the USA[33] and the Netherlands.[34] In this respect, Gullifer notes that 'judicial confirmation of the validity of subordination agreements is very much to be welcomed',[35] given their prevalence in corporate finance. Contractual subordination stems from the principle of freedom of contract and does not negatively impact the interests of creditors. It does not create an unfair advantage; rather, creditors simply agree on how conflicts between their claims should be addressed in the distribution of the debtor's assets. Nevertheless, there may be concerns with a subordination agreement if the lender (parent company) that agreed to subordinate its claim becomes insolvent. In such a scenario, the agreement could potentially harm its creditors. The subordination agreement would then be subject to scrutiny under transaction avoidance rules (e.g. as a transaction at an undervalue), and factors such as the benefits granted to the subordinated lender (e.g. higher interest rates, suggesting a higher return for increased risk) are likely to influence the court's analysis. Disputes could also concern the interpretation of subordination clauses, the ranking of subordinated creditors among themselves, and their position relative to other creditors. **6.26**

To the extent that contractual subordination is based on the principle of freedom of contract and generally does not interfere with the equal treatment of creditors or their legitimate expectations, it will not be further discussed in this book. Instead, I will focus on statutory subordination. Unlike contractual subordination, statutory subordination is not based on a contract; it is prescribed by law and typically applies to the claims of insiders, including those of shareholders and group affiliates. The following sections explore national law approaches to statutory subordination. **6.27**

32 *Re Maxwell Communications Corp* [1993] 1 WLR 1402, holding that there were no principles of insolvency law or public policy that precluded a contract between a company and creditor whereby, if the company was insolvent, the debt was to be subordinated in the winding up to the payment of debt owed to other unsecured creditors. See also *Re SSSL Realisations* [2004] EWHC 1760 (Ch), dealing with subordination of intercompany debt.

33 11 U.S. Code § 510(a), providing that a contractual subordination agreement is enforceable 'to the same extent that such agreement is enforceable under applicable nonbankruptcy law'. This rule codifies pre-Bankruptcy Code case law. *In re Credit Industrial Corp.*, 366 F.2d 402 (2d Cir. 1966). The scope and enforceability of subordination agreements are determined by state law. *Wilmington Trust Co. v. Tribune Co.*, 2014 U.S. Dist. LEXIS 82782 (D. Del. June 18, 2014).

34 Dutch Civil Code, Article 3:277(2). Rb.'s-Gravenhage 28 October 2009, *JOR* 2010/317, *RI* 2010/21 (*Van der Eng c.s./SNSPF, Andalucia Projects*). N.B. Pannevis, Achtergestelde vorderingen (Onderneming en recht nr. 114) (diss. Nijmegen), Deventer: Wolters Kluwer, 2019.

35 R. Goode and L. Gullifer, Goode and Gullifer on Legal Problems of Credit and Security, 6th edn, Sweet & Maxwell, 2017, para. 5-61.

6.4.2 The UK: subordination for claims of shareholders *qua* shareholders

6.28 English law treats claims arising from intra-group financial arrangements *pari passu* with other unsecured claims. In the 1933 case *Matthew Ellis & Co. Ltd*,[36] the debtor, facing financial difficulty, obtained a loan from its chairman and controlling shareholder, Mr Arthur Tipper. The loan was provided to ensure the operational continuity of the debtor and was secured by a floating charge over the debtor's assets. It was agreed that part of this money was used to cover the past debt owed to the principal supplier of goods, of which Mr Tipper was a partner. This payment was a precondition for future supplies and the only means of keeping the debtor's business operational.

6.29 The liquidator contested the validity of the security, arguing that the money did not come to the debtor free from obligation and that the debtor merely acted as a conduit. However, the court refused the liquidator's application and found that the debtor 'did secure a valuable advantage in the continuation of the supply of goods …' and that 'the transaction must be considered as a whole and not split up'.[37] The fact that the loan and security involved an insider had no effect on the court's reasoning.

6.30 Another relevant case involving the claim of a shareholder is *Soden v. British & Commonwealth Holdings Plc*.[38] In 1988, British & Commonwealth Holdings Plc (B&C) acquired the entire share capital of Atlantic Computers (Atlantic). The acquisition proved disastrous, and Atlantic, along with B&C, went into administration. B&C brought proceedings against Atlantic for damages, alleging negligent misrepresentations made by Atlantic to induce B&C to purchase its shares. The question was whether this claim should be subordinated under section 74(2)(f) of the Insolvency Act 1986. According to this section:

> a sum due to any member of the company (in his character of a member) by way of dividends, profits or otherwise is not deemed to be a debt of the company, payable to that member in a case of competition between himself and any other creditor not a member of the company …

6.31 The administrators of Atlantic submitted that 'the basic principle applicable was that "members come last"', implying that members of a company (shareholders) should not receive any payment until outside creditors are paid in full. They considered it a 'manifest absurdity' if B&C, as a shareholder in its wholly owned subsidiary, was allowed to claim as damages the sums calculated with

---

36 *In re Matthew Ellis Ltd* [1933] Ch. 458.

37 Ibid.

38 *Soden and Another v. British & Commonwealth Holdings Plc. (In Administration)* [1997] 4 All ER 353.

reference to the price of shares based on the misrepresentation related to their acquisition. The House of Lords did not agree with this position and declined to subordinate the shareholder's claim.

The court distinguished between two types of shareholder claims: (i) sums due to a member 'in his character of a member', which were interpreted as sums falling due under or by virtue of the 'statutory contract' between a shareholder and the company and the members inter se – a memorandum and articles of association, and (ii) sums due to a member 'otherwise than in his character as a member'. Subordination in this case applied solely to rights and liabilities created by the constitutional documents of a company or those conferred and imposed on shareholders by the Companies Act. The court did not accept the principle that 'members [always] come last', ruling instead that 'a member having a cause of action independent of the statutory contract is in no worse a position than any other creditor'.[39] The principle dictates that the rights of shareholders *qua shareholders* come last, reflecting the trade-off for limited liability.[40] Since the cause of action in this case did not stem from corporate membership but rather from a misrepresentation made by the debtor during the purchase of existing shares from a third party, the court did not impose subordination. 6.32

Therefore, a narrow interpretation of the 'character of a member' was adopted. If a shareholder holds a claim in its capacity of a creditor (e.g. a claim for loan repayment or a subrogation claim), such a claim will not be subordinated. As a result, claims of insiders under intra-group financial transactions generally rank *pari passu* with unsecured creditors. This means that in insolvency, such claims could be set off against an obligation of contribution.[41] 6.33

English law has not developed a general doctrine of equitable subordination.[42] This is not to say that there has been no critique of the current approach to 6.34

39 Ibid.

40 For early cases, see *Re Addlestone Linoleum Co* (1887) 37 Ch.D. 191, ruling that the claimant who is induced to acquire his shares by subscription falls within the class of those who are not allowed to compete with general creditors. See also *Houldsworth v. City of Glasgow Bank* (1888) 5 App. Cas. 317, holding that a shareholder could not sue for damages for misrepresentation made by the company on the occasion of the issue (as opposed to the purchase) of its shares unless he first rescinded the contract, and that once the company had gone into liquidation such a rescission was impossible. See P. Wood, Principles of International Insolvency, 2nd edn, Sweet & Maxwell, 2007, para. 11-073.

41 V. Finch and D. Milman, Corporate Insolvency Law: Perspectives and Principles, 3rd edn, CUP, 2017, p. 533.

42 K. van Zwieten, Goode on Principles of Corporate Insolvency Law, 5th edn, Sweet & Maxwell, 2018, para. 8-30, suggesting that this outcome may be explained by the existence of statutory provisions, such as those enabling subordination of claims of creditor-directors found guilty of fraudulent or wrongful trading (ss. 215(4) and 246ZC of the Insolvency Act 1986).

shareholder loans. The famous Report of the Review Committee on Insolvency Law and Practice, also known as the Cork Report, recognised the issue:

> The strength of the case of those who seek a change in the law – and radical at that – can be seen if a simple and perhaps extreme example is taken. A wholly-owned subsidiary company is under-capitalised. It relies virtually wholly on moneys lent by the parent. Its affairs are conducted by and in the interest of the parent and they are mismanaged ... The subsidiary becomes insolvent and goes into liquidation. The parent company declines all liability for its subsidiary's debt to external creditors, and competes with them by submitting a proof in respect of its loan. The result is that, out of the total funds realised by the liquidator for distribution among the creditors, a substantial proportion goes to the parent company. We recognize that a law which permits such an outcome is undoubtedly a defective law.[43]

6.35 The Cork Report made several recommendations for reforms, ranging from joint and several liability of group entities, to the subordination of shareholder loans if they can be properly characterised as capital contributions. It proposed distinguishing between debts arising from ordinary intra-group trading activities and debts 'which in substance represent long term working capital and which arise from finance provided by the parent company'.[44] However, no legislation addressing the subordination of insider claims was adopted in the UK, nor has it been the focus of recent insolvency law reforms.

6.4.3 The USA: equitable subordination and debt recharacterisation

6.4.3.1 Equitable subordination: undoing wrongdoing

6.36 The doctrine of equitable subordination in the USA allows courts to subordinate the claim of one creditor to the claims of other creditors when the former has engaged in inequitable behaviour, resulting in an unjustified advantage or injury to other creditors of the distressed entity. The doctrine is therefore limited to reordering priorities and does not permit the disallowance of claims as such. In other words, it does not deal with the validity or invalidity of claims. Notably, equitable subordination is not restricted in its personal scope and may, in principle, apply to any creditor involved in some form of misconduct.[45]

---

43 Insolvency Law and Practice: Report of the Review Committee, Cmnd 8558, 1982, pp. 435–436.

44 Ibid., para. 1960.

45 See e.g. *Enron Corp. v. Ave. Special Situations Fund II, LP (In re Enron Corp.)*, 333 B.R. 205 (Bankr. S.D.N.Y. 2005); *Developmental Specialists, Inc. v. Hamilton Bank, N.A. (In re Model Imperial, Inc.)*, 250 B.R. 776 (Bankr. S.D. Fl. 2000). Traditionally, equitable subordination was inapplicable to ordinary creditors, as opposed to insiders. For external creditors, inequitable conduct warranting subordination must be 'gross and egregious, tantamount to fraud, misrepresentation, overreaching or spoliation, or involving moral turpitude'. See *In re Eufaula Indus. Auth.*, 266 B.R. 483, 489 (B.A.P. 10th Cir. 2001).

The doctrine of equitable subordination finds its origins in the famous 1939 cases of *Taylor v. Standard Gas & Electric*[46] (often referred to as the *Deep Rock* case) and *Pepper v. Litton*.[47] In *Deep Rock*, the US Supreme Court considered a claim of Standard Gas & Electric Company (Standard), the corporate parent, against its insolvent subsidiary – Deep Rock Oil Corporation (Deep Rock). Standard ran an open account with thousands of transactions between Standard and Deep Rock from 1919 to 1933. Many of these transactions were attacked as fraudulent, with allegations that Standard had made Deep Rock its mere agent or instrumentality. **6.37**

The Supreme Court held that '[f]rom the outset Deep Rock was insufficiently capitalised, was top heavy with debt and was in parlous financial condition. Standard so managed its affairs as always to have a stranglehold upon it'.[48] Due to findings of abuses by the parent company and inadequate capitalisation of the subsidiary, the Supreme Court ruled that the claim of the parent against its subsidiary should only participate in the reorganisation plan of the subsidiary in subordination to the preferred stock of the subsidiary.[49] **6.38**

Since 1978, the doctrine of equitable subordination has been codified in § 510(c) of the US Bankruptcy Code, which states that: **6.39**

> … the court may:
> (1) under principles of equitable subordination, subordinate for purposes of distribution all or part of an allowed claim to all or part of another allowed claim or all or part of an allowed interest to all or part of another allowed interest; or
> (2) order that any lien securing such a subordinated claim be transferred to the estate.[50]

The 'principles of equitable subordination' are not defined in the US Bankruptcy Code. As reflected in Congressional records, the development of **6.40**

46 *Taylor v. Standard Gas & Elec. Co.*, 306 U.S. 307 (1939).
47 *Pepper v. Litton*, 308 U.S. 295 (1939).
48 *Taylor v. Standard Gas & Elec. Co.*, 306 U.S. 307, 315 (1939).
49 *Pepper v. Litton*, 308 U.S. 295, 307 (1939), confirming the equitable power of courts 'to sift the circumstances surrounding any claim to see that injustice or unfairness is not done in administration of the bankrupt estate'.
50 11 U.S. Code § 510(c).

these principles was intentionally left to courts.[51] This makes equitable subordination 'a potentially vague standard'.[52]

6.41 Case law has formulated a number of requirements to guide courts in their application of the doctrine. In the widely quoted pre-reform case *In re Mobile Steel Corp.*,[53] a three-prong test for equitable subordination was proposed: (i) the claimant must have engaged in some type of inequitable conduct; (ii) this misconduct must have resulted in injury to the creditors of the bankrupt or conferred an unfair advantage on the claimant; and (iii) equitable subordination of the claim must not be inconsistent with the provisions of the US Bankruptcy Code. While the second (injury or unfair advantage) and the third (consistency with the law) prongs of the test are relatively unambiguous, the first element, namely 'inequitable conduct', or as one court has described it, conduct 'that shocks one's good conscience',[54] is not precise.

6.42 Courts acknowledge that equitable subordination is an extraordinary remedy, not a penalty, and should be used sparingly.[55] When dealing with the claims of insiders, the doctrine has been applied in situations involving: (i) fraud, illegality or breach of fiduciary duty; (ii) undercapitalisation; and (iii) control or use of the debtor as an alter ego for the benefit of a claimant.[56] Also, courts apply higher levels of scrutiny to the claims of insiders and are often willing to shift the burden to such insiders to prove both the good faith of the transaction and its inherent fairness.[57]

---

51 124 Cong.Rec.H 11095, H 11113 (Sept. 28, 1978), stating: 'It is intended that the term "principles of equitable subordination" follow existing case law and leave to the courts development of this principle. To date, under existing law, a claim is generally subordinated only if holder of such claim is guilty of inequitable conduct.' Interestingly, the initial bill introduced in the House of Representatives (H.R. 31, 94th Cong. (1976)) and the Senate (H.R. 31, 94th Cong. (1976)) prescribed a blanket subordination of all claims of insiders and their affiliates. Congress rejected this statutory language.

52 A.J. Levitin, Business Bankruptcy: Financial Restructuring and Modern Commercial Markets, Wolters Kluwer, 2016, p. 957, adding that 'as a standard, it is difficult to say exactly what will trigger or not trigger equitable subordination'. J. Kilborn, National Report for the United States, in D. Faber et al. (eds), Ranking and Priority of Creditors, OUP, 2016, para. 19.40, noting that the equitable nature 'makes application of this doctrine inherently difficult to predict'.

53 *Benjamin v. Diamond (In re Mobile Steel Co.)*, 563 F.2d 692 (5th Cir. 1977). The proposed formula was implicitly endorsed by the US Supreme Court in *United States v. Noland*, 517 U.S. 535 (1996).

54 *In re 80 Nassau Associates*, 169 B.R. 832, 837 (Bankr. S.D.N.Y. 1994).

55 See e.g. *In re Alternate Fuels, Inc.*, 789 F.3d 1139 (10th Cir. 2015); *In re Vetter Assets Service, LLC*, 609 B.R. 279 (Bankr. W.D. Okla. 2019); *In re Lifschultz Fast Freight*, 132 F.3d 339, 347 (7th Cir. 1997), holding that '[w]rongful or unpredictable subordination spawns legal uncertainty of a particular type: the risk that a court may refuse to honor an otherwise binding agreement on amorphous grounds of equity'.

56 *In re Fabricators, Inc.*, 926 F.2d 1458, 1467 (5th Cir. 1991); *In re Monahan Ford Corp. of Flushing*, 340 B.R. 1, 44 (Bankr. E.D.N.Y. 2006).

57 *Benjamin v. Diamond (In re Mobile Steel Co.)*, 563 F.2d 692 (5th Cir. 1977); *In re Virginia Broadband, LLC.*, 521 B.R. 539 (Bankr. W.D. Va. 2014); *In re Mid-Town Produce Terminal, Inc.*, 599 F.2d 389, 392 (10th Cir. 1979), noting that '[b]ecause there is incentive and opportunity to take advantage, dominant

In *In re Herby's Foods Inc.*,[58] the court ordered the subordination of shareholder loans based on the premise that the debtor's capital was insufficient to support its operations and that the debtor was already insolvent at the time of acquisition by the shareholder. However, the court noted that undercapitalisation alone was not sufficient to justify equitable subordination. Thus, additional grounds or factors for subordination were necessary. Among other factors, the court pointed out that: (i) the insiders never injected any equity capital into Herby's, 'electing instead to advance funds through tardily perfected secured loans made at times when no bona fide third-party lender would have done so'; (ii) the parent company's loan was not initially reflected on the debtor's books, and when it was finally booked, it was listed as an unsecured loan; (iii) the security interests were perfected only after the debtor stopped making interest payments; (iv) the aggregate size of the debtor's unsecured debt to its trade creditors increased fivefold, a result partially attributed to the shareholder's misrepresentations, which led outside creditors to increase their credit exposure to Herby's. The court considered these factors collectively as indicative of inequitable behaviour, which justified the subordination of the shareholder loans. **6.43**

Fact-sensitive analysis is a characteristic feature of cases involving equitable subordination. For example, in contrast to the previous case, in *In re SI Restructuring, Inc.*,[59] the court did not subordinate the loan granted by shareholders, even though the loan was secured. It concluded that the proceeds of the loan were used to pay unsecured creditors and to keep the company in operation. According to the court, this meant that unsecured creditors, as a class, were not harmed by the granting of security. The argument that the creditors were harmed due to so called 'deepening insolvency' and the value of the debtor deteriorating from the 'prolonging an insolvent corporation's life through bad debt' was rejected by the court.[60] **6.44**

---

shareholders and other insiders' loans in a bankruptcy situation are subject to special scrutiny'. However, *In re LightSquared Inc.*, 511 B.R. 253, 348 (Bankr. S.D.N.Y. 2014), stating that 'courts in this District have held that there is no different or heightened standard by which to judge a non-insider's conduct, though there may be fewer traditional grounds available because neither undercapitalization nor breach of fiduciary duty applies to the conduct of a non-insider'.

58 *In re Herby's Foods, Inc.*, 2 F.3d 128 (5th Cir. 1993).

59 *In re SI Restructuring Inc.*, 532 F.3d 355 (5th Cir. 2008).

60 Under the theory of 'deepening insolvency', directors may be held liable for prolonging the debtor company's life to the detriment of creditors. This theory is controversial and has been rejected by several courts. For example, the Delaware Supreme Court did not recognise deepening insolvency as an independent cause of action. See *Trenwick Am. Litig. Trust v. Billet (Trenwick)*, 931 A.2d 438 (Del. 2007).

6.45 Another case addressing secured loans of shareholders is *In re Phase I Molecular Toxicology Inc.*[61] In this case, the court refused to subordinate the loans, despite the fact that the loans were made when the thinly capitalised debtor was unable to secure outside financing. The court reasoned that the purpose of these loans was to cover the debtor's operating expenses until the anticipated sale of a subsidiary, which was expected to generate significant funds. The court also considered that the provision of collateral to secure the shareholder loans was not unreasonable and did not rise to the level of inequitable conduct.

6.46 In summary, the doctrine of equitable subordination has been developed as a remedy to address inequitable conduct and restore justice or balance among creditors. Although not limited to insiders, the degree of culpable behaviour and the burden of proof required in cases involving internal and external creditors differ.[62] Yet the mere fact of an insider relationship is insufficient to warrant subordination.[63] As noted in one case, insiders are often 'the persons most interested in restoring and reviving the debtor, and such bona fide efforts should be viewed with approval'.[64] The prevailing fact-based analysis demands more than a simple crisis or undercapitalisation of the debtor at the time of financing. A showing of deception about the debtor's financial condition or some other misconduct is necessary.

6.4.3.2 Debt recharacterisation: discovering parties' intentions

6.47 Alongside equitable subordination, US courts acknowledge their power to reclassify debt (11 U.S. Code, § 101(12)) as an equity interest (11 U.S. Code, § 101(16)) and to treat a loan as a capital contribution. There is no specific provision in the US Bankruptcy Code that allows claim recharacterisation. Some courts derive the right to recharacterise a debt claim as equity from general equitable powers.[65] Other courts base their recharacterisation mandate on the

---

61 *In re Phase I Molecular Toxicology, Inc.*, 287 B.R. 571 (Bankr. D.N.M. 2002).

62 C.J. Tabb, Law of Bankruptcy, 4th edn, West Academic Publishing, 2016, p. 714, observing that '[i]nequitable conduct sufficient to support a finding of equitable subordination is much easier to establish in the case of a creditor who is an *insider* or an *alter ego* of the debtor' and, conversely, '[c]ourts are very reluctant to subordinate the claim of a noninsider creditor'.

63 Collier on Bankruptcy, 16th edn, 2022, Vol. 4, ¶ 510.05.

64 *In re Hyperion Enterprises, Inc.*, 158 B.R. 555 (D.R.I. 1993); cited with approval in *In re AutoStyle Plastics, Inc.*, 269 F.3d 726, 745 (6th Cir. 2001), adding that '[i]nsider transactions are more closely scrutinized, not because the insider relationship makes them inherently wrong, but because insiders "usually have greater opportunities for … inequitable conduct"'. See also *In re Rego Crescent Corp.*, 23 B.R. 958, 964 (Bankr. E.D.N.Y. 1982), holding that 'the penalty for attempting to save the corporation should not be subordination'.

65 11 U.S. Code § 105(a), which states that bankruptcy judges have the authority to 'issue any order, process or judgment that is necessary or appropriate to carry out the provisions' of the US Bankruptcy Code. See *In re Dornier Aviation, Inc.*, 453 F.3d 225 (4th Cir. 2006).

statutory authority to allow or disallow claims under state law.[66] In practice, the economic effect of debt recharacterisation is similar to the subordination of a claim pursuant to equitable subordination, as both actions place the claim behind the claims of other creditors, making its satisfaction unlikely.[67] Nevertheless, it is accepted that the two doctrines are distinct, serve different purposes and involve different considerations.

In *In re AutoStyle Plastics*,[68] it was explained that recharacterisation determines the existence of debt by focusing on the underlying substance of the disputed transaction, while equitable subordination answers the question of whether a claim should be subordinated due to the creditor's inequitable conduct. If the claim is recharacterised, the equitable subordination analysis does not come into play.[69] **6.48**

Despite the predominant view that the US Bankruptcy Code authorises courts to recharacterise claims, the circuits have taken different approaches in identifying the legal framework for such recharacterisation.[70] Most courts use flexible and multi-factor tests to determine when a debt claim can be recharacterised as equity. **6.49**

Wheaton identified three separate lines of federal case law addressing recharacterisation.[71] **6.50**

The first line of cases is represented by the two-pronged test, pursuant to which a shareholder loan may be deemed a capital contribution in two circumstances: (i) the debtor was initially undercapitalised; or (ii) no other disinterested lender would have extended loans at the time they were made.[72] This test is not widely applied, as it may discourage an insider from providing a loan to **6.51**

66 11 U.S. Code § 502(b), which permits courts to disallow debt claims that state law classifies as equity. See *In re Lothian Oil*, 650 F.3d 539, 542 (5th Cir. 2011), also confirming that 'recharacterization extends beyond insiders and is part of the bankruptcy courts' authority to allow and disallow claims under 11 U.S.C. § 502'. The court applied Texas law and ruled in favour of recharacterisation. For critique of the split between the courts and support of sole reliance on state law, see J.M. Wilton and W.A. McGee, The Past and Future of Debt Recharacterization, The Business Law, Vol. 74, Winter 2018–2019, pp. 91–125.

67 R. Craig, Groups of companies: the parent subsidiary relationship and creditors remedies, PhD thesis, University of Durham, 1999, p. 322.

68 *In re AutoStyle Plastics, Inc.*, 269 F.3d 726 (6th Cir. 2001).

69 *United States v. Colorado Invesco, Inc.*, 902 F.Supp. 1339 (D. Colo. 1995); *Sinclair v. Barr (In re Mid–Town Produce Terminal, Inc.)*, 599 F.2d 389, 393 (10th Cir. 1979), noting that 'the usual procedure is to first determine whether the transaction was a contribution to capital rather than a loan'.

70 Collier on Bankruptcy, 16th edn, 2022, Vol. 4, ¶ 510.02, noting that '[c]ourts have adopted various multi-factored tests borrowed from nonbankruptcy case law to define the recharacterization inquiry'.

71 C. Wheaton, Clearing a Minefield of Insolvency Law: Toward Debt Recharacterization as a Supplement to the Bankruptcy Code, Santa Clara Law Review, Vol. 55, 2015, pp. 769–798.

72 *Estes v. N & D Props., Inc.*, 799 F.2d 726, 733 (11th Cir. 1986).

a distressed company, even if the insider is acting in the best interests of the company and its creditors.

6.52 The second line of cases includes a few early decisions in which courts refused to apply the doctrine of recharacterisation based on the lack of authority to recharacterise loans. In *In re Pacific Express*, the court stated that '[w]here there is a specific provision governing these determinations [§ 510(c), equitable subordination], it is inconsistent with the Bankruptcy Code to allow such determinations to be made under different standards through the use of a court's equitable powers'.[73] It seems that this position is no longer supported or followed.[74]

6.53 The third and by far the most prevalent position embraces the multi-factor tests, largely inspired by tax law cases concerning tax benefits of insider loans granted to solvent companies. These tests were never designed to apply to recharacterise loans extended to insolvent companies in the context of intra-group financing.[75] They addressed the tax treatment of interest expense as an important revenue issue. The most commonly cited case in this respect is *Roth Steel Tube Co. v. C.I.R.*, which determined the following catalogue of eleven factors to be used in making the capital contribution vs. loan determination:

> (1) the names given to the instruments, if any, evidencing the indebtedness; (2) the presence or absence of a fixed maturity date and schedule of payments; (3) the presence or absence of a fixed rate of interest and interest payments; (4) the source of repayments; (5) the adequacy or inadequacy of capitalization; (6) the identity of interest between the creditor and the stockholder; (7) the security, if any, for the advances; (8) the corporation's ability to obtain financing from outside lending institutions; (9) the extent to which the advances were subordinated to the claims of outside creditors; (10) the extent to which the advances were used to acquire capital assets; and (11) the presence or absence of a sinking fund to provide repayments.[76]

---

73 *In re Pacific Express, Inc.*, 69 B.R. 112, 115 (9th Cir. BAP 1986); *In re Pinetree Partners, Ltd.*, 87 B.R. 481 (Bankr. N.D. Ohio 1988) (following *In re Pacific Express*).

74 *In re Fitness Holdings Intern.*, 714 F.3d 1141, 1147 (9th Cir. 2013), noting that '[b]ecause we hold that a court may recharacterize an obligation that does not constitute "debt" under state law, we disagree with *In re Pacific Express, Inc*'.

75 *In re Rego Crescent Corp.*, 23 B.R. 958, 962 (Bankr. E.D.N.Y. 1982), commenting on the use of tax law tests that 'the legal questions and policy considerations underlying that determination [dividend vs. loan for tax purposes] are so removed from determining whether money advanced should be considered capital contributions or loans for bankruptcy purposes that those cases are in no way relevant to the inquiry before this court'.

76 *Roth Steel Tube Co. v. Commissioner of Internal Revenue*, 800 F.2d 625, 630 (6th Cir. 1986). Another often cited case is *Fin Hay Realty Co. v. U.S.*, 398 F.2d 694, 696 (3d Cir. 1968), proposing a list of sixteen distinguishing factors. Also, *Estate of Mixon v. United States*, 464 F.2d 394 (5th Cir. 1972), adopting a thirteen-factor test.

Under this multi-factor test, no single factor is seen as controlling or decisive.[77] Instead, all the factors need to be considered. Notably, the insider status, undercapitalisation and dire financial circumstances surrounding the infusion of cash alone have been regarded as insufficient to cause debt recharacterisation.[78] 6.54

The variability of tests and plurality of factors that may dictate the outcome of a case have been criticised as problematic from the standpoint of predictability.[79] Furthermore, courts have acknowledged that recharacterisation does not depend on how many of the relevant factors are met; they also assign different weight to these factors. In one case, it was noted that 'no mechanical scorecard suffices. And none should, for Kabuki outcomes elude difficult fact patterns.'[80] In our view, predictability of Kabuki outcomes can actually be a virtue, especially from the perspective of group (insider) financiers, without any wrongful conduct on their part. The reason is that the totality-of-the-facts-in-each-case test affords courts wide discretion to recharacterise insider debt as equity. This creates legal uncertainty and compels insiders to engage in a box-ticking exercise to comply with formalities typical of debt instruments. After all, carefully documented loans are less likely to be recharacterised, but uncertainty may still remain. For example, in *In re AtlanticRancher*,[81] the court recharacterised an insider loan, despite the fact that the loan was properly documented, used for working capital and treated as debt on the debtor's books. Yet, when making the decision to recharacterise, the court held that the insider never made any effort to collect the debt or to foreclose on his collateral. It noted that the creditor 'recognized that if he attempted to exercise his rights as a secured creditor it would have put the company out of business'.[82] According to the 6.55

77 In cases involving recharacterisation, courts typically go over all the factors under the prevailing test. See e.g. *In re Lyondell Chemical Company*, 544 B.R. 75 (Bankr. S.D.N.Y. 2016); *In re Live Primary, LLC*, 626 B.R. 171 (Bankr. S.D.N.Y. 2021).

78 *In re Dornier Aviation, Inc.*, 453 F.3d 225 (4th Cir. 2006); *In re SubMicron Systems Corp.*, 432 F.3d 448 (3d Cir. 2006).

79 D.A. Skeel and G. Krause-Vilmar, Recharacterization and the Nonhindrance of Creditors, EBOR, Vol. 7, 2006, p. 278, arguing that there are two intractable problems with the 'welter of factors'. The first being that many of such factors 'are either unhelpful or used in precisely the wrong way'. The second problem is that the list of factors 'tended to distort court's analysis of what should and should not be honored as a loan'. H.A. Goehausen, You Said You Were Going to Do What to My Loan? The Inequitable Doctrine of Recharacterization, DePaul Business and Commercial Law Journal, Vol. 4, 2005, p. 133, noting that the doctrine has spawned 'conflicting standards and inconsistent judicial decisions' and pointing out that since the doctrine does not require a showing of bad faith or misconduct on the part of a lender, 'it is easier for a trustee or creditor to be successful in a recharacterization action then in a claim for equitable subordination'.

80 *In re SubMicron Systems Corp.*, 432 F.3d 448, 456 (3d Cir. 2006).

81 *In re AtlanticRancher*, Inc., 279 B.R. 411 (Bankr. D. Mass. 2002).

82 Ibid., at 437.

court, the creditor's behaviour signalled that the debt was not treated as a loan but rather as an investment.

6.56 To conclude, the boundaries of the recharacterisation doctrine in the USA are not clear. First, the very legal basis of the doctrine is disputable. While some US courts rely on the equitable powers granted to them under § 105(a) of the US Bankruptcy Code, other courts adhere to the view that the power to recharacterise should be derived from state law. Second, different multi-factor tests are developed to determine whether an insider loan should be treated as an equity contribution. These tests may produce inconsistent and unpredictable results. They could also have a chilling effect on the willingness of insiders to extend financing to a financially distressed group member or to refuse to foreclose on collateral or collect the loan in hopes of rescuing such a group member.[83] Third, the parallel existence of two doctrines – equitable subordination and recharacterisation – with some overlapping elements or factors (e.g. undercapitalisation) and similar results is hard to justify. It may lead to confusion and further complicate the position of internal creditors.

6.4.4 The Netherlands: conflicting authorities

6.57 The issue of statutory subordination of shareholder loans is not fully settled in the Netherlands.[84] The Dutch Bankruptcy Act does not contain express rules on shareholder loans, and the relevant case law presents mixed outcomes.

6.58 In *Oude Grote Bevelsborg q.q./Louwerier q.q.*,[85] the District Court of Breda ruled in favour of subordinating an intercompany claim. The case concerned a claim of the parent company, Stichting Ambacht, against its subsidiary, Ambacht B.V., which relied heavily on the parent for staff, equipment and materials. When Stichting Ambacht went bankrupt, Ambacht B.V. became insolvent. The trustee of the parent company submitted a claim in the bankruptcy proceedings of Ambacht B.V. The trustee of the subsidiary did not dispute the existence of the claim but argued that it should be subordinated and treated as a capital contribution. If subordination was ordered, ordinary creditors would

83 For a similar view, see S. Mba, New Financing for Distressed Businesses in the Context of Business Restructuring Law, Springer, 2019, p. 52. Mba refers to the situation around recharacterisation tests as a 'doctrinal bedlam'. J.M. Wilton and W.A. McGee, The Past and Future of Debt Recharacterization, The Business Law, Vol. 74, Winter 2018-2019, p. 106, noting that the use of various tests leads to unpredictable results 'that discourage out-of-court workouts and reorganization of insolvent businesses'.

84 J. Barneveld and F. Corpeleijn, Financiering met risicomijdend vermogen? Over de aandeelhouderslening in faillissement, TvI 2014/39.

85 Rb. Breda 7 July 2010, *JOR* 2010/293 (*Oude Grote Bevelsborg q.q./Louwerier q.q.*).

receive the full payment on their claims. Without subordination, the payouts would drop to 40–45 per cent.

6.59 The court considered the method of financing and the relationships between the group entities. It noted that in special circumstances, there may be grounds to treat a claim as subordinated, even if there was no contractual basis for it. In answering the question of whether, in the present case, there was a reason to treat the parent's claim differently from the claim of other creditors, the court considered both the method of financing and the interrelationship between the group entities. The court concluded that the claim of Stichting Ambacht against Ambacht B.V. should be considered an informal provision of capital, subordinated to the claims of other creditors. It took into account close business integration of the two companies. The companies conducted similar business activities, used the same staff, and even completed work of each other, only deciding afterwards whether to assign such work to Stichting Ambacht or Ambacht B.V. Moreover, the subsidiary's survival depended on its parent's support, and its insolvency followed directly from the parent's financial collapse. Given these circumstances, the court deemed it would be 'contrary to reasonableness and fairness for a controlling shareholder that has established the company, had absolute control over the company and has maintained it through the current-account financing, to share in the proceeds of the insolvency estate in the same way as unsecured creditors'.[86]

6.60 This line of reasoning was not upheld in *P&O Partner/Wind Holding*.[87] In this case, the debtor company, a developer and manufacturer of offshore wind turbines, was declared bankrupt on 30 June 2009. Wind Holding B.V. (Wind), which held a 90 per cent ownership stake in the debtor, also subsequently became insolvent. Under a loan facility agreement dated 1 October 2008, Wind had transferred over EUR 10 million to the debtor between 31 December 2008 and 8 May 2009. This was the claim submitted by Wind in the insolvency proceedings of the debtor. One of the debtor's creditors, P&O

86 Ibid. Also Gerechtshof Amsterdam 5 November 2005, *JOR* 2007/51, m.nt. S.M. Bartman (*Carrier 1*), where the court approved the unequal treatment of the parent company under the restructuring plan (the parent was promised a smaller distribution of 5.6 per cent compared to other unsecured creditors receiving 33 per cent). The court concluded that the plan was the only feasible compromise and that the loan to the wholly owned subsidiary, in the given situation, at least partly had the character of a capital injection. No specific reasoning was given for classifying the loan as 'capital replacement', but the first-instance court focused on the fact that the loan was provided at a time and under conditions that would not be accepted by any third party. Commenting on *Carrier 1*, Bartman questioned whether, in the absence of a clear legal basis for a distinction between capital-replacing and other loans, the court's motivation would stand in cassation.

87 Gerechtshof Arnhem-Leeuwarden 10 March 2015, *JOR* 2015/160, m.nt. J. Barneveld (*P&O Partner/Wind Holding*).

Partner B.V. (P&O), argued that the shareholder loan must be subordinated. The court disagreed.

6.61 First, it referred to Article 3:277(1) of the Dutch Civil Code, which states that creditors have an equal right to recover their claims from the debtor's assets, except for cases where priority is granted by law. Second, the court acknowledged that a debtor and a creditor may contractually agree on subordination (Article 3:277(2) BW). It did not follow from the loan documentation that such an agreement was reached in the case at hand. P&O submitted that the parties had decided to convert the loan into equity, and in line with the judgment in the above case, the loan should be treated as an informal capital contribution. However, the conversion from debt to equity was not finalised, nor was it proven that the parties had always intended to convert the loan into equity. Third, the court noted that Wind's loan to the debtor was an intercompany or shareholder loan, which had no special status under Dutch law, in the sense that Dutch law did not prescribe its subordination. It could not be deduced from case law and literature that the prevailing doctrine supported subordination or that subordination was desirable. Fourth, the court accepted that unlawful behaviour of the parent company may result in its liability towards the subsidiary's creditors under Article 6:162 BW as a tortious act. It is generally accepted that a parent company must take into account the interests of (future) creditors of its subsidiary when financing such a subsidiary. This is relevant where, in the absence of any real prospects of survival, the subsidiary is financed by shareholder loans, which could mislead creditors and create the impression of creditworthiness, while it would have been in the interest of creditors to cease the debtor's activities. Finally, the court mentioned that subordination could possibly be construed on the basis of the principle of reasonableness and fairness.[88] In the given case, however, this principle was not breached.

6.62 In summary, the limited case law from Dutch courts concerning subordination of shareholder loans does not lead to a clear conclusion. The Dutch Bankruptcy Act does not explicitly address this issue, and the Dutch Supreme Court has yet to take a position. What is clear, however, is that insider claims are not automatically subordinated. If such subordination is available at all, it is reserved for cases involving harmful behaviour by an insider. In this context,

88 On reasonableness and fairness as applied to creditors, see F.M.J. Verstijlen, De faillissementscurator, W.E.J. Tjeenk Willink, 1998, p. 73ff; M.J.M. Franken, Verificatie van vorderingen, redelijkheid en billijkheid tussen schuldeisers onderling: een gemiste kans?, in N.E.D. Faber et al., De bewindvoerder, een octopus, Serie Onderneming en Recht deel 44, Deventer: Kluwer, 2008.

subordination might be seen as compensation for improper conduct.[89] An insider might also be viewed as acting unlawfully if it disregards the standards of reasonableness and fairness expected of creditors. This brings the Dutch approach closer to the US doctrine of equitable subordination, as both require some form of inequitable conduct and reject the notion that insider status alone justifies subordination.

Yet, one should exercise caution when drawing any parallels. There are several reasons why making a comparison may be difficult or undesirable, including: (i) the inherent ambiguity of the term 'inequitable conduct' and the boundaries of 'reasonableness and fairness'; (ii) the fact that, unlike the US Bankruptcy Code, the Dutch Bankruptcy Act does not contain any specific rules on subordination; (iii) the lack of internal coherence in the application of the subordination rules and standards. This is explained by the fact-sensitive analysis characterising cases involving intercompany financing and the subordination of insider debt. This contrasts with UK law, which only subordinates shareholder claims closely tied to shareholder status (e.g. payment of dividends) and does not prescribe subordination of shareholder loans. **6.63**

6.5 SHAREHOLDER LOANS: TO SUBORDINATE OR NOT TO SUBORDINATE?

There is no *communis opinio* or widely held view as to whether financing provided by related parties should be subordinated in insolvency, and if so, under which conditions and with what exceptions, if any. The landscape of national responses to these questions is equally divided.[90] Arguments in favour of subordination typically include: (i) facilitation of early insolvency filings, which should prevent the build-up of non-performing loans and minimise creditor **6.64**

89 N.B. Pannevis, Achtergestelde vorderingen (Onderneming en recht nr. 114) (diss. Nijmegen), Deventer: Wolters Kluwer, 2019, 2.4.

90 For an overview of arguments in favour and against subordination, see R. de Weijs, J. de Vries and A. Jonkers, Corporate Finance for Lawyers, Edward Elgar Publishing, 2023, Chapter 6.

losses;[91] (ii) responsibility for the consequences of financial decisions;[92] and (iii) the risk reallocation and risk shifting role of debt financing, and the incentives of shareholders vs. outside creditors.[93] The analysis of these arguments falls outside the scope of this book. Instead, I will focus on the issue of intra-group financial support.

6.65 Intra-group financial support may facilitate efficient restructuring. It is widely recognised that businesses need money, and struggling businesses need it the most. Money is required to support the continued operation of the debtor during its negotiations with creditors and to implement the restructuring plan upon confirmation. The preservation of operational continuity may be equally important when contemplating the sale of the business as a going concern, as any interruption might result in a reduction in its price. Access to funds is critical to ensure business continuity and timely payments to critical suppliers of goods and services, lessors, employees, insurance providers and other stakeholders.[94]

6.66 In groups of companies, a common source of funds can be within the group and include both solvent group entities and group members already subject

---

91 BGH, Urteil vom 16. Oktober 1989 - Az. II ZR 307/88, noting that the recharacterisation of shareholder loans is not solely intended to prevent the shareholder from satisfying its claims before or alongside creditors, but it should also rule out the delay in a crisis response and curb any further reduction of remaining assets at the expense of creditors. Yet the correlation between subordination of shareholder loans and early insolvency filings is not obvious. See W. Meilicke, Das Eigenkapitalersatzrecht - eine deutsche Fehlentwicklung, GmbH-Rundschau, 2007, ss. 225-236. See also A. Cahn, Equitable Subordination of Shareholder Loans? EBOR, Vol. 7, 2006, p. 300, observing that 'given the uncertainties inherent in calculating expected values and the fact that shareholders are not likely to put substantial amount of fresh money at stake if they do not have good reason to expect a successful turnaround, the chances in practice of fostering overinvestment are probably negligible'.

92 BGH, Urteil vom 26 März 1984 - II ZR 171/83, noting that a shareholder cannot choose a less risky form of financial support to the detriment of other creditors. Hence, if the company is in financial distress, shareholders should take special responsibility for the consequences of financial decisions. It appears that 'responsibility for consequences of financial decisions' is linked to the power of shareholders to direct the company and decide what to do with it once it has entered a crisis period. If the company is in a crisis, its shareholders should decide whether to liquidate it or to provide the necessary funding. However, it is not apparent why such funding should be extended in the form of equity.

93 R.J. de Weijs and M. Good, Shareholders' and Creditors' Entitlements on Insolvency: Who Wins Where? Butterworths Journal of International Banking and Financial Law, November 2015, p. 643, observing that shareholder loans 'dramatically change the risk profile of the company' and prompt 'shareholders to have the company make riskier investments'. This problem is inherent in the corporate form, where shareholders do not internalise losses and costs of failure due to limited liability. The risk-bearing nature of equity contributions creates an incentive for shareholders to monitor management and engage in corporate governance. Equating the position of shareholders with that of creditors leads to risk reallocation and weakens the said incentive. The risks are externalised from shareholder to creditors. Subordination rules aim to restore the shareholder-creditor balance and create a disincentive to pursue inefficient and unjustifiably risky strategies, and engage in the 'gamble for resurrection'.

94 UNCITRAL Legislative Guide, Part two, Ch. II, para. 94.

to insolvency proceedings. For illustrative purposes, the Singapore case is of interest. Based on the mix of empirical data and case studies on Singapore schemes covering the period from 1996 to 2019, Wan et al. have observed that 'when companies are approaching insolvency or financial distress, controlling shareholders do not unnecessarily hold out; ... they add value (in the provision of financial support) and are often critical to the success of restructuring efforts'.[95] The authors conclude that new financing by controlling shareholders is one of the conditions or essential predictors of the effectiveness of schemes.[96]

The value of new financing is not simply intuitive. A positive effect of rescue financing on the chances of business survival is highlighted in a number of empirical studies.[97] Some of them conclude that debtors with debtor in possession (DIP) financing are more likely to successfully emerge from Chapter 11 compared to the companies that did not receive such financing.[98] The positive impact of post-petition financing on reorganisation is accepted by the American Bankruptcy Institute (ABI) Commission to Study the Reform of Chapter 11 (ABI Commission). It recognised the need for a robust and competitive post-petition financing market and the value that it provides to distressed firms.[99] The importance of rescue financing is also pointed out in the non-US context.[100] Tsioli emphasises that rescue financing 'counteracts potential value-destructive "lingering" of the case, moves it along more briskly and as such helps preserve the debtor's going concern value'.[101] 6.67

What are the effects of subordination? 6.68

95 W.Y. Wan, C. Watters and G. McCormack, Schemes of Arrangement in Singapore: Empirical and Comparative Analyses, American Bankruptcy Law Journal, Vol. 94, 2020, p. 486.

96 Ibid., p. 502.

97 The term 'rescue financing' is mainly used in the EU and the UK, whereas the term 'DIP financing' is prevalent in the USA.

98 S. Dahiya et al., Debtor-in-possession financing and bankruptcy resolution: Empirical evidence, Journal of Financial Economics, Vol. 69, 2003, pp. 259–280, finding that DIP-financed companies had a shorter reorganisation period. The authors did not find evidence of overinvestment (e.g. the undertaking of risky projects and projects with negative NPV). U.S. Dhillon, T. Noe and G.G. Ramírez, Debtor-in-possession financing and the resolution of uncertainty in Chapter 11 reorganisations, Journal of Financial Stability, Vol. 3, 2007, pp. 238–260, concluding that DIP financing resolves information asymmetries regarding the value of the firm and is correlated with successful reorganisations.

99 ABI Commission to Study the Reform of Chapter 11, Final Report and Recommendations, 2014, p. 77.

100 L. Stanghellini et al. (eds), Best Practices in European Restructuring. Contractualised Distress Resolution in the Shadow of the Law, Wolters Kluwer, 2018, p. 60, referring to Italian quantitative and qualitative analysis, underlining the importance of new financing to rescue businesses in distress. It is observed that commonly new finance comes from the debtor's shareholders.

101 L. Tsioli, Rescue financing under a 'viability spotlight', Journal of Corporate Law Studies, Vol. 22, 2022, p. 858. Tsioli also highlights the risks related to the exercise of creditor control through DIP financing.

In the analysis of the economic effects of subordination rules, Gelter argues that '[even] though subordination has some beneficial effects, it deters some desirable rescue attempts and is an insufficient deterrent for some undesirable ones'.[102] A similar argument was made by other scholars.[103] For instance, Van Zwieten notes that 'a rule mandating the subordination of related party creditor claims would likely limit the availability of insider capital even in circumstances where it might reasonably be expected to increase firm value …'[104] She points out that a rule that imposes mandatory subordination of related-party debt claims 'seems highly unattractive, given the potential for related party loans to be value-enhancing for the firm'.[105] De Weijs, who generally supports subordination, still notes that the prevention of desirable rescue attempts is '[o]ne of the strongest and most serious critiques as to subordination rules relates to rescue attempts'.[106]

6.69 Relying on a statistical hypothesis testing, Gelter distinguishes two types of errors relevant to subordination. Type I error occurs if inefficient (negative expected value) rescue attempts are not prevented, so that the life of a dying business is artificially extended (overinvestment). This leads to the accumulation of debt and results in a dissipation of the firm's value to the detriment of creditors. Subordination partly internalises risk with shareholders and can therefore facilitate a timely exit of inefficient firms from the market.[107] Type II error arises when efficient firms are liquidated instead of being saved

102 M. Gelter, The subordination of shareholder loans in bankruptcy, International Review of Law and Economics, Vol. 26, 2006, p. 478.

103 S. Mba, New Financing for Distressed Businesses in the Context of Business Restructuring Law, Springer, 2019, p. 55, noting with respect to the German approach that 'it would appear that the law does not countenance the need to support the superstructure on which informal distress financing rests, one of which is the provision of restructuring financing and an increasingly important source of this financing being insider/shareholder financing'. See also H. Eidenmüller, Comparative Corporate Insolvency Law, in J.N. Gordon and W-G. Ringe (eds), The Oxford Handbook of Corporate Law and Governance, OUP, 2018, p. 1024, stating that 'a subordination rule discourages debt financing by shareholders if the company is in financial distress, and the shareholders may be the only available financing source in such a setting. As a consequence, the prospects for a restructuring of the firm might be greatly reduced.' M.R. Tucker, Debt Recharacterization During an Economic Trough: Trashing Historical Tests to Avoid Discouraging Insider Lending, Ohio State Law Journal, Vol. 71, 2010, p. 191, arguing that '[c]ourts must not inadvertently prohibit a company's most readily available source of funding [insider financing] by imposing on insiders an unreasonable fear of loan invalidation because of the existing capricious doctrine of debt recharacterization'.

104 K. van Zwieten, Related Party Transactions in Insolvency, in L. Enriques and T.H. Tröger (eds), The Law and Finance of Related Party Transactions, CUP, 2019, p. 275.

105 Ibid., p. 274. According to Van Zwieten, a more attractive route to prevent misuse of related-party transactions is a director-targeting personal liability rule. A similar position is taken by Eidenmüller.

106 R.J. de Weijs, Hybrid finance by means of shareholder loans, in R. de Weijs, J. de Vries and A. Jonkers, Corporate Finance for Lawyers, Edward Elgar Publishing, 2023.

107 M. Gelter, The subordination of shareholder loans in bankruptcy, International Review of Law and Economics, Vol. 26, 2006, p. 486.

(underinvestment).[108] The extent or degree to which subordination reduces overinvestment and increases underinvestment is not entirely clear,[109] and requires empirical evaluation. Yet, assuming that there are instances where subordination discourages the provision of intra-group loans to economically viable group entities and thereby prevents efficient rescue attempts (i.e. Type II error), the overall outcome may be detrimental to social welfare. Armour, Hertig and Kanda explain this by noting that:

> The rationale [of subordination] is to deter overinvestment in distressed firms, but such doctrines must walk a tightrope between deterring this and permitting controlling shareholders to make legitimate efforts to rescue failing firms through the injections of new debt capital. Perhaps reflecting these difficulties, this doctrine is not applied in France or the UK.[110]

This is why, for instance, following the recent reforms seeking to encourage shareholders to provide loans to their distressed companies, subordination rules were weakened in Italy. Under reformed Italian law, subordination does not apply to claims of shareholders and other parties exercising direction and control over the debtor arising from loans and guarantees granted by them for the purposes of a *concordato preventive* or debt restructuring agreement up to 80 per cent of the original claim.[111] In this 80 per cent part, financing is subject to the special regime of *prededuzione*, which gives priority over unsecured creditors. The remaining 20 per cent is subordinated. By contrast, while the German StaRUG allows a plan to incorporate new financing agreements, including those from shareholders (shareholder loans), if the debtor subsequently enters bankruptcy proceedings, shareholder loans under the plan remain shareholder loans, which means that they are subordinated in insolvency distribution (§ 39(1)(5) InsO). Besides, security granted to subordinated debt is widely avoidable.[112] 6.70

The difficulty lies in finding a balance between preventing overinvestment in economically non-viable enterprises through intra-group loans, on the one hand, and protecting and encouraging transactions that aim at value creation 6.71

---

108 Ibid. Gelter seems to view subordination as a way of penalising shareholders. See ibid., p. 479.

109 S. Landuyt, A Capital Question, Should Shareholder Loans be Automatically Subordinated?, in D. Bruloot (ed), Belgian and European perspectives on creditor protection in closed companies, Intersentia, 2019, p. 142, arguing that it is 'unlikely that in case of the subordination of shareholder loans the costs of the underinvestment problem will outweigh the benefits generated by the deterrence of excessive risk-taking'.

110 J. Armour, G. Hertig and H. Kanda, Transactions with creditors, in R. Kraakman et al. (eds), The Anatomy of Corporate Law, OUP, 2017, p. 132.

111 Codice della crisi d'impresa e dell'insolvenza (Decreto Legislativo 12 gennaio 2019, n. 14), Articles 102(1) and 292(2).

112 InsO, §135.

and efficient allocation of resources and liquidity within the group, on the other hand. My view is that blanket subordination of all insider loans does not establish this balance, as it fails to distinguish between value-enhancing and value-destroying rescue attempts. In other words, it may be disproportionate.

6.72 The provision of intra-group loans in a situation of financial distress (absent external financing on comparable terms) can contribute to the maximisation of enterprise value and the preservation of the debtor's business, from which outside creditors and other stakeholders, like employees, can benefit. The mere fact that financing comes from an insider does not change this. However, to mitigate the risk of inefficient rescue attempts and the externalisation of costs, a supervised and controlled legal framework for rescue financing should be considered (see Chapter 10). Should the law provide for shareholder loan subordination, this framework could consider that if the rescue attempt has a positive expected value, subordination will not apply. This would mitigate the problem of underinvestment while discouraging overinvestment.

6.6 CONCLUSION

6.73 At the beginning of this chapter, I compared intra-group, inward-looking financing to the blood flow within a human body. Just like the circulatory system, wherein blood circulates and transports nutrients, such as amino acids and oxygen, to different organs of the body, the provision of capital and liquidity to group entities could be vital for their continued operation and survival. A centralised cash management or cash-pooling system, typical for many large enterprise groups like Lehman Brothers, may be seen as the closest analogue to the circulatory system (to the extent that it is possible to compare a living organism with an artificial construct such as a legal entity or an enterprise group). This chapter focuses on intra-group loans, which constitute a common way to reallocate liquidity within groups of companies.

6.74 One issue that is specific to intra-group loans is their potential subordination in insolvency. It means that shareholder loans are repaid after unsecured creditors. It has been shown that countries adopt very different approaches to the issue of shareholder loan subordination. While countries like Germany, Brazil and Spain have strict subordination rules mandating subordination in almost all cases, in the UK, only sums due to a shareholder 'in his character of' a shareholder, narrowly interpreted (e.g. dividends), are subject to subordination. In the USA, the doctrines of equitable subordination and debt recharacterisation were developed over time. The former aims to remedy inequitable conduct and restore justice among creditors. The latter is not explicitly based on the statute, has unclear boundaries, and relies on different multi-factor tests. In the Netherlands, there is no settled stance on subordination. Dutch law does not contain rules prescribing subordination, leaving only a limited possibility for subordinating insider claims in cases involving improper conduct or behaviour that violates the standards of reasonableness and fairness.

The wide range of approaches to the subordination of insider loans is underpinned by a variety of views on the pros and cons of subordination. Some authors argue that subordination facilitates timely insolvency filings and exit of economically non-viable firms from the market. It is also suggested that subordination could respond to risk-shifting behaviour of shareholders, prevent the externalisation of losses, promote better corporate governance, and preserve creditors' status as residual claimants in insolvency. These arguments reflect the differences between internal and external creditors, discussed in section 6.3. At the same time, other scholars note that a non-subordinated shareholder loan aligns the interests of a shareholder with those of external creditors, whereas the risks of misuse of related-party transactions are better tackled by transaction avoidance and directors' liability rules. UNCITRAL adds that subordination might threaten the viability of the subordinated group entity (as it is likely to receive nothing in the insolvency of the borrower), harm its creditors and cause detriment to the reorganisation of the group as a whole.[113] 6.75

Perhaps the strongest and most important criticism of subordination is that it is overreaching and disproportionate, and that it discourages efficient, value-enhancing rescue attempts. There is nothing morally reprehensible about intra-group loans. However, there is a fine line between, on the one hand, deterring overinvestment in inefficient, economically non-viable enterprises and combating group opportunism, and on the other hand, encouraging insiders (e.g. group entities) to make legitimate, value-creating efforts to save financially distressed but economically viable firms, mitigating the problem of underinvestment and contributing to the preservation and maximisation of estate value. Finding a balance is crucial in the context of rescue financing – financing provided to a struggling company to ensure the continuity of its operations during restructuring negotiations with creditors or to facilitate the implementation of the plan. 6.76

113 UNCITRAL Legislative Guide, Part three, Ch. II, para. 88. See similarly, I. Mevorach, Transaction Avoidance in Bankruptcy of Corporate Groups, ECFR, Vol. 8, 2011, p. 251, noting that the 'prospect of equitable subordination of intra-group debts increases the risk of non-payment to the subordinated party and therefore induces the creditors of that company to investigate the other affiliates' creditworthiness'.

7

FACING UNCERTAINTY: INTRA-GROUP FINANCING AND TRANSACTION AVOIDANCE

7.1 INTRODUCTION

7.01 In many jurisdictions, transactions between or involving group entities face increased scrutiny, as do other related-party transactions[1] – especially if such transactions are concluded in the vicinity of insolvency. This is a common approach across many national legal systems.[2] It can be attributed to the information asymmetry that often exists between internal (related) and external (non-related) creditors (see section 6.3). The former usually have a better awareness of the debtor's financial situation. In the group context, this awareness concerns the financial soundness of group entities and the entire group. Additionally, due to their control advantage and risk-shifting incentives in the vicinity of insolvency, shareholders can be incentivised and have the power to engage in value-destroying behaviour, whether in the form of overinvestment or value extraction.[3] The value extraction might be arranged through various

1 UNCITRAL Legislative Guide, Part two, Ch. II, para. 182.

2 Control over related-party transactions is not limited to the area of insolvency law. For example, it emerges in the rules imposing prohibitions and introducing procedural safeguards, mandatory disclosures, requirements for external independent advice and ex post standard-based judicial review. L. Enriques, Related Party Transactions, in J.N. Gordon and W-G. Ringe (eds), The Oxford Handbook of Corporate Law and Governance, OUP, 2018, pp. 506–531.

3 R.J. Mokal, Corporate Insolvency Law: Theory and Application, OUP, 2005, p. 307, explaining that 'in the twilight period while the company is distressed but not yet subject to formal insolvency proceedings,

means, from a transfer at an undervalue, assumption of liability, to a preferential payment of intercompany debt, e.g. via setting-off an intercompany claim. There are other examples of transactions that could be detrimental to external creditors of separate group entities.[4]

The danger of group opportunism is only a part of the picture. Related-party transactions are not *per se* problematic in the sense that they do not always or often harm the collective interest of creditors. Intra-group loans may facilitate efficient allocation of liquidity within the group and mitigate the problem of underinvestment (lack of incentives to finance value-creating projects). Cross-guarantees are used to secure beneficial conditions (e.g. lower interest rates and larger amounts) from outside lenders and help address the debt overhang problem (a situation where the firm's high debt levels act as a disincentive to new investment). Both intra-group loans and cross-guarantees promote financing – whether from inside or outside the group. The previous chapter noted that subordination disincentivises intra-group lending. This chapter focuses on transaction avoidance. **7.02**

Transaction avoidance can have an economic effect similar to that of subordination, as both increase credit risk for a counterparty.[5] This follows from the fact that subordination and transaction avoidance rules limit 'the ability of debtors to engage in the transactions in the first instance'.[6] The word 'ability' is not used here in the factual sense (parties may still proceed with a transaction at their own risk), but rather in the economic sense. Transaction avoidance creates a chilling or deterrent effect. A financier is likely to be reluctant to finance restructuring efforts if it has to face transaction avoidance, should the restructuring attempt fail. Think of an intra-group guarantee. Will an external creditor, such as a bank, be willing to grant a loan to a distressed group entity, knowing that the guarantee offered by another group entity is likely to **7.03**

---

its assets are under the control of decision-makers who do not have the correct incentives to use them so as to benefit the company's new residual owners [creditors]'.

4 One such example is conduit-pipe financing. See R. de Weijs and M. Baltjes, Opening the Door for the Opportunistic Use of Interim Financing: A Critical Assessment of the EU Draft Directive on Preventive Restructuring Frameworks, International Insolvency Review, Vol. 27, 2018, p. 227, describing a situation where the granting of finance is not intended for the benefit of the recipient company but is instead used to pay off the debts for which the shareholder gave a guarantee. Also H. Bennett, Late Floating Charges, in J. Armour and H. Bennett (eds), Vulnerable Transactions in Corporate Insolvency, Hart Publishing, 2003, p. 201

5 A. Muscat, The Liability of the Holding Company for the Debts of its Insolvent Subsidiaries, Dartmouth Publishing Company, 1996, p. 238, viewing equitable subordination as a functional substitute to fraudulent conveyance law.

6 D.G. Baird and T.H. Jackson, Fraudulent Conveyance Law and Its Proper Domain, Vanderbilt Law Review, Vol. 38, 1985, p. 834, pointing out that 'in considering a legal rule such as fraudulent conveyance law, overbroad rules may be more pernicious than underbroad rules'.

be avoided if the guarantor itself ends up in insolvency? On this, Mevorach argues (and I fully agree) that routine attacks on intra-group guarantees in insolvency 'may deter lenders from providing funding in circumstances where the only security can be given by an affiliate knowing that the guarantee is likely to be attacked in the case of the guarantor liquidation'.[7]

7.04 Yet, cross-guarantees present substantial problems for transaction avoidance law, precisely because they are often driven by group interest and might not entail clear and direct benefits to group guarantors. This chapter examines the application of transaction avoidance rules and logic to intercompany guarantees as an example of a widely used group financing transaction. Section 7.2 examines national transaction avoidance law and concludes that legal uncertainty is inherent in the review of group guarantees. This uncertainty relates to the acceptance of group economic reality or 'group considerations' in transaction avoidance. Section 7.3 explores the difficulties of ex post review of intra-group transactions. Section 7.4 concludes.

7.2 'GROUP CONSIDERATIONS' IN INSOLVENCY TRANSACTION AVOIDANCE

7.2.1 Transaction avoidance and group specificity

7.05 The issue of validity and enforceability of cross-guarantees is of crucial importance. It makes a huge difference in terms of the size of creditor recovery and the overall dynamics of group insolvency. Historically, the review of transactions has fallen under the domain of transaction avoidance law. Roman law knew a remedial action for the rescission of conveyance in fraud of creditors, commonly known as *actio Pauliana*.[8] This action was available both in and outside insolvency.[9]

7.06 Transaction avoidance rules contribute to the achievement of various principles of insolvency law. Most notably, they seek to protect creditors from the diminution of assets available to them in insolvency, thereby promoting the preservation and maximisation of the insolvency estate value and ensuring

---

7 I. Mevorach, Insolvency within Multinational Enterprise Groups, OUP, 2009, p. 293. Also I. Mevorach, Transaction Avoidance in Bankruptcy of Corporate Groups, ECFR, Vol. 8, 2011, p. 249, observing that 'in a group scenario it may well be that intra-group guarantees … are the only way to secure any credit for the distressed affiliate and gain breathing-space for the group as a whole'.

8 R. Obenchain, The Roman Law of Bankruptcy, The Notre Dame Lawyer, Vol. 3, 1928, p. 200.

9 I. Pretelli, Cross-Border Credit Protection Against Fraudulent Transfers of Assets: Actio Pauliana in the Conflict of Laws, Yearbook of Private International Law, Vol. 13, 2011, p. 595, noting that the remedy was available to both *curator bonorum* and the creditors individually.

equal treatment of creditors.[10] UNCITRAL identifies three types of transactions that are subject to avoidance, found in most legal systems: (i) transactions intended to defeat, hinder or delay creditors from collecting their claims; (ii) transactions at an undervalue; (iii) preferential transactions.[11] The existence of different grounds for invalidating transactions (transaction avoidance risk) can influence parties' willingness to engage in a transaction in the first place. For example, a financier may decide not to grant a loan if there is a high risk that a group guarantee that should secure the loan might be successfully challenged in the future. This becomes problematic if the 'averted' loan transaction was, in fact, a value-creating one.

In this chapter, we do not aim to offer a detailed account of transaction avoidance law in specific jurisdictions.[12] Given the constraints of space and the main focus of this book, our attention is on group specificity. The central question revolves around the recognition and treatment of the group reality within the context of transaction avoidance law. Why does it matter? UNCITRAL observes that: 7.07

> Some transactions that might appear to be preferential or undervalued as between the immediate parties might be considered differently when viewed in the broader context of an enterprise group, where the benefits and detriments of transactions might be more widely assigned.[13]

In other words, the benefits and detriments of an intra-group transaction can be affected by the sheer economic position of the debtor within the group. Let's consider an example of a subsidiary that extends a guarantee benefiting a parent company. The guarantee may be a precondition for an external lender to provide financing to the parent company, or it may allow the parent company to negotiate better credit terms. While the subsidiary may not directly benefit from this transaction, it could still benefit indirectly by preserving the borrower's solvency, preventing the triggering of cross-defaults, ensuring a steady supply of goods and services from the borrower, or for other group-related reasons.[14] 7.08

---

10 K. van Zwieten, Goode on Principles of Corporate Insolvency Law, 5th student edn, Sweet & Maxwell, 2019, para. 13-03, explaining that 'avoidance provisions may thus be seen as necessary both to preserve the company's net assets and to ensure equality of distribution, at least among classes of creditors'.

11 UNCITRAL Legislative Guide, Part two, Ch. II, para. 170.

12 For an overview of national approaches to transaction avoidance in insolvency law, see R. Bork and M. Veder, Harmonisation of Transactions Avoidance Laws, 1st edn, Intersentia, 2022.

13 UNCITRAL Legislative Guide, Part three, Ch. II, para. 75.

14 See an example of this reasoning in the Decision of the Russian Supreme Court No. 310-ЭС20-18954 from 25 March 2021 (*Spar Lipetsk*), holding with respect to liability of a director of a subsidiary, which provided a guarantee: 'By itself, the issuance of such guarantees in favour of a credit institution insisting

7.09 Group-mindful application of transaction avoidance rules becomes particularly important in the context of insolvency and pre-insolvency rescue financing. In this respect, the World Bank opines that insolvency systems should 'permit an enterprise group member subject to insolvency proceedings to provide or facilitate post-commencement finance or other kind of financial assistance to other enterprises in the group which are also subject to insolvency proceedings'.[15] Similarly, UNCITRAL argues that insolvency law should permit an enterprise group member subject to insolvency proceedings to advance post-commencement finance to other group entities subject to insolvency proceedings, or grant security interest or guarantee in their favour.[16]

7.10 The reasoning is that, in specific circumstances – however limited they may be – intra-group support provided by one insolvent group member to another insolvent group member may serve the interests of both, e.g. by ensuring the continued operation or survival of the providing entity's business or preserving and enhancing its estate value.[17] UNCITRAL asserts, more generally, that the assessment of short and long-term implications for group members should permit, even if only in the short term, some detriment to the interests of an individual group entity and its creditors (short-term harm v. long-term gain).[18] Nevertheless, this does not mean that group interest can serve as a cover-up or justification for intra-group transactions that injure the creditors of an individual group entity, where a short-term detriment is *not* offset by long-term gain.

7.11 The next sections will examine the position of English, US and Dutch law on transaction avoidance in group insolvencies. It is impossible to analyse all types of transactions, which is why I will focus on a cross-guarantee, a transaction common in group financing (Chapter 5). This type of transaction is challenging to evaluate from the perspective of an individual group company that incurs a contingent obligation to pay to a guaranteed creditor. In fact, it may appear as a pure gift with no consideration being paid to the guarantor.

---

on additional security does not reveal the signs of unreasonableness or dishonesty in the behaviour of the guarantor's management ... even in a situation where the guarantor, acting in group interest and not with the purpose to injure creditors, assumes joint and several obligations to the bank in an amount exceeding its financial capabilities, believing that in the future the result of the group's activities will allow it to pay off the obligations of its members to creditors' (author's translation).

15 The World Bank, Principles for Effective Insolvency and Creditor/debtor Regimes, 2021, C16.2.

16 UNCITRAL Legislative Guide, Part three, Recommendations 211–213.

17 Ibid., Ch. II, para. 66. See also para. 71, adding that the particular interest of the providing entity may relate to the outcome for the entire group, especially if there is a high degree of integration and reliance between businesses of the group entities.

18 UNCITRAL Legislative Guide, Part four, Section two, para. 4.

7.2.2 The UK: measuring the value for the creditor and guarantor

Section 238 of the Insolvency Act 1986 provides that if a company has entered into a transaction at an undervalue at a relevant time (i.e. within two years leading up to the onset of insolvency),[19] an IP may apply to the court for relief, restoring the position to what it would have been if the company had not entered into that transaction. Importantly, the law adds that the debtor must be unable to pay its debts at the relevant time or should become unable to do so in consequence of the transaction – only then the time becomes 'relevant'.[20] The inability to pay debts is presumed, unless the contrary is demonstrated, if the transaction is entered into by a person who is connected to the debtor company.[21] **7.12**

The Insolvency Act 1986 specifies that a transaction at an undervalue could be a gift (transfer of an asset for no consideration) or a contract for no consideration (e.g. a voluntary release of a debt), or a disposition for consideration worth *significantly* less than the value of the return consideration.[22] It is recognised that a guarantee transaction is not a gift or a no-consideration contract, even if the recipient of funds from the creditor – the borrower-principal debtor – is a different entity and the objective value of the advance to the guarantor is nil.[23] In fact, the consideration is the advance made to the borrower because this is 'the act exacted by the surety as the price of his guarantee'.[24] The fact that the advance is made to the principal debtor rather than the guarantor does not automatically render the guarantee a transaction at an undervalue.[25] **7.13**

Besides, not every undervalued transaction can be avoided. Section 238(5) of the Insolvency Act 1986 provides a defence on the basis that there may be a legitimate reason for a party, such as a guarantor, to enter into a transaction at an undervalue. This defence applies if the transaction is entered into: (i) in good faith and for the purpose of carrying out the party's own business; and in the circumstances, where (ii) at the time there were reasonable grounds to **7.14**

19 Insolvency Act 1986, s. 240(1).

20 Insolvency Act 1986, s. 240(2).

21 Ibid. For a definition of a 'connected party', see s. 249 of the Insolvency Act 1986, mentioning among such parties 'an associate of the company'. In most cases, group members will be associates of each other and therefore constitute connected parties. See s. 435 of the Insolvency Act 1986. An outside lender will typically not be a connected party.

22 Insolvency Act 1986, s. 238(4).

23 K. van Zwieten, Goode on Principles of Corporate Insolvency Law, 5th edn, Sweet & Maxwell, 2018, paras. 13-23 and 13-32; D. Spahos, Lenders, Borrowing Groups of Companies and Corporate Guarantees: An Insolvency Perspective, Journal of Corporate Law Studies, Vol. 1, 2001, p. 336.

24 K. van Zwieten, Goode on Principles of Corporate Insolvency Law, 5th student edn, Sweet & Maxwell, 2019, para. 13-32. See also J.G. Doyle, Insolvency Litigation, Sweet & Maxwell, 1999, p. 205.

25 Ibid. (Van Zwieten), para. 13-32.

believe that the transaction in question would benefit the party. The assessment of whether there were such reasonable grounds is done objectively. For the defence to be available, it is not necessary for the transaction to have been beneficial in practice. Both elements (good faith and propriety of purpose and reasonableness) must be established at the same time.[26] If any of the elements is not present, the transaction remains vulnerable.

7.15 The first question to answer is whether a cross-guarantee qualifies as a transaction at an undervalue. The 'value' refers to the amount that a reasonably well-informed purchaser is willing, in arm's-length negotiations, to pay for an asset.[27] Where there is a market for an asset, its value can be determined by comparing the price of a substitute asset in the market.[28] However, when the asset is unique, such a comparison may not be possible. Because there is generally no market for corporate guarantees, determining the guarantee's market value and equality of exchange is difficult.

7.16 According to Goode, the crucial question is 'whether the benefit conferred on the creditor by the issue of the guarantee is significantly greater than the value to the surety of the advance to the principal debtor'.[29] Therefore, the balancing exercise involves measuring the value of the guarantee to the creditor, on the one hand, and the value of the guaranteed financing for the guarantor, on the other hand.[30] Should there be a *significant* difference between these two values, the transaction avoidance rules are triggered.[31] This approach is unusual

---

26 *Wallach v. Secretary of State for Trade and Industry* [2006] EWHC 989 (Ch). The burden of proof in establishing the defence rests on the party seeking to defend the transaction against its avoidance under s. 238.

27 *Phillips (Liquidator of AJ Bekhor & Co) v. Brewin Dolphin Bell Lawrie Ltd* [2001] 1 WLR 143, at 30.

28 *Re Brabon, Treharne v. Brabon* [2001] BCLC 11, at 38; *Spencer v. The Commonwealth* (1907) 5 CLR 418, at 431.

29 R. Goode, Principles of Corporate Insolvency Law, 4th edn, Sweet & Maxwell, 2011, para. 13-34. Also R. Goode and L. Gullifer, Goode and Gullifer on Legal Problems of Credit and Security, 6th edn, Sweet & Maxwell, 2017, para. 8-37, pointing out that 'in deciding whether a guarantee gives rise to a transaction at an undervalue the act which constitutes the transaction is the giving of the guarantee, not the creditor's subsequent call under the guarantee'.

30 This line of thinking was adopted in *Tailby v. HSBC Bank Plc* [2015] BPIR 143 (case on s. 339), pointing out that the value of the guarantee was originally minimal, while at the same time there was a real commercial benefit to the guarantor on several levels. See *Levy McCallum Ltd v. Allen* [2007] N.I Ch. 3, where the principal borrower and the guarantor belonged to the same group of companies and the guarantor extended the guarantee trying to improve its chances of receiving payment from the principal debtor.

31 D. Spahos, Lenders, Borrowing Groups of Companies and Corporate Guarantees: An Insolvency Perspective, Journal of Corporate Law Studies, Vol. 1, 2001, p. 338, highlighting that 'only where the value of the impeached guarantee significantly exceeds the value of the economic benefit flowing to the surety will section 238 come into play'. See, however, R. Bork, Transactions at an Undervalue – A Comparison of English and German Law, Journal of Corporate Law Studies, Vol. 14, 2014, p. 473, arguing that '[e]ven if indirect advantages, like the support of a parent company's interest in the financing of its subsidiary, are taken into account, these advantages will normally be of significantly less value than the security …'.

because the 'value' of a transaction is commonly assessed from the viewpoint of the debtor company (in our case, a group guarantor), and not from that of a third party (in our case, an outside lender). For instance, in *MC Bacon*, Millett J. observed that the assessment of the transaction requires 'a comparison to be made between the value obtained by the company for the transaction and the value of consideration provided by the company. Both values must be ... considered from the company's point of view.'[32]

However, the case of a guarantee transaction is somewhat special. Since a guarantee creates a contingent liability that may never crystallise, its value to the creditor and guarantor is often linked or (negatively) correlated. The more value the guarantee provides to the creditor (i.e. the more protection it offers), arguably the less value and the higher the risk or exposure it entails for the guarantor. In this respect, Goode suggests several factors to consider when assessing the value of a guarantee: 7.17

- **Principal debtor's financial strength**. If the principal debtor's financial position is strong and likely to remain stable, and the guarantee is unlikely to be called upon, it may be argued that such a guarantee holds relatively small value for the creditor,[33] as the creditor can receive full satisfaction from the principal debtor. The principal debtor's financial strength also correlates with the level of the guarantor's risk. The stronger the principal debtor, the smaller the guarantor's risk.
- **Existence of security (e.g. mortgage, charge) furnished by the principal debtor**. When the principal debtor provides *in rem* security to the creditor, it not only improves the creditor's position but also positively affects the guarantor. If the guarantor ends up paying, it will have the right to be subrogated to the security held by the creditor, thereby reducing the guarantor's risk.
- **Presence of other guarantors guaranteeing the same obligation**. If the guarantor pays in discharge of common liability, it generally acquires the right to seek contribution from the co-guarantors, who are likely to be members of the same group of companies. This, in turn, may reduce the risks for the paying guarantor.[34]

---

32 *Re MC Bacon Ltd (No. 1)* [1990] BCC 78, at 92.

33 K. van Zwieten, Goode on Principles of Corporate Insolvency Law, 5th student edn, Sweet & Maxwell, 2019, para. 13-33. Where the principal debtor is 'on the rocks' and the guarantee merely staves off disaster, the guarantee will most certainly constitute a transaction at an undervalue (see para. 13-34). However, it is noted that in practice 'it is unlikely that a guarantee will be impeached as a transaction at an undervalue except where it is clearly of no benefit to the surety company'. For a similar position, see G.D. Vinter, Project Finance: A Legal Guide, 3rd edn, Sweet & Maxwell, 2006, p. 375. Also, R. Goode and L. Gullifer, Goode and Gullifer on Legal Problems of Credit and Security, 6th edn, Sweet & Maxwell, 2017, para. 8-37, concluding that 'in the ordinary way a guarantee is unlikely to be held a transaction at an undervalue unless there is both a serious risk of default and no benefit to the surety ...'.

34 K. van Zwieten, Goode on Principles of Corporate Insolvency Law, 5th edn, Sweet & Maxwell, 2018, paras. 13-33 and 13-34.

7.18 The second question is whether, even if there is an undervalue, the defence of section 238(5) of the Insolvency Act 1986 is available. Parry and Shivji consider this question in the context of intra-group support and conclude that there is nothing to prevent the defence from being applicable where one group entity makes a payment for the benefit of another. However, what ultimately matters is the benefit received by the paying entity, rather than the benefit enjoyed by the group as a whole.[35] Nevertheless, such benefit may arise from the fact that the receiving entity 'needs funds in order to complete a particular contract so as to avoid liquidation and to avoid taking the entire group with it'.[36] The common economic goal and survival of the entire group could be taken into account when evaluating the benefits of the transaction from the providing entity's perspective. But if this entity itself is on the verge of insolvency or already insolvent, determining the benefit becomes challenging. It is difficult to argue that the payment was made to carry out *its own business* in such circumstances.[37] Similarly, if the group entity receiving intra-group support is irredeemably insolvent, particularly due to the non-viability of its business core, the defence is more likely to fail.

7.19 The defence of section 238(5) can also apply to intercompany guarantees. For this to work, it must be demonstrated that the guarantor acted in good faith and had reasonable grounds to believe that the guarantee was for the guarantor's own benefit. The benefit received by the guarantor is, therefore, one of the key elements. In the group context, it may be the case that the guarantor receives an indirect benefit if its interests are aligned with or dependent on those of the principal debtor, and the guarantee was issued as part of a group restructuring – a group-related benefit.[38]

---

35 E. Ferran and L.C. Ho, Principles of Corporate Finance Law, 2nd edn, OUP, 2014, p. 35, noting that 'since the interests of a failing company are identified with those of its own creditors rather than those of its shareholders or of the collective interests of the group's creditors, actions taken in the interests of the group will be particularly vulnerable under these sections [s. 238 and s. 239 Insolvency Act 1986]'. *Re Genosyis Technology* [2006] EWHC 989 (Ch), at 25, drawing the line between the interests of the English group entity and those of other group entities with application to directors' duties.

36 R. Parry and S. Shivji, Transactions at an Undervalue (Insolvency Act 1986, ss. 238 and 339), in R. Parry et al. (eds), Transaction Avoidance in Insolvencies, 3rd edn, OUP, 2018, para. 4.166; A. Muscat, The Liability of the Holding Company for the Debts of its Insolvent Subsidiaries, Dartmouth Publishing Company, 1996, p. 232, noting that 'many such guarantees should be saved from the clutches of section 238 on the basis of the defence [of section 238(5)]'.

37 Ibid. (Parry and Shivji), para. 4.167.

38 Ibid., para. 4.171. See also J. Armour, Transactions at an Undervalue, in J. Armour and H. Bennett (eds), Vulnerable Transactions in Corporate Insolvency, Hart Publishing, 2003, p. 70, discussing indirect consideration in the context of an upstream guarantee and giving an example, where the subsidiary (guarantor) relies upon the parent company for much of its business and the guarantee is necessary for the parent's continued trading. For a sceptical view on group-related indirect benefits, see J. O'Donovan, Lender Liability, English edn, Sweet & Maxwell, 2005, para. 10.80, arguing that the 'court may not value very highly the intangible benefits of operating in a group …'.

The analysis of the benefits can be carried out for different types of guarantees: downstream, cross-stream and upstream guarantees. For a downstream guarantee, it is easier to see the benefit, as it could arise from the enhancement of the subsidiary's position, in which shares are held by the parent company-guarantor. For a cross-stream guarantee, the situation is less straightforward. The benefit may emerge if the advance made to a sister company is made available to the guarantor or if it is used to refinance the entire group. Finally, assessing the guarantor's benefit for an upstream guarantee is a matter of considerable difficulty. Again, the benefit may be observed if the advance received by the parent is shared with the guarantor or if it is used to ensure group restructuring, upon which the guarantor's own survival is based. Another factor to consider is whether the guarantor receives a fee for providing the guarantee, which might salvage the guarantee from avoidance.[39] But then, there remains a question of whether the fee is adequate and whether the relevant values are *significantly* different, given the risks assumed by the guarantor. 7.20

In considering potential benefits to the guarantor, regard must be had to what the provision of a guarantee sought to achieve (i.e. the motives of the guarantor). Hence, if the guarantee was extended to support the principal debtor's gamble for resurrection[40] or its last-ditch attempt to avoid insolvency, regardless of how unlikely its success, there may be little potential benefit for the guarantor. Instead, there is a real risk of the guarantee being called in. The benefits and risk also depend on the presence of adequate security that the guarantor can 'inherit' and on the existence of other guarantors. Of course, the real effect of these safeguards will depend on the value of the security and the financial position of co-guarantors. Interestingly, while the mental element (subjective intent) of the guarantor plays a role in determining the availability of the defence, the law does not establish a similar element on the counterparty's (i.e. outsider lender's) side.[41] 7.21

To sum up, group guarantees present unique challenges for transaction avoidance rules. This is because the law requires the assessment of the present value of a contingent right conferred on the creditor by the guarantee and its relation to the benefit received by the guarantor from the advance made to the principal 7.22

---

39 Ibid. (Parry and Shivji), para. 4.179. Note, however, that in most cases, the consideration for a guarantee consists entirely of some advantage given to the principal debtor by the creditor. This may include forbearance from suing the principal debtor or granting a loan to the principal debtor. G. Andrews and R. Millett, Law of Guarantees, 4th edn, Sweet & Maxwell, 2005, para. 2-008.

40 Posner refers to 'gambling for resurrection' as the 'incentive of a firm at risk of insolvency to roll the dice …' R.A. Posner, The Crisis of Capitalist Democracy, HUP, 2010, p. 91.

41 G. McCormack, National Report for the UK, in R. Bork and M. Veder, Harmonisation of Transaction Avoidance Laws, Intersentia, 2022, p. 1294.

debtor. In practice, various factors can impact this fact-intensive inquiry and influence the value of the guarantee to the creditor and guarantor. These factors may include group considerations, such as the recovery of the group and the risks that may arise from group destabilisation.

7.23 English law provides a defence of good faith, propriety of purpose and reasonableness, which might alter the outcome and 'save' an otherwise undervalued transaction. That being said, it is generally true that the higher the risk of default by the principal obligor (e.g. due to financial distress or insolvency), the more likely it is that the guarantee will fall under close scrutiny. This applies to both the assessment of the guarantee's value and the use of the defence.

7.2.3 The USA: in search for future and indirect benefits

7.24 When it comes to US law, the relevant provisions concern the remedy for fraudulent transfers. As explained in Collier on Bankruptcy, fraudulent transfer law provides the possibility 'to avoid transactions which unfairly or improperly deplete a debtor's assets or that unfairly or improperly dilute the claims against those assets'.[42]

7.25 The US Bankruptcy Code permits a trustee[43] to challenge (avoid) any transfer of an interest of the debtor in property, or any obligation incurred by the debtor, that was made or incurred on or within two years before the date of the bankruptcy filing. A transfer made or an obligation incurred prior to the beginning of the statutory look-back period is invulnerable to an attack as fraudulent. A look-back period may, however, be longer if the action is brought using state fraudulent transfer law.[44] Notably, a transfer or obligation incurred after the bankruptcy filing cannot be considered a fraudulent transfer. But if it is 'unauthorised', it may still be subject to avoidance.[45] I will focus on pre-petition intra-group transactions, such as cross-guarantees, that fall under the rules on fraudulent transfers.

---

42 Collier on Bankruptcy, 16th edn, 2022, Vol. 5, ¶ 548.01.

43 Note that § 548 vests the power to avoid fraudulent transfers in the bankruptcy trustee, but in Chapter 11, § 1107 expands the definition of a 'trustee' to include a debtor in possession.

44 The law allows the trustee to avoid any transfer of an interest of the debtor in property or any obligation incurred by the debtor that would otherwise be available to debtor's creditors under state law. 11 U.S. Code § 544(b). Many US states enacted a version of the Uniform Fraudulent Transfers Act, or its slightly modified successor, the Uniform Voidable Transactions Act.

45 11 U.S. Code § 549(a). Filing a bankruptcy petition transforms all debtor's property into property of the estate (11 U.S. Code § 541(a)(1)). From that moment, transfers of the debtor's property are prohibited, unless they fall within a statutory exception, such as transfers authorised under the Bankruptcy Code (e.g. transfers in the ordinary course of business) or by the court.

A transaction may be challenged if the debtor (i) made a transfer or incurred liability with the actual intent to hinder, delay or defraud creditors ('actual' fraudulent transfers);[46] or (ii) received less than a reasonable equivalent value in exchange for such a transfer or obligation ('constructive' fraudulent transfers).[47] 7.26

The first fraudulent conveyance statutes permitted reversal of transactions only if the debtor's ill intent was proven. Yet finding such intent can be difficult if the debtor does not cooperate and the transaction has a legitimate business purpose unrelated to injuring creditors.[48] Usually, intercompany guarantees are legitimate business transactions that are not made to defraud creditors. In contrast, the application of constructive fraudulent transfer rules is not premised on showing the debtor's intent to harm creditors' interests. Instead, it requires some extra pre-requisites or 'plus' factors that make a transaction suspicious and typically signal an increased likelihood of harm. These factors include, inter alia, the debtor's insolvency at the time of the transaction, the debtor becoming insolvent as a result of the transfer or the assumption of an obligation, or the debtor incurring debts beyond its ability to pay as they mature.[49] If the guarantor is insolvent when providing a guarantee, or becomes insolvent as a result of it, or is left with unreasonably small capital, therefore making insolvency highly likely, the guarantee is vulnerable to a fraudulent transfer attack. 7.27

The rules on constructively fraudulent transfers are often used to challenge intra-group support transactions. The purpose of voiding transfers that are not supported by 'reasonably equivalent value' is to protect creditors against the depletion of the debtor's estate.[50] As Clark pointed out, 'be just before you are generous'.[51] When deciding what constitutes 'reasonably equivalent value', the definition of 'value' given in the US Bankruptcy Code is relevant. According to this definition, 'value' means 'property, or satisfaction or securing of a present 7.28

46 11 U.S. Code § 548(a)(1)(A).
47 11 U.S. Code § 548(a)(1)(B)(i).
48 A prima facie case of fraudulent intent can be established by offering proof of various badges of fraud. These badges include, among others, '(1) a close relationship among the parties to the transaction; (2) secret and hasty transfer not in the usual course of business; (3) inadequacy of consideration; (4) transferor's knowledge of the creditor's claim and the transferor's inability to pay it; (5) use of dummies or fictitious parties; and (6) retention of control of property by the transferor after the conveyance'. *Rosener v. Majestic Mgmt. (In re OODC, LLC)*, 321 B.R. 128, 140 (Bankr. D. Del. 2005).
49 11 U.S. Code § 548(a)(1)(B)(ii).
50 *In re Rodriguez*, 895 F.2d 725, 727 (11th Cir. 1990).
51 R.C. Clark, The Duties of the Corporate Debtor to its Creditors, Harvard Law Review, Vol. 90, 1977, p. 510.

or antecedent debt of the debtor …'[52] The application of this definition to cross-guarantees is problematic, as in most cases, a guarantor does not receive any payment as consideration. As a general rule, obligations incurred by the debtor (guarantor) solely for the benefit of a third party (borrower) are treated as not being supported by reasonably equivalent value.[53] However, in recognition of group realities and contemporary financial practices, in several cases courts have departed from an earlier, stricter approach to the value determination, and acknowledged that future or indirect benefits might be accepted.[54] Collier on Bankruptcy identifies three circumstances in which an indirect benefit was recognised (not specifically or solely in the guarantee context):

> (i) the debtor and the third party are closely related or share an identity of interests, so that what benefits one will benefit the other on something close to a dollar-for-dollar basis; or (ii) the debtor had the actual use and benefit of the goods or services for which the third party was obligated, again on something close to a dollar-for-dollar basis; or (iii) when the transfer also satisfied an obligation for which the debtor was liable.[55]

7.29 The intercompany guarantee and, more generally, group financing relationships can fall under these circumstances. For example, in *Mellon Bank*, the court found reasonably equivalent value for the debtor's guarantee of an affiliate's debt when the loan strengthened the corporate group as a whole, so that the guarantor would benefit from the synergy within the group.[56] In *In re Young*, the court explained that the correct way to determine value was not to define it 'only in terms of tangible property or marketable financial value', but instead to 'examine … all aspects of the transaction and carefully measure … the value of all benefits and burdens to the debtor, direct or indirect, including "indirect economic benefits"'.[57] In *Telefest Inc.*, it was first stressed

---

52 11 U.S. Code § 548(d)(2)(A). Note that whereas 'value' is defined, 'reasonably equivalent value' is not. For example, the Third Circuit described it as follows: 'The touchstone is whether the transaction conferred realizable commercial value on the debtor reasonably equivalent to the commercial value of the assets transferred. Thus, when the debtor is a going concern and its realizable going concern after the transaction is equal to or exceeds its going concern value before the transaction, reasonably equivalent value has been received.' *Mellon Bank, N.A. v. Metro Communications, Inc.*, 945 F.2d 635, 647 (3rd Cir. 1991).

53 *Tourtellot v. Huntington Nat'l Bank (In re Renegade Holdings, Inc.)*, 457 B.R. 441, 444 (Bankr. M.D.N.C. 2011); *Rubin v. Mfrs. Hanover Trust Co.*, 661 F.2d 979, 991 (2d Cir. 1981).

54 *Rubin v. Manufacturers Hanover Trust Co.*, 661 F2d 979, 991 (2d Cir. 1981), holding that 'the transaction's benefit to the debtor need not be direct; it may come indirectly through benefit to a third person'. *In re Image Worldwide, Ltd.*, 139 F.3d 574, 578 (7th Cir. 1998), noting that '[i]ntercorporate guarantees are routine business practice, and their potential voidability creates a risk for unwary lenders'.

55 Collier on Bankruptcy, 16th edn, 2022, Vol. 5, ¶ 548.05[2][b].

56 *Mellon Bank, N.A. v. Metro Communications, Inc.*, 945 F.2d 635, 647 (3rd Cir. 1991). The court pointed out that indirect benefits included intangibles such as goodwill and an increased ability to borrow working capital.

57 *United States v. Crystal Evangelical Free Church (In re Young)*, 82 F.3d 1407, 1415 (8th Cir. 1996), vacated on other grounds.

that requiring a direct flow of capital to a guarantor to avoid a finding of a fraudulent transfer 'is inhibitory of contemporary financing practices, which recognise that cross-guarantees are often needed because of the unequal abilities of interrelated corporate entities to collateralise loans'.[58] The court then indicated that indirect benefits to a guarantor can exist when 'the transaction of which the guaranty is a part may safeguard an important source of supply, or an important customer for the guarantor'.[59] It suggested that 'substantial indirect benefits may result from the general relationship between the parent company and its subsidiaries, rather than the particular transaction giving rise to the guaranty'.[60] In *Fairchild*, the cross-stream financing was insulated from transaction avoidance, as the companies – the debtor-aircraft manufacturer and the debtor's affiliate, a commuter airline – shared an identity of interest, and the debtor benefited from the continued operation of the airline.[61]

It is important to keep in mind that while cross-guarantees may enhance the overall value of the enterprise group, including the guarantor, they can also merely shift risk from one group entity to another or support a resurrection gamble, particularly if no viable enterprise exists. In the case concerning the insolvency of TOUSA Inc. and its subsidiaries, formerly one of the largest homebuilding enterprises in the USA, it was concluded that the argument of bankruptcy prevention (survival of the group) cited to prove the benefit for the subsidiaries-lien providers arising from financing acquired by their borrower-parent was not persuasive. The bankruptcy court observed that 'not every transfer that decreases the odds of bankruptcy for a corporation can be justified'.[62] It did not decide whether a chance to avoid bankruptcy can in principle constitute 'reasonably equivalent value'. Instead, it found that in the case at hand, financing secured by the subsidiaries' liens only delayed the inevitable collapse, as '[i]n contrast to the surprise attack at Pearl Harbor, the warnings about the collapse of TOUSA [debtor] made that event as foreseeable as the bombing of Nagasaki after President Truman's ultimatum'.[63] Notably, the court in the first instance, whose judgment was affirmed on appeal, examined the group characteristics. It noted that the insolvency of the parent company would not necessarily have caused the subsidiaries to declare bankruptcy, and 7.30

58 *Telefest, Inc. v. VU-TV, Inc.*, 591 F.Supp. 1368, 1379 (D.C.N.J. 1984).
59 Ibid., at 1381.
60 Ibid. See also *In re Tryit Enterprises*, 121 B.R. 217 (Bankr. S.D. Tex. 1990), refusing to annul cross-guarantees on the basis that they were necessary for the optimal (group) financing arrangement.
61 *Matter of Fairchild Aircraft Corp.*, 6 F.3d 1119, 1126 (C.A.5 (Tex.) 1993).
62 *In re Tousa*, 680 F.3d 1298, 1311 (11th Cir. 2012).
63 Ibid., at 1313.

that the subsidiaries could have operated as independent entities without the services provided by the parent.[64]

7.31 *TOUSA* brings into focus the fraudulent transfer risk in financial arrangements within complex corporate families, especially where the borrower and the affiliated guarantors are financially distressed or when their insolvency is foreseeable at the time of the transaction. It also shows that the avoidance risk increases if the borrower is non-viable, and if the guarantor can function independently of its group affiliates.

7.32 As mentioned in the previous section, the analysis of benefits stemming from a corporate guarantee or its reasonable equivalent value may differ in situations where the guarantee is provided by the corporate parent (downstream guarantee). In the USA, courts tend to presume that the parent corporation receives a benefit in the form of increased stock value flowing from the increased strength and value of its subsidiary when the subsidiary obtains a loan guaranteed by the parent.[65] Therefore, downstream guarantees are largely shielded from attacks under fraudulent transfer rules.[66] Some courts have recognised this important point and noted that the otherwise applicable presumption of indirect benefits arising from a downstream guarantee does not apply if the subsidiary, whose obligation is guaranteed by the parent, is insolvent at the time of the transaction in which the guarantee is extended.[67]

---

64 *In re Tousa, Inc.*, 422 B.R. 783, 847 (Bankr. S.D. Fla. 2009).

65 *In re Royal Crown Bottlers of N. Am., Inc.*, 23. B.R. 28, 30 (Bankr. N.D. Ala. 1982), stating that 'the passing to a subsidiary of the consideration for a transfer by a debtor-parent may be presumed to be substantial ...'; *Branch v. Fed. Deposit Ins. Corp.*, 825 F.Supp. 384, 400 (D. Mass. 1993), noting that the 'Court is aware of no case in which transfers to a solvent subsidiary have been determined to be for less than equivalent value'. P. Blumberg, Intragroup (Upstream, Cross-Stream, and Downstream) Guarantees under the Uniform Fraudulent Transfer Act, Cardozo Law Review, Vol. 9, 1987, p. 701, explaining that in case of a downstream guarantee 'additional liability incurred by the parent is offset by a comparable increase in the value of its equity interest'. R.K. Rasmussen, Guarantees and Section 548(a)(2) of the Bankruptcy Code, The University of Chicago Law Review, Vol. 52, 1985, p. 215, arguing that when a debtor guarantees the obligations of its wholly owned subsidiary, 'there should be a rebuttable presumption that the debtor received a reasonably equivalent value through indirect benefits'.

66 *Branch v. Fed. Deposit Ins. Corp.*, 825 F.Supp. 384, 389 (D. Mass. 1993) ('Generally, transfers to a solvent subsidiary are considered to be for reasonably equivalent value, because, since the parent is the sole shareholder of the subsidiary corporation, any benefit received by the subsidiary is also a benefit to the parent'). See, however, R. Squire, Distress-triggered Liabilities and the Agency Costs of Debt, in B.E. Adler (ed), Research Handbook on Corporate Bankruptcy Law, Edward Elgar Publishing, 2020, p. 137, stating that 'a downstream guarantee – despite being the variety least vulnerable to fraudulent-transfer attack – typically produces a larger distortive transfer than an otherwise equivalent cross-stream guarantee, as the parent's equity stake in the subsidiary increases the correlation between the two entities' insolvency risks'.

67 *In re Renegade Holdings*, Inc., 457 B.R. 441, 445 (Bankr. M.D.N.C. 2011), at 446 also noting that 'the totality of the circumstances to be considered in assessing and weighing value versus obligation in this case includes the insolvency ... and whether the enterprise involving the Debtors and PTM [subsidiary-borrower] was *commercially viable*' (emphasis added). Also, *In re Duque Rodriguez*, 77 B.R. 937, 939 (Bankr. S.D. Fla. 1987).

In summary, the US Bankruptcy Code's approach to avoiding intra-group guarantees shares certain similarities with the Insolvency Act 1986. Both require a fact-intensive analysis of the benefits (value) of the transaction at the time of its conclusion. This analysis can include future and indirect benefits, such as those arising from relationships and synergies with the principal debtor or from group operations – especially in closely integrated, interdependent corporate groups.[68] As in the UK, it is more challenging to defend an intra-group transfer (e.g. a guarantee, collateral or provision of capital) if, at the time of transfer, the guarantor and/or the principal debtor were insolvent or nearing insolvency. The type of guarantee (downstream, upstream or cross-stream) is equally important. Downstream guarantees are generally less vulnerable to fraudulent transfer claims, though they may still be subject to avoidance as constructively fraudulent transfers if the subsidiary-borrower was insolvent at the time when the parent company extended the guarantee. In terms of differences, whereas the UK approach looks at whether there is a significant imbalance between the benefits (value) of the guarantee to the creditor and the value generated by the loan to the guarantor, the US approach mainly focuses on the benefits to the guarantor, whether direct or indirect. In practice, this difference may have limited impact, as both values tend to be correlated. 7.33

7.2.4 The Netherlands: *Faillissementspauliana*

The Dutch Bankruptcy Act sets out rules for transaction avoidance related to insolvency (*actio pauliana*) in Articles 42–51. There are two principal sets of rules.[69] One of them, namely Article 42 Fw, governs the avoidance (annulment) of legal acts that the debtor had no prior obligation to perform. A legal act is considered obligatory if the debtor is legally obliged to perform it or, in other words, when a prior enforceable legal obligation existed for the debtor to perform the legal act in question.[70] If such a legal obligation exists, a legal act can only be challenged on the basis of Article 47 Fw, and not Article 42 Fw. Understandably, the requirements for avoiding obligatory legal acts are stricter than those for non-obligatory acts. In this section, I will first address 7.34

68 Greer et al. argue (and we concur) that where 'the parties involved are genuinely interdependent in some form or where the guaranty will enable the guarantor and affiliate for which it has provided a guaranty to realize genuinely synergistic gains …, the courts should protect the transfer, notwithstanding the fact that the estate may have been somewhat diminished by the transaction'. B.E. Greer, J.S. Moss and N.B. Herther-Spiro, Guarantees in Bankruptcy: A Primer II, Norton Annual Survey of Bankruptcy Law, 2014 edn, p. 209.

69 On both sets of rules, see B. Wessels, Gevolgen van faillietverklaring (Wessels Insolventierecht nr. III), 5e druk, Deventer: Wolters Kluwer, 2019, paras. 3017-3273.

70 R.J. de Weijs and D.G.J. Heems, GS Faillissementswet, commentaar op art. 42 Fw; R.D. Vriesendorp, Insolventierecht, Deventer: Wolters Kluwer, 2021.

avoidance under Article 47 Fw and then proceed with the rule under Article 42 Fw (see Figure 7.1).

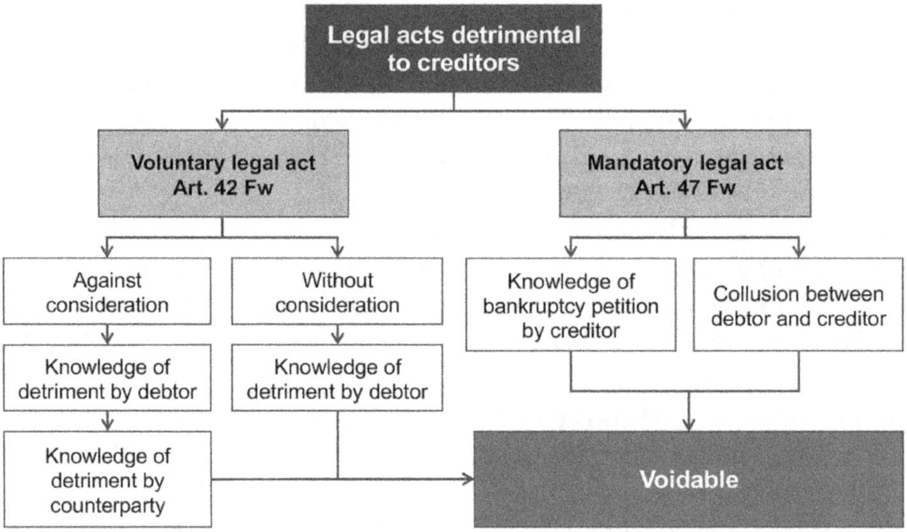

Note: This figure is based on N.B. Pannevis, The European harmonisation of avoidance rules, a Dutch perspective on reshaping an age-old instrument, Tvl 2023/12, p. 78.

Figure 7.1 Transaction avoidance in Dutch insolvency law

7.35 A guarantee may qualify as an obligatory legal act if the guarantor committed to providing it before the actual issuance, such as when a lender extends credit to a borrower contingent on a future guarantee.[71] According to Article 47 Fw, the performance of a due and demandable (payable) obligation (*opeisbare schuld*) can be annulled based on fraudulent conveyance, but only if it is demonstrated that either the other party was aware of a pending bankruptcy petition or the performance occurred due to consultations (*overleg*) between the debtor and creditor with the intent to favour that creditor. According to the Dutch Supreme Court, this second criterion requires collusion.[72] Unlike

71 R.J. de Weijs and D.G.J. Heems, GS Faillissementswet, commentaar op art. 42 Fw, observing that a broad interpretation should be given to what may constitute an obligatory legal act, and that it may encompass the creation of a security right. See HR 1 February 2013, *JOR* 2013/155, *NJ* 2013/156 (*Van Leuveren q.q./ ING*), dealing with silent pledging of future claims by means of a collective deed construction (*verzamelpandakteconstructie*). Yet, if the prior legal obligation exists, the creation of such a prior legal obligation may itself be challenged under Article 42 Fw.

72 HR 24 March 1995, *NJ* 1995/628 (*Gispen q.q./IFN*).

Article 42 Fw (see further below), Article 47 Fw does not distinguish between gratuitous legal acts and legal acts for consideration.

As noted in the previous paragraph, for a successful challenge under Article 47 Fw, the creditor must be aware of the bankruptcy petition, or there must be collusion between the debtor and creditor. These elements must be restrictively interpreted. Regarding the creditor awareness, it is not sufficient for the creditor to merely know of the debtor's impending or unavoidable insolvency;[73] instead, it must be shown that the creditor had knowledge of the filed bankruptcy petition. This rule is easy to apply in practice, which, according to the legislator's intent, should facilitate transactional certainty. Unless the creditor and the guarantor share the same directors or a creditor has been explicitly notified of the bankruptcy filing, it will be difficult to demonstrate that the creditor was aware of the filed petition. 7.36

Proving collusion under Article 47 Fw is even more challenging, as it demands more than mere awareness of disadvantage;[74] the debtor and creditor must share an actual intent to favour the creditor.[75] In *Cikam/Siemon qq*, the Dutch Supreme Court upheld the judgment of the Court of Appeal, which assumed collusion (subject to rebuttal) based on a close relationship between the creditor and debtor – specifically, shared officers and mutual knowledge of the debtor's financial troubles.[76] In contrast, demonstrating collusion is difficult if the guaranteed creditor is unrelated to the debtor. 7.37

In practice, it is more likely that an IP will challenge a guarantee under Article 42 Fw, which applies to voluntary (non-obligatory) legal acts. After all, intercompany guarantees are usually provided without a prior obligation to grant them. Importantly, the use of the parent company's power of instruction over the subsidiary-guarantor, whether legal or economic, does not make the guarantee an obligatory legal act.[77] 7.38

According to Article 42 Fw, if a debtor performs a voluntary act before the start of bankruptcy proceedings and if it knew or should have known that 7.39

---

73 HR 29 June 2001, *JOR* 2001/220, *NJ* 2001/662 (*Meijs qq/Bank of Tokyo*).

74 HR 20 November 1998, *NJ* 1999/611 (*Verkerk Varkenshandel/Tiethoff q.q.*).

75 HR 24 March 1995, *NJ* 1995/628, m.nt. P. van Schilfgaarde (*Gispen q.q./IFN*). R.D. Vriesendorp, Art. 47 FW: een geamputeerde tentakel of verdient de curator meer? in S.C.J.J. Kortmann e.a. (red.), De curator, een octopus, Zwolle: W.E.J. Tjeenk Willink, 1996, pp. 65–79; R.D. Vriesendorp, Enkele grenzen van artikel 47 Fw verkend: een machtig wapen voor de curator of een dode letter, Insolad Jaarboek 2014, Deventer: Kluwer 2015, pp. 165–193.

76 HR 7 March 2003, *JOR* 2003/102, *NJ* 2003/429 (*Cikam/Siemon q.q.*).

77 Even if there is economic necessity, perceived or real, to perform a legal act, this does not mean that such legal act is mandatory. HR 10 December 1976, *NJ* 1977/617 (*Eneca/BACM*).

this act would harm creditors' recovery rights, this legal act (*rechtshandeling*) is voidable on the ground of fraudulent conveyance and may be nullified on the application of an insolvency practitioner. This rule is designed to protect creditors from legal acts that prejudice them in insolvency. It targets (1) actions that reduce creditors' recovery and damage both the debtor and creditors (e.g. selling property below market value or assuming new debts without equivalent value – undervalued transactions); and (2) actions that are neutral to the debtor itself but interfere with the *pari passu* principle, such as selectively paying a single creditor in the vicinity of insolvency at the expense of other creditors (preferential transaction).[78]

7.40 For an avoidance action to succeed under Dutch law, several conditions must be met: (i) the legal act must be optional or voluntary, meaning it is not required by law or a pre-existing contract; (ii) the act must prejudice creditors, which is interpreted broadly; and (iii) there must be knowledge of that prejudice at the time the legal act is performed. Hence, mere prejudice is insufficient. It is required that the debtor acted with knowledge of the prejudice, that is to say that it knew or should have known that its creditors' ability to recover would be hindered by the act.

7.41 Relevant to the element of knowledge, Dutch law distinguishes between gratuitous legal acts and legal acts done for consideration. In the case of the former, only the debtor's knowledge is relevant. It is presumed that such knowledge exists if the legal act was performed within one year before the declaration of bankruptcy.[79] In *Van Doorn Beheer/Thielen q.q.*, the court ruled that a guarantee granted by the subsidiary to finance the purchase of its shares from the parent company was an act for no consideration.[80] Also, if a security right (personal or *in rem*) is granted for a loan which has already been extended – without such security right being a precondition for the loan – the provision of security may be regarded as a gratuitous legal act, unless there is some form of consideration (e.g. a deferral on loan repayment, a reduced interest rate or continued financing under a revolving credit facility).[81] If the guarantor derives some benefit

78 B. Wessels, Gevolgen van faillietverklaring (Wessels Insolventierecht nr. III), 5e druk, Deventer: Wolters Kluwer, 2019; R.J. van der Weijden, De faillissementspauliana (Onderneming en recht nr. 75) (diss. Nijmegen), Deventer: Kluwer, 2012, pp. 68–77.

79 Dutch Bankruptcy Act, Article 45.

80 Gerechtshof Arnhem-Leeuwarden 12 February 2013, ECLI:NL:GHARL:2013:822, *JOR* 2014/78; Gerechtshof Arnhem-Leeuwarden, 12 September 2017, ECLI:NL:GHARL:2017:8021, finding that the payment made by the subsidiary to a lawyer of its parent company was an act for no consideration.

81 R.J. de Weijs, Faillissementspauliana, Insolvenzanfechtung en Transaction Avoidance in Insolvencies. Naar een geobjectiveerde regeling van schuldeisersbenadeling (Recht en Praktijk nr. InsR1) (diss. Amsterdam UvA), Deventer: Kluwer, 2010, 4.2.1.2.3.

from the financing of another party, such as obtaining direct or indirect access to credit, then the guarantee will not be regarded as a gratuitous legal act.[82]

To annul a legal act made for consideration, both the debtor and the counterparty must be aware of the prejudice caused by the act. It is important to note that the debtor and counterparty do not need to have the intention to harm or disadvantage the creditors, nor is it necessary for the parties to foresee the extent of the prejudice or identify the injured parties.[83] Instead, it must be shown that both the debtor and the counterparty could have foreseen with a reasonable degree of probability the debtor's insolvency and the resulting financial deficit at the time of the legal act.[84] Thus, if the counterparty, such as a financier, is aware or should be aware of the debtor's (i.e. guarantor's) financial distress, knowledge of the prejudice can be attributed to the counterparty. **7.42**

In practice, proving knowledge or awareness might be difficult.[85] For this reason, Article 43 Fw establishes a number of presumptions. These presumptions apply to non-mandatory legal acts that took place within one year before the bankruptcy order was made. They cover instances that indicate the suspicious nature of a legal act, either because of the nature of the act itself (e.g. when performance is not yet due, *niet-opeisbare schuld*) or the parties involved.[86] For example, knowledge of the prejudice is presumed if the transaction involves another company within the same enterprise group.[87] In the case of a guarantee, however, a creditor is often a non-related party (outside lender), which makes the presumption inapplicable. However, if the financier is a group member, the presumption will apply. **7.43**

For the purposes of this section, another presumption is relevant. Under this presumption, knowledge of prejudice exists if the value of an obligation on the part of the debtor *significantly* exceeds that of the obligation on the other **7.44**

82 A. Jonkers, Selective Perforation by Means of Guarantees: Dutch Law, in The 800-Pound Gorilla. Limits to Group Structures and Asset Partitioning in Insolvency, NACIIL 2018 report, Eleven International Publishing, 2019, p. 79, noting that 'even guarantees for which no direct premium is paid will usually be viewed as "for consideration"'.

83 R.J. de Weijs and D.G.J. Heems, GS Faillissementswet, commentaar op art. 42 Fw.

84 HR 22 December 2009, *NJ* 2010/273 *(ABN/Van Dooren q.q. III)*. Read further R.J. van der Weijden, Wetenschap van benadeling in de zin van art. 42 Fw en de voorzienbaarheid van het faillissement van de schuldenaar, MvV, afl. 10, 2017, pp. 285–289.

85 G. van Dijck, De Faillissementspauliana: Revisie van een Relict (proefschrift), 2016, p. 84, noting that 75 per cent of the surveyed IPs indicated that it was (very) difficult to demonstrate knowledge of prejudice in situations where no presumption applied.

86 G.F. van der Feltz, Geschiedenis van de Wet op het Faillissement en de Surséance van Betaling, Haarlem: De Erven F. Bohn, 1896, pp. 442–443.

87 Dutch Bankruptcy Act, Article 43(1)(6).

side.[88] An example of this can be an agreement in which the debtor sells an asset for a fraction of its market value or pays substantially more when buying an asset.[89] Such a manifest discrepancy in the price suggests that the transaction is suspicious. Similarly, if the debtor takes on joint and several liability for another's debt without any benefit in return, this imbalance raises concerns.[90] As observed in the previous sections, in intra-group transactions, like cross-guarantees, determining the value or benefit received by the guarantor can be challenging, as it requires an analysis of complex interdependencies and indirect benefits within the group. Ultimately, a court has to assess the upside to the guarantor and determine whether this upside is proportionate to the liability incurred. If the guarantor has not benefited from the advance made to the borrower, the transaction is likely to be deemed undervalued and open to challenge.

7.45 Dutch courts recognise the realities of enterprise groups and group interest as legally relevant factors, although in different contexts. For example, they have confirmed the existence of a 'duty of group management' (*concernleidingsplicht*) for a parent company within an integrated enterprise group, which encompasses an obligation to actively oversee subsidiaries in order to prevent insolvency or minimise losses.[91] A parent company may therefore be liable in tort (6:162 BW) where the group structure has been set up with inherent risks for creditors of a subsidiary, and where the parent company discontinues financial support to a subsidiary, while its appearance of creditworthiness misleads creditors.[92] Directors of the subsidiary could take into account group interest; however, this group interest cannot override the subsidiary's own interests.[93]

7.46 Thus, when reviewing intra-group financial transactions, various group-related circumstances may be taken into account. A court will consider which entity used the loan (e.g. whether the guarantor had access to the funds) and other relevant facts.[94] Evaluating a single transaction may not reveal the full picture,

---

88 Dutch Bankruptcy Act, Article 43(1)(1).

89 R.J. van der Weijden, De Faillissementspauliana, Deventer: Kluwer, 2012, p. 143.

90 F.M.J. Verstijlen, in *T&C Insolventierecht*, commentaar op art. 42.

91 HR 21 December 2001, *NJ* 2005/96 (*Sobi/Hurks*).

92 HR 11 September 2009, *NJ* 2009/565, *JOR* 2009/309 (*Comsys/Van den End q.q.*).

93 HR 26 October 2001, *NJ* 2002/94 (*Juno*). S. Bartman, Dutch Supreme Court at a Loss over Groups, European Company Law, Vol. 13, 2016, p. 125. See also HR 7 July 2017, *NJ* 2018/363 (*Oi Brasil Holdings Coöperatief/Citadel e.a.*) and *NJ* 2018/364, m.nt. F.M.J. Verstijlen *(Portugal Telecom International Finance/Citicorp Trustee Company e.a.*). The court noted with respect to Article 242 Fw (withdrawal of suspension of payments), that an IP may take into account the interests of the group in his decision. Yet the court pointed out that in bankruptcy proceedings, the starting point was the separate legal personality of group entities.

94 HR 13 July 2012, *JOR* 2012/306 (*Janssen q.q./JVS*).

as the issuance of a guarantee can enhance credit availability, which may support the entire group and create wider benefits. These benefits may arise, for instance, if outside financial injections make it possible to invest in other parts of the group to fund profitable activities or to stabilise various parts of the group, including the guarantor.[95] Dutch law recognises that a legal act that in itself leads to the prejudice of creditors but which forms part of a set of legal acts (*samenstel van rechtshandelingen*) that does not result in any prejudice, cannot be annulled. This rule is deduced from the rationale of *faillissementspauliana* and has been upheld by the Dutch Supreme Court.[96] The 'disadvantage' of the contested legal act can therefore, under certain (rather limited) circumstances, be mitigated or offset by the 'advantage' (*gunstige gevolgen*) that lies outside the contested legal act.[97] Yet, this advantage should be conferred on creditors of the debtor (guarantor), and not solely on another group member (principal debtor-borrower) and its creditors.[98]

In summary, intra-group guarantees may be subject to avoidance (*actio pauliana*) pursuant to the Dutch Bankruptcy Act. For a non-Dutch lawyer, the law can seem like a labyrinth. Different rules apply, depending on whether the guarantee constitutes the performance of a due and enforceable (payable) obligation or whether it was granted without prior commitment. Most guarantees likely fall under the category of non-obligatory legal acts. In these cases, unless the transaction is gratuitous, the trustee must demonstrate detriment and that both parties were aware of its prejudicial impact on the guarantor's creditors. This is challenging, as it requires proof that the guarantee was given when the lender could have anticipated the guarantor's insolvency with a reasonable degree of probability. As a result, intercompany guarantees made over a year before insolvency proceedings are generally hard to annul. 7.47

For transactions concluded within a one-year suspect period, the evidentiary presumption of knowledge applies if the transaction was undervalued. As illustrated in the English and US law sections, determining the value of a group guarantee and showing that it is not substantially lower than the assumed obligation is problematic. Dutch courts may consider group reality and recognise indirect benefits for the guarantor. The extent of this recognition is not 7.48

95 HR 8 April 2003, *JOR* 2003/160 (*Rivier de Loh/Van de Wetering*), dealing with an internal obligation to contribute in group relationships.

96 HR 10 December 1976, *Nl* 1977/617 (*Curatoren Eneca/BACM*); HR 22 March 1991, *NJ* 1992/214, m.nt. Van Schilfgaarde (*Loeffen q.q./Mees & Hope II*); HR 9 June 2006, *NJ* 2007/21, m.nt. Van Schilfgaarde (*Smit/Van Hees q.q.*); HR 19 December 2008, *NJ* 2009/220 (*Curatoren AHC/Air Holland c.s.*).

97 R.J. van der Weijden, De faillissementspauliana, Deventer: Kluwer, 2012, 5.5.1.

98 Ibid.

clear and will depend on the totality of facts. In examining these facts, courts could hypothesise what would have been the outcome if the guarantee had not been granted.[99] This retrospective, context-dependent analysis introduces legal uncertainty, making intra-group guarantees particularly susceptible to avoidance actions.

7.3 DIFFICULTIES OF EX POST SUBSTANTIVE REVIEW

7.49 The insolvency law frameworks of the UK, the US and the Netherlands all provide mechanisms for challenging intra-group financial transactions, including cross-guarantees. While there are important differences across these jurisdictions – such as the length of suspect periods, requirements regarding knowledge of the counterparty and available defences – there are notable similarities. For example, in all three jurisdictions, a cross-guarantee may be subject to transaction avoidance as a transaction at an undervalue. Undervalued transactions are harmful to creditors because they reduce the insolvency estate value, otherwise available to creditors. The determination of whether a group guarantee is such a transaction involves a fact-intensive analysis. This analysis may include the assessment of:

- direct and indirect benefits received by a guarantor;
- the financial positions of both the guarantor and the principal debtor at the time of the transaction;
- the degree of legal and economic integration within the group;
- the type of guarantee: upstream, downstream or cross-stream.

7.50 With a certain, inevitable degree of generalisation, it can be observed that the risk of avoidance increases under the following conditions: (i) the benefits of the guarantee are more distant or vague for the guarantor; (ii) the financial positions of the guarantor or the principal debtor are unstable at the time of the transaction; (iii) the group is less integrated, meaning the continued existence of the guarantor is less dependent on the principal debtor or other group entities; and (iv) the guarantee is upstream or cross-stream.

99 HR 19 October 2001, *NJ* 2001/654, *JOR* 2001/269, m.nt. NEDF *(Diepstraten q.q./ Gilhuis)*; Parket bij de HR, 16 October 2020, 19/05439, Conclusie B.F. Assink (*Volkerink q.q./Rabobank*), r.o. 3.17, arguing that what is required is 'although not always simple – a realistic, measurable assessment of what concretely would have happened if that legal act had not taken place, making the judgment of probability intrinsically contextual'.

Ex post (judicial) review of a debtor's transactions is essential for protecting creditors' rights.[100] Transaction avoidance rules contribute to the achievement of the principles of estate value maximisation and equal treatment of creditors. Moreover, an insolvency transaction avoidance procedure might also allow creditor participation or even initiation,[101] fostering an active role for creditors and contributing to procedural fairness. That said, there are important downsides and difficulties related to an ex post substantive review, especially when applied to intra-group financing. 7.51

First, when applying rules on avoidance of undervalued transactions, determining reasonably equivalent value is often problematic.[102] This is especially true for intercompany guarantees where no relevant market benchmark exists. Courts have to assess the true economic value of such transactions, which may entail an inquiry into complex business structures and group interdependencies. This is because, in many instances, a group entity acting as a guarantor does not receive a direct benefit from providing the guarantee; instead, it may derive indirect benefits related to the group's overall operations. Courts may be required to consider, with the benefit of hindsight, what might have happened had the guarantee not been provided. As Mevorach points out, evaluating the true economic effect of a transaction, or a series of related transactions, 'makes the law potent but also somewhat unpredictable'.[103] 7.52

Second, transaction avoidance law is often connected to the issue of directors' liability and the decision-making process. After all, it is directors or a chief executive officer (CEO) who make the decisions to enter into transactions that 7.53

100 A. Keay, The Harmonization of the Avoidance Rules in European Union Insolvencies, International & Comparative Law Quarterly, Vol. 66, 2016, p. 84, observing that the avoidance provisions promote collectivism and fairness among creditors, and protect them from unfair diminution of the insolvency estate.

101 An example of the law that allows creditors to initiate insolvency *pauliana* actions is Article 61.9(2) of the Russian Bankruptcy Act. In the jurisdictions studied in this book, creditors' right to challenge a debtor's transactions is limited. See e.g. Article 49 Fw, according to which only an IP is authorised to challenge legal acts under Articles 42 and 47 Fw. However, creditors can compel an IP to challenge a legal act pursuant to Article 69 Fw. In the UK, with respect to transactions at an undervalue and preferences, only an IP (liquidator, administrator) has standing (ss. 238 and 239 of the Insolvency Act 1986). Yet transactions defrauding creditors can be challenged by any 'victim' of a transaction, which includes creditors (s. 424, providing that in insolvency proceedings, a victim can apply for an order only with the leave of the court). The US law gives a bankruptcy trustee or a DIP the sole authority to pursue fraudulent transfer actions (11 U.S. Code § 548). However, courts have allowed creditors' committees or individual creditors to commence litigation on behalf of the estate (derivative standing) under narrowly defined circumstances, e.g. where a DIP or a trustee unjustifiably refused either to pursue the claim or to consent to the movant's prosecution of the claim on behalf of the estate. *Official Comm. of Unsecured Creditors v. Meltzer*, 589 B.R. 6, 16 (D. Me. 2018); *In re Know Weigh, L.L.C.*, 576 B.R. 189, 210 (Bankr. C.D. Cal. 2017).

102 D.G. Baird, Legal Approaches to Restricting Distributions to Shareholders: The Role of Fraudulent Transfer Law, EBOR, Vol. 7, 2006, p. 211, noting that '[v]aluations by their nature are uncertain'.

103 I. Mevorach, Transaction Avoidance in Bankruptcy of Corporate Groups, ECFR, Vol. 8, 2011, p. 243.

might later be challenged. Directors can be held personally liable for permitting a company to engage in a transaction that is subsequently declared void in insolvency.[104] However, especially in the shadow of insolvency, making the 'right' choices is very difficult. As aptly spotted by Licht, the 'vicinity-of-insolvency duties form a notoriously murky area, where legal space warps. The contours of this area are fuzzy'.[105] On the one hand, directors are influenced by cognitive biases, such as self-serving bias, positive outcome or optimism bias and illusion of control.[106] On the other hand, the irregularity of events of financial distress (compared to the business-as-usual), significant complexity imposed by diversity of interests, including the interests of other group companies, the lack of adequate information,and uncertainty about the future, coupled with significant time pressure, further complicate directors' ability to select the best course of action. Both cognitive biases and the irregularity of crisis situations indicate that ex post control may be a less suitable strategy for protecting creditors' rights or guiding directors' behaviour ex ante, at the time of the crisis.

7.54 Third, the effectiveness of ex post judicial review is highly dependent on the sophistication and experience of the judiciary. As discussed, the review of intra-group transactions involves nuanced assessments of indirect benefits, awareness of prejudice, calculation of reasonably equivalent value and the significance of an imbalance. Judges have considerable discretion in evaluating these factors, and such assessment might be time-consuming and costly for the parties involved. The difficulty in evaluating cross-guarantees makes ex post review less desirable in jurisdictions where the judiciary is less sophisticated and reliable.[107] This problem is exacerbated by the fact that ex post review is clouded by hindsight and outcome biases, as transactions are assessed with full knowledge of adverse outcomes.[108] Interestingly, cognitive biases cannot be

---

104 UNCITRAL Legislative Guide, Part four, Section two, para. 7.

105 A.N. Licht, My Creditor's Keeper: Escalation of Commitment and Custodial Fiduciary Duties in the Vicinity of Insolvency, Washington University Law Review, Vol. 98, 2021, p. 1732.

106 On cognitive biases in vicinity-of-insolvency decision-making, see M-W. Hung and W-H. Tsai, Managerial Optimism, CEO Retention, and Corporate Performance: Evidence from Bankruptcy-filing firms, Journal of Economics and Finance, Vol. 44, 2020, p. 506, studying the data on bankruptcy-filing firms in the USA, and concluding that managerial optimism is detrimental to operating performance at filing and survival probability. See also F. Drescher, Insolvency Timing and Managerial Decision-Making, Springer Gabler, 2014, p. 84, arguing that the 'context factors of the insolvency timing decisions are very likely to aggravate the manager's cognitive limitations'.

107 A. Gurrea-Martínez, Towards an Optimal Model of Directors' Duties in the Zone of Insolvency: An Economic and Comparative Approach, Journal of Corporate Law Studies, Vol. 21, 2021, pp. 389-390, arguing that 'in jurisdictions without sophisticated and reliable judicial systems … the discretion of courts should be reduced'.

108 N. Strohmaier et al., Hindsight Bias and Outcome Bias in Judging Directors' Liability and the Role of Free Will Beliefs, Journal of Applied Social Psychology, Vol. 51, 2020, pp. 141-158, finding that professional

eliminated even in countries with experienced judges. Although knowledge or awareness about the existence of judgmental heuristics and biases may help avoid certain straightforward mistakes, they are unlikely to mitigate hindsight bias.[109] The combination of biases with the inherent uncertainty and complexity of ex post evaluation could contribute to the over-deterrence of intra-group financing.[110]

The lack of predictability in applying transaction avoidance rules to intra-group transactions, such as intercompany guarantees, is problematic for a number of reasons. Legal uncertainty surrounding ex post review is harmful to the principle of protection of legitimate expectations. It can contribute to the increased cost of finance due to the risk of a guarantee being annulled ex post and result in foregone transactions. This is not bad if these transactions are value-destroying (overinvestment, debt dilution, etc.) and harm existing creditors of the guarantor. However, it is undesirable if it leads to the under-investment problem, as a result of which value-enhancing transactions and rescue attempts do not occur. 7.55

7.4 CONCLUSION

In the realm of enterprise group insolvency, there are many possibilities but few certainties. This observation also holds true for the rules regulating intra-group financing transactions. The application of these rules is often context specific and is marred by legal uncertainty. Some of this uncertainty stems from insolvency law itself, described by Goode and Gullifer as 'one of the most technical and, in some respects, one of the most arbitrary branches of law'.[111] Additionally, the complexity of intra-group dynamics, the diverse financial 7.56

legal investigators such as judges and lawyers are affected by hindsight and outcome biases when assessing directors' conduct. A. Gurrea-Martínez, The Avoidance of Pre-Bankruptcy Transactions: An Economic and Comparative Approach, Chicago-Kent Law Review, Vol. 93, 2018, p. 714, observing that 'hindsight bias will incentivize creditors, judges, and trustees to think that the transaction potentially challenged was harmful ex ante, even if it, at the moment of entering into the transaction, it looked reasonable'.

109 G. Mandel, Patently Non-Obvious: Empirical Demonstration that the Hindsight Bias Renders Patent Decisions Irrational, Ohio State Law Journal, Vol. 67, 2006, pp. 1391-1463; D. Hardman, Judgment and Decision-Making: Psychological Perspectives, BPS Blackwell, 2009, p. 37.

110 A.M. Pacces, Procedural and Substantive Review of Related Party Transactions: The Case for Noncontrolling Shareholder-Dependent Directors, in L. Enriques and T.H. Tröger (eds), The Law and Finance of Related Party Transactions, CUP, 2019, pp. 182-183, commenting with respect to ex post substantive review of related-party transactions (not specifically in the insolvency context), that 'fundamental incompetence of courts to evaluate the efficiency of RPTs stems from the same rationale behind judges' abstention from second-guessing business judgment' and arguing that 'substantive ex-post review tends to over-deter RPTs as it leads courts to second-guess, with hindsight bias, the decision to enter into RPTs'.

111 R. Goode and L. Gullifer, Goode and Gullifer on Legal Problems of Credit and Security, 6th edn, Sweet & Maxwell, 2017, para. 8-16.

and operational structures within groups, and the varying degrees of interdependence among group entities further contribute to this uncertainty. This chapter explored one aspect of insolvency law – transaction avoidance, which is a form of ex post review. This review involves substantively assessing a transaction against certain standards.

7.57 When dealing with transactions involving group entities, UNCITRAL points out that intra-group transactions may need to be 'considered differently when viewed in the broader context of an enterprise group, where the benefits and detriments of transactions might be more widely assigned'.[112] It has been observed that national legal systems are in principle capable of taking the group context (e.g. group integration and interdependence) into account when reviewing transactions. For example, US courts have, when applying the remedy of fraudulent transfers, looked beyond a single entity and considered whether entities in a group were closely related and shared the 'identity of interest'. There may be some room for group considerations in English and Dutch transaction avoidance law, even though the full extent of their recognition and impact remains unclear. A common challenge lies in estimating indirect benefits stemming from the extension of a cross-guarantee. This evaluation is problematic due to the difficulty of determining the (market) value of a guarantee ex post and a lot of uncertainty that such determination creates. This underscores the need for specialised courts equipped to handle complex insolvency and valuation disputes.

7.58 Based on the analysis of UK, US and Dutch law, the following conclusions are drawn:

- The application of insolvency transaction avoidance rules to intra-group transactions, such as group guarantees, lacks certainty. It involves a fact-intensive analysis in which various considerations may play a role, including the existence of co-guarantors (against whom a claim for contribution can be filed) or an *in rem* security interest that the guarantor can 'inherit' through the right of subrogation. These considerations affect the guarantor's risk.
- Any ex post assessment of transactions can be affected by various cognitive biases, which may unjustifiably influence a court's decision. Such cognitive biases cannot be fully eliminated, even if they are acknowledged by decision-makers.
- The vaguer and more distant the value or conferred benefit for the guarantor is, the more vulnerable the guarantee becomes to a future avoidance action.
- A transaction becomes even more vulnerable to transaction avoidance if, at the time of the transaction, either the principal debtor or the guarantor is financially

112 UNCITRAL Legislative Guide, Part three, Ch. II, para. 75.

distressed or insolvent, making the risk of harm to their creditors more pronounced or expected.

- Upstream or cross-stream support transactions, including upstream and cross-stream guarantees, are more vulnerable to an avoidance challenge compared to downstream support transactions, such as downstream guarantees.

While ex post review of intra-group financial transactions is necessary as a form of judicial protection, ensuring equal treatment of creditors and estate value preservation, the design of avoidance provisions – dating back to Roman law – makes it difficult to apply to transactions involving group members. As mentioned in Chapter 2, a group of companies is a relatively recent phenomenon. The quest is to achieve a balance between, on the one hand, maximising insolvency estate value, which depends on whether the transaction is properly compensated – not an easy calculation to be made ex ante and evaluated ex post, and, on the other hand, ensuring contractual predictability and legal certainty for the parties involved: principal debtor-borrower, group guarantor and outside lender. Transaction avoidance law is not shaped in a way that allows one to clearly foresee whether group support transactions, such as cross-guarantees, are voidable. This is partially caused by the ambiguity in recognising 'indirect' and 'group' benefits. The legal uncertainty is problematic from a principle-based perspective, as it undermines legitimate expectations and transaction certainty. Furthermore, avoidance risk may deter efficient, value-enhancing transactions, which runs counter to the principle of estate value maximisation. **7.59**

PART V

GROUP-SENSITIVE INSOLVENCY LAW: TOOLS AND SOLUTIONS

8

GROUP DEBT DELEVERAGING AND DEBT ADJUSTMENT: THIRD-PARTY RELEASES

8.1 INTRODUCTION

This part of the book explores various tools and solutions for the specific concerns or problems discussed in Part IV. It is important to clarify that the legal instruments (such as transaction avoidance and statutory subordination) or the transactions (such as cross-guarantees and intra-group loans) themselves are not inherently problematic. In fact, they often pursue legitimate goals and can be value-creating and beneficial. For example, as noted in Chapter 7, transaction avoidance rules play a crucial role in maximising estate value and ensuring equal treatment of creditors. Hence, transaction avoidance can be seen as a solution to the problems of fraudulent and undervalued transactions, as well as unfair preferences. Similarly, typical group-related transactions, such as cross-guarantees and intra-group loans may contribute to the efficient attraction and allocation of funds within an enterprise group, thereby facilitating the creation of value. However, as noted earlier, the same legal instruments and transactions can also present challenges or exacerbate problems in the context of group insolvency. **8.01**

For instance, Chapter 7 discussed the problematic application of transaction avoidance law to transactions involving group entities. It was observed that transactions like group guarantees are frequently driven by group considerations **8.02** or group interest. As a consequence, there may be no direct benefit for a group entity providing a guarantee. Given the legal separateness of group entities, recognising indirect benefits and assessing the true economic effect of a cross-guarantee could be challenging and might result in legal uncertainty. But let's assume that this transaction withstands legal scrutiny and is deemed valid and enforceable – meaning it is not void *ab initio* and does not get annulled when avoidance rules are invoked. In such a case, the group guarantee will likely impact the dynamics of group insolvency and restructuring. The exact ways in which this could happen were outlined in Chapter 5, dealing with various ex ante and ex post effects of cross-guarantees.

8.03 This chapter covers the response to the insolvency-related (ex post) effects produced by cross-guarantees and similar cross-entity liability arrangements. Given the group interconnectedness and synergies, as well as the complexities created by the triangle of rights and liabilities (the principal debtor – creditor – group guarantor), more and more jurisdictions are adopting rules that provide for the possibility to restructure obligations of third parties, like group guarantors, through a single proceeding opened with respect to one group entity ('anchor' debtor[1]). Such restructuring is made possible via so-called 'third-party releases'. In this chapter, I analyse this novel legal instrument or tool, which can be used to deleverage or adjust the debt of several group entities.[2]

8.04 This chapter proceeds as follows. Section 8.2.1 outlines the rationale behind third-party releases. It is followed by a comparative analysis, examining the availability of and conditions for third-party releases in three core jurisdictions: the UK (section 8.2.2), the USA (section 8.2.3) and the Netherlands (section 8.2.4). This analysis reveals that the countries adopt divergent views on the availability and desirability of third-party releases, largely due to their significant impact on creditors' rights in the absence of specific bankruptcy law protections. Section 8.3 concludes with a summary of the main findings and a proposal of elements or considerations to guide the design and application of rules on third-party releases.

---

1 The term 'anchor debtor' is borrowed from G. Ray Warner and M. Veder, Enterprise Group Restructuring: Dutch Options and United States Enforcement, European Insolvency and Restructuring Journal, 2021-7, 2021, pp. 1–52.

2 Different considerations might apply to third-party releases outside the enterprise group context. These non-group instances include, inter alia, releases of insurance companies, directors, legal and financial advisors and tortfeasors in mass tort litigation. These cases often raise distinct legal and moral questions and touch upon different policy reasons. Therefore, they fall outside the scope of this book.

8.2 THIRD-PARTY RELEASES

8.2.1 Rationale behind third-party releases

8.05 As follows from Chapter 5, typically, the insolvency of the principal debtor does not affect the rights of creditors against group guarantors, co-debtors and collateral providers. If it did, the protective function of these contractual arrangements would be compromised (see Figure 8.1).

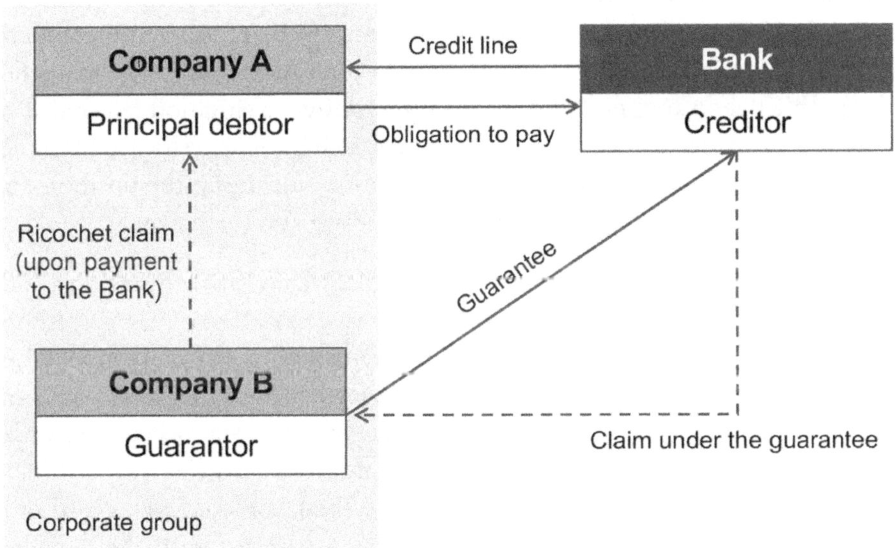

Figure 8.1 Triangle of rights and liabilities in group financing

8.06 Imagine that Company A initiates insolvency or restructuring proceedings, in which the claim of the Bank is altered. The fact that the Bank's claim against the principal debtor (Company A) has been reduced or completely written down in a non-consensual way generally shall not affect the Bank's rights under the guarantee.[3] Yet, this is not the end of our consideration.

8.07 In integrated groups, where the fates of group entities are intertwined or closely tied together, the successful restructuring of a group entity often requires the preservation of group synergies and the survival of other group members. The

3 A situation is different if the creditor voluntarily discharges the principal debtor of its liability (workout). In this case, because of the accessory nature of a guarantee or suretyship, the corresponding liability of a guarantor could be discharged or reduced accordingly.

debtor might rely on these other group entities to implement its reorganisation plan and sustain operations post-restructuring. The American Bankruptcy Institute recognised that this support could take the form of 'service, collaboration, funding, business commitments, or other means that allow the debtor to achieve its objectives in the chapter 11 case or in its postconfirmation operations'.[4] Be that as it may, third parties acting as guarantors, co-debtors and collateral providers[5] can be reluctant to contribute to the restructuring plan or extend assistance thereafter if they remain exposed to creditor claims and are liable despite the confirmation of the debtor's restructuring plan. They might also be forced into insolvent liquidation or end up being sold to a competitor. This can have a significant effect on the economic viability of the anchor debtor. This debtor may end up failing in the future – a situation referred to as the 'orphan restructuring problem'. Therefore, a single-entity-focused restructuring without due consideration of group reality, including the position and interests of group members, risks being short-lived and inefficient.

8.08 While group guarantors can initiate separate insolvency proceedings, this adds coordination challenges and transaction costs, especially if parallel proceedings are opened across several jurisdictions. The Oi Brazil case (see section 1.1.3) demonstrates how multiple proceedings can lead to inefficiencies, increased costs and delays. In addition to the redundancy of multiple proceedings, Veder and Thery observe that the duplication of proceedings gives an additional opportunity to dissenting creditors to exercise their holdout leverage, 'if only it were for the litigation risk, costs and timing associated with the remedies available in the second proceedings'.[6] A coordinated distress resolution within an enterprise group – especially where the group is international – is promoted by procedural centralisation. Such centralisation entails the concentration of separate insolvency proceedings in a single forum or court. It also manifests itself in situations where obligations of several group entities are restructured via a single proceeding opened with respect to one of them.

8.09 In recent decades, the restructuring of liabilities within corporate groups has increasingly used plans that incorporate third-party releases, which enable the

---

4 ABI Commission to Study the Reform of Chapter 11, Final Report and Recommendations (ABI Commission), 2014, p. 255.

5 In US literature and case law, such third parties are referred to as 'non-debtors'. See e.g. ABI Commission, p. 253. This term may be confusing since these parties are obligated to the creditor and are, in this sense, debtors, although not always the principal ones (e.g. surety). Nevertheless, the term 'non-debtor' can still be useful to signal that such a person is not subject to an insolvency or restructuring proceeding of its own.

6 M. Veder and A. Thery, The Release of Third Party Guarantees in Pre-insolvency Restructuring Plans, in D. Faber, B. Schuijling and N. Vermunt (eds), Trust and Good Faith Across Borders, Liber Amicorum Prof. Dr. S.C.J.J. Kortmann, Wolters Kluwer, 2017.

resolution of claims not only against the principal debtor but also against its affiliates acting as guarantors, co-debtors and collateral providers. In essence, a third-party release extends the legal effect of debt restructuring and addresses the complexities of group financing by sanctioning a group-wide solution. Historically, third-party releases have been available in common law jurisdictions, such as Australia,[7] Canada,[8] Singapore,[9] Ireland,[10] the Cayman Islands[11] and the UK.[12] More recently, however, this tool has also been adopted by civil law jurisdictions, including Germany and the Netherlands.

8.2.2 The UK: third-party releases in schemes of arrangement

English schemes of arrangement require some 'give and take' on each side, as opposed to mere surrender or forfeiture.[13] The question is whether this 'give and take' and the underlying arrangement are only available to the principal debtor and its creditors or can also extend to third parties. In *Re T&N Ltd.*, the court ruled for the latter.[14] The case was decided under the Companies Act 1985 (s. 425) and concerned actual and potential claims of employees and former employees of T&N Limited and fifty-seven associated companies (debtors) for damages due to personal injuries from exposure to asbestos. Under the scheme, the debtors and employees (claimants) agreed not to assert their claims against liability insurers, on the condition that the insurers would establish a fund of £36.74 million to be held in trust to pay the damages whenever they are established. It was objected that the proposed scheme did not constitute an arrangement between T&N Limited and its creditors but instead represented a compromise between the debtors and insurers since the scheme did not compromise the rights of claimants against the scheme companies. The court dismissed this objection and affirmed the scheme. It held that the term 'arrangement' had a broad meaning, which encompassed a settlement of litigation between T&N Limited and insurers to the extent 8.10

7 *Re Opes Prime Stockbroking Ltd* [2009] FCA 813; *Re Tiger Resources Ltd.* [2019] FCA 2186.

8 *ATB Financial v. Metcalfe & Mansfield Alternative Investments II Corp.*, 2008 ONCA 587 (Ont. C.A.).

9 *Pathfinder Strategic Credit LP v. Empire Capital Resources PTE Ltd.* [2019] SGCA 29.

10 *In the matter of Nordic Aviation Capital Designated Activity Company* [2020] No. 162 COS.

11 *Re Sphinx Group of Companies*, Grand Court of the Cayman Islands, unreported, 5 May 2010.

12 Although this book focuses on the release of group guarantors, co-debtors and collateral providers, releases can also extend to other parties, such as directors, officers and professional advisers. For an overview of the types of parties included in releases and the rationale for these releases, see *In the matter of Yuzhou Group Holdings Company Limited* [2024] HKCFI 3098, at 37, noting that a release of liability for directors, officers and professional advisers 'particularly when it is expressed in general or unqualified terms, cannot be said to be necessary for the implementation of the scheme'.

13 *Re NFU Development Trust Ltd* [1972] 1 WLR 1548; *Re Lehman Brothers International (Europe) (in admin.)* [2018] EWHC 1980 (Ch); [2019] BCC 115, at 64.

14 *Re T&N Ltd. (No. 3)* [2006] EWHC 1447 (Ch).

that the settlement ('not immediately') affected the position of the debtors and was effectively a 'tripartite matter'. According to the court, the scheme was 'an integral part of a single proposal affecting all the parties'.[15]

8.11 This broad interpretation of the scope of schemes of arrangement was affirmed in *Re Lehman Brothers International (Europe)*, where the court noted that it was 'entirely logical' to extend the jurisdiction to approve a scheme that varies or releases creditors' claims against both the principal debtor and third parties 'designed to recover the same loss'.[16] Claims subject to a release can be contractual or tortious in nature, as in the T&N case, and can be secured or unsecured. Importantly, the English court ruled that the release of a third party should be ancillary to the arrangement between the principal debtor and its own creditors, and that such a release must be 'necessary in order to give effect' to the arrangement. This 'necessity' requirement became known as the '*Lehman necessity*'.[17] Another qualification added by the court was that the rights of creditors against third parties should be closely connected with their rights against the principal debtor. On this point, the court highlighted that 'the decision in T&N Ltd (No. 3) [was] near the outer limits of the scope of s. 895'.[18]

8.12 A more recent case, *Far East Capital Limited*,[19] involved a discharge of obligations under two sets of notes in return for a payment by the debtor of a settlement amount. The scheme included the release of third parties – group entities that provided guarantees and security for the notes. Additionally, the release was given to other identified 'protected parties' who had been involved in the preparation, negotiation or implementation of the scheme. In *Van Gansewinkel Groep BV and others*, the court held that a release should be 'necessary to give legal or commercial effect to the compromise or arrangement between the scheme company and its creditors'.[20] The case concerned the release of group members under guarantees. In *La Seda De Barcelona*,[21] the court sanctioned a scheme that provided for the release of a third-party – group member Artenius under the guarantee agreement, in exchange for Artenius releasing other group members of its own claims. Thus, the release of Artenius benefited the

15 Ibid., at 52.

16 *Lehman Brothers International (Europe), Re Insolvency Act 1986* [2009] EWCA Civ 1161, at 63.

17 *Re Gategroup Guarantee Limited* [2021] EWHC 304 (Ch), at 163, noting that '[w]here the alteration of creditors' rights against third parties is both ancillary to the arrangement between the company and its creditors and necessary to ensure the effectiveness of that arrangement, then they will be permitted'.

18 *Lehman Brothers International (Europe), Re Insolvency Act 1986* [2009] EWCA Civ 1161, at 83.

19 *In the matter of Far East Capital Limited S.A.* [2017] EWHC 2878 (Ch).

20 *Re Van Gansewinkel Groep BV* [2015] EWHC 2151 (Ch).

21 *In Re La Seda de Barcelona SA* [2010] EWHC 1364 (Ch).

scheme creditors because its release of the debtor and other group companies improved their financial position. In the alternative scenario, Artenius' claims could have triggered 'insolvency of a company which would have escalated group bankruptcy proceedings'.[22]

In *Noble Group Limited*,[23] the scheme was part of a complex group restructuring where, in return for writing off creditors' claims, the creditors received debt instruments issued by the newly incorporated companies. Additionally, the scheme entailed the release of claims against the debtor's management, a group of its senior creditors, their related parties and officers, directors, employees, agents, advisors and representatives. It encompassed claims relating to the scheme claims and the preparation, negotiation, sanctioning or implementation of the scheme. The court acknowledged the breadth of the suggested release to include any claims arising from or related to the scheme claims. This, however, was not found to be problematic. When sanctioning the scheme with a third-party release, it mentioned that an issue could arise where a scheme creditor has a more 'tangential' claim against the to-be-released third party (e.g. a claim by a creditor in negligence against an independent financial adviser who advised that creditor to purchase financial instruments). The court noted that this could affect class composition, because only some, but not all, scheme creditors would be entitled to pursue such a claim. **8.13**

In sum, English schemes of arrangement are flexible and commercially driven in their approach to third-party releases. It is well-established that, in certain circumstances, a scheme can, as part of the arrangement between the scheme company (the 'anchor' debtor) and a creditor, require the creditor to give up or vary its rights against a third party – a person other than the scheme company. Claims arising from various types of intercompany liability arrangements (guarantees, co-debtorship, third-party collateral), facilitating group interconnectedness and interdependence, are commonly eligible for release. This is because such a release can be viewed as necessary to give effect to the proposed arrangement. Without it, the guaranteed creditor is entitled to sue the guarantor, who, in turn, could claim the full amount from the principal debtor (the scheme company) based on the guarantor's right to indemnity (section 5.5.3.1). This indemnity claim can defeat the purpose of the whole scheme, as the principal debtor would remain liable for the very amount that the scheme was designed to compromise. **8.14**

22 Ibid., at 19.
23 *In the Matter of Noble Group Limited* [2018] EWHC 3092 (Ch).

8.15 The mechanism most commonly used to achieve a release of group guarantors in English schemes of arrangement involves including a clause in the plan that grants authority to a nominated person to execute a deed of release or variation on behalf of the scheme creditors in favour of third parties.[24] This release can be granted where the 'anchor debtor' is a principal debtor,[25] one of the principal debtors[26] or a guarantor.[27] Three aspects are worth emphasising concerning third-party releases under English law.

8.16 First, a wide range of 'third parties' may benefit from a release. These can include both related parties (e.g. group entities, their directors and officers) and non-affiliated parties (e.g. insurers, auditors, legal and financial advisors).[28] Second, claims subject to a release can be contractual (e.g. based on a guarantee, co-debtorship or collateral arrangement) or non-contractual (e.g. arising in tort), secured or unsecured. Third, there are certain requirements imposed on third-party releases. Payne distinguishes four of them:[29]

- A scheme should involve a genuine 'give and take'. This does not necessarily entail equal monetary consideration and can include indirect benefits in the short or long run (e.g. financial stability of the group as a whole). English courts do not always rigorously scrutinise this requirement.[30]

---

24 *Re Noble Group Ltd (sanction)* [2019] 2 BCLC 548, at 24; *Re Van Gansewinkel Groep BV* [2015] Bus LR 1046, at 16.

25 *Re APCOA Parking Holdings GmbH* [2014] EWHC 3849 (Ch), 2014 WL 5833966; *In the Matter of Noble Group Limited* [2018] EWHC 3092 (Ch).

26 *Re NN2 Newco Ltd* [2019] EWHC 1917 (Ch). In this case, NN2 was specifically incorporated in England for the purposes of facilitating a scheme of arrangement. Upon incorporation, NN2 voluntarily became co-issuer and co-obligor under financial obligations, assuming joint and several liability under the debt instruments. The court noted that such a technique to create jurisdiction for a scheme was not abusive. Also, *Re Codere (UK) Ltd* [2015] EWHC 3778 (Ch).

27 *In the Matter of Swissport Fuelling Ltd* [2020] EWHC 1499 (Ch). In this case, a scheme company was a guarantor rather than a borrower. It was incorporated in England and Wales. The borrowers were incorporated in Luxembourg and Switzerland and might not have been able to establish a sufficient connection with the UK. Under the credit agreement, the borrowers did not have a right of contribution or indemnity against the guarantors, so a claim against them would not ricochet against the scheme guarantor. In order to change this and create such a ricochet claim, the scheme company entered into a deed in favour of the borrowers. Under this deed, it assumed the position of a primary obligor, alongside the borrowers, so that each of them would have a right of contribution against the other.

28 C. Pilkington, Schemes of Arrangement in Corporate Restructuring, Sweet & Maxwell, 2017, para. 9-001, noting that there are four main categories of third parties for whose benefit a release is often granted, namely: (i) third-party security providers (e.g. operating company guarantors); (ii) advisers; (iii) directors; and (iv) administrators or liquidators.

29 J. Payne, Schemes of Arrangement: Theory, Structure and Operation, CUP, 2014, pp. 23–24.

30 *In the matter of Syncreon Group BV* [2019] EWHC 2412 (Ch), 2019 WL 04279919, at 26, briefly noting that the scheme companies confirmed the need of third-party releases 'in order to give full effect to the schemes' and that such releases are 'a relatively regular feature of the schemes'. The court mentioned that the release provisions were explained to creditors.

- Creditors' rights against a third party must be sufficiently closely connected with their claims against the principal debtor. This typically includes claims under guarantees, co-debtorship and collateral arrangements but may also extend to other claims that could impact the success of the scheme and the obligations of the principal debtor. The review of recent cases shows that the requirement of 'close connection' is not closely examined by courts.[31] In any case, claims under cross-guarantees are seen as closely connected to the creditor's claim against the principal debtor, as both seek to recover the same loss.
- Creditors' rights against a third party must be personal rather than proprietary, meaning they should not be based on the creditor's title over specific assets.
- A creditor should benefit from a release of its rights against the third party 'to the extent that if it were to exercise them this would adversely affect what it might recover under the scheme'.[32]

The question remains whether the scheme of arrangement can be approved if, as a result of a third-party release, the guaranteed creditor is disadvantaged. It is essential to note that the majority of English schemes of arrangement are uncontested. Therefore, the issue of third-party releases and their fairness is rarely explicitly addressed by English courts. Compliance of third-party releases with the constitutional protection of private property was discussed by the High Court of Ireland in *Re Ballantyne RE Plc*. In this case, the court observed that 'the requirement to obtain the sanction of the Court for a scheme of arrangement …, which sanction will not be granted if this scheme is unfair, inequitable, improperly coercive or unreasonable …, combined with the requirement for a special majority at the relevant scheme meeting as a pre condition for such sanction …, represents a fair, reasonable and proportionate balance … of the various potentially competing interests involved in a scheme of arrangement'.[33] **8.17**

English courts are likely to follow the same approach. They are generally unwilling to replace the will of the majority of creditors with their own views on the commercial merits or on what is reasonable.[34] When deciding whether to sanction a scheme, courts consider whether there are reasons to doubt that the majority of creditors have made a decision that a reasonable creditor would have arrived at when assessing the proposal. Yet it is important to keep in mind that the court's sanctioning of a scheme is not a rubber-stamping exercise, even **8.18**

31 See *In the Matter of Noble Group Limited* [2018] EWHC 3092 (Ch), at 25, noting that '[t]he jurisdiction is not … limited to guarantees and claims closely connected to scheme claims'.

32 J. Payne, Schemes of Arrangement: Theory, Structure and Operation, CUP, 2014, p. 31.

33 *Re Ballantyne RE Plc & Companies Act 2014* [2019] IEHC 407, at 130.

34 *Re Equitable Life Assurance Society* [2002] EWHC 140 (Ch). See G. McCormack, The European Restructuring Directive, Edward Elgar Publishing, 2021, paras. 6.47-6.50, describing the 'creditor democracy' approach adopted with respect to schemes of arrangement.

if the scheme is supported by the majority of voting creditors.[35] In considering the general fairness of a scheme, the court may scrutinise a third-party release and its effect on a guaranteed creditor. If the release is fully disclosed and is not manifestly unfair, it is likely to be sanctioned by the court.[36] This might be the case where evidence demonstrates that an insolvent liquidation is a likely scenario if the scheme is not approved, and that the scheme provides each scheme creditor with a better return than they would receive in an insolvency proceeding.[37]

8.19 Conversely, if a scheme of arrangement with a third-party release deprives a guaranteed creditor of the benefits of the guarantee and places it in a worse position compared to an alternative scenario, there can be significant concerns about the fairness of the release and the scheme itself. This was confirmed in the context of CVAs. For example, in *Mourant & Co Trustees Ltd v. Sixty UK Ltd*, the court found that a CVA would deprive landlords of guarantees they would otherwise retain in the alternative liquidation.[38] The guarantees for the remainder of the leases, having obvious commercial value, were given to protect the landlords in case of tenant default. The court refused to sanction the release. Therefore, fairness is a critical issue, particularly when a creditor has a more tangential claim against a third party, such as a claim based on a guarantee, that could be compromised by a third-party release. In these cases, the courts may be more inclined to scrutinise the fairness of the scheme more closely.[39]

8.20 The existence of a separate claim could also be relevant for class composition.[40] A recent case that highlights this issue is *Gategroup*, where the company, a

---

35 *Re Stemcor Trade Finance Limited* [2015] EWHC 2803 (Ch); *Re Sunbird Business Services Limited* [2020] EWHC 2493 (Ch); *Re All Scheme Limited* [2021] EWHC 1401 (Ch) (given specific circumstances of the case, such as low level of creditor turnout, limited financial sophistication and literacy of creditors, unsatisfactory presentation of realistically probable alternatives to the scheme, the court questioned fairness of the scheme whereby creditors were to suffer a 90 per cent haircut, while shareholders retained their economic interest in the group).

36 C. Pilkington, Schemes of Arrangement in Corporate Restructuring, Sweet & Maxwell, 2017, para. 9-021.

37 *Re Lecta Paper UK Ltd* [2020] EWHC 382 (Ch), at 29. The relevance of the comparator to the scheme, or the counterfactual of what would be an alternative if the proposed scheme does not proceed, was considered in *Re Stronghold Insurance Co Ltd* [2019] BCLC 11, at 49, stating that '… only by identifying the comparator can the likely practical effect of what is proposed be assessed and the likelihood of sensible discussion between the holders of rights so affected and between them and others with different rights be weighed fairly'.

38 *Mourant & Co Trustees Ltd v. Sixty UK Ltd* [2010] BCC 882.

39 See *Re Virgin Active Holdings Limited* [2021] EWHC 1246 (Ch), at 206.

40 *Re Noble Group Ltd* [2018] EWHC 3092 (Ch), at 26, suggesting that 'issues of class composition could arise on the facts if, for example, some but not all scheme creditors had such a claim against a third-party adviser'. The leading case on class composition is *Sovereign Life Assurance v. Dodd* [1892] 2 QB 573, per

global leader in airline catering, faced significant business downturns due to the Covid-19 pandemic. To avoid insolvency, a Part 26A restructuring plan was proposed,[41] involving two groups of creditors: Bondholders and Senior Lenders. The rights of these creditors were guaranteed by the specifically incorporated Plan Company via the Deed Poll, under which the Plan Company undertook to indemnify the creditors in respect of the obligations of primary obligors. It is important to note that the primary obligors under bonds and loans were *different group entities*. The key question in this case was whether Bondholders and Senior Lenders should be placed in a single class. The court ruled that they should not be, as their claims were considered 'materially different, being against different entities [different obligors]'.[42] The court also highlighted that the rights conferred by the plan on the respective creditors were different. For example, maturity dates were not the same, reflecting the existing contractual rights. The relevance of the rights against third parties (e.g. group guarantors) for class composition has been confirmed more recently.[43]

8.2.3 The USA: third-party releases in Chapter 11

Explaining the attractiveness of Chapter 11 among foreign companies, McCormack mentions several factors: (i) the worldwide automatic stay; (ii) the DIP regime; (iii) developed rules on rescue financing; (iv) cram down possibilities; and (v) procedural consolidation.[44] The availability of third-party releases is not cited. Until recently, the position of US bankruptcy law on non-consensual non-debtor or third-party releases was unsettled. To clarify the current US approach, three points should be made. 8.21

First, US courts distinguish between temporary injunctions staying the enforcement and suits against third parties, and permanent releases of claims against them. While it is generally accepted that injunctions to protect third parties, such as guarantors or co-debtors, can be granted in certain circumstances, permanent third-party releases are more contentious and, in most 8.22

Bowen LJ at 583, holding that a class must be confined to those persons whose rights are not so dissimilar as to make it impossible for them to consult together with a view to their common interest. Other relevant cases include *Re Hawk Insurance Co Ltd* [2001] EWCA Civ 241 and *Re UDL Holdings Ltd* [2002] 1 HKC 172.

41 In *Re Virgin Atlantic Airways Ltd* [2020] EWHC 2191 (Ch), at 45–48, it was concluded that the same approach to class constitution applies to a Part 26A plan as to a Part 26 scheme of arrangement.

42 *Re Gategroup Guarantee Limited* [2021] EWHC 304 (Ch), at 189.

43 *Virgin Active Holdings Ltd & Ors, Re Part 26A of The Companies Act 2006* [2021] EWHC 814 (Ch), at 81.

44 G. McCormack, Bankruptcy Forum Shopping: The UK and US as Venues of Choice for Foreign Companies, International and Comparative Law Quarterly, Vol. 63, 2014, p. 827.

cases, would not be approved. The next chapter of the book extensively covers the issue of the extension of insolvency stays to the benefit of third parties.

8.23 Second, US courts usually approve consensual third-party releases offered in connection with a bankruptcy reorganisation plan.[45] Differing opinions, however, exist on what constitutes valid 'consent' and whether deemed or implied consent suffices to sanction a third-party release.[46] Some courts hold that voting in favour of a reorganisation plan is sufficient to assume consent to a third-party release included therein.[47] Other courts require manifest assent to the release, so that mere voting for a plan is not enough.[48] The third category of courts considers abstaining from voting or failing to opt out as consent.[49] The Commission established by the American Bankruptcy Institute to study the reform of Chapter 11 in its report favours express consent to the release, which covers: (i) voting for a plan that includes a third-party release; (ii) a separate point on the ballot indicating consent to a release; or (iii) a separate agreement with the affected creditor approving the release.[50] Until the US Supreme Court clarifies what 'consent' is sufficient to sanction a third-party release, divergent approaches are likely to persist.

8.24 Third, non-consensual third-party releases are particularly problematic in US bankruptcy law. Divergent views on the admissibility and desirability of non-consensual third-party releases are reflected in both scholarly,[51] and judicial positions. Given that US statutory law does not expressly permit third-party

45 *In re SunEdison, Inc.*, 576 B.R. 453, 458 (Bankr. S.D.N.Y. 2017); *In re Specialty Equip. Cos., Inc.*, 3 F.3d 1043, 1047 (7th Cir. 1993).

46 See D. Coco, Third-Party Bankruptcy Releases: An Analysis of Consent Through the Lenses of Due Process and Contract Law, Fordham Law Review, Vol. 88, 2019, p. 233, arguing that the existing divergence in case law leads to inconsistent application of the US Bankruptcy Code, raises due process concerns and causes forum shopping.

47 *In re Chassix Holdings Inc.*, 533 B.R. 64 (Bankr. S.D.N.Y. 2015); *In re Zenith Elecs. Corp.*, 241 B.R. 92, 111 (Bankr. D. Del. 1999).

48 *In re Digital Impact, Inc.*, 223 B.R. 1, 14–15 (Bankr. N.D. Okla. 1998), emphasising that the court 'must ascertain whether the creditor unambiguously manifested assent to the release of the nondebtor from liability on its debt'.

49 *In re DBSD N. Am., Inc.*, 419 B.R. 179, 217–19 (Bankr. S.D.N.Y. 2009), holding that '[e]xcept for those who voted against the Plan, or who abstained and then opted out, … Third Party Release provision [is] consensual'. *In re Indianapolis Downs, LLC*, 486 B.R. 286, 306 (Bankr. D. Del. 2013), stressing that 'parties were provided detailed instructions on how to opt out, and had the opportunity to do so by marking their ballots'.

50 ABI Commission to Study the Reform of Chapter 11, Final Report and Recommendations, 2014, p. 255.

51 In support of third-party releases, see A. Casey and J. Macey, In Defense of Chapter 11 for Mass Torts, University of Chicago Law Review, Vol. 90, 2023, pp. 973–1021; E.J. Janger, Aggregation and Abuse: Mass Torts in Bankruptcy, Fordham Law Review, Vol. 91, 2022, pp. 362–383. For a critical position on non-consensual third-party releases, see L.D. Simon, Bankruptcy Grifters, The Yale Law Journal, Vol. 131, 2022, pp. 1154–1216; R. Brubaker, Mandatory Aggregation of Mass Tort Litigation in Bankruptcy, The Yale Law Journal Forum, Vol. 131, 2022, pp. 960–1009.

releases except in asbestos-related liability,[52] courts have adopted various approaches and tests. A few circuits (Ninth,[53] Tenth[54] and Fifth[55]) have taken a restrictive view on third-party releases, ruling that § 524(e) prohibits them.[56] Other circuits have avoided this narrow interpretation and, under certain limited conditions, were willing to approve third-party releases. These courts focused on § 105(a), which grants US courts the equitable power to 'issue any order, process, or judgment that is necessary or appropriate to carry out the provisions of [the US Bankruptcy Code]'.[57] Yet, even for them, the permissibility of third-party releases has not resulted in a single judicial standard.[58]

The hesitation of US courts in approving non-consensual releases can also be explained by the risks of their abuse. As the court in *Metromedia* warned, 'a nondebtor release is a device that lends itself to abuse ... In form, it is a release; in effect, it may operate as a bankruptcy discharge arranged without a filing and without the safeguards of the Code.'[59] **8.25**

The availability of third-party releases has entered the spotlight in view of Purdue Pharma's Chapter 11 plan. This plan included a settlement with the Sackler family, whereby, in exchange for the release of all opioid-related claims against over 1,000 individuals and entities related to the Sackler family ('shareholder released parties'), the Sacklers initially agreed to provide USD 4.275 billion towards the insolvency estate; that figure reached appr. USD 6 **8.26**

52 11 U.S. Code § 524(g)(1)(B). Even in asbestos-related cases, it is not entirely clear whether liability, other than the derivative liability of the debtor, can be released. J.M. Silverstein, Overlooking Tort Claimants' Best Interests: Non-Debtor Releases in Asbestos Bankruptcies, UMKC Law Review, Vol. 78, 2009, p. 63, arguing that the language of this section 'suggests that supplemental injunctions may not extinguish rights against a third party arising from the *third party's independent conduct*' (original emphasis).

53 *Resorts Int'l, Inc. v. Lowenschuss (In re Lowenschuss)*, 67 F.3d 1394, 1402 (9th Cir. 1995), restating that '[t]his court has repeatedly held, without exception, that § 524(e) precludes bankruptcy courts from discharging the liabilities of nondebtors'.

54 *Landsing Diversified Props.-II v. First Nat'l Bank & Trust Co. of Tulsa (In re W. Real Estate Fund, Inc.)*, 922 F.2d 592, 601 (10th Cir. 1990), holding that 'Congress did not intend such [discharge of debt] to third-party bystanders'.

55 *Bank of N.Y. Tr. Co. v. Official Unsecured Creditors' Comm. (In re Pac. Lumber Co.)*, 584 F.3d 229, 252 (5th Cir. 2009).

56 For criticism of the position that § 524(e) bars third-party releases, see R. Brubaker, Bankruptcy Injunctions and Complex Litigation: A Critical Reappraisal of Non-Debtor Releases in Chapter 11 Reorganizations, University of Illinois Law Review, Vol. 4, 1997, p. 971, arguing that while 'a bankruptcy court does, indeed, lack the authority to approve a nonconsensual release of creditors' non-debtor claims, courts' and commentators' reliance upon section 524(e) as a statutory prohibition is misguided and unfortunate. Section 524(e) is necessary, as a matter of mere mechanics, to prevent the debtor's discharge from automatically discharging co-debtors and guarantors, through the operation of common-law suretyship rules that release secondary obligors upon release of the primary obligor'.

57 11 U.S. Code § 105(a).

58 See e.g. *In re Dow Corning Corp.*, 280 F.3d 648, 658 (6th Cir. 2002); *In re Millennium Lab Holdings II, LLC.*, 945 F.3d 126, 137 (C.A.3 (Del.) 2019).

59 *In re Metromedia Fiber Network, Inc.*, 416 F.3d 136, 142 (2nd Cir. 2005).

billion on appeal. The plan was approved by well above the 75 per cent supermajority in each class of creditors and was confirmed by the bankruptcy court in September 2021.[60] The court emphasised that the settlement was necessary for the plan and that the plan was reasonable and fair. On appeal, this confirmation order was vacated. The district court concluded, in a rather broad statement, that the Bankruptcy Code did not authorise non-consensual non-debtor releases.[61] The Court of Appeals overturned the district court's ruling and held that the bankruptcy court's initial approval of the releases was appropriate.[62] The fate of this long saga – and perhaps of non-consensual third-party releases in the USA, more generally – was now in the hands of the US Supreme Court.

8.27 On 27 June 2024, the US Supreme Court ruled in the case of *Harrington v. Purdue Pharma*,[63] in a 5–4 decision, that the non-consensual non-debtor releases included in the company's plan of reorganisation were impermissible under the US Bankruptcy Code, as lacking statutory basis. Writing for the majority, Justice Gorsuch concluded that the Bankruptcy Code 'does not authorize a release and injunction that, as part of a plan of reorganization under Chapter 11, effectively seeks to discharge claims against a nondebtor without the consent of affected claimants'.[64] According to the majority, the catch-all provision in § 1123(b)(6) which provides that a Chapter 11 plan may 'include any other appropriate provision not inconsistent with the applicable provisions of this title' must be read in light of its surrounding provisions that only concern the rights and responsibilities of the debtor, and not third parties.[65] While holding that non-consensual non-debtor releases are not authorised under the Bankruptcy Code, the court did not express a view on what qualifies as a consensual release and did not opine on whether its holding applies to 'a plan that provides for the full satisfaction of claims against a third-party nondebtor'.

---

60 *In re Purdue Pharma L.P.*, 633 B.R. 53 (Bankr. S.D.N.Y. 2021).

61 *In re Purdue Pharma, L.P.*, 635 B.R. 26 (S.D.N.Y. 2021).

62 *In re Purdue Pharma L.P.*, No. 22-110, 2023 WL 3700458 (2d Cir. May 30, 2023).

63 *Harrington v. Purdue Pharma L.P.*, 603 U.S. 204 (2024) (2024) <https://www.supremecourt.gov/opinions/23pdf/23-124_8nk0.pdf> accessed 10 October 2024. For a discussion of this judgment, see Episode 55 of INSOL Talks <https://www.insol.org/focus-groups/academic-group/events-and-podcasts> accessed 10 October 2024.

64 Ibid., p. 19.

65 Additionally, the court noted that the 'Sacklers have not filed for bankruptcy and have not placed virtually all their assets on the table for distribution to creditors, yet they seek what essentially amounts to a discharge'. According to court, no provision of the law authorised that kind of relief.

8.2.4 The Netherlands: third-party releases in WHOA schemes

8.2.4.1 General release framework

Prior to the adoption of the WHOA, Dutch law did not have statutory rules addressing third-party releases. Outside the WHOA framework, examined below, the possibility of releasing third parties in plans adopted in bankruptcy and suspension of payments procedures remains unclear. In academic literature, the predominant view seems to be that such releases are only available if the creditor consents to a release.[66] 8.28

This position is substantiated with reference to the nature of a plan, which is seen as an agreement between the debtor and its creditors, and which therefore requires creditor consent (*aanvaarding*). In other words, the binding effect of a release arises from such consent rather than from court approval of a plan. The release provisions are believed to be extraneous to a plan (*akkoordvreemde bepalingen*), as they do not concern the debtor–creditor relationship but regulate creditor–third party relationship. Some authors, including Vriesendorp and Hermans,[67] and Tollenaar[68] argue that a plan should be able to affect creditors' rights against third parties, even over creditors' disagreement. Be that as it may, in practice, third-party releases have been included in bankruptcy and suspension of payments plans.[69] They purported to release, among others, debtors' directors, bankruptcy trustees, direct and indirect shareholders, group members, their insurers and advisors from potential liability vis-à-vis creditors who were part of the plan. Yet these third-party releases were either not challenged or not invoked after plan approval. Hence, the limits of what could be agreed in a plan have not been tested in courts. The same is true for WHOA plans that contain releases of directors, board members, agents and other parties, whose 'releases' are not based on any specific statutory provision.[70] This is different for releases of group members discussed below. 8.29

---

66 S.C.J.J. Kortmann, Derden in het faillissementsrecht (1997) 46 AA 5, pp. 59–60; A.D.W. Soedira, Het Akkoord. Een wetenschappelijke proeve op het gebied van de rechtsgeleerdheid (Onderneming en recht, nr. 60) (diss. Nijmegen), Deventer: Kluwer, 2011, pp. 93–96; A.M. Mennens, Het dwangakkoord buiten surseance en faillissement (Onderneming en recht nr. 118), Deventer: Wolters Kluwer, 2020, p. 495ff; B. Wessels, Het Akkoord (Wessels Insolventierecht nr. VI), 5e druk, Wolters Kluwer, 2020, 6159ff; K. Harmsen, Lehman Brothers: een akkoord in strijd met de Faillissementswet, TvI 2013/28.

67 R. Hermans and R.D. Vriesendorp, Het dwangakkoord in het insolventierecht: vrijheid in gebondenheid? TvI 2014/10.

68 N.W.A. Tollenaar, Het pre-insolventieakkoord. Grondslagen en raamwerk (diss. Groningen), Deventer: Wolters Kluwer, 2016, pp. 300–302.

69 Rb. Amsterdam 22 March 2013, *JOR* 2013/191, m.nt. W.J.M. van Andel (*Lehman Brothers Treasury Co. B.V.*); Rb. Amsterdam 23 September 2021, *JOR* 2022/17, m.nt. R.J. van Galen (*Steinhoff International Holdings N.V.*).

70 Rb. Amsterdam 21 June 2023, ECLI:NL:RBAMS:2023:4152 (*Steinhoff International Holdings N.V.*), 12.10., noting that the 'court sees no grounds for rejecting the homologation request in the foregoing,

8.30 As previously noted, the starting point is that a WHOA scheme, just like any other procedure under the Dutch Bankruptcy Act, does not affect creditors' rights against third parties, such as guarantors and co-debtors, who are liable for the debt of the debtor proposing the plan.[71] In the context of group financing, where several group members provide security or act as co-borrowers, this means that restructuring the obligations of one group member does not alter creditor's rights against other group members, which remain liable for the restructured debts. This liability can push these other group members into insolvency, potentially destabilising the operational and financial interdependence in the group and thus jeopardising the restructured debtor's own survival. If so, the goal of rescuing a viable business will not be achieved. With this in mind and to facilitate restructuring within enterprise groups, the Dutch Bankruptcy Act in its articles on WHOA schemes, provides an exception to the general rule of 'no-third-party-effect'. It offers a debtor or a restructuring expert an option to propose the restructuring of group obligations under a single plan.[72] Without this option, each group member would need to commence individual proceedings to restructure obligations under the guarantees.

8.31 The WHOA introduced Article 372 Fw, which allows a WHOA plan to modify the rights of creditors against third parties (non-debtors) that must belong to the debtor's corporate group. This is possible provided that these group entities have not proposed their own restructuring plan for the obligations in question. The definition of a 'group' under Dutch law was discussed in section 2.3. The following paragraphs will first examine the scope of the third-party release provisions, and then outline the conditions necessary for approval of a third-party release.

8.32 When it comes to the personal scope, a WHOA plan can amend the rights of creditors against group entities, provided that the rights against such entities entail the payment or provision of security for the obligations of the debtor or obligations for which these legal entities are liable together with or alongside the debtor. Going back to the example of a group mentioned earlier, if Company A is the principal debtor (borrower) and Company B provides a guarantee to secure Company A's obligation to the Bank, a WHOA plan

---

noting that the court will not rule on whether the Release Clause can be invoked by or against third parties after homologation'.

71 Dutch Bankruptcy Act, Article 370(2) and Article 160.

72 A restructuring expert (*herstructureringsdeskundige*) is an independent insolvency officer who can be appointed by the court to develop and propose a WHOA plan to the debtor's creditors and shareholders, or to some of them. See Article 371 Fw. The appointment of a restructuring expert does not mean that the debtor ceases to be a debtor in possession; the debtor does not lose any powers other than those related to the WHOA plan.

adopted for Company A can amend the Bank's claim against Company B. This scenario is relatively simple. However, the WHOA's application may be less clear-cut in other cases, two of which are identified in Figure 8.2.

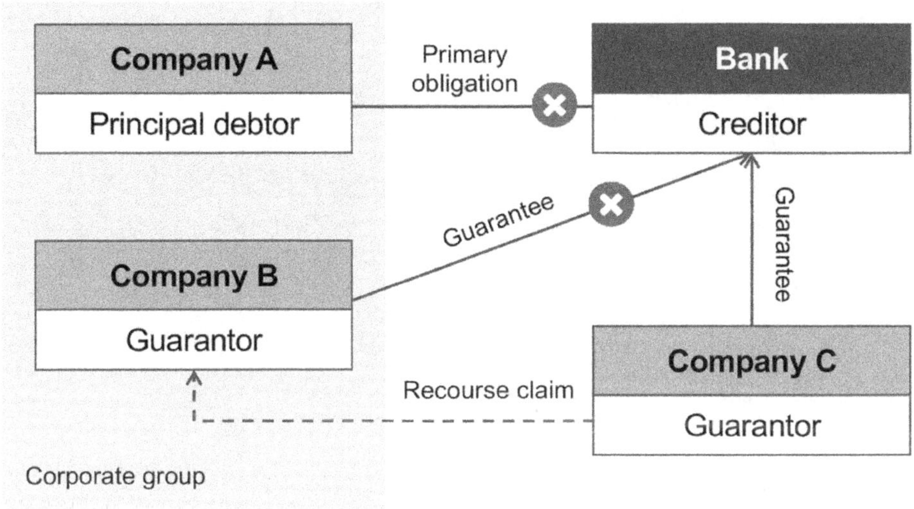

Figure 8.2 Third-party release with a non-group guarantor (Case 1)

The first case has the same facts, except that there is a non-group entity, Company C, which has also guaranteed Company A's obligations. Let us assume that upon payment to the Bank, Company C is entitled to collect from Company B in full. Company A initiates a WHOA procedure and proposes a plan that releases the obligations of Company B, so that the Bank cannot force it to pay. However, this WHOA plan does not release Company C from its obligations under the guarantee, since Company C is not part of the enterprise group. This is why the Bank is not prevented from suing Company C for the full outstanding amount. In turn, Company C can sue Company B based on a *regres* claim. If such a claim threatens the group restructuring, a third-party release is of limited use. This example demonstrates the limitations of the Dutch approach to third-party releases. While it is clear that a WHOA scheme can release group entities from obligations owed by the debtor, it is less clear whether it can release a non-debtor group entity (Company B) from obligations owed to its own creditors. Given this uncertainty, Company B may need to initiate its own WHOA procedure and restructure debts owed to Company C (see Figure 8.3). 8.33

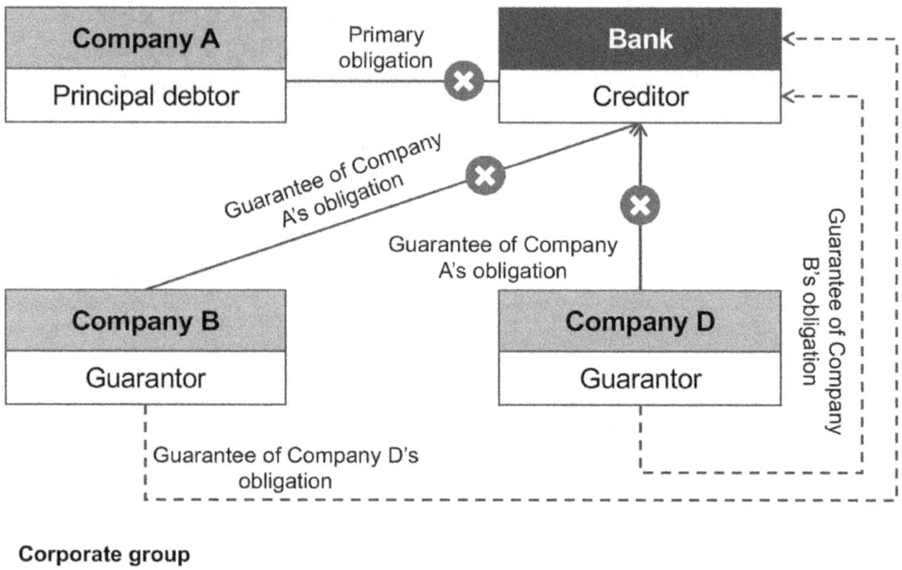

Figure 8.3 Third-party release and cross-guarantees between guarantors (Case 2)

8.34 The second case involves the same group of companies, but there is another group entity, Company D, that has extended a guarantee to the Bank. Thus, there are two group members, Company B and Company D, acting as guarantors for Company A's obligation (first-level guarantees). In addition to guaranteeing the debt of the principal debtor, Company A, Company B and Company D have guaranteed the obligations of each other (second-level guarantees). In other words, the guarantors have cross-guaranteed each other's obligations to the Bank, and in this way, they have become the principal debtors to each other. As in the case above, the WHOA plan releases the initial, first-level guarantees. Does it also release second-level guarantees?

8.35 As a general rule, a surety is liable for the original debt, even if such debt has been restructured in a WHOA plan. Therefore, one could argue that the second-level guaranteed debt survives the release of the first-level guarantees. However, the question remains whether a WHOA plan can also release second-level obligations. Providing a definitive answer to this question is difficult. Article 372 Fw specifies that a WHOA plan may amend the rights of creditors against group members, but only if the creditors' rights against such group members are intended to satisfy or secure the performance of obligations of the scheme debtor or obligations for which those legal persons are liable with or in addition to the scheme debtor. In our case, Company B and Company D have guaranteed each other's obligations. These obligations are separate and distinct from the obligations of the scheme company (Company A). Consequently, we are dealing with two separate *principal* obligations. Since neither of the guarantors – each being the principal debtor to the other – is subject to a WHOA scheme, their own separate obligations may not be released by Company A's plan. Yet, if Company A has also provided a guarantee securing the obligations of its guarantors (which is unlikely), such a release would be possible, as the WHOA debtor would be a holder of the principal obligation.

One possible way to solve this puzzle is to open separate WHOA procedures for Company B and Company D and release their obligations in such procedures.[73] However, this approach creates costs and weakens the legal framework for third-party releases, which aims to resolve intra-group obligations in one go. Nevertheless, one may argue that the obligations of the guarantors (Company B and Company D) under second-level guarantees are derived from the primary obligation of the scheme debtor (Company A), and hence should be capable of being released in the latter's WHOA plan. **8.36**

8.2.4.2 Conditions for a third-party release

The Dutch Bankruptcy Act lists several conditions for third-party releases. **8.37**

- First, claims against third parties should be ancillary to the obligations of the anchor debtor – a scheme company.[74] This means that the right of a creditor against a third party should involve the payment of or security for the obligations of the anchor debtor, or the obligations for which the third party is liable together with the anchor debtor. The obligations of group members capable of being released in a WHOA plan are given a broad interpretation and may include, inter alia, liabilities arising from the relationship of suretyship, co-debtorship and a 403-statement. It is also possible to release group obligations in a situation where the anchor debtor is not the principal debtor but a (co-)guarantor.[75] In this respect, Dutch law aligns with English case law with its flexibility. Yet, unlike English law, Dutch law does not (explicitly) provide for releases of persons other than group members, such as directors, insurers, legal and financial advisers.
- Second, a third party benefiting from a release must itself be in a state of financial distress,[76] so that it can reasonably be assumed that it will not be able to continue

73 N.B. Pannevis, Insolventierecht, Deventer: Wolters Kluwer, 2022, 29.4.4., observing that if 'the co-debtors wish to restructure their own debts in addition to their liability for the debt of the plan provider, for which they are jointly and severally liable, they could offer their own plans at the same time. Then there will be several plans. These plans can be handled jointly and, for example, be offered in a single document ...' Rb. Amsterdam 5 August 2021, ECLI:NL:RBAMS:2021:6519, *JOR* 2022/102, m.nt. R. van den Sigtenhorst.

74 Dutch Bankruptcy Act, Article 372(1)(a).

75 R. van den Sigtenhorst, in T&C Insolventierecht, commentaar op art. 372 Fw.

76 Dutch Bankruptcy Act, Article 372(1)(b).

paying its debts as they fall due.[77] The foreseen financial distress may be connected to the enforcement of a guarantee or another intra-group liability arrangement. In integrated groups, group financial distress normally entails impending insolvency not only of the principal debtor but also of group guarantors. The requirement of financial distress is added to prevent situations in which creditors are barred from pursuing their claims against solvent group members.

- Third, the group entities concerned need to consent to the release, or the plan should be proposed by a restructuring expert pursuant to Article 371 Fw.[78]
- Fourth, the court should have jurisdiction over third parties in a situation where these legal entities would themselves offer a restructuring plan.[79] In a public procedure, this amounts to either the presence of COMI or establishment (as defined under the EIR Recast) of all relevant group entities in the Netherlands,[80] or of the presence of their COMI or establishment in a non-EU jurisdiction (or in Denmark, as it falls outside the EIR Recast regime).[81] In a non-public WHOA procedure, sufficient connection to the Netherlands suffices.[82]

8.38 Additionally, the law stipulates that when deciding on the request to confirm a WHOA plan that restructures claims against guarantors, a court, on its own initiative (*ex officio*) or upon request, assesses whether the proposed plan 'in respect of these third parties' (*ten aanzien van deze rechtspersonen*) complies with the general confirmation criteria contained in Article 384 Fw.[83] In other words, the statutory confirmation criteria should be satisfied with respect to each third party, whose obligations are restructured via the plan. This is a rather peculiar norm that does not have analogues in US or UK law.

---

77 Dutch Bankruptcy Act, Article 370(1). The Explanatory Memorandum defines this access criterion as 'imminent insolvency' or 'unavoidable insolvency'. MvT, *Kamerstukken II* 2018/19, 35249, 3. This is a situation where the debtor has not yet ceased to pay its debts and is still able to meet its current obligations, but the debtor foresees that there is no realistic prospect of averting future insolvency if its debts are not restructured.

78 Dutch Bankruptcy Act, Article 372(1)(c).

79 Dutch Bankruptcy Act, Article 372(1)(d).

80 The public WHOA scheme (*De openbare akkoordprocedure buiten faillissement*) is covered by the jurisdictional rules of the EIR Recast. See Regulation (EU) 2021/2260 of 15 December 2021 amending Regulation (EU) 2015/848 on insolvency proceedings to replace its Annexes A and B. A non-public WHOA scheme does not fall within the scope of the EIR Recast.

81 Dutch Bankruptcy Act, Article 369(7). Where COMI of a group entity is not in the EU (or is in Denmark), rendering the EIR Recast inapplicable, the jurisdiction of Dutch courts with respect to a public WHOA proceeding is determined on the basis of Article 3 of the Dutch Code of Civil Procedure. For the discussion of jurisdictional aspects of WHOA schemes and third-party releases, see R. Warner and M. Veder, Enterprise Group Restructuring: Dutch Options and United States Enforcement, European Insolvency and Restructuring Journal, 2021-7, 2021.

82 Dutch Code of Civil Procedure, Article 3, establishes a flexible jurisdictional basis, under which Dutch courts have jurisdiction when either the applicant or, where there are multiple applicants, one of them has its domicile or habitual residence in the Netherlands, or when the case is otherwise sufficiently connected to the Dutch legal system. Such connection may result from jointly owed or guaranteed debt with a Dutch group member. See MvT, *Kamerstukken II* 2018/19, 35249, nr. 3.

83 Dutch Bankruptcy Act, Article 372(2)(b).

Following this norm, for example, similar to the scheme company, the guarantor must be in a state of impending financial distress. The plan or supplementing documents, as prescribed by Article 375 Fw, should encompass all relevant information covering the group entities benefiting from a third-party release, as though these entities were to offer separate WHOA plans. This comprehensive information should include details about their financial position, as well as a properly documented statement of income and expenditures.[84] Since the group plan, referred to in the Dutch parliamentary documents as a 'broad agreement' ('*breed akkoord*' in Dutch),[85] must meet the conditions related to disclosure and content with respect to each third party, some authors suggest that such a plan effectively incorporates 'mini-plans' offered by relevant group companies.[86] I will revisit this view and explore potential problems it may create later in this chapter. **8.39**

For the approval of a WHOA plan, a crucial issue is the formation of classes of creditors. Once it is determined which creditors are affected by the plan, the next question is whether these creditors will vote in one class or whether the plan provides for a class division. This division must meet the requirements of Article 374 Fw, which states that the division of creditors into classes should consider the rights that creditors have in the event of the realisation of the debtor's assets in bankruptcy or the rights given to them under the plan. Creditors should be allocated to separate classes if their rights are so different that they cannot be said to be in a comparable position. One court explained that 'a correct class division gives meaning to the vote and a democratic justification for attributing legal effect to the majority opinion'.[87] **8.40**

In any event, creditors with different ranks in insolvency must be placed into separate classes.[88] The question is whether creditors with claims against group guarantors should be placed in a separate class(es). The answer will depend on whether the rights of such creditors against the guarantors are affected by **8.41**

84 Dutch Bankruptcy Act, Article 375(2)(a) and 375(3)(d). See N.W.A. Tollenaar, Het pre-insolventieakkoord. Grondslagen en raamwerk (diss. Groningen), Deventer: Wolters Kluwer, 2016, 8.11, explaining that information about the financial position of a third party needs to be provided to enable the affected creditors to make an informed decision about the proposed amendment or waiver of claims against the third party.

85 *Kamerstukken II* 2018/19, 35249, nr. 3, p. 44.

86 R. van den Sigtenhorst, in T&C Insolventierecht, commentaar op art. 372 Fw. Also, R. van den Sigtenhorst, Herstructurering van groepen onder de WHOA, in C.M. Harmsen & M.L.H. Reumers (red.), De WHOA van wet naar recht (Recht & Praktijk, nr. InsR18), Deventer: Wolters Kluwer, 2021, 8.3.4; A.M. Mennens, Het dwangakkoord buiten surseance en faillissement (Onderneming en recht nr. 118), Deventer: Wolters Kluwer, 2020, 7.7.3.3.

87 Rb. Amsterdam 24 December 2021, ECLI:NL:RBAMS:2021:7643, r.o. 7.8.2.

88 Dutch Bankruptcy Act, Article 374(1).

the plan. In a recent case, a creditor argued that its position was significantly different from other unsecured creditors because it could enforce a guarantee if the principal debtor went bankrupt. Hence, the creditor contended that it should be placed in a separate class. The court rejected this argument and stated that the existence of a claim against the guarantor did not influence the position of the creditor under the plan or its potential recovery in a bankruptcy scenario.[89] It is important to note that the case at hand did not involve a third-party release.[90]

8.42 The outcome might be different if the creditor's rights against the guarantor are restructured in the plan. The reason for this is that the guaranteed creditor's position will be distinct from that of creditors who only have a claim against the principal debtor, and this distinct position would be specifically addressed (or altered) by the plan. As a result, guaranteed creditors subject to the effects of a third-party release should constitute a separate class or classes of creditors.[91] The division of different guaranteed creditors into separate classes may be justified when their positions in the alternative scenario (e.g. insolvent liquidation) are not identical. This could arise, for example, if their rights under the guarantees are enforceable against different group companies, leading to varying recovery rates. Consequently, the impact of the WHOA plan on guaranteed creditors would differ, necessitating their classification into separate classes. Yet, there are instances where different guaranteed creditors could

---

89 Rb. Limburg 8 October 2021, *JOR* 2022/20, m.nt. Tekstra. The same was held in Rb. Amsterdam 24 December 2021, ECLI:NL:RBAMS:2021:7643, r.o. 7.8.1. Similarly, the Grand Court of the Cayman Islands in *In the Matter of Ocean Rig UDW Incorporated, Drill Rigs Holdings Incorporated, Drillships Financing Holdings Incorporated and Drillships Ocean Ventures Incorporated (each in provisional liquidation)* 2017 (2) CILR 495 held that for the purpose of class composition, the 'fact that certain creditors had rights against other entities within the group was irrelevant as rights against third parties were not to be taken into account'. It should be noted that in this case, the guarantor companies were subject to separate schemes and no third-party release was involved.

90 However, Rb. Midden-Nederland 10 November 2021, ECLI:NL:RBMNE:2021:5531, *JOR* 2022/21, mr. drs. N.B. Pannevis. In this case, the court seems to indicate that the fact that a creditor may sue several jointly and severally liable debtors, each proposing a plan, may impact the class formation, because for such a creditor the (overall) rate of recovery is higher compared to creditors who can only sue individual debtors.

91 N.W.A. Tollenaar, Het pre-insolventieakkoord. Grondslagen en raamwerk (diss. Groningen), Deventer: Wolters Kluwer, 2016, 8.11; A.M. Mennens, Het dwangakkoord buiten surseance en faillissement (Onderneming en recht nr. 118), Deventer: Wolters Kluwer, 2020, 7.7.3.3. R. van den Sigtenhorst, Herstructurering van groepen onder de WHOA, in C.M. Harmsen & M.L.H. Reumers (red.), De WHOA van wet naar recht (Recht & Praktijk, nr. InsR18), Deventer: Wolters Kluwer, 2021, 8.3.4, stating that it may be possible to put guaranteed creditors in the same class with non-guaranteed creditors, provided that (1) the position of the guaranteed creditors in bankruptcy, and (2) their rights under the plan do not differ to such an extent that there is no comparable position with creditors of the principal debtor with whom they are placed in one class. According to Van den Sigtenhorst, this is conceivable within groups, 'certainly when there is a large or even complete financial interdependence'. One can imagine a situation where group guarantees do not substantially affect the recovery rates of guaranteed creditors, for example, because the guarantors are hopelessly insolvent.

potentially be grouped in the same class. One such example involves bondholders under two separate note programs, both secured by cross-guarantees offered by the same group members.[92] In this particular scenario, it might be easier to demonstrate that the recovery positions in the alternative scenario and under the plan are not significantly different, making it unnecessary to divide them into separate classes.

Dutch law establishes the best-interest-of-creditors test as a key safeguard to protect the rights of creditors and shareholders. According to this test, 'the court may refuse to confirm the plan … if there is prima facie evidence that [the objecting] creditors or shareholders are worse off under the plan than they would have been in a liquidation of the debtor's assets in bankruptcy'.[93] This provision ensures that a creditor cannot be forced to accept a smaller share of the value under the plan than it would receive in bankruptcy. If the creditor retains its claim against the guarantor, only the value of the principal debtor is considered.[94] **8.43**

However, the situation changes when a WHOA plan includes a third-party release. A creditor whose rights under the guarantee are restructured and who did not support the plan may object to the plan's approval, citing a violation of the best-interest-of-creditors test. If the creditor's claim against the guarantor is restructured, the court may need to assess the payment the creditor would have received if it could enforce this claim. This exercise is inherently uncertain because it requires the court to explore a hypothetical scenario based on assumptions that are themselves uncertain. When examining intercompany guarantees, this issue becomes even more complex due to the need to examine the financial strength of the guarantor and determine the value of its assets and liabilities, including group liabilities and future contribution claims. This problem is not new, as it mirrors issues faced in transaction avoidance, where the difficulty of determining the value of a group guarantee and 'predicting' an alternative (no-guarantee) scenario was emphasised (Chapter 7). If the guarantor is insolvent or may become insolvent as a result of enforcement under the **8.44**

92 See *Pathfinder Strategic Credit LP and another v. Empire Capital Resources Pte Ltd* [2019] SGCA 29, in which the issue of classification of guaranteed creditors was discussed. The question was whether the holders of different notes (2015 Noteholders and 2017 Noteholders), guaranteed by different group entities, should be classified as a single class for the purpose of voting on the scheme. The court observed that, assuming the alternative scenario is insolvent liquidation, the 2015 and 2017 Noteholders would be affected differently by the plan – the recovery rates in insolvency are different, but in the proposed scheme both creditors receive the same treatment. However, in the court's view, the difference in the recovery rates (i.e. 3 per cent) was not significant enough to call for separate classes.

93 Dutch Bankruptcy Act, Article 384(3).

94 Rb. Limburg 8 October 2021, ECLI:NL:RBLIM:2021:8851, r.o. 3.3.21.

guarantee, the determination of prospective creditor payouts in its bankruptcy will have to be conducted.

8.2.4.3 Potential impediments to third-party releases

8.45 The view of a group plan as encompassing mini-plans with respect to group guarantors might cause problems in practice. Two potential problems are discussed below.

8.46 First, let's imagine that a class of guaranteed creditors does not support the plan. Yet, for the WHOA plan to be approved and crammed down on dissenting classes, if necessary, at least *one* in-the-money class of creditors must accept the plan.[95] If we treat a third-party release as part of a separate mini-plan for the guarantor, and if we assume that the class of guaranteed creditors is the only class relevant for this mini-plan (because the rights of other creditors or shareholders of the guarantor are not affected), the requirement of having 'at-le ast-one-in-the-money-supporting-class' may not be satisfied. As a result, the mini-plan, along with the third-party release contained therein, may fail to take effect. This could pose a significant obstacle to implementing third-party releases.

8.47 Second, another issue arises from the Dutch version of the absolute priority rule (APR). Under the Dutch Bankruptcy Act, the court must refuse to confirm the plan if the distribution of value under the plan deviates to the disadvantage of the class that did not accept the plan, compared to the ranking that would apply in the debtor's bankruptcy proceedings under Book 3, Title 10 of the Dutch Civil Code.[96] If we adopt the perspective that a release forms part of a separate mini-plan, this plan must comply with key requirements, including the APR. If the affected class of guaranteed creditors does not support the plan, compliance with APR may be problematic, since the mini-plan would likely only affect the guaranteed creditors, while the rights of lower-ranking creditors and shareholders of the guarantor would remain unaffected by the plan.[97] After all, creditors and shareholders not involved in the plan will retain their entire claim against the group guarantor.

---

95 Dutch Bankruptcy Act, Article 383(1).

96 Dutch Bankruptcy Act, Article 384(4)(b).

97 These potential obstacles to the adoption of a group plan were highlighted by A.M. Mennens, Het dwangakkoord buiten surseance en faillissement (Onderneming en recht nr. 118), Deventer: Wolters Kluwer, 2020, 7.7.3.3. Notably, the problem related to the APR rule is not as acute in the UK, since this rule was not enacted as a principle for the exercise of discretion on sanctioning schemes of arrangement or Part 26A plans. *Re Virgin Active Holdings Limited* [2021] EWHC 1246 (Ch), at 289. See also, *Houst Limited* [2022] EWHC 1941, at 33, noting that a departure from the priority applicable in the relevant alternative 'is not in itself, unlike the position in the closest equivalent procedure in United States federal bankruptcy law,

The first problem creates a strong holdout position for a class of guaranteed creditors, which effectively blocks the possibility of cramming down this class. This essentially gives the class a veto right, which could be viewed as an instrument of oppression by the minority. This is why, in this particular case, it is preferable to look at the group plan alone,[98] instead of subdividing it into mini-plans. This interpretation is supported by the wording of Article 383(1) Fw, which states that at least one class of creditors must accept *the plan* (and not one class *per each mini-plan*). It can also be inferred from the wording of Article 372(2)(b) Fw, which only refers to compliance with the requirements of Article 384 Fw and does not mention Article 383(1) Fw. The absence of a reference to Article 383(1) Fw in the final text of the WHOA is especially notable in view of the fact that the Explanatory Memorandum contained such a reference to Article 383(1).[99] **8.48**

The advocated 'group approach' should facilitate estate value maximisation, making third-party releases a workable tool with the benefits of reduced transaction costs and expedient debt restructuring. As long as the best-interest-of-creditors test is complied with, and the distribution of reorganisation value under the plan is fair, the 'group approach' appears balanced and does not disproportionately encroach on the principles of equal treatment of creditors, protection of legitimate expectations and party autonomy. **8.49**

As for the second problem, it can also lead to a holdout position of a guaranteed creditor. This time, however, it might be more difficult to overcome because, in the absence of substantive consolidation, the APR applies at an entity level rather than a group level.[100] This follows from the doctrine of entity separateness, meaning that the guarantor has its own pool of creditors (liabilities) and assets, separate from those of the principal debtor. As a result, creditors are ranked separately per legal entity, in accordance with the **8.50**

---

the Chapter 11 plan, fatal to the success of the plan'. Yet, when exercising discretion to impose a plan on a dissenting class of creditors, courts will examine whether differences in treatment of the different classes of creditors *inter se* can be justified. In other words, courts analyse whether the distribution of the benefits of the restructuring (i.e. restructuring surplus) among classes is fair. See *Strategic Value Capital Solutions Master Fund LP and others v AGPS BondCo PLC* [2024] EWCA Civ 24.

98 This approach was taken by the US court *in JPMorgan Chase Bank v. Charter Commc'ns Operating, LLC (In re Charter Commc'ns)*, 419 B.R. 221, 266 (Bankr. S.D.N.Y. 2009). In this case, the group plan involved a group entity with only one creditor and this creditor voted against the plan. Section 1129(a)(10) Bankruptcy Code provides that a court cannot confirm a plan unless at least one class of impaired claims approves the plan. Yet the US court ruled that '[i]t is appropriate to test compliance with section 1129(a)(10) on a per-plan basis, not … on a per-debtor basis'.

99 *Kamerstukken II* 2018/19, 35249, 3.

100 The same applies to the best-interest-of-creditors test, which prescribes determination of liquidation value per entity.

statutory order of priority ('waterfall'). One should keep in mind that the APR ensures a fair distribution of reorganisation value, which refers to the value of the company after the plan approval and implementation.[101] To determine whether the reorganisation value is fairly distributed, the size of a creditor's claim is compared to the relative claim that this creditor has in the reorganisation value. If the reorganisation value exceeds the total debts, there is no priority issue, as each class receives 100 per cent, and creditors affected by the plan are fully compensated.[102]

8.51 The situation is different if the reorganisation value is insufficient to cover all debts. In this case, if a class votes against the plan, it must be determined whether that class receives its share of the reorganisation value of the relevant entity under the plan in accordance with the statutory waterfall. Since the Dutch Bankruptcy Act mandates compliance with the APR in respect of third parties (such as group guarantors), it becomes difficult to justify releasing or amending a creditor's claim against a guarantor while leaving the guarantor's shareholders unaffected. A strict application of the APR suggests that shareholders cannot retain their shareholdings in the guarantor company against the will of (classes of) creditors unless the creditors have been fully compensated.

8.52 One way to address the described problem is to arrange restructuring at the parent company level. If the shareholders are wiped out at this top level, the issues caused by the APR can be resolved more easily, as the creditors' claims will be addressed within the restructuring process of the group's ultimate parent, potentially eliminating the concern of separate priority rules for each guarantor entity. Alternatively, it may be argued that the value of the shares in the third-party guarantor is effectively zero, meaning that allowing shareholders to retain their equity does not confer any value ahead of creditors. The success of this argument, however, will depend on the interpretation of 'value' under Article 384(4)(b) Fw – that is, whether worthless shares can be considered as having value.[103] In my opinion, even if the equity interest in the guarantor does not have a positive present market value, the power to control it and the right to share in future profits could be deemed to give such equity potential value.

---

101 Rb. Amsterdam 2 September 2021, ECLI:NL:RBAMS:2021:6521, r.o. 10.8.

102 Rb. Amsterdam 3 November 2021, ECLI:NL:RBAMS:2021:6522, r.o. 9.17.

103 Note that the Dutch version of the APR refers to the distribution of 'value' realised under the plan, whereas US law mentions 'any property'. In the past, some parties in US bankruptcy proceedings argued that the interest they retained under the plan was valueless and therefore did not constitute property. However, this argument did not survive the scrutiny of the US Supreme Court. See *Norwest Bank Worthington v. Ahlers*, 485 U.S. 197 (1988).

Finally, it is worth noting that the Dutch APR is not strict and allows for an exception. When the distribution deviates from the statutory priority of claims (the bankruptcy 'waterfall'), the debtor needs to demonstrate: (i) reasonable grounds for such a deviation; and (ii) that the interests of the dissenting creditors are not harmed under the plan.[104] The term 'reasonable grounds' is not clearly defined, but in a group context, it could involve considering the total reorganisation value generated or realised by the group plan, which might otherwise be lost if the plan were not accepted. Therefore, for the purpose of determining the fairness of distribution, one may consider the total (group) reorganisation value and the *relative* entitlement of the creditor to such reorganisation value. The contribution to a plan by the guarantor's shareholders (new value exception) might also be taken into account.[105] 8.53

In extreme cases, holdout behaviour by a guaranteed creditor could be qualified as an abuse of power.[106] That being said, we should keep in mind that the concept of abuse of power is narrowly interpreted and cannot serve as a general solution to the problem. Ultimately, the rigid application of the APR to each affected group member can undermine the effectiveness of third-party releases for enterprise groups. Thus, the safest – and seemingly the most popular – option is to avoid cross-class cram downs by securing consensual approval of third-party releases.[107] 8.54

104 Dutch Bankruptcy Act, Article 384(4)(b). R. van den Sigtenhorst, in T&C Insolventierecht, commentaar op art. 384 Fw, observing with regard to the second requirement that it 'can hardly be understood in any other way than a repetition of the best interest test concretely for those who object ...' See Rb. Den Haag 23 July 2021, ECLI:NL:RBDHA:2021:8121.

105 N. Tollenaar, Pre-Insolvency Proceedings: A Normative Foundation and Framework, OUP, 2018, para. 6.97, observing that under the new value exception, shareholders can retain their investment, 'even if dissenting senior classes are not fully satisfied, if in consideration for their retained interest they contribute new funds or new value that is at least equal to the value of their retained interest'. For the discussion of new value exception, APR and the position of shareholders, see Rb. Midden-Nederland 31 March 2022, ECLI:NL:RBMNE:2022:1329, r.o. 4.42ff, *JOR* 2022/240, m.nt. R. van den Sigtenhorst, noting that a shareholder may preserve a stake in the debtor if he acquires this stake at market price by contributing new money. Such a contribution must be in reasonable proportion to the value that is obtained or retained. In scrutinising the new money exception and the adequacy of the shareholder contribution, the court considered the fact that no other party, including the dissenting creditor, was willing to provide the funds necessary to implement the restructuring.

106 Dutch Civil Code, Article 3:13. See HR 12 August 2005, *NJ* 2006/230 (*Groenemeijer/Payroll*); HR 24 March 2017, *NJ* 2017/466 (*Mondia/V&D*), dealing with the possibility to force one or several creditors to join the agreement proposed by the debtor out of court, where the majority of creditors have already agreed to the agreement, and the holdout creditor's behaviour is regarded an abuse of rights.

107 Rb. Amsterdam 21 maart 2024, ECLI:NL:RBAMS:2024:1674 (*McDermott*); Rb. Amsterdam 2 augustus 2023, ECLI:NL:RBAMS:2023:6160, *JOR* 2024/18 (*Diebold Nixdorf*) with reference to Rb. Amsterdam 8 juni 2023, ECLI:NL:RBAMS:2023:6159, *RI* 2023/103 (*Diebold Nixdorf*).

8.3 CONCLUSIONS AND SUGGESTIONS

8.3.1 Overview of main findings

8.55 Third-party releases are born out of commercial necessity. They synchronise legal responses to business and financing models, addressing the complexity of group interdependences facilitated by intra-group liability arrangements. They ensure a 'single point of entry' to the resolution of group crises, saving costs that would otherwise arise from multiple proceedings. But the significance of third-party releases goes beyond mere cost-saving. They provide the liberating effect of debt alteration or discharge to third (non-debtor) parties. I will refer to this effect as the 'extension effect'. The economic benefits of third-party releases are clear. They protect the continuity of an enterprise against the destabilising function of cross-guarantees. Alternatively, the simultaneous enforcement of cross-entity obligations for the full amount may result in the destruction of enterprise value.

8.56 A good example of a case where the parallel enforcement of debt under cross-entity liability arrangements greatly complicated a centralised group restructuring is Oi Brazil (section 1.1.3). This case featured an integrated cross-border group of companies with a complex centralised financing structure, involving special purpose financing entities in the Netherlands, guarantees extended by the parent and operating companies in Brazil, and intercompany loans. In such a case, third-party releases – either at the level of operating companies or financing companies – can save costs, prevent conflicting judgments, accelerate group reorganisation and promote the preservation and maximisation of value.

8.57 However, the extension effect does not sit well with the traditional entity-by-entity approach to corporate insolvency. It also interferes with personal security rights, such as guarantees, which are based on the principle of entity separateness. Thus, it implicates freedom of contract to the extent that it affects the rights of creditors against third parties and the obligations of these third parties. Non-consensual amendment or discharge of creditors' claims is an extraordinary feature of restructuring or insolvency proceedings. But in the case of third-party releases, these effects are achieved without opening such proceedings with respect to third parties benefiting from releases. This explains why third-party releases are controversial and treated differently across jurisdictions.

8.58 English courts adhere to a pro-release approach and consider third-party releases a common practice in schemes of arrangement. Most English schemes deal with financial indebtedness, restructure group obligations and are approved without opposition. In contrast, US courts have adopted restrictive approaches to the availability of non-consensual third-party releases. This negative attitude to third-party releases was driven almost exclusively by their use in mass tort bankruptcies. In a recent judgment in *Purdue Pharma*, the US Supreme Court concluded that the Bankruptcy Code did not authorise non-consensual third-party releases. The Dutch WHOA framework tailors third-party releases to address financial distress in enterprise groups and includes safeguards to protect affected creditors.

As indicated above, third-party releases may contribute to the preservation and maximisation of estate value. However, they can also disrupt the protective function of group guarantees and other cross-liability arrangements. Any limitation of rights under these arrangements constitutes an interference with freedom of contract and party autonomy. A release may also conflict with the principle of equal treatment of creditors if the substantive rights of a guaranteed creditor against a guarantor are altered (e.g. reduced or written down) under the plan, while non-guaranteed creditors do not lose such rights, for they never had them in the first place. This results in different (less favourable) treatment for guaranteed creditors compared to non-guaranteed creditors. Finally, if the rules on third-party releases and their application are unpredictable, unclear and non-uniform, the protection of creditors' legitimate expectations is at stake. 8.59

Weakening the protection afforded by intra-group guarantees, co-debtorship and collateral arrangements is likely to reduce the amount a guaranteed creditor can recover upon the debtor's default, potentially causing the creditor's own financial distress or insolvency. This diminishes the economic value of cross-guarantees, potentially resulting in higher borrowing costs and a decrease in credit availability.[108] 8.60

8.3.2 Suggestions on third-party releases in a group context

In pursuit of a balanced solution, the following suggestions can be made regarding third-party releases in a group context. 8.61

First, a third-party release should comply with the best-interest-of-creditors test. This test protects creditor entitlements, promotes substantive fairness and 8.62

108 P.M. Boyle, Non-Debtor Liability in Chapter 11: Validity of Third-Party Discharge in Bankruptcy, Fordham Law Review, Vol. 61, 1992, p. 443, noting that the 'availability of the guarantee may reduce the cost of credit because the interest rate on loans will decrease as the risk of default decreases'.

ensures the protection of property rights. For a guaranteed creditor, this test should be applied with the existence of a claim against a third party in mind. This may require assessing what the guaranteed creditor would have received had it pursued a lawsuit against the guarantor, co-debtor or collateral provider. I propose to call this assessment the 'group best-interest-of-creditors' test.

8.63 Admittedly, applying the 'group best-interest-of-creditors' test may face practical complications and require comprehensive disclosures from a non-debtor seeking to benefit from a release. Nevertheless, these are necessary sacrifices to ensure that a creditor is not deprived of the benefits afforded by a valid and effective personal or proprietary security arrangement. A valid claim against a third party is a property right that should not be taken away without adequate compensation.[109] This is precisely why a guaranteed creditor should not be worse off under the restructuring plan containing a third-party release than in an alternative scenario – typically insolvency – where the creditor retains its right to sue the third party. Any other solution risks being disproportionate and would undermine the protective function of the relevant security arrangement. This suggestion aims to safeguard the value of existing creditor entitlements, promote substantive fairness and ensure the protection of property rights.

8.64 **Second,** given the diversity of groups, their financial arrangements and crisis situations, it is impossible to come up with a simple, bullet-proof, universal formula to determine whether a third-party release is desirable or justified. Instead, I identify circumstances where the case for third-party releases is strong and where it is weak.

8.65 The case for approving a third-party release is stronger when:

- *The release is consensual.* If the creditor consents to the release, such release should not raise any objections, as it is in line with party autonomy and does not negatively affect the insolvency estate or the rights of other creditors.
- *The release involves a derivative claim.* This applies when the claim belongs to the debtor rather than the creditor. However, claims under cross-guarantees, co-debtorship and other intra-group liability arrangements are not derivative, as they belong to the guaranteed creditor and not the debtor.
- *Existence of recourse claims.* A third party, such as a guarantor, may be entitled to file a recourse claim (e.g. indemnity or *regres*) in full against the debtor, undermining

109 J.L. Schroeder and D.G. Carlson, Third Party Releases Under the Bankruptcy Code After Purdue Pharma, American Bankruptcy Institute Law Review, Vol. 31, 2023, p. 3, arguing that a release of creditors' claims against third parties 'constitutes an expropriation of property owned by individual creditors'. The authors refer to reorganisation plans that contain this type of release, and which do not provide for adequate compensation, as 'theft plans'.

the success of its restructuring efforts. This is the 'ricochet problem', described in Chapter 5. If not addressed, this problem can lead to a failed restructuring and reduced estate value.

- *The release is part of a purely financial restructuring involving sophisticated parties.* Well-informed, sophisticated and strongly adjusting creditors are better positioned to diversify their risks and seek guidance from professional advisors. As a result, conflicts between weak and strong creditors are less likely to occur, reducing concerns about the fairness and foreseeability of a third-party release in a purely financial restructuring.
- *An enterprise group is integrated, and the likely failure of a third party resulting from the enforcement of a guarantee will have a significant detrimental effect on the debtor's own survival.* This is the case where the group member benefiting from a release plays an important role within the anchor debtor's group of companies or is an integral part of the anchor debtor's restructuring. Any failure to address this may lead to the 'orphan restructuring problem', described in Chapter 5. In essence, the orphan restructuring problem harms the principle of estate value preservation and maximisation as applied to a group context.
- *The release is necessary to facilitate efficient, speedy and cost-effective restructuring.* This can be particularly advantageous for international enterprise groups, like Oi Brazil, where the opening of multiple proceedings against group entities in different countries significantly complicates a centralised group solution and leads to excessive costs, substantial delays, holdout behaviour and even conflicting judgments.

By contrast, the need for a third-party release may be called into question when: 8.66

- *None of the elements mentioned above are present.*
- *The third party is not financially distressed and does not become financially distressed as a result of the enforcement of the guarantee or collateral.* If the third party is solvent, liquid and able to satisfy the debt without becoming insolvent or illiquid, the case for a third-party release is weaker. Discharging the liability of a third party solely because the principal debtor is in financial distress and unable to fully satisfy the creditor's claim is difficult to justify. Interference with contractual rights is hard to substantiate if the guarantor, co-debtor or collateral provider is not financially distressed or insolvent. In such a case, the protection of legitimate expectations, freedom of contract and party autonomy should prevail.
- *The case involves a piecemeal liquidation rather than business preservation.* In a piecemeal liquidation, the need to preserve the debtor's going concern value is limited, and therefore, a third-party release – being first and foremost a restructuring tool aimed at business preservation – is less necessary. Worth noting is that business preservation does not necessarily require maintaining the business within current companies and may be achieved through a business sale.

Third, the strict application of certain national rules can create roadblocks to the efficient use of third-party releases. As discussed in the sections on 8.67

WHOA schemes, these rules may not allow third-party releases when the guarantors are outside the debtor's group or when they provide separate guarantees securing debts of each other. Additional challenges may arise from conditions imposed on third-party releases, such as requirements to have at least one supporting class of creditors and adherence to the APR for each group entity involved. If these requirements must be met for a third party whose obligations are being modified or released, guaranteed creditors may effectively acquire veto power, rendering third-party releases less practical or even unfeasible outside consensual plans. The need for law to be applied in a commercially sensible way, particularly in financial restructuring cases, in my view, justifies a flexible application of certain rules and special consideration given to group reorganisation value. However, the key safeguard of the 'group best-interest-of-creditors-test' should remain in full force.

9

INSOLVENCY STAY ON CREDITOR ACTION AND ITS EXTENSION TO GROUP ENTITIES

9.1 INTRODUCTION

A stay of individual enforcement actions and the replacement of such actions 9.01
with a collective enforcement process are among the cornerstones of modern insolvency law. They aim to preserve the value of the insolvency estate and facilitate its efficient administration.[1] Thus, a stay effectively addresses the common pool problem. Jackson explains that:

> To the extent that a non-piecemeal collective process (whether in the form of liquidation or reorganization) is likely to increase the aggregate value of the pool of assets, its substitution for individual remedies would be advantageous to the creditors as a group. This is derived from the commonplace notion: that a collection of assets is sometimes more valuable than the same assets would be if spread to the winds. It is often referred to as the surplus of a going concern value over a liquidation value.[2]

1 UNCITRAL Legislative Guide on Insolvency Law, Part two, 2004, Ch. II, para. 26; O. Couwenberg and S.J. Lubben, Essential Corporate Bankruptcy Law, EBOR, Vol. 16, 2015, p. 49; T.H. Jackson, The Logic and Limits of Bankruptcy Law, Harvard University Press, 1986, p. 14.

2 T.H. Jackson, The Logic and Limits of Bankruptcy Law, Harvard University Press, 1986, p. 14.

9.02 A stay plays an equally important role in proceedings aimed at rescuing ailing companies, as it provides the debtor with breathing space, safeguards its going concern value and strengthens its position in negotiations with creditors.[3] Without a stay, creditors could seize assets essential for carrying out the business, jeopardising any prospects for successful restructuring. By blocking the actions of individual creditors that might frustrate restructuring efforts, even if these efforts are supported by the majority of creditors, a stay mitigates the anti-commons problem.[4] Whereas the commons problem addresses the collective action problem arising from the large number of creditors and the difficulty of coordinating their actions, the anti-commons problem stems from the fragmented and conflicting interests among creditors.[5] In addition to preserving the value of the insolvency estate, a stay also ensures equality of distribution among creditors (*paritas creditorum*) by preventing the grab race.[6]

9.03 The importance of a stay is emphasised by various standard-setting organisations, including the World Bank,[7] UNCITRAL,[8] FSB[9] and EBRD.[10] The Restructuring Directive acknowledges that a 'debtor should be able to benefit from a temporary stay of individual enforcement actions ... with the aim of supporting the negotiations on a restructuring plan, in order to be able to continue operating or at least to preserve the value of its estate during the negotiations'.[11]

---

3 See H.R. Rep. No. 95-595, 95th Cong., 1st Sess. 340 (1977), noting that a stay 'gives the debtor a breathing spell from his creditors. It stops all collection efforts, all harassment, and all foreclosure actions. It permits the debtor to attempt a repayment or reorganization plan, or simply to be relieved of the financial pressures that drove him into bankruptcy'.

4 On the problem of holdouts and the tragedy of anti-commons in insolvency and restructuring, see R.J. de Weijs, Harmonisation of European Insolvency Law and the Need to Tackle Two Common Problems: Common Pool and Anticommons, International Insolvency Review, Vol. 21, 2012, pp. 67-83. See, generally, M.A. Heller, The Tragedy of the Anticommons: Property in the Transition from Marx to Markets, Harvard Law Review, Vol. 111, 1998, pp. 621-688.

5 D.G. Baird and R.K. Rasmussen, Antibankruptcy, The Yale Law Journal, Vol. 119, 2010, p. 648.

6 See, however, B. Wessels and S. Madaus (eds), Rescue of Business in Europe: A European Law Institute Instrument, OUP, 2020, p. 195, observing that 'a stay does not primarily serve to guarantee equal treatment of creditors, but rather serves to protect the realisation of the intention of the debtor to restructure its business'.

7 World Bank, Principles for Effective Insolvency and Creditor/Debtor Regimes, 2021, C5, stating that the 'injunctive relief (stay) should be as wide and all-encompassing as possible, extending to an interest in assets used, occupied, or in the possession of the debtor'.

8 UNCITRAL Legislative Guide (2004), Part two, Ch. II, para. 26ff.

9 FSB Key Attributes of Effective Resolution Regimes for Financial Institutions, 2014, KA 3.2. referring to the power of resolution authorities to impose a stay on creditor actions to attach assets or otherwise collect money or property from a bank, and the power to temporarily stay the exercise of early termination rights that may otherwise be triggered upon entry of a bank into resolution.

10 EBRD Core Principles of an Effective Insolvency System, September 2020, Principle 6.

11 Restructuring Directive, Recital 32, Articles 6 and 7.

This chapter discusses the stays available to companies in financial distress. It is no coincidence that it follows the chapter on third-party releases. A stay – when extended to group guarantors, co-debtors, or collateral providers – ensures the effectiveness of a third-party release. But even without such a release, it can be employed to address the problems created by the triangle of rights and liabilities (see Chapter 5), even if only temporarily. **9.04**

This chapter proceeds as follows. First, I describe the main features of how a stay is regulated in the chosen national legal systems (section 9.2). This study demonstrates that the availability, design and scope of a stay vary across jurisdictions, and sometimes even within the same jurisdiction, depending on the applicable procedure. For instance, in the UK, an automatic stay applies in administration but is not available in schemes of arrangement or CVAs. Besides, a stay binds secured creditors in administration, but not in liquidation. Under Dutch law, secured creditors are generally unaffected by bankruptcy. In contrast, under US bankruptcy law, a wide-ranging stay is automatically imposed on both secured and unsecured creditors. Second, since this book primarily focuses on group financial arrangements, I explore whether an enforcement stay can have an extension effect. In other words, I look into the personal scope of a stay and examine whether it can be extended to cover third parties, such as group entities acting as guarantors, co-debtors and collateral providers (section 9.3), even if they are not themselves subject to an insolvency or restructuring proceeding. Section 9.4 provides suggestions on when a group-wide extension of a stay may be desirable. **9.05**

9.2 ENFORCEMENT STAYS IN NATIONAL LAW

9.2.1 The UK: patchwork of different rules and procedures

The rules on enforcement stays are found in the laws of many jurisdictions. However, the scope of these rules and the mode of their operation (e.g. automatic vs. non-automatic, general stay vs. selective stay, and the duration of the stay) vary depending on the type of procedure or the creditor concerned.[12] **9.06**

English law is not homogeneous. It offers a menu of procedures that can be used in situations of financial distress, including winding up by the court, administration, administrative receivership, CVAs, and more recently, a standalone moratorium. While these procedures are part of the Insolvency Act **9.07**

12 G. McCormack, A. Keay, S. Brown and J. Dahlgreen, Study on a new approach to business failure and insolvency, 2016, pp. 230–231.

1986, schemes of arrangement, often relied on to restructure debts of financially distressed firms, fall under the Companies Act 2006. The existence, purpose and scope of a stay depend on the applicable procedure. For example, differences can be observed between a liquidation stay applicable upon making a winding-up order,[13] and an administration stay applicable during administration.[14] A liquidation stay 'is designed to avoid the unnecessary expenditure of assets otherwise available for distribution amongst creditors and to support the replacement of a creditor's right to establish a claim by judgment in an action with a right to lodge a proof of debt'.[15] This stay does not affect the right of a secured creditor to enforce security or other real rights, as the goal of liquidation is not rehabilitation but the disposal of the debtor's assets and distribution of the proceeds among creditors.[16] By contrast, administration imposes a statutory moratorium on the enforcement of most types of claims, including secured ones.[17] Therefore, no steps may be taken to enforce security over the debtor's property except with the consent of an administrator or court permission.[18] This stay is designed to facilitate the preservation of the debtor's business as a going concern. Yet, historically, administration in the UK has been associated with the end of reorganisation prospects.[19]

9.08 The CIGA introduced a new, stand-alone moratorium procedure aimed at providing the debtor with a breathing space to explore its restructuring options free from creditor action.[20] Its scope is broadly similar to an administration stay, with some differences. When a company invokes a moratorium, it is entitled to a 'payment holiday' for its pre-moratorium debt, which includes both (i) debts due before the moratorium, and (ii) debts that fall due during the moratorium but arise from obligations incurred before the moratorium.[21] Certain debts are excluded from the moratorium, such as the monitor's remuneration or expenses, amounts payable for goods or services supplied during the moratorium, rent for a period during the moratorium and wages or salary arising from a contract of employment.[22] While the payment holiday in

13 Insolvency Act 1986, s. 130(2).

14 Insolvency Act 1986, Schedule B1, para. 43.

15 *Gardner v. Lemma Europe Insurance Company Ltd* [2016] EWCA Civ 484, at 2.

16 *Heis & Ors (Administrators of MF Global UK Ltd.) v. MF Global Inc.* [2012] EWHC 3068 (Ch), at 33.

17 Administration does not affect the enforceability of a security interest under a financial collateral arrangement. See Regulation 8(1)(a), Financial Collateral Arrangements (No. 2) Regulations 2003.

18 Insolvency Act 1986, Schedule B1, para. 43.

19 S. Paterson, Corporate Reorganization Law and Forces of Change, OUP, 2020, p. 239.

20 Insolvency Act 1986, Part A1. Between 26 June 2020 and 30 September 2024, 57 moratoriums were obtained. See Official Statistics. Monthly Insolvency Statistics, 18 October 2024.

21 Insolvency Act 1986, Part A1, Ch. 4, s. A18(3).

22 Ibid.

principle applies to both unsecured and secured creditors,[23] it does not extend to 'debts … arising under a contract or other instrument involving financial services'.[24] This exclusion covers loan agreements.[25] Consequently, unless the lender consents to a payment holiday, the debtor must continue making payments under a loan agreement, regardless of whether the payment obligation arises before or after the moratorium begins. This may reduce the attractiveness of the moratorium procedure in practice.[26]

Unlike the procedures described above, which in one way or another encompass a stay, the Companies Act 2006 does not prescribe a stay. Neither schemes of arrangement (Part 26) nor restructuring plans (Part 26A) provide the debtor with a break. The absence of a stay leaves the company exposed to creditor actions during the period when the proposed restructuring is negotiated and implemented. This exposure is not insignificant, considering it can take at least eight weeks from the proposal of a scheme to its sanctioning by the court.[27] In some cases, courts have recognised their jurisdiction to order a stay of proceedings initiated by a creditor against the debtor to recover debt, pending the implementation of a scheme of arrangement. This jurisdiction is usually based on the UK Civil Procedure Rules (CPR) and the court's case management powers.[28] Additionally, a scheme of arrangement or a restructuring plan may be accompanied by a freestanding moratorium (Part A1), which can support the negotiation of a scheme or restructuring plan. Yet, as noted above, this moratorium does not apply to contracts involving financial services. Alternatively, a standstill agreement can be entered into with a selected group of financial creditors. A standstill agreement is a useful contractual solution, 9.09

23 In addition, a moratorium imposes a restriction on the enforcement of security over the debtor's property, subject to specified exceptions (e.g. financial collateral). See Insolvency Act 1986, Part A1, Ch. 4, s. A21(1)(s).

24 Insolvency Act 1986, Part A1, Ch. 4, s. A18(3).

25 Insolvency Act 1986, Schedule ZA2. See *Minor Hotel Group MEA DMCC v. Dymant & Anor* [2022] EWHC 340 (Ch), at 14, observing that the 'exclusion of finance debts from the "payment holiday" effects of a moratorium is somewhat surprising: but is the clear meaning of the amended Act'.

26 J. Payne, An Assessment of the UK Restructuring Moratorium, Lloyd's Maritime and Commercial Law Quarterly, 2021, p. 465, explaining that 'for the moratorium to be fully effective the company will need to have the support of its lenders, and possibly enter into some form of waiver or standstill agreement with them'.

27 J. Payne, Schemes of Arrangement: Theory, Structure and Operation, CUP, 2021, p. 239.

28 *BlueCrest Mercantile BV v. Vietnam Shipbuilding Industry Group* [2013] EWHC 1146 (Comm). The court stated that the scheme of arrangement had a reasonable prospect of success, and relied on CPR, Rule 3.1(2)(f). Under this rule, the court has the power to 'stay the whole or part of any proceedings or judgment either generally or until a specified date or event'. *Sea Assets Ltd v. PT Garuda Indonesia*, 27 June 2001, unreported. Another case where the CPR were relied on to order a stay is *Riverside CREM 3 Ltd v Virgin Active Health Clubs Ltd* [2021] EWHC 746 (Ch), at 34, establishing that the 'process under Part 26A should be permitted to proceed without being impeded by a judgment being entered or enforced'.

especially for situations where creditors are not numerous and have homogeneous interests.

9.10 The last procedure worth mentioning is a company voluntary arrangement (CVA),[29] valued as a debt restructuring mechanism.[30] If a CVA runs in parallel with a winding-up or administration, it benefits from the statutory moratorium. Besides, prior to the CIGA, the law allowed directors of 'eligible companies' to take steps to obtain a moratorium if they intended to make a proposal for a CVA – a so-called small company moratorium.[31] This was available to companies meeting certain criteria related to turnover, balance sheet, or the number of employees.[32] The small company moratorium regime was not widely used,[33] and was replaced by the standalone moratorium, discussed above. Outside these special cases, entry into a CVA does not attract a moratorium. In the absence of a moratorium, a CVA can alter obligations and impose new payment terms, so that creditors would only be able to institute any action if these terms have not been complied with by the debtor.[34] However, creditors not bound by the CVA face no such restrictions and can initiate any action based on their claims.

9.11 Describing the corporate reorganisation toolbox in the UK and the USA, Paterson emphasises the striking difference between 'relative weakness of available moratorium (or stay) protection in English corporate reorganization law when compared with the US'.[35] The following section examines the scope and operation of the automatic stay under US bankruptcy law.

---

29 Insolvency Act 1986, Part I.

30 See e.g. *Discovery (Northampton) Ltd v. Debenhams Retail Ltd* [2019] EWHC 2441 (Ch). Note, however, that a CVA does not bind preferential and secured creditors without their consent. Insolvency Act 1986, s. 4.

31 Insolvency Act 1986, Schedule A1 (abolished by the CIGA).

32 Ibid. Section 382(3), Companies Act 2006. I. Fletcher, The Law of Insolvency, 5th edn, Sweet & Maxwell, 2017, paras. 15-054 to 15-059.

33 P. Walton, C. Umfreville and L. Jacobs, A Snapshot of Company Voluntary Arrangements: Success, Failure and Proposals for Reform, International Insolvency Review, Vol. 29, 2020, p. 269.

34 On this point, it has been noted that a moratorium is 'an almost universal feature of a concluded CVA, although its effect is confined to those bound by the CVA'. K. van Zwieten, Goode on Principles of Corporate Insolvency Law, 5th edn, Sweet & Maxwell, 2018, para. 11-54. See also J. Payne, Schemes of Arrangement: Theory, Structure and Operation, OUP, 2014, p. 216, observing that 'a CVA will only have this effect [a stay] if its terms so provide. Without such a term any creditor, even one bound by a CVA, is free to pursue his claims by action, whereas with such a term, creditors bound by the CVA are not free to pursue their claims, save for those creditors outside the CVA (e.g. the secured creditors)'.

35 S. Paterson, Corporate Reorganization Law and Forces of Change, OUP, 2020, p. 239.

9.2.2 The USA: broad, automatic and worldwide stay

The filing of a bankruptcy petition in the USA automatically opens the bankruptcy case and triggers a worldwide stay binding on the debtor's creditors, whether secured or unsecured. The stay is akin to a statutory injunction, as a result of which '[i]nstead of an uncontrolled self-help scramble for the debtor's assets, creditor claims must be dealt with in an orderly manner under the supervision and control of the bankruptcy court'.[36] Actions carried out in violation of a stay – whether or not a party had knowledge of the bankruptcy filing – are deemed void *ab initio*,[37] and, when intentional, may be punishable as contempt of court. **9.12**

The stay covers the commencement or continuation of any judicial, administrative or other action or proceeding against the debtor that was, or could have been, commenced before the Chapter 11 case, as well as the recovery of a claim against the debtor that arose before the commencement of the case.[38] Importantly, a claim arises at the time when the obligation is incurred, and not when it is due.[39] Lawsuits based on post-petition claims are not stayed unless the debtor seeks and obtains injunctive relief from the bankruptcy court. The stay precludes creditors from enforcing pre-petition judgments, perfecting or enforcing pre-petition liens, foreclosing on collateral, terminating executory contracts on account of pre-petition default (as executory contracts are considered property of the estate), setting-off pre-petition debts arising from different transactions, etc.[40] In sum, the automatic stay is extensive and normally remains in place for the whole duration of the bankruptcy procedure.[41] **9.13**

There are myriad exceptions to the automatic stay. They include, inter alia, enforcement by a governmental unit of a 'police and regulatory power', including protection of public health, safety and welfare,[42] commencement or continuation of a criminal action or proceeding against the debtor,[43] and the exercise of contractual rights under various financial contracts (e.g. repos, commodity **9.14**

---

36 C.J. Tabb, Law of Bankruptcy, 4th edn, West Academic Publishing, 2016, p. 235.

37 A minority of courts holds the view that acts taken in violation of the stay are voidable. See e.g. *In re Coho Res., Inc.*, 345 F.3d 338, 344 (5th Cir. 2003).

38 11 U.S. Code § 362(a)(1). For the broad definition of a 'claim' see § 101(5).

39 Collier on Bankruptcy, 16th edn, 2022, Vol. 3, ¶ 362.03[3][a].

40 11 U.S. Code § 362(a)(2)–(8).

41 11 U.S. Code § 362(c)(2).

42 11 U.S. Code § 362(b)(4). Note that the police power exception in principle does not affect the stay applicable to the enforcement of a money judgment even if it is connected to the government's police and regulatory powers.

43 11 U.S. Code § 362(b)(1).

contracts, forward contracts, securities contracts, swap agreements).[44] Parties to these contracts enjoy the privilege to the extent that they are not limited in exercising their right 'to cause the liquidation, termination, or acceleration' of the contract by the prohibition of ipso facto clauses.

9.15 Unlike a liquidation stay in the UK, or the stays discussed below in Dutch bankruptcy and suspension of payments procedures, a stay under the US Bankruptcy Code also binds secured creditors. In specific circumstances, a secured creditor can request relief from the stay. In fact, motions related to stay relief are among the most common forms of litigation in bankruptcy procedures.[45] The law stipulates that:

> On request of a party in interest and after notice and a hearing, the court shall grant relief from the stay provided under subsection (a) of this section, such as by terminating, annulling, modifying, or conditioning such stay –
> (1) for cause, including the lack of adequate protection of an interest in property of such party in interest;
> (2) with respect to a stay of an act against property under subsection (a) of this section, if –
> (A) the debtor does not have an equity in such property; and
> (B) such property is not necessary to an effective reorganization;[46]

9.16 This provision aims to establish a balance between the interests of a debtor and unsecured creditors in a reorganisation process, on the one hand, and the interests of secured creditors and other property rights holders, on the other hand. If the value of collateral declines during a stay, the interests of a secured creditor are affected and require adequate protection. Conversely, the absence of any decline in the value of collateral might be regarded as a lack of impairment of the creditor's rights, indicating that these rights are adequately protected.

9.17 'Adequate protection' is a flexible concept that should be assessed against the facts and circumstances of each case.[47] The purpose of ensuring adequate pro-

---

44 11 U.S. Code § 362(b)(6), (7), (17), (27). A.J. Levitin, Business Bankruptcy: Financial Restructuring and Modern Commercial Markets, Wolters Kluwer, 2016, p. 266, noting that the 'anti-forfeiture principle and the general policy of favoring reorganization are not limitations on financial contract creditors' and that their exemption from a stay 'is essentially the ultra super-priority'. Also, S.J. Lubben, Subsidizing Liquidity or Subsidizing Markets: Safe Harbors, Derivatives, and Finance, American Bankruptcy Law Journal, Vol. 91, 2017, p. 472, observing that 'the bankruptcy court has no ability to stay the exercise of safe harbor rights or the commencement of closeout netting'.

45 C.J. Tabb, Law of Bankruptcy, 4th edn, West Academic Publishing, 2016, p. 285.

46 11 U.S. Code § 362(d).

47 H. Rep. No. 595, 95th Cong., 1st Sess. 343-4 (1977), U.S. Code Cong. & Admin. News 1978, p. 5787. See also *In re Alyucan Interstate Corp.*, 12 B.R. 803 (Bankr. D. Utah 1981); *In re Bushee*, 319 B.R. 542, 551 (Bankr. E.D. Tenn. 2004), noting that the 'determination of whether a creditor's interest is adequately protected is not an exact science nor does it involve a precise arithmetic computation. Rather, it is

tection as a prerequisite for the continuation of an automatic stay is to guarantee that the creditor receives the value for which they bargained prior to the bankruptcy.[48] This is rooted in the property interest protections of the Fifth Amendment to the US Constitution.[49] In practice, adequate protection can take various forms. It may involve cash payments (lump sum or, more commonly, periodic) offsetting depreciation of the property's value, as well as additional or replacement collateral. A secured creditor is entitled to the protection of the collateral value and not of the rights in a specific asset provided as collateral.[50] Arguably, in many cases, a distressed debtor lacks the necessary liquidity and unencumbered assets to offer as collateral. This is why the third means of adequate protection becomes particularly important, namely, 'granting such other relief … as will result in the realization by such entity of the indubitable equivalent of such entity's interest in such property'.[51]

The US Bankruptcy Code does not define 'indubitable equivalent'.[52] The phrase originated in the context of a plan cram-down, where it refers to the 'unquestionable value of a lender's secured interest in the collateral'.[53] This catch-all term gives the courts significant flexibility and discretion to determine what protection is appropriate in a given situation. Some courts have found that adequate protection can be achieved through: (i) the existence of an equity cushion shielding the interests of a secured creditor from loss due to a decrease in the property's value;[54] (ii) a third-party guarantee;[55] and (iii) the 9.18

pragmatic and synthetic, requiring a court to balance all relevant factors in a particular case, including the value of the collateral, whether the collateral is likely to depreciate over time, the debtor's prospects for a successful reorganization and the debtor's performance under the plan. Other considerations may include the balancing of hardships between the parties and whether the creditor's property interest is being unduly jeopardized.'

48 *In re DB Capital Holdings, LLC*, 454 B.R. 804, 816–17 (Bankr. D. Col. 2011); *In re O'Connor*, 808 F.2d 1393, 1396 (10th Cir. 1987).

49 *Wright v. Union Central Life Ins. Co.*, 311 U.S. 273 (1940). See, however, C.J. Tabb, The Bankruptcy Clause, the Fifth Amendment, and the Limited Rights of Secured Creditors in Bankruptcy, University of Illinois Law Review, Vol. 2015, 2015, pp. 765-809, arguing that the Fifth Amendment is not relevant in considering the constitutional rights of secured creditors in bankruptcy.

50 *Wright v. Union Central Life Ins. Co.*, 311 U.S. 273 (1940).

51 11 U.S. Code § 361.

52 The phrase 'indubitable equivalent' has its genesis in the opinion of Judge Learned Hand, writing for the court in *In re Murel Holding Corporation*, 75 F.2d 941 (2nd Cir. 1935). For the background of this phrase, see *In re Colrud*, 45 B.R. 169 (Bankr. D. Alaska 1984).

53 *In re Philadelphia Newspapers, LLC*, 599 F.3d 298, 310 (3d Cir. 2010).

54 *In re Norton*, 347 B.R. 291, 298 (Bankr. E.D. Tenn. 2006); *In re Mellor*, 734 F.2d 1396, 1400 n. 2 (9th Cir. 1984); *In re Roane*, 14 B.R. 542 (E.D. Pa. 1981). The equity cushion of 20 per cent or more is usually deemed to be sufficient by courts. An equity cushion of 0 per cent to 11 per cent has generally been held insufficient, and case law is divided on whether a cushion of 12 per cent to 20 per cent constitutes adequate protection. For a summary of case law, see *In re Big Dog II, LLC*, 602 B.R. 64 (Bankr. N.D. Fla. 2019).

55 *In re Harrow Leasing Corp.*, 35 B.R. 916 (Bankr. E.D. Pa. 1983); *In re Swedeland Dev. Group, Inc.*, 16 F.3d 552, 564 (3d Cir. 1994), noting that the sufficiency of a guaranty would depend on the financial strength of

maintenance of insurance on the creditor's collateral or leased property, protecting the collateral against loss or depreciation.[56] Notably, granting administrative priority to a claim does not constitute adequate protection, as 'such protection is too uncertain to be meaningful'.[57]

9.19 The preceding paragraphs discussed relief from the automatic stay 'for cause', such as due to the lack of adequate protection of an interest in property. Even if the equity cushion is found to be adequate or the debtor is able to provide an alternative means of adequate protection, relief from the stay can nevertheless be granted to a creditor, provided that the requirements of the second test of § 362(d) of the US Bankruptcy Code are met. Under this test, a stay shall be lifted if: (i) the debtor has no equity in the property of the bankruptcy estate; *and* (ii) this property is not necessary for an effective reorganisation.[58] Both requirements must be met.

9.20 To satisfy the first requirement, the value of the property should not exceed the debts secured by all liens and other encumbrances on such property.[59] Valuation is determined case by case, taking into account the nature of the debtor's business, market conditions, the debtor's prospects for rehabilitation and the type of collateral. If the debtor maintains equity in the property, the stay cannot be lifted under this provision. But even if the debtor lacks such equity, relief from the stay will be denied if the debtor needs the property in question for a successful reorganisation. To satisfy this requirement, the debtor must show that the property is essential for an *effective* reorganisation which is in prospect.[60] This means that there must be 'a reasonable possibility of a successful reorganization within a reasonable time'[61] (feasibility) and that the property in question is necessary for this reorganisation (necessity). If relief from the stay is requested early in the bankruptcy process, the burden on the

---

the guarantor. However, *In re C.F. Simonin's Sons, Inc.*, 28 B.R. 707, 712 (Bankr. E.D.N.C. 1983), holding that '[e]ven if there was undisputable evidence of the creditworthiness of the guarantors, the chance to pursue a guarantor with its uncertainties and costs is not adequate protection'.

56 *In re Powell*, 223 B.R. 225, 234 (Bankr. N.D. Ala. 1998), stating that 'adequate protection may include providing proof of an enforceable insurance policy on the collateral and/or proof of proper maintenance of the property'.

57 S. Rep. No. 95-595, 95th Cong., 2d Sess., at 54 (1978).

58 11 U.S. Code § 362(d)(2).

59 *In re Garsal Realty, Inc.*, 98 B.R. 140 (Bankr. N.D.N.Y. 1989); *Sutton v. Bank One, Texas, Nat'l Ass'n*, 904 F.2d 327 (5th Cir. 1990).

60 *In re HSD Partners, LLC*, 451 B.R. 636, 638 (Bankr. S.D. Ga. 2011), noting that for property to be necessary to an effective reorganisation, it must be 'logically required for a reorganization which has a reasonable possibility of succeeding within a reasonable time'.

61 *United Savings Ass'n v. Timbers of Inwood Forest Associates, Ltd.*, 484 U.S. 365, 98 L. Ed. 2d 740, 108 S. Ct. 626 (1988).

debtor tends to be less stringent. As the case progresses, this burden becomes heavier.[62]

In sum, a stay on creditor actions under the US Bankruptcy Code is distinguishable from that available in the UK. Unlike the complex puzzle of procedures and tools found in the Insolvency Act 1986 and the Companies Act 2006, some of which do not provide for a stay, US Chapter 11 acts as a single gateway to corporate restructurings. It offers an automatic and extensive stay that precludes the commencement and continuation of proceedings aimed at recovery on a pre-petition claim, as well as collection and foreclosure actions by the debtor's creditors, including secured ones. Nevertheless, it seeks to maintain a balance by granting secured creditors the right to request relief from an automatic stay. This contributes to the growing influence of secured creditors over firms in bankruptcy. The following section will show that Dutch law is even more protective of the interests of secured creditors. **9.21**

9.2.3 The Netherlands: moratoriums and cooling-off periods

In the Netherlands, as in the UK and the USA, there is no statutory stay in an out-of-court workout. This section discusses three relevant statutory procedures in the Dutch Bankruptcy Act: (i) suspension of payments (*surseance van betaling*); (ii) bankruptcy (*faillissement*); and (iii) WHOA scheme or plan (*onderhands akkoord*), introduced in section 3.3.3. **9.22**

A suspension of payments provides for a stay or moratorium (*schorsing van executie*) effective from the day on which a suspension of payments is (provisionally) granted. As a result, the debtor cannot be forced to pay debts subject to the suspension, and all executions initiated to recover such debts are suspended.[63] This applies not only to the payment of a sum of money but also includes, in line with Article 6:30 BW, every form of satisfaction in the broadest sense.[64] The stay applies to pre-filing claims and claims based on pre-existing relationships at the time of filing.[65] It is important to note that the stay is only effective against unsecured creditors and only lasts as long as the **9.23**

---

62 *Matter of Holly's, Inc.*, 140 B.R. 643 (Bankr. W.D. Mich. 1992); *In re Ashgrove Apartments of DeKalb County, Ltd.*, 121 B.R. 752 (Bankr. S.D. Ohio 1990); *In re Brian Wise Trucking, Inc.*, 386 B.R. 215 (Bankr. N.D. Ind. 2008).

63 Dutch Bankruptcy Act, Article 230(1).

64 HR 23 October 1981, *NJ* 1982/173, m.nt. B. Wachter (*Gemeente Heiloo/Orthopedagogisch Centrum Noord-Holland c.s.*); Rb.s'-Hertogenbosch 20 October 2010, *JOR* 2011/28, m.nt. W.J.M. van Andel, concerning an obligation to provide a bank guarantee.

65 Ibid. HR 19 April 2013, *NJ* 2013/291, m.nt. F.M.J. Verstijlen (*Koot Beheer/Tideman qq*); HR 23 March 2018, *NJ* 2018/290, m.nt. F.M.J. Verstijlen (*Credit Suisse Brazil (Bahamas)/Jongepier qq*). This interpretation also follows from Article 233 Fw.

suspension remains in effect.[66] Thus, it does not bind creditors with priority.[67] Priority arises from a pledge, mortgage, privilege or other grounds laid down in law.[68] Insofar as a claim cannot be recovered from the assets on which the priority rests, such a claim is subject to a stay. Some authors have cited the fact that priority claims, especially secured claims, remain unaffected by the stay as one of the primary reasons why the suspension of payments is considered an inefficient reorganisation procedure, often acting as a gateway to bankruptcy.[69]

9.24 Dutch law provides limited relief against secured creditors. The court may, upon request or *ex officio*, order a cooling-off period (*afkoelingsperiode*), during which any power to recover from the insolvency estate or to claim assets under the debtor's control cannot be exercised, except with the authorisation of the court or, if appointed, a supervisory judge (*rechter-commissaris*).[70] A cooling-off period can be granted for up to two months, with a possible extension for another two months. This aligns with the objectives of the suspension of payments, as this procedure primarily aims to ensure the continuity of the debtor's business. Yet the limited duration of a cooling-off period reflects the understanding that it constitutes a significant limitation of (secured) creditors' rights.[71] The court has the authority to restrict the application of a cooling-off period to specific creditors and attach specific conditions.[72]

9.25 A stay in bankruptcy proceedings is similar to that applicable in the suspension of payments. Dutch law mandates a stay on enforcement actions brought by individual creditors upon the commencement of bankruptcy.[73] Consequently, individual enforcement actions cease as soon as a bankruptcy order is pronounced. The basic rule is that creditors can only assert their claims by

---

66 In principle, the provisional suspension of payments (and its stay) is first granted for a period of two months, with one extension of up to two more months. During this period, creditors must be consulted by the court to reassess the validity of the suspension of payments. See Article 215 Fw and the National procedural regulations in bankruptcy cases (*Landelijk procesreglement verzoekschriftprocedures insolventiezaken rechtbanken*), 1 July 2023, at 2.3.1. When a court grants a final suspension of payments, this is for a maximum of one and a half years. Before this period expires, the debtor may request an extension for a maximum of one and a half years once or several times, with the court reassessing whether the debtor still qualifies for the suspension of payments each time. Article 223(2) Fw.

67 Dutch Bankruptcy Act, Article 232.

68 Dutch Civil Code, Article 3:278(1).

69 R.J. van Galen, De surseance als echte reorganisatieprocedure, TvI 2015/23, pp. 151–152; R.D. Vriesendorp, Insolventierecht, 2e druk, Deventer: Wolters Kluwer, 2021.

70 Dutch Bankruptcy Act, Article 241(a)(1). Note that the exception is made for *boedelschuldeisers* – creditors with post-commencement or estate claims. HR 19 April 2013, ECLI:NL:HR:2013:BY6108, *NJ* 2013/291, m.nt. F.M.J. Verstijlen (*Koot Beheer/Tideman*). Also, B. Wessels, Vereffening van de boedel (Wessels Insolventierecht nr. VII), 5e druk, Deventer: Wolters Kluwer, 2021/7075.

71 Rb. Amsterdam 4 December 2013, ECLI:NL:RBAMS:2013:8883, *RI* 2014/46, *JOR* 2014/340.

72 Dutch Bankruptcy Act, Article 241(a)(2).

73 Dutch Bankruptcy Act, Article 33.

submitting them for verification, and these claims cannot be enforced outside of bankruptcy.[74] This follows from the 'fixation principle' (*fixatiebeginsel*), under which the legal position of all parties involved becomes 'fixed' or 'immutable' upon bankruptcy. The fixation principle offers creditors protection against any reduction in the assets of the estate available for distribution in bankruptcy and against increases in the debtor's liabilities that could reduce bankruptcy payouts.[75] However, as with the suspension of payments, a bankruptcy stay does not apply to secured creditors, who can enforce their security rights and sell the pledged or mortgaged asset as if bankruptcy had not occurred.[76] This 'separatist' position of secured creditors dates back to the inception of the Dutch Bankruptcy Act of 1893 (in force since 1896) and is intended to promote lending.[77]

As in the suspension of payment, in a bankruptcy, a cooling-off period might be imposed by a supervisory judge, either at the request of an interested party or *ex officio*.[78] The purpose of this cooling-off period is to enable an IP to investigate which assets belong to the estate and which should be preserved, for example, with a view to the continuation of the debtor and/or a going concern sale of its business.[79] The maximum duration of a cooling-off period is four months, consisting of an initial two months plus a possible extension of up to two months, including any cooling-off granted in the preceding suspension of payments.[80] 9.26

Lastly, a cooling-off period can also accompany negotiations of a WHOA scheme. The Dutch Bankruptcy Act stipulates that a debtor or a restructuring expert, if appointed, may request the court to order a cooling-off period if the 9.27

74 Dutch Bankruptcy Act, Articles 26 and 110.

75 HR 28 January 2022, ECLI:NL:HR:2022:80, r.o. 3.2.1, *NJ* 2022/50; HR 18 December 1987, *NJ* 1988/340, m.nt. G (*OAR/ABN*).

76 Dutch Bankruptcy Act, Article 57. F.M.J. Verstijlen and F.M. van Nieuwstadt, Stelling: De separatistenpositie voor zekerheidsgerechtigden moet worden afgeschaft, TvI, 2005/14; G.D. Hoekstra, De positie van de pandhouder in het faillissementsrecht (diss. Groningen), Den Haag: Boom Juridische Uitgevers, 2007, p. 132-135.

77 E.F. Verheul, GS Faillissementswet, commentaar op art. 57 Fw. For criticism of creditor separatism, see S.C.J.J. Kortmann, Het faillissement, een paradijs voor banken (afscheidsrede Nijmegen), Nijmegen: Radboud Universiteit, 2017.

78 Dutch Bankruptcy Act, Article 63(a). If the applicant, whether a debtor or a creditor, requests a cooling-off period at the moment of the bankruptcy filing, the cooling-off period is ordered by the court. See M.J. van der Aa, De afkoelingsperiode in faillissement (diss. RUG), Kluwer, 2007; B. Wessels, Gevolgen van faillietverklaring (1) Wessels Insolventierecht nr. II, 5e druk, Deventer: Wolters Kluwer, 2019/2596ff.

79 Parl. Gesch. Wijziging Rv. e.a.w., Inv. 3, 5 en 6, p. 414; S.C.J.J. Kortmann and N.E.D. Faber (red.), Geschiedenis van de Faillissementswet. Wetswijzigingen, Zwolle: W.E.J. Tjeenk Willink, 1995, pp. 203-204.

80 Rb. Amsterdam 4 December 2013, *JOR* 2014/340, ruling that a cooling-off period in the suspension of payments is deducted from the term of a cooling-off period in the subsequent bankruptcy.

debtor has submitted a declaration regarding the preparation of a WHOA plan and has proposed a plan or undertakes to propose such a plan within two months.[81] Therefore, in a WHOA procedure, there is no automatic stay. However, if the court grants a cooling-off period, during this period (maximum four months with a possible extension to a total of eight months): (i) third parties cannot enforce their rights against the debtor's assets without leave from the court; (ii) the court can lift attachments at the debtor's request; and (iii) the review of requests to open bankruptcy or suspension of payments proceedings is suspended.[82] When a general cooling-off period is announced, the suspension of individual enforcement rights in principle applies to all creditors. Yet, if the cooling-off order is directed at a specific group of creditors, only those creditors are prevented from enforcing claims against the debtor's assets.

9.28 The cooling-off period can be ordered if there is *prima facie* evidence that it is necessary for the debtor to continue its business during the preparation and negotiation of a WHOA plan. Moreover, at the time when the cooling-off period is announced, it should be reasonable to assume that the interests of the debtor's joint creditors are served by this measure and that it would not materially prejudice the interests of third parties.[83] The cooling-off period is in the interest of creditors if the preserved going concern value and potential payouts exceed the liquidation value. As for material prejudice, insofar as collateral is established on the debtor's property, no such prejudice exists if the collateral value remains stable during the cooling-off period.[84]

9.29 When considering the imposition of a cooling-off period, courts conduct a balancing exercise, taking into account potential payouts expected without the cooling-off period (i.e. in bankruptcy), the viability of the debtor and the likelihood of successfully adopting a WHOA plan.[85] Available evidence shows that courts are likely to grant cooling-off requests with an approval rate of over 80 per cent, whether to support the continuity of the debtor's business during

81 Dutch Bankruptcy Act, Article 376(1). Rb. Overijssel 16 July 2021, ECLI:NL:RBOVE:2021:2907, r.o. 3.6, *RI* 2021/82.

82 Dutch Bankruptcy Act, Article 376(2).

83 Dutch Bankruptcy Act, Article 376(4). Rb. Den Haag 15 January 2021, ECLI:NL:RBDHA:2021:198, r.o. 4.6ff, *RI* 2021/25, *JOR* 2021/77.

84 Rb. Oost-Brabant, 25 February 2022, ECLI:NL:RBOBR:2022:916, r.o. 4.9–4.11.

85 Rb. Rotterdam 8 March 2021, *JOR* 2021/247, m.nt. Mennens; Rb. Oost-Brabant, 17 September 2021, r.o. 3.7., *RI* 2022/6, noting that the necessity of a cooling-off period is substantiated by the fact that the WHOA plan, if successfully implemented, would lead to a better result for creditors than the alternative of bankruptcy.

restructuring or to facilitate an orderly liquidation of a non-viable company.[86] If the statutory requirements for a cooling-off period are no longer met, the court must lift the stay, either at the request of the debtor, a third party or on its own initiative.[87]

9.2.4 Summary of national law approaches

This section highlights the diversity of rules regarding a stay across different jurisdictions. This relates to: **9.30**

- *Availability of a stay*, protecting the debtor against creditors' claims. For example, a stay is a feature of English administration and liquidation proceedings, Dutch bankruptcy and suspension of payments and US bankruptcy proceedings. At the same time, certain procedures available to financially distressed debtors (e.g. English schemes of arrangement, CVAs and restructuring plans) do not come with a statutory stay.
- *Operation of a stay*. A stay may be automatic and connected to the opening of a proceeding. This is the case in US Chapter 11, English administration and Dutch bankruptcy and suspension of payments proceedings. By contrast, the Dutch cooling-off period available in a WHOA scheme can only be granted upon filing by the debtor or a restructuring expert. In the UK, procedures that do not trigger a stay (as mentioned above) could be supplemented by a stand-alone moratorium.
- *Duration of a stay*. Another characteristic of a stay is its length. In some cases, the duration of a stay coincides with the duration of the procedure (e.g. English administration, US Chapter 11, Dutch bankruptcy), while in other instances, the maximum length of a stay is prescribed by law (e.g. English moratorium, cooling-off periods supporting WHOA schemes).
- *Scope of a stay*. This refers to the types of creditors and/or obligations covered by the stay. A category of creditors who often enjoy priority and may be carved out of a stay are secured creditors. For example, an English liquidation stay and a stay triggered by Dutch bankruptcy and suspension of payments filings do not affect secured creditors, who can proceed with enforcing their security rights. Conversely, a US bankruptcy stay, English administration stay and Dutch cooling-off period cover or may cover enforcement rights of secured creditors. In addition to creditors protected by *in rem* security rights, exemptions from a stay could apply to parties in financial contracts. For example, the new UK moratorium procedure does not affect contracts 'involving financial services', such as loan agreements, while the Chapter 11 stay does not affect contractual rights of counterparties to financial contracts (e.g. swap and repurchase agreements).

---

86 R.D. Vriesendorp et al., One year and 100 court decisions later: Dutch restructuring scheme in practice, 23 March 2022. The bill implementing the Restructuring Directive in the Netherlands explicitly authorises granting a stay to support an orderly winding up of the debtor company.

87 Dutch Bankruptcy Act, Article 376(10).

9.31 This diversity of regulatory frameworks concerning a stay can be explained by the differences in the applicable procedures and their intended purposes (e.g. liquidation-oriented v. rescue oriented, pre-insolvency v. insolvency, court-supervised v. out-of-court procedures). However, these important factors alone cannot fully explain the variations in the design and qualities of a stay across jurisdictions. In this regard, Wessels and Madaus convincingly argue that 'a "stay" serves as a tool to balance, on the one hand, the interests involved with restructuring a viable business, and, on the other hand, the interests of certainty, predictability and stability of contractual positions'.[88] This balancing exercise naturally results in different solutions, influenced by the normative commitment to freedom of contract (traditionally strong in the UK) and the organisational and institutional environment in which legal rules are developed and applied.

9.32 Paterson notes that in the UK, until the early 2000s, large corporate reorganisations operated outside the court system, and since the 2000s, most reorganisations have been confined to financial liabilities.[89] In contrast, the US Bankruptcy Code was adopted with a range of tools to implement full operational and financial restructurings, reflecting the prevailing circumstances at that time. Whether these tools, including the automatic stay – the US bankruptcy law's core institution – retain their importance amid changing corporate structures and the move towards the service economy is questioned by some scholars.[90]

9.33 In terms of operation, an automatic stay maximises legal certainty, yet it may be less justified from the perspective of proportionality when compared to a tailored and court-ordered stay.[91] After all, a stay on creditor actions hinders creditors' enforcement rights.[92] This is why the duration of a stay could be limited, and its extension might depend on showing that it continues to

---

88 B. Wessels and S. Madaus, Rescue of Business in Europe: A European Law Institute Instrument, OUP, 2020, p. 195.

89 S. Paterson, Corporate Reorganization Law and Forces of Change, OUP, 2020, p. 2.

90 M.J. Roe, Three Ages of Bankruptcy, Harvard Law Review, Vol. 7, 2017, pp. 187–219; J. Armour, A. Hsu and A. Walters, The Costs and Benefits of Secured Creditor Control in Bankruptcy: Evidence from the UK, Review of Law & Economics, Vol. 8, 2012, pp. 101–135, noting that the UK market practice of all-encompassing security interest with a single bank gave it effective control over the debtor's assets, and that English law effectively allowed a private liquidation via administrative receivership, making a stay unnecessary. This stood in stark contrast to US bankruptcy law, underpinned by the concept of a bargain among the debtor's creditors, supported by a wide-ranging stay.

91 R. Bork, Rescuing Companies in England and Germany, OUP, 2012, paras. 10.04–10.07.

92 L. Stanghellini et al. (eds), Best Practices in European Restructuring: Contractualised Distress Resolution in the Shadow of the Law, Wolters Kluwer, 2018, p. 117, observing that 'a stay directly impinges on creditors' legal and contractual rights, limiting them' and arguing that 'the longer the stay, the higher the confidence should be in the fact that the stay is maximising value for the creditors'.

serve its purpose.[93] Regarding the scope, a far-reaching stay binding secured creditors facilitates equal treatment of creditors. It may also contribute to the preservation of the debtor's estate value and the development of a restructuring plan. However, the need to ensure adequate protection of the property rights of secured creditors and the value of security justifies lifting a stay in certain circumstances.[94] Given the main focus of this book, the following section will address the group insolvency context.

9.3 EXTENSION OF AN ENFORCEMENT STAY TO GROUP ENTITIES

9.3.1 A stay and group insolvency

One of the key features of recent restructuring reforms is that they provide the possibility of staying individual enforcement actions, giving the debtor breathing space, protecting its going concern value and improving its position in negotiations with creditors. However, the success of restructuring or insolvency proceedings often depends on the preservation of financial and operational links within the group of companies. The threat of enforcement against the debtor's affiliates (co-debtors, guarantors, collateral providers) may significantly weaken the debtor's bargaining power. One way to secure a stay for group companies is to initiate separate proceedings for each of them. Arguably, this could drive up transaction costs and substantially complicate coordinated group restructuring. The question is whether, in order to preserve the overall value of the group enterprise, a stay can (and should) be extended to the debtor's group members and, if so, under what conditions. **9.34**

In essence, the rationale behind an intra-group extension of a stay overlaps with that of a third-party release discussed in the previous chapter. Both tools aim to preserve enterprise value, ensure a coordinated response to financial distress and give the debtor additional leverage in negotiations with creditors. However, there is a distinction between them. While a third-party release entails group debt deleveraging or debt adjustment, the extension of a stay does **9.35**

93 See e.g. Article 376(5) Fw. See Rb. Den Haag 3 September 2021, r.o. 4.4., *RI* 2021/91 (*ADO Den Haag*), extending the cooling-off period for a Dutch association football club and referring to the progress made in reaching a plan (extensive consultation with stakeholders, completed class formation, establishment of a data room with important documents, etc.).

94 Restructuring Directive, Article 6(9)(c); Article 376(10) Fw; 11 U.S. Code § 362(d). On lifting of the administration stay, see *Bristol Airport Plc v. Powdrill* [1990] Ch 744; *Re Atlantic Computer Systems Plc (No 1)* [1992] Ch 505; *Mackay v. Kaupthing Singer* [2013] EWHC 2533 (Ch). In the UK, the underlying principle is that an administration for the benefit of unsecured creditors should not be conducted at the expense of those who have proprietary rights which they are seeking to exercise, save to the extent that this may be unavoidable and even then, this will usually be acceptable only to a very limited extent.

not affect the existence and extent of third-party liability. It simply provides these third parties with a temporary break or interim protection to facilitate the adoption of a group solution, whatever that may be (e.g. a group business sale as a going concern or restructuring of group members' obligations). In this sense, the extension of a stay is less intrusive compared to a third-party release. The extended stay can be used on its own or in combination with a third-party release. Without a stay, the release may be less effective since, until the confirmation of a plan with a third-party release, a guaranteed creditor can enforce its claim against the guarantor.

9.36 UNCITRAL considers the extension of a stay to the debtor's affiliates to be beneficial, especially in cases where there is 'interrelatedness of the business of the group'.[95] This is likely to occur when financing is arranged on a group basis. The Restructuring Directive does not explicitly authorise such an extension;[96] however, it acknowledges that, if provided under national law, a stay should be able to apply for the benefit of third parties, including guarantors and collateral providers.[97] Ultimately, the Directive offers limited guidance on the nature of third parties (e.g. whether they should be group entities or not) or the conditions under which a stay can be extended to shield third parties.

9.37 Under English law, there is no express statutory authority to extend the benefits of a stay to third parties. As a result, a group guarantor seeking to benefit from a stay will need to initiate its own procedure, such as administration or a moratorium.[98] The statutory language does not support the extension of a stay to non-debtors. For example, the Insolvency Act 1986 specifies that the administration stay applies to a company in administration,[99] and the liquidation stay applies to a company against which a winding-up order has been made.[100] Similarly, in the case of a stand-alone moratorium, the law stipulates that it is available to an eligible company upon filing or lodging documents at the court.[101] Hence, the availability of a stay is linked to the opening or filing for the opening of an insolvency procedure by a specific entity. Since the UK does not seem to offer the possibility to extend a stay to third parties, the next

95 UNCITRAL Legislative Guide, Part three, 2010, Ch. II, para. 40.

96 Restructuring Directive, Articles 6 and 7.

97 Restructuring Directive, Recital 32.

98 The UK is not the only jurisdiction that adheres to this approach. In *State Bank of India vs. V. Ramakrishnan and Ors.* (14.08.2018 - SC), the Supreme Court of India, interpreting section 14 of the Insolvency and Bankruptcy Code 2016, clarified that the insolvency moratorium could not be extended to the debtor's personal guarantor.

99 Insolvency Act 1986, Schedule B1, para. 43.

100 Insolvency Act 1986, s. 130(2).

101 Insolvency Act 1986, Part A1.

paragraphs will examine jurisdictions that either allow extended stays through case law (the USA) or directly approve them in statute (the Netherlands).

9.3.2 The USA: limited possibility of a stay extension

As a general rule, the automatic stay does not extend to third parties.[102] This position is based on the language of the US Bankruptcy Code, which states that the bankruptcy petition 'operates as a stay, applicable to all entities, of … any act to collect, assess, or recover a claim *against the debtor* that arose before the commencement of the case under this title'[103] (emphasis added). Thus, the bankruptcy stay applies only to the debtor, property of the debtor or property of the estate, and does not cover proceedings against non-debtor parties, such as group guarantors or co-debtors. **9.38**

Nevertheless, the power of a court to enjoin actions against third parties has been recognised in exceptional circumstances, where these actions interfere improperly with the purposes of bankruptcy law or when 'there is such an identity between the debtor and the third-party defendant that … a judgment against the third-party defendant will in effect be a judgment or finding against the debtor'.[104] Courts have also permitted the extension of a stay when a claim against a third party is considered to have 'an immediate adverse economic consequence for the debtor's estate'[105] and when protection by a stay is believed to be 'essential to the debtor's efforts of reorganization'.[106] For example, in *Caesars*, the court issued an injunction preventing indenture trustees and holders of notes issued by the debtor from pursuing lawsuits against the debtor's corporate parent, which was acting as a guarantor.[107] The court accepted that the debtor's reorganisation heavily relied on the parent's financial contribution, which would have been undermined by guarantee litigation. According to the court, extending the stay served the public interest in a successful reorganisation, as 'reorganizations preserve value for creditors and ultimately the public'.[108] **9.39**

---

102 *Credit Alliance Corp. v. Williams*, 851 F.2d 119, 121 (4th Circ. 1988); *In re S.I Acquisition, Inc.*, 817 F.2d 1142, 1147 (5th Cir. 1987); *In re Supermercado Gamboa*, 68 B.R. 230, 232 (Bankr. D.P.R. 1986); *Reliant Energy Servs., Inc. v. Enron Canada Corp.*, 349 F.3d 816, 825 (5th Cir. 2003).

103 11 U.S. Code § 362(a)(6).

104 *Reliant Energy Services, Inc. v. Enron Can. Corp.*, 349 F.3d 816, 825 (5th Cir. 2003).

105 *Ritchie Capital Management, L.L.C. v. Jeffries*, 653 F.3d 755, 763 (8th Cir. 2011), citing *Queenie, Ltd v. Nygard Int'l*, 321 F.3d 282, 287–88 (2d Cir. 2003).

106 *In re Union Trust Philadelphia, LLC*, 460 B.R. 644, 658 (E.D. Pa. 2011); *In re Hart*, 530 B.R. 293, 308 (Bankr. E.D. Pa. 2015); *In re Saxby's Coffee Worldwide, LLC*, 440 B.R. 369, 386 (Bankr. E.D. Pa. 2009).

107 *In re Caesars Entertainment Operating Co., Inc.*, 561 B.R. 441 (Bankr. N.D. Ill. 2016).

108 Ibid., at 453. *In re Integrated Health Services, Inc.*, 281 B.R. 231, 239 (Bankr. D. Del. 2002), confirming that '[p]romoting a successful reorganization is one of the most important public interests'.

9.40 Two observations can be made regarding the approach of US courts to the extension of a bankruptcy stay to group affiliates.

9.41 First, the legal basis for extending a stay to non-debtor parties is not clear. Some courts base their decisions on § 105(a) of the US Bankruptcy Code and the equitable power to grant an injunction to enjoin third-party litigation.[109] According to § 105(a), the 'court may issue any order, process, or judgment that is necessary or appropriate to carry out the provisions of this title'.[110] However, it has been pointed out that § 105(a) does not constitute an independent source of subject matter jurisdiction or a repository of substantive rights. Instead, it allows the court to issue an order when 'necessary or appropriate' to carry out the provisions of the Bankruptcy Code, for example, § 362(a).[111] Other courts rely solely on § 362(a) when extending the stay, even though this section does not explicitly provide for such an extension.[112] Thus, it remains uncertain whether the basis for extension lies in § 105(a) alone, in conjunction with § 362(a) or solely in § 362(a).

9.42 Second, it has been observed that case law on the extension of a bankruptcy stay is rather 'confusing' when it comes to the appropriate standard or test.[113] It is evident, however, that the possibility to enjoin litigation against third parties is limited and depends on the facts of each case. Normally, the party seeking the extension should meet the test applicable to injunction actions, including, among other things, a reasonable likelihood of successful reorganisation and the possibility that the debtor would suffer some cognizable prejudice or irreparable injury as a result of the creditor's lawsuit against the third party. The latter can be demonstrated if the third party has a right of indemnity against the debtor.[114] While the general approach remains restrictive, US courts have

---

109 *In re Calpine Corp.*, 365 B.R. 401, 409 (S.D.N.Y. 2007). In this case, the court first noted that the request by the debtor for an injunction under the Bankruptcy Code, authorising the court to issue any order, is treated as a request for a preliminary injunction. It stated that the following factors should be evaluated: (1) whether there is a likelihood of successful reorganisation; (2) whether there is imminent irreparable harm to the estate in the absence of an injunction (whether there is imminent, substantial and irreparable threat to the reorganisation process); (3) whether the balance of harms tips in favour of the moving party; and (4) whether the public interest weighs in favour of an injunction.

110 11 U.S. Code § 105(a).

111 *In re Bora Bora, Inc.*, 424 B.R. 17, 23 (Bankr. D.P.R. 2010); *In re Continental Airlines*, 203 F.3d 203, 211 (3d Cir. 2000), observing that section 105(a) does not 'create substantive rights that would otherwise be unavailable under the Bankruptcy Code'.

112 See e.g. *In re QA3 Fin. Corp.*, 2011 WL 2678591 (Bankr. D. Neb. 2011).

113 S. Maza, Enjoining Third Party Litigation under §362, Norton Journal of Bankruptcy Law & Practice, Vol. 26, 2017 (online version).

114 *First Nat'l Bank v. Kanawha Trace Dev. Partners*, 87 B.R. 892 (Bankr. E.D. Va. 1988); *In re Lomas Fin. Corp.*, 117 B.R. 64 (S.D.N.Y. 1990); *Rivera-Olivera v. Antares Oil Services*, 482 B.R. 44 (D.P.R. 2012), extending a stay to third parties and noting that the process established by the bankruptcy court allows third parties to submit proofs of claim for indemnification or contribution against the debtors, and because

been willing to extend a stay or grant an injunction to enjoin actions against the debtor's affiliates when necessary for a successful restructuring. This is particularly the case when there is compelling evidence that the debtor's reorganisation would be severely hampered if the lawsuit against a non-debtor group entity were to proceed. Courts retain broad discretion in determining whether a bankruptcy stay can be extended. The need for a group-wide extension is somewhat reduced due to the common practice of simultaneous bankruptcy filings by all or the majority of entities comprising the group.[115] As a consequence, each group entity secures a separate automatic stay.

While the extension of an enforcement stay in the USA is not group-specific – it can benefit debtors' directors, insurers and even third parties who allegedly participated in a Ponzi scheme[116] – the Netherlands has implemented reforms designed to provide effective tools to address financial distress within enterprise groups. Among other things, Dutch law permits the extension of a cooling-off period to group affiliates as part of a WHOA scheme.[117] **9.43**

9.3.3 The Netherlands: extension of a stay to group entities

The previous chapter showed that Dutch law responds to the group environment and permits a WHOA plan to modify creditors' rights against legal entities that form one enterprise group with the debtor – a third-party release.[118] The rights of creditors towards the debtor's affiliates must aim to satisfy or to secure the performance of the debtor's obligations (e.g. cross-guarantees, provision of collateral) or the obligations for which such legal entities are liable **9.44**

---

certain third parties in this case have submitted or will submit such claims against the debtors, a judgment against non-debtor third parties may constitute a judgment against the debtors, which, in turn, could negatively impact the liquidation process.

115 This practice is supported by the 'affiliate-filing rule' of 28 U.S. Code § 1408, which allows a company to file a bankruptcy petition in a district where its affiliate is already the debtor in a pending title 11 case. Under Rule 1015(b) of the Federal Rules of Bankruptcy Procedure, if a joint petition or two or more petitions are pending in the same court by or against a debtor and an affiliate, the court may order the joint administration of the estates. These rules promote the reorganisation of an entire business enterprise in a centralised manner. Another reason for group-wide filings may be the unavailability of non-consensual third-party releases in the USA (see section 8.2.3).

116 *In re Madoff*, 848 F.Supp.2d 469 (S.D.N.Y. 2012), granting a § 105(a) injunction and barring the bankrupt investment firm's customers from bringing class action lawsuits against third parties with whom the trustee was on the brink of settling pending fraudulent transfer action lawsuits.

117 Legal systems that include rules for the extension of an enforcement stay in a group scenario are Germany and Singapore. In Germany, StaRUG, § 49(3) permits the extension of a stay of actions arising from intragroup liability arrangements to protect group guarantors and collateral providers. Similarly, in Singapore, according to IRDA section 65(1), the court may, on the application of a company that is a subsidiary, a holding company or an ultimate holding company (related company) of the subject company (debtor), restrain the commencement or continuation of any proceedings or enforcement actions, including enforcement of security rights, against a related company.

118 Dutch Bankruptcy Act, Article 372(1).

with the debtor (e.g. co-debtorship). Among other requirements, the law states that a group entity subject to a release must be in a situation where it may reasonably be assumed that it will be unable to continue paying its debts. Hence, there has to be a threat of insolvency that justifies a court's intervention. Other requirements include the consent of the to-be-released group entity, the court's jurisdiction over it and compliance with substantive requirements, including the best-interest-of-creditors test.[119]

9.45 If a WHOA plan seeks to amend creditors' rights against a non-debtor group entity, the debtor can request the court to extend a cooling-off period to that group entity.[120] This extension is premised on the proposed amendment of creditors' rights against that group entity through the plan. This is why, to be eligible for an extended stay, the relevant group entity must meet the conditions set for a third-party release, such as being in a state of financial distress. Dutch courts have approved extended cooling-off periods in many recent restructurings of large enterprises.[121] In *Vroon*, the court granted a stay to two top Dutch companies, as well as some 100+ subsidiaries. How did the court establish its jurisdiction?

9.46 As both petitioning entities were registered in the Netherlands, the jurisdiction of Dutch courts over them was relatively straightforward.[122] However, the same cannot be said about foreign subsidiaries, jointly and severally liable under cross-guarantees. Assuming jurisdiction over non-Dutch group companies,[123] the Dutch court referred to the parliamentary history of the WHOA, showing that when one or more plans are offered involving a restructuring of the debts of several legal entities that form a group, it is sufficient for at least one of the debtors to have a centre of main interests or an establishment in the Netherlands.[124] In principle, even if one group debtor has a sufficient connection to the Netherlands, this may be enough to establish the jurisdiction of Dutch courts over foreign group entities covered by the non-public WHOA scheme. The application of Dutch law and its 'sufficient connection' test to determine the jurisdiction of Dutch courts is possible because non-public WHOA schemes – unlike their public counterparts – do not fall within the scope of the EIR Recast. As a result, they are not bound by the latter's strict

119 Dutch Bankruptcy Act, Article 384(3).

120 Dutch Bankruptcy Act, Article 372(3), together with Article 376(1).

121 See e.g. Rechtbank Amsterdam, 8 juni 2023, ECLI:NL:RBAMS:2023:6159 (*Diebold*).

122 Article 369(7)(b) Fw, in conjunction with Article 3 of the Code of Civil Procedure and Article 1:10(2) of the Dutch Civil Code.

123 Rechtbank Zeeland-West-Brabant, 24 november 2022, ECLI:NL:RBZWB:2022:8629, noot mr. drs. M.M. Hoving.

124 Memorie van Toelichting (Kamerstukken II 2018/19, 35249, nr. 3, p. 32). Article 372(3) Fw.

requirements of COMI or establishment. The open and flexible jurisdictional standard applicable to non-public WHOA schemes creates the possibility to restructure group obligations in a centralised way. It seems, however, that the group-wide stay was voluntarily complied with by creditors, and its jurisdictional reach was not challenged abroad.[125]

Without extending a cooling-off period to group guarantors, in some cases, it may be too late to implement a third-party release. By the time of plan confirmation, the assets of such group guarantors might have been dismembered, and their business could be destroyed. In a recent case involving a group engaged in international e-commerce business, the court approved the extension of a cooling-off period to the debtors' corporate shareholders. The court observed that: (i) the debtors and their shareholders were organisationally and financially interconnected and formed an economic unit within the meaning of Article 2:24b BW (see section 2.3); (ii) the shareholders were jointly and severally liable for the debts owed to financiers by the debtors; and (iii) the successful restructuring required an amendment of creditors' rights against the shareholder-guarantors, pursuant to the proposed third-party releases.[126] The court linked the necessity to extend the cooling-off period to the operational and financial interdependence of group entities and the proposed restructuring through third-party releases. 9.47

The extension of a cooling-off period to the debtor's affiliates must not materially prejudice the interests of a guaranteed creditor. This requirement can be inferred from the general provisions applicable to a cooling-off period.[127] If, during the extended cooling-off period, the financial position of a group guarantor significantly deteriorates, or if such an entity is involved in value-destroying activities, it should be possible to lift the extended stay. The same rule applies if the value of third-party collateral diminishes during the cooling-off period. This rule is necessary for maintaining a balance between the interests of all parties involved and resembles the adequate protection requirement of the US Bankruptcy Code. 9.48

125 I. Kokorin, Parallel Restructurings: Challenges and Opportunities, TvI 2024/12, 2024, pp. 103–113.

126 Rb. Oost-Brabant 25 February 2022, ECLI:NL:RBOBR:2022:916, r.o. 4.13; Rb. Amsterdam 15 February 2021, ECLI:NL:RBAMS:2021:6516, granting the request to order a cooling-off period and extend it to the debtor's affiliates and observing that: (i) a temporary stay is necessary for the continuation of the debtor's business; (ii) the plan offers higher payouts to the creditors compared to bankruptcy; and (iii) the bankruptcy is unavoidable without a cooling-off period and the plan.

127 Dutch Bankruptcy Act, Article 376(4)(b).

9.4 CONCLUSIONS AND SUGGESTIONS

9.4.1 Overview of main findings

9.49 A stay on individual enforcement actions is a defining feature of most insolvency law regimes. It serves to preserve the value of the insolvency estate, facilitates its efficient administration, and promotes the restructuring of viable enterprises. In this chapter, I have demonstrated that laws differ when it comes to the availability, operation (automatic vs. non-automatic), duration (limited in time vs. applying throughout the entire procedure) and scope (general vs. targeted) of a stay.

9.50 Among the laws studied in this book, the automatic stay provided by the US Bankruptcy Code stands out as the most powerful, with an extremely broad scope. In contrast, Dutch bankruptcy and suspension of payments procedures do not affect secured creditors unless the court orders a temporary cooling-off period. Without it, secured creditors can enforce their security rights as if there were no bankruptcy. UK law offers a patchwork of rules and procedures that can be used either on a stand-alone basis or in combination with other procedures.

9.51 Another area where national laws diverge is whether a stay can be extended to third parties, including the debtor's group members, which are not themselves subject to the relevant insolvency or restructuring procedure but are linked to the debtor through various cross-liability arrangements (e.g. intra-group guarantees, co-debtorship). The review of national legal systems reveals a variety of attitudes and criteria for extending a stay to benefit the debtor's affiliates, which are summarised in Table 9.1.

9.52 Given the group economic reality, extending a protective shield to the debtor's affiliates may contribute to the efficient restructuring of a group enterprise. It can help preserve group synergies, maintain the operational continuity of group members, and strengthen the debtor's bargaining power. While English law does not seem to permit such an extension, US and Dutch laws are more flexible and, to some extent, allow courts to enjoin actions against third parties.

9.53 In the US, bankruptcy courts tend to enjoin actions against non-debtor parties in rare and exceptional circumstances. The exact configuration of these circumstances remains somewhat ambiguous, depends on specific facts, and may vary from one court to another. Moreover, the legal basis for the extension of a stay is disputable. However, courts often grant injunctions that benefit group companies if it is deemed essential for the debtor's reorganisation or if

Table 9.1 Extension of a stay to third parties

Question	The USA	The Netherlands
Is the extension of a stay to third parties available?	Only available in exceptional circumstances.	Explicitly available in WHOA schemes.
Who can request the extension of a stay?	Debtor or a third party.	Debtor or restructuring expert, if appointed.
Who can benefit from the extension of a stay?	Broad category of persons (e.g. group entities, officers, insurance companies).	Group entities that have secured the obligation of the debtor (guarantor, collateral provider) or are liable with the debtor (co-debtors).
What are the requirements for the extension of a stay?	Different considerations, inter alia, (i) identity between the debtor and a third party; (ii) a claim against a third party has an immediate adverse effect on the debtor's estate; (iii) a stay is essential to debtor's reorganisation efforts.	(i) A WHOA plan entails the amendment of creditors' rights against the related (group) company, (ii) this group company is in financial distress, (iii) it gives its consent, and (iv) the court has jurisdiction over it. The extension of a cooling-off period must not materially prejudice the creditor's interests.

failing to do so could result in immediate adverse economic consequences for the debtor's estate.

Dutch law, by contrast, clearly permits the extension of a stay to the debtor's affiliates within the WHOA framework. It places a cooling-off period in the context of a WHOA restructuring plan, which aims to amend creditors' rights against related group members (i.e. third-party release) and targets the debtor's guarantors, collateral providers or co-debtors. Thus, Dutch law makes the extension of a stay conditional on a particular type of contractual relationship, the amendment of creditors' rights against a third party in a WHOA scheme and the financial position of such a third party. Essentially, the extension of a stay plays an ancillary role, supporting the effectiveness of a (future) restructuring plan. 9.54

9.4.2 Suggestions on the extension of a stay to group entities

Based on an overview of national law approaches and in pursuit of a balanced solution, the following suggestions can be made regarding the extension of a stay in the group context. 9.55

9.56 **First**, the extension of a stay on individual enforcement actions to non-debtor group entities may be useful as a tool for preserving and maximising estate value, and specifically the group enterprise value (see section 4.3.1). However, the extension of a stay should not be automatic. Non-debtor group entities are not themselves subject to insolvency proceedings and, therefore, should not automatically benefit from insolvency law protections, including the insolvency stay. Granting an automatic extension of a stay would excessively limit creditors' rights and unduly restrict the protective function of intercompany guarantees and other forms of cross-liability arrangements. Instead, any extension of a stay should be carried out following notice and a court hearing, ensuring that affected creditors have an opportunity to be heard. This approach aligns with the notion of (procedural) fairness.

9.57 **Second**, the case for extending an enforcement stay to group affiliates is stronger in the following scenarios:

- The first scenario is when an enterprise group is integrated, and the non-debtor group company is or may become financially distressed or insolvent as a result of the creditor's enforcement action. In this case, the extension of a stay to protect another group company can be justified if that company plays an integral and necessary role in the anchor debtor's restructuring or future operations.
- The second scenario is when the debtor's restructuring plan envisages a third-party release. If a creditor of the to-be-released group company (e.g. group guarantor, co-debtor or collateral provider) is allowed to pursue its claim against this company and collect on its claim before a release takes effect, the third-party release could become futile. Paraphrasing the well-known legal maxim 'Justice delayed is justice denied', we could say, 'An extension of a stay delayed is a third-party release denied'.

9.58 By contrast, the extension of an enforcement stay appears to be less justified where:

- The creditor's action against a non-debtor group company is unlikely to jeopardise or frustrate a restructuring attempt of the anchor debtor and does not disrupt the debtor's business during negotiations with creditors. This may be the case where the group is not integrated (i.e. in decentralised groups), and the businesses of the debtor and its group affiliates are not aligned, dependent or synergetic (section 2.4). In such cases, the extension of a stay is simply unnecessary. The necessity requirement is an integral part of the proportionality analysis (section 4.4.2). If the extension of a stay is not necessary for the debtor's successful restructuring, it is unlikely to be proportional. Furthermore, if the debtor's affiliate requires insolvency law protection, it can secure it by filing its own insolvency petition.
- A debtor's group affiliate is solvent and liquid, and the creditor's action does not undermine its solvency or liquidity. In a case like this, there is generally no reason

for financial relief or insolvency protection. Limiting contractual rights exercised against solvent entities is more likely to be disproportionate. However, in rare circumstances, a stay covering a solvent group guarantor, co-debtor or collateral provider could be proportionate, particularly if it aims to protect an asset (e.g. production equipment) that is central to the business of the entire group or the anchor debtor.[128] Nevertheless, any extension of an insolvency stay to solvent companies should be subject to strict scrutiny by the court.

Third, the extension of a stay should, in principle, be available to achieve the goal of business preservation, regardless of whether the business remains within its current legal entities or is sold and transferred to new entities. This means that the extension of an enforcement stay should be used to preserve and ensure the continuation of economically viable businesses whose going concern value exceeds their liquidation value. If the debtor's assets are to be liquidated on a piecemeal basis, the extension of a stay may be unnecessary or ill-suited to facilitate value preservation. **9.59**

However, there are instances where the non-viability of an anchor debtor, a third party (e.g. a group guarantor) or the entire group enterprise should not preclude the extension of a stay. Such an extension may be needed to facilitate an orderly liquidation of a non-viable business, as exemplified in the Nortel Networks case (section 1.1.2). In that case, a unified approach to the sale of the group's assets resulted in USD 7.3 billion – an amount that could not have been attained if the assets were sold on an entity-by-entity basis.[129] In cases like this, the extension of a stay makes it possible to preserve the pool of assets spread across different group entities. These assets can then be bundled and sold together to secure the highest purchase price possible. One might simply need a group-wide stay, even if on a temporary basis, to preserve the global pool of assets, which are more valuable when sold collectively. **9.60**

Thus, there are situations in which an extended stay is value-maintaining or value-increasing, even if the underlying business is not viable and the debtors are to be liquidated with their assets sold to the highest bidder on the market. Notably, this approach differs from the one adopted in the chapter on third-party releases, where I argued that such releases should be reserved for cases seeking going-concern value preservation, not asset liquidation. **9.61**

---

128 UNCITRAL Legislative Guide, Part three, 2010, Ch. II, para. 41. However, UNICTRAL recognises that ordering insolvency-related relief with respect to a solvent group member may conflict with the protection of property rights and raise constitutional law questions. See para. 42.

129 J.L. Westbrook, Corporate Formalism in a Global Economy, in J.P. Sarra and B. Romaine (eds), Annual Review of Insolvency Law, Toronto: Carswell, 2015, observing that the sale of Nortel's assets 'realized far more than the parties had expected, no doubt because of the global nature of the sale'.

9.62 **Fourth**, and finally, a restraint on enforcement actions against third parties should not unfairly prejudice the rights of an affected creditor (e.g. a guaranteed creditor, a creditor benefiting from third-party collateral) or cause substantial detriment to it. Such detriment may arise if the value of collateral held by the debtor's affiliate significantly depreciates during a stay or if the guaranteed creditor's claim is made worse, potentially resulting in uncompensated loss. This can happen in a situation where the debtor or a group guarantor engage in opportunistic value-destroying behaviour or misconduct, such as strategic stripping of assets from the guarantor or co-debtor to place them out of the creditor's reach, to the detriment of a guaranteed creditor. In cases like this, it should be possible to terminate the extension of a stay. This suggestion is inspired by the approach adopted in the Netherlands, where a cooling-off period can be lifted if the interests of a creditor are materially prejudiced, and the US bankruptcy rule for lifting an automatic stay 'for cause, including the lack of adequate protection'. The option to lift an extended stay for valid reasons ensures proportionality in the application of this legal tool. It helps strike a balance between the principles of estate value preservation and the protection of trust and legitimate expectations.

10

INTRA-GROUP RESCUE FINANCING: SAFE HARBOURS AND PRE-EMPTIVE STRATEGIES

10.1 INTRODUCTION

This chapter should be seen as a response to the concerns raised in Chapter 6, which covers the subordination of intra-group claims, and Chapter 7, which addresses the avoidance of transactions involving group members. These chapters highlight various issues associated with intra-group financing, two of which warrant particular attention. The first is the problem of underinvestment, which occurs when socially desirable, value-creating projects and rescue attempts do not take place (section 6.5). Insolvency law rules that provide for the avoidance of related-party transactions or the subordination of insider claims can potentially discourage efficient intra-group rescue financing, because they amplify risks for assisting companies (e.g. guarantors, lenders, collateral providers). As a result, the principle of estate value preservation and maximisation may be compromised. The second problem concerns the lack of legal certainty regarding the avoidance of transactions common in group financing, such as cross-guarantees and the provision of collateral, in cases where a guarantor or collateral provider themselves faces financial difficulties and becomes insolvent (section 7.3). 10.01

10.02 The absence of predictability and sufficient clarity regarding the permissibility of intra-group transfers – whether through intra-group loans, provision of guarantees or collateral or other transactions – in going concern and gone concern scenarios to manage financial distress and maximise value is troubling. The key question is how to find a balance between discouraging overinvestment, asset shifting, asset dilution and other forms of opportunistic behaviour, while at the same time avoiding underinvestment and facilitating the efficient allocation of resources among group entities. This chapter addresses this question.

10.03 There are different strategies that may be adopted to find a balance. This chapter focuses on two such strategies: (i) ex ante authorisation of transactions within a regulated and supervised framework, a safe harbour, as an ad hoc response to financial distress (section 10.2), and (ii) several pre-emptive financial arrangements commonly used among banking groups (section 10.3). Section 10.4 concludes with my suggestions.

10.04 Thus, I examine both private and public law responses to the balancing problem and draw conclusions from developments in corporate insolvency and bank resolution. Figure 10.1 places the discussed strategies along a timeline, reflecting the demise curve of the company's financial situation. Transaction avoidance rules primarily apply to transactions entered into by the debtor before an insolvency filing, but at a time when the debtor is either insolvent, foreseeably insolvent, or otherwise financially distressed.[1] Hence, ex post judicial review of transactions is placed in the middle column. Ex ante authorisation is available post-filing, whether carried out in an insolvency or pre-insolvency

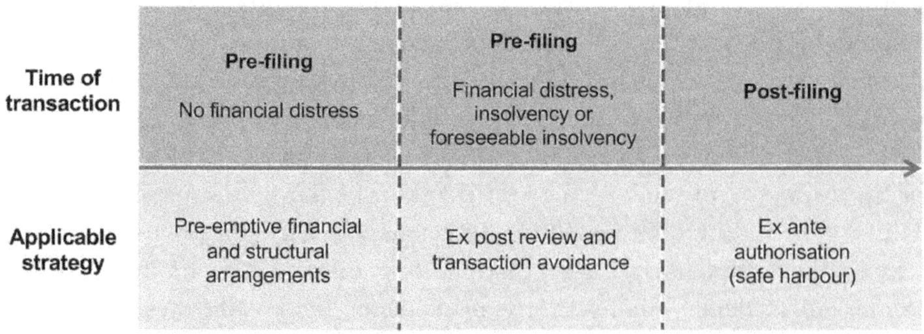

Figure 10.1 Strategies addressing group financial transactions

1 R. Bork and M. Veder, Harmonisation of Transactions Avoidance Laws, 1st edn, Intersentia, 2022, paras. 3.15 and 4.32, explaining that transaction avoidance law commonly addresses transactions concluded or performed prior to the opening of insolvency (liquidation) proceedings. In most legal systems, upon the opening of such proceedings, the rights of disposal and administration over the debtor's estate are shifted

procedure (e.g. preventive restructuring framework) and is positioned on the right side of the figure. Finally, pre-emptive arrangements are established long before insolvency, when the debtor is entirely solvent and liquid, and are situated on the left side of the figure.

10.2 EX ANTE APPROVAL MECHANISMS AND SAFE HARBOURS

10.2.1 Three types of safe harbours

The past years have witnessed the introduction of safe harbour rules into national laws. Before discussing these rules, it is important to clarify the term 'safe harbour', as it is used in different contexts and can refer to different things. **10.05**

First, a safe harbour regime may involve a carve-out of specific types of legal relationships (e.g. certain types of contracts or payments) from otherwise applicable legislation. For example, the US Bankruptcy Code establishes a safe harbour for certain types of financial transactions by granting them immunity from transaction avoidance,[2] and insulating them from the prohibition of ipso facto clauses.[3] Similarly, in the UK, the recently introduced limitations on ipso facto clauses do not apply to most financial agreements (e.g. securities contracts, swap agreements, etc.).[4] These carve-outs are meant to preserve liquidity, instil confidence in financial markets and mitigate systemic risk.[5] **10.06**

Second, a safe harbour could encompass the protection of corporate officers from personal insolvency-related liability. An example of such a safe harbour can be found in Australian law, which lays down an exception to insolvency trading liability for directors.[6] This exception applies when a director, in the **10.07**

---

to an IP. Transactions occurring after the commencement of insolvency proceedings typically need to be entered into by an IP, with his approval, or the approval by the court.

2 11 U.S. Code § 546(e). C.W. Mooney Jr., The Bankruptcy Code's Safe Harbors for Settlement Payments and Securities Contracts: When Is Safe Too Safe? Texas International Law Journal, Vol. 49, 2014, pp. 245–269.

3 11 U.S. Code § 555 (securities contracts), § 556 (commodities and forward contracts), § 559 (repos), § 560 (swap agreements).

4 Insolvency Act 1986, s. 233B(10), Schedule 4ZZA.

5 Whether bankruptcy carve-outs for financial contracts actually reduce systemic risk remains debatable. See M.J. Roe, Derivatives and repos in bankruptcy, in B.E. Adler (ed), Research Handbook on Corporate Bankruptcy Law, Edward Elgar Publishing, 2020, p. 103, arguing that the carve-outs for derivatives and repos reduce incentives for market discipline, encourage more short-term financing and therefore unfavourably affect financial stability. See also, R. Mokal, Liquidity, Systemic Risk, and the Bankruptcy Treatment of Financial Contracts, Brooklyn Journal of Corporate, Financial and Commercial Law, Vol. 10, 2015, pp. 15–96.

6 Treasury Laws Amendment (2017 Enterprise Incentives No. 2) Act 2017. See also Explanatory Memorandum, General outline and financial impact, Treasury Laws Amendment (2017 Enterprise Incentives No. 2) Bill 2017 (Cth).

vicinity of insolvency, engages in 'one or more courses of action that are reasonably likely to lead to a better outcome for the company' and 'the debt is incurred, or the disposition is made, directly or indirectly in connection with any such course of action'.[7] In this context, 'a better outcome' means 'an outcome that is better for the company than the immediate appointment of an administrator, or liquidator, of the company'.[8] The Australian safe harbour regime strikes a balance between creditor protection, discouragement of misconduct and encouragement of entrepreneurship and restructuring efforts.[9] While it does not provide absolute legal certainty and predictability, this safe harbour aims to assist directors and those dealing with them navigate 'the legal minefield which surrounds attempts at business rescue'.[10] Importantly, however, the safe harbour does not offer protection against transaction avoidance actions.[11]

10.08 Third, while the first type of safe harbours exempts certain contracts from specific rules and the second grants protection to directors of financially distressed companies, the third type of safe harbours takes the form of an antecedent approval mechanism, establishing screening and ex ante authorisation of transactions.[12] This safe harbour is of particular interest, as it can address some of the problems inherent in ex post judicial review, such as hindsight bias and uncertainty of outcomes. A well-structured and cost-efficient ex ante approval regime can promote the principle of protection of trust and certainty of transactions, mitigate information asymmetries, avert opportunistic behaviour and contribute to value preservation by facilitating the provision of rescue financing. In the following paragraphs, I explore these safe harbours as established in Dutch and US law.

10.09 UK law is excluded from my analysis because it lacks a tailored regime that facilitates rescue financing. Some priority may be granted to financing attracted by an administrator in the course of administration; such financing

7 Corporations Act 2001, s. 588GA.

8 Corporations Act 2001, s. 588GA(7).

9 S. Steele, I. Ramsay and M. Webster, Insolvency Law Reform in Australia and Singapore: Directors' Liability for Insolvent Trading and Wrongful Trading, International Insolvency Review, Vol. 28, 2019, pp. 363-391.

10 J. Harris and A. Hargovan, Potential Liability for Directors During Corporate Restructuring: Comparative Perspectives, in P.J. Omar and J.L.L. Gant (eds), Research Handbook on Corporate Restructuring, Edward Elgar Publishing, 2021, p. 164.

11 Compare with the safe harbour under § 546(e) US Bankruptcy Code, which applies to financial contracts.

12 For a brief overview of safe harbours in Belgian, French, German, Spanish and Italian law, see B. Wessels and S. Madaus (eds), Rescue of Business in Europe: A European Law Institute Instrument, OUP, 2020, pp. 246-250.

qualifies as an administrative expense.[13] In a standalone moratorium, priority for rescue financing can arise from the provision of a security interest over the debtor's property.[14] However, neither schemes of arrangement, restructuring plans nor CVAs are supported by a rescue financing regime. Several proposals have been put forward to encourage lenders to provide rescue financing in the UK.[15] They included granting security to new lenders over property already subject to charges, in priority to existing charge holders.[16] These proposals did not receive a positive response.[17] When it comes to rescue finance in the UK, it is pointed out that a market-based response has naturally emerged. If the business is deemed viable, additional funding is typically extended by existing or new credit providers on a consensual basis.[18]

10.2.2 The Netherlands: safe harbour under the WHOA

The third type of safe harbour has recently been incorporated into Dutch law. **10.10** To make rescue financing more attractive, the Dutch legislator initially considered setting up a safe harbour that would offer protection against transaction avoidance for security rights created in the period between the proposal of a restructuring plan and its voting.[19] No distinction was made between new and old financing, and no specific safeguards against abuse were included.[20] In the final version of the WHOA, the legal framework for the protection of rescue financing was refined. According to Article 42a Fw (in the version applicable since 1 January 2023),

13 Insolvency Act 1986, Schedule 1, para. 3, under which an administrator has the 'power to raise or borrow money and grant security therefor over the property of the company'.

14 Insolvency Act 1986, s. A26, under which the debtor may grant security over its property if the monitor gives his consent, which can only be given if the monitor believes the grant of security will support the rescue of the debtor as a going concern.

15 The Cork Committee recommended that if the administration order is discharged 'all creditors should revert to the position as it was when the original application was made, subject to the rights of priority of payment to anyone who in the meantime has given money or advanced credit to the administrator, to enable the company's business to be carried on as a going concern'. Insolvency Law and Practice: Report of the Review Committee, 1982, para. 514.

16 Insolvency Service, Encouraging Company Rescue – A consultation, London: DTI, June 2009. The Insolvency Service, A Review of the Corporate Insolvency Framework: A Consultation on Options for Reform, May 2016, para. 10.21.

17 Insolvency and Corporate Governance, Government Response, 26 August 2018, pp. 75–77.

18 Ibid. See J. Payne and J. Sarra, Tripping the Light Fantastic: A Comparative Analysis of the European Commission's Proposals for New and Interim Financing of Insolvent Businesses, International Insolvency Review, Vol. 27, 2018, p. 184.

19 Continuity of Enterprises Act II (*Wet Continuïteit Ondernemingen II*), 2014, Article 42a. See F.M.J. Verstijlen, Ondersteunende voorzieningen in de WHOA, TvI 2020/4.

20 F.M.J. Verstijlen, Flankerende voorzieningen in de Wet Homologatie onderhands akkoord ter voorkoming van faillissement, in Preadviezen van de Vereniging Handelsrecht, Uitgeverij Paris, 2017, p. 137, noting the desirability of a more cautious and fine-tuned approach.

> The preceding article [Article 42, dealing with transaction avoidance] may not be invoked to annul a legal act performed after the debtor has submitted a declaration to the clerk of the court as meant in Article 370(3) or after the court has appointed a restructuring expert … if the court, upon the debtor's request, has granted prior approval of that act. The court shall grant the requested approval if, at the time of the approval it can reasonably be assumed that:
>
> a. the performance of a legal act is necessary to:
>   1. allow the debtor to continue its business during the preparation of a plan …, or
>   2. allow the debtor to prepare the plan …, to put it to the vote, or to have it approved by the court in accordance with Article 384.
>
> b. this legal act would be in the interests of the general body of creditors and would not materially prejudice the interests of any individual creditors.

10.11 The Explanatory Memorandum to the WHOA clarifies that this article deals with situations where an attempt is made to adopt a restructuring plan, and financing is provided in that context. Such financing should be necessary to sustain the debtor's business during the plan's preparation. Article 42a Fw allows the debtor to petition the court for authorisation to perform certain acts, such as granting a security right necessary to obtain new financing. The debtor can attract new financing during the preparation of a plan and establish security rights for it, without these legal acts being exposed to the risk of avoidance, should the WHOA plan fail and bankruptcy ensue.

10.12 To obtain court approval: (i) the debtor must initiate the preparation of a restructuring plan and submit the relevant statement to the court; (ii) financing must be essential to ensure the continuity of the debtor's business during restructuring negotiations; and (iii) the legal act in question must benefit the debtor's joint creditors and not entail any material detriment to any individual creditor. This is typically the case where creditors are likely to be better off under the WHOA plan than in an alternative (bankruptcy) scenario.[21] Once court approval is secured, the legal act cannot be annulled in future bankruptcy proceedings. Importantly, Article 42a Fw does not distinguish between external and internal creditors (e.g. group entities), both of whom can, in principle, rely on it.

10.13 The operation of Article 42a Fw may be complicated when several group entities are involved in a restructuring attempt. Consider a scenario where one group entity, Company A, obtains financing from a Creditor. As part of this financial arrangement, another group entity, Company B, provides a guarantee or collateral to the Creditor. The court overseeing the restructuring of Company A authorises the financing under Article 42a Fw. The question

21 Rb. Noord-Nederland 26 March 2021, ECLI:NL:RBNNE:2021:1100, r.o. 2.13.

then arises whether the protective shield of the court's approval extends to cover the guarantee and collateral. I argue that this is not the case. Dutch law respects entity separateness.[22] When the court in Company A's proceedings assesses whether financing is necessary to sustain Company A's operations and whether it materially harms the interests of its creditors, it does not, and for practical reasons cannot, evaluate these aspects as they pertain to Company B. This is because Company B is not subject to the restructuring scheme, nor is it under the jurisdiction of the court. It is true that Article 372 Fw, discussed in Chapter 8, enables the restructuring of cross-guarantees via a single WHOA plan. However, this article does not deal with transaction avoidance. It only permits a valid (non-annulled) cross-guarantee to be released and contains distinct rules designed to safeguard the interests of the guaranteed creditor.[23]

If the restructuring of Company A fails and Company B enters bankruptcy proceedings, the guarantee and collateral could be subject to an *actio pauliana* challenge by Company B's IP under Article 42 Fw, or, as the case may be, Article 47 Fw. The IP representing Company B may argue that the transactions in question are disadvantageous, as the guarantee has increased the guarantor's liability and the pledged assets are no longer available to its creditors, while all the benefits of the financing were enjoyed by another entity, Company A. Thus, the safe harbour may not provide certainty at the moment when the lending decision is made. One might argue that the guarantee itself is covered by the protective shield of Article 42a Fw simply because it is approved by the court as part of the new financing package, and the Creditor would not have extended the loan without the guarantee. However, this view is not persuasive, as it effectively deprives the guarantor's creditors of the protections offered by transaction avoidance rules. In other words, it is disproportionate. As noted above, the decision by a judge to approve financing is based on Company A's situation (and that of its creditors), and does not give consideration to the effects on Company B or its creditors, just as the position of the Creditor providing rescue financing is irrelevant to the court's assessment. **10.14**

This example illustrates the limits of an ex ante approval mechanism within the context of enterprise groups. The reason is that Article 42a Fw, much **10.15**

22 Rb. Noord-Holland 19 February 2021, ECLI:NL:RBNHO:2021:1398, *JOR* 2021/101, m.nt. Tollenaar (*Jurlights*). The court observed that 'it is questionable whether the law offers the option of offering a plan for several companies in this combined manner. After all, the basic principle is that a separate agreement is offered for each company, in which the individual company identity and separate assets are respected.' Separate plans should be submitted for each group entity, except in cases where the restructured debts are covered by the provisions of Article 372 Fw.

23 Dutch Bankruptcy Act, Articles 372 and 384.

like Articles 17 and 18 of the EU Preventive Restructuring Directive, does not expressly address group restructurings. While the Directive mentions that third-party guarantees are covered by financial assistance that deserves protection,[24] it does not specify how this can be arranged in practice, especially when the guarantee might adversely affect the guarantor's own creditors. One potential solution can be proposed. The WHOA's flexibility means that it can be used to implement group restructurings. Separate WHOA schemes could be initiated for Company A and Company B, allowing Article 42a Fw to be invoked for the approval of both the loan and the associated guarantee through two parallel yet coordinated WHOA schemes. In this scenario, the court would be able to consider the implications of the guarantee for creditors of Company B. Consequently, the protection of rescue financing would encompass the entire package of transactions. This also means that the safeguards of Article 42a Fw and other relevant articles of the Bankruptcy Act would apply to all relevant group members. Admittedly, the opening of separate proceedings is not ideal due to transaction costs. Yet, it may be a necessary sacrifice to ensure procedural fairness and the substantive protection of creditors' rights.

10.2.3 The USA: DIP financing as a group effort

10.16 The special treatment of post-petition or DIP financing in the USA can be traced back to the nineteenth century large-scale corporate reorganisations, when lenders were afforded special priority for financing reorganisation efforts, often for distressed railroad companies.[25] At that time, loans were used to support businesses during the lengthy restructuring process. Today, DIP financing is considered to be 'the most publicized feature of bankruptcy reorganizations'.[26] In Chapter 11, it grants a debtor access to the liquidity necessary to finance a restructuring effort, ensuring uninterrupted operating activity and preventing value-depleting piecemeal liquidation. This, among other things, explains the popularity of Chapter 11 among non-US incorporated debtors and their groups.

10.17 The rules governing DIP financing can be found in § 364 of the US Bankruptcy Code. These rules incentivise both new and existing lenders to provide

---

24 Restructuring Directive, Recital 66.

25 D.A. Skeel Jr., The Past, Present and Future of Debtor-in-Possession Financing, Cardozo Law Review, Vol. 25, 2004, pp. 1905–1934; D.A. Skeel Jr., Debt's Dominion: A History of Bankruptcy Law in America, Princeton University Press, 2001, p. 48, noting more generally that 'the history of corporate reorganization is the history of nineteenth-century railroad failure'.

26 G.G. Triantis, A Theory of the Regulation of Debtor-in-Possession Financing, Vanderbilt Law Review, Vol. 46, 1993, p. 901.

financing to struggling debtors. They do so in several ways, offering varying degrees of protection and priority, ranging from administrative expense priority to senior secured credit priority. This creates a ladder of priority that courts can authorise if financing cannot be otherwise obtained. The higher the stair (i.e. level of priority), the more demanding the associated conditions become. Without delving into the complex regulation of DIP financing, it suffices to point out that US law does not make any exceptions related to the composition of rescue financiers. Therefore, the benefits of the DIP financing regime are available to insider lenders as well. A recent example illustrating this is the bankruptcy case of LATAM Airlines Group S.A. and its group affiliates, in which shareholder DIP financing was authorised.[27] However, despite the fact that the identity of a DIP financier is of lesser importance, courts apply heightened scrutiny when assessing the *bona fides* of transactions involving related parties.[28]

The US approach is quite distinct, primarily due to the practice of group members filing bankruptcy petitions simultaneously to have their cases jointly administered.[29] This 'group filing' is made possible by several notable features of US law. First, the US Bankruptcy Code permits a debtor to file for bankruptcy in any bankruptcy court where a case concerning the debtor's affiliate is pending.[30] This promotes procedural consolidation and enables a single court, or even a single judge, to oversee the restructuring of the entire group. Second, the flexible and COMI-independent jurisdictional criteria for opening a Chapter 11 case allow group companies, including foreign affiliates, to implement a group restructuring in the USA in a centralised manner. There is no requirement that all (or any) group members have their COMI in the USA.[31] Third, Chapter 11 does not mandate material insolvency of a debtor 10.18

27 Order Granting Motion to Approve Debtor in Possession Financing [ECF No. 1091] *In re LATAM Airlines Group S.A.*, No. 20-11254 (JLG) (Bankr. S.D.N.Y. 2020). The DIP financing involved two existing shareholders, Qatar Airways Investments (UK) Ltd and Costa Verde Aeronautica S.A., which held appr. 32 per cent of LATAM's stock.

28 *In re Innkeepers USA Tr.*, 442 B.R. 227 (Bankr. S.D.N.Y. 2010); *In re Papercraft Corp.*, 211 B.R. 813 (W.D. Pa. 1997); *Carlson v. Hallinan*, 925 A.2d 506 (Del. Ch. 2006).

29 S.J. Lubben, American Business Bankruptcy: A Primer, Edward Elgar Publishing, 2021, pp. 109–110.

30 28 U.S. Code § 1408(2). The wide range of permissible bankruptcy venue options, resulting in a concentration of bankruptcy cases in a few districts, has attracted some criticism. See the Bankruptcy Venue Reform Act of 2021, which seeks to limit the 'affiliate-filing rule'.

31 For a bankruptcy jurisdiction, 'a dollar, a dime, or a peppercorn' of property in the US suffices. *In re Theresa Mctague* (1996) 198 BR 428, 431. A. Walters, United States' bankruptcy jurisdiction over foreign entities: exorbitant or congruent? Journal of Corporate Law Studies, Vol. 17, 2017, pp. 367–404; G. Ray Warner, Conflicting Norms: Impact of the Model Law on Chapter 11's Global Restructuring Role, International Insolvency Review, Vol. 28, 2019, p. 275, calling the US approach to international insolvency jurisdiction and its global reach 'aggressive universalist'.

as an entry threshold.[32] As a result, it removes the access barrier in the form of the insolvency requirement and thereby permits participation of different group entities, whether solvent or insolvent, in a group reorganisation.[33]

10.19 The affiliate-filing rule, flexible jurisdictional standards and the absence of an insolvency requirement, among other factors, have made the USA a preferred destination for the restructuring of enterprise groups, such as Aeromexico, Avianca and LATAM. Most importantly for this section, these features allow DIP financing to be organised and sanctioned at the group level. In fact, it is common for US courts to approve DIP financing provided to the group, where one group entity acts as the borrower and other members of the group, each subject to its own bankruptcy proceeding, guarantee the borrower's obligations under the DIP financing.[34]

10.20 Before exploring a few examples, it is important to highlight an important feature of US law that ensures the effectiveness of DIP orders and safeguards legal certainty. In Chapter 11, a debtor cannot obtain financing outside the ordinary course of business without a court order.[35] Since it is not always clear whether an action is within the ordinary course of business, debtors often seek approval of DIP financing as part of a first-day motion package.[36] Another common motion is a request for the approval of cash management systems.[37] Although the law stipulates that a court may authorise DIP financing *after notice and hearing*, when financing is urgently needed to continue business operations or protect assets, US courts are willing to authorise it without an actual hearing.[38] The degree of the courts' involvement and control over DIP

32 P. Blumberg et al., Blumberg on Corporate Groups, 2nd edn, Wolters Kluwer, 2021, § 89.03, observing that '[s]olvency of the subsidiary does not present any hurdle to the institution of voluntary proceedings with respect to the subsidiary and therefore does not present any hurdle to subsequent procedural or substantive consolidation with the proceedings of its insolvent parent'.

33 *In re General Growth Properties, Inc.*, 409 B.R. 43, 63 (Bankr. S.D.N.Y. 2009), noting that 'a judgment on an issue as sensitive and fact-specific as whether to file a Chapter 11 petition can be based in good faith on consideration of the interests of the group as well as the interests of the individual debtor'.

34 *In re Patriot Coal Corp.*, 2012 WL 3728168 (Bankr. S.D.N.Y. 2012); *In re EWGS Intermediary, LLC*, 2013 WL 6978584, at 6 (Bankr. D. Del. 2013), holding that the debtors (group members) have an immediate need to obtain 'Post-Petition Financing in order to, among other things, permit the orderly continuation of the operation of their operating businesses, preserve jobs for their employees, maintain vendor support and minimize the disruption of their business operations, manage and preserve the assets of the Debtors' bankruptcy estates … in order to maximize the recoveries to creditors of the Estates'.

35 11 U.S. Code, § 364(b)-(d).

36 Collier on Bankruptcy, 16th edn., 2022, Vol. 10, ¶ 6003.01.

37 *In re Colad Group, Inc.*, 324 B.R. 208, 216-17 (Bankr. W.D.N.Y. 2005).

38 11 U.S. Code § 102(1)(b). *Morlan v. Universal Guar. Life Ins. Co.*, 298 F.3d 609, 618 (7th Cir. 2002), observing that a 'notice and a hearing' really means 'notice and the opportunity for a hearing'.

financing and its terms is limited.[39] What is crucial to note is that, under the US Bankruptcy Code, if the court authorises DIP financing, any reversal or modification of such authorisation on appeal does not affect the validity of any debt incurred, or any priority or lien granted to an entity that extended credit in good faith.[40] This 'enhanced' safe harbour is of utmost importance for post-petition lenders. It has a practical effect of mooting appeals against orders authorising DIP financing, as long as: (i) the lender or group of lenders acted in good faith in extending new credit; and (ii) the creditor challenging the authorisation does not obtain a stay pending an appeal.[41]

An example of a case in which DIP financing was granted at a group level is the restructuring of Babcock and Wilcox Company, Inc. (B&W) and two of its wholly owned subsidiaries. The debtors filed voluntary Chapter 11 petitions, and the court administratively consolidated the cases under Bankruptcy Rule 1015(b). The debtors also submitted a motion seeking authorisation to enter into a post-petition financing arrangement with Citicorp North America, Inc. (CNA). Under this arrangement, the debtors were to receive a USD 300 million revolving line of credit and a letter of credit facility that allowed them to continue doing business. As part of the agreement, CNA would hold a claim against the assets of all the debtors, and this claim would be accorded super-priority administrative expense status. The agreement stipulated that if any group entity made payments to CNA in excess of the funds actually received by that entity, the said entity would acquire a super-priority claim under § 364(c)(1) against the other debtors, subordinate only to CNA's claim. 10.21

The court approved DIP financing, finding that it was 'necessary to the collective health of the debtors and that all the debtors would benefit from the agreement'.[42] This decision was made despite objections from a creditor of one of the group members. This creditor argued that the agreement did not apportion the super-priority administrative expenses based on the amounts actually 10.22

39 L. Tsioli, Rescue financing under a 'viability spotlight', Journal of Corporate Law Studies, Vol. 22, 2022, p. 851, observing that 'the statutory model of DIP financing leaves the court with de facto very little power to restrict excessive creditor control in light of the fear of becoming the one "stopping the music on a case" ...' The limited involvement of courts makes the role of the creditors' committee (as a watchdog in the DIP process) crucial.

40 11 U.S. Code § 364(e).

41 *In re Revco D.S., Inc.*, 901 F.2d 1359, 1364 (6th Cir. 1990). See, however, *In re Swedeland Dev. Group, Inc.*, 16 F.3d 552, 562 (3d Cir. 1994), noting that '[w]e see no reason why section 364(e) should be understood to protect a lender with respect to money it has not disbursed'. Also, Collier on Bankruptcy, 16th edn, 2022, Vol. 3, ¶ 364.08, arguing that in 'view of the extraordinary protection provided by section 364(e), the better approach is to protect only the lender's actual reliance interest, and not its expectation interest'.

42 *Clyde Bergemann, Inc. v. Babcock & Wilcox Co. (In re Babcock & Wilcox Co.)*, 250 F.3d 955, 957 (5th Cir. 2001).

used by each individual debtor, resulting in de facto substantive consolidation that benefited certain entities and their creditors while disadvantaging others. The court disagreed and concluded that the DIP financing order did not combine the assets or liabilities of the debtors. The group entities effectively acted as guarantors for the post-petition financing. They maintained separate insolvency estates and, as noted above, acquired a super-priority claim against other debtors for any amounts paid to CNA in excess of the funds received from it.

10.23 The B&W group case is notable because it involves collective post-petition financing for related debtors in cases that are jointly administered but not substantively consolidated.[43] The DIP financing was authorised for the corporate group, with the DIP financier obtaining full recourse and priority against the assets of its constituent members, regardless of which group entity ultimately benefited from the DIP financing. Widen notes that the practice of approving DIP financing, whereby the DIP lender receives priority in the consolidated assets of a group of companies 'recognizes the corporate group as a single entity post-petition for the purposes of obtaining financing' and 'creates the equivalent of an intercompany family of guarantees to protect the DIP lender'.[44]

10.24 To conclude, ex ante authorisation of rescue financing can be a valuable addition to ex post judicial review. Yet, it cannot and should not fully substitute such ex post review, as it plays a crucial role in safeguarding creditors' rights and remains a fallback option. The effectiveness of a safe harbour as a tool to ensure legal certainty, promote intra-group financing in a crisis and filter out opportunistic and harmful transactions depends on its design and implementation. As is often the case, the devil is in the detail. This is also true when using a safe harbour in a group context. If a safe harbour does not accurately reflect the group reality, its efficiency may be limited. This is because it could fail to establish a balance between the interests of individual group entities and their creditors.

10.25 If restructuring and the attraction of rescue financing are a team (group) effort, the relevant group entities should be involved in the authorisation process, and the creditors of those group entities should be sufficiently protected. Whether this is achievable in practice depends on a variety of factors, from rules on international insolvency jurisdiction (e.g. whether a centralised group solution is possible) to the specific conditions for accessing restructuring or insolvency

43 For a similar DIP financing arrangement involving intercompany guarantees, see *In re Solidus Networks, Inc.*, Not Reported in B.R., 2008 WL 8462968 (9th Cir. BAP 2008).

44 W.H. Widen, Prevalence of Substantive Consolidation in Large Bankruptcies from 2000 to 2004: Preliminary Results, American Bankruptcy Institute Law Review, Vol. 14, 2006, p. 57.

proceedings (e.g. whether insolvency is a prerequisite). In this regard, the US Bankruptcy Code offers a framework that facilitates group restructuring efforts and incorporates intra-group DIP financing as an integral part. It provides the whole package, including welcoming jurisdictional standards, a low threshold for entry, procedural consolidation and an 'enhanced' safe harbour arising from court-authorised DIP financing.

10.3 PRE-EMPTIVE FINANCIAL ARRANGEMENTS IN BANKING GROUPS

10.3.1 Bank resolution: from reaction to pre-emption

The preceding sections discussed the strategy of ex ante authorisation of rescue financing, which applies when an entity experiences financial distress and requires access to rescue financing. In other words, it is an ad hoc crisis-triggered strategy. By contrast, after the Global Financial Crisis (GFC), legislators in the EU and other regions shifted their focus from reactive measures to pre-emptive and proactive strategies, particularly in the area of bank regulation. Unlike ad hoc strategies, proactive measures are designed and implemented during periods of stability, when there are no signs of financial distress or insolvency. The rationale for this anticipatory crisis preparation lies in the recognition that no business is immune to insolvency and that failures are nearly inevitable within complex systems – a lesson underscored by the GFC.[45] Hence, it is logical to make systems less complex and limit the negative consequences of failures. One way to achieve this is through group recovery and resolution planning. 10.26

The requirement for banks to adopt recovery or resolution plans, commonly known as 'living wills', has been introduced in the USA[46] and the EU.[47] These plans serve several important purposes.[48] First, detailed and up-to-date plans provide resolution and other authorities with the necessary information to 10.27

45 S.L. Schwarcz, Regulating Complexity in Financial Markets, Washington University Law Review, Vol. 87, 2009, p. 248.

46 Dodd-Frank Act, Section 165(d). US law does not separate recovery and resolution planning.

47 BRRD, Title II. Under the BRRD, recovery plans are drawn up by banks themselves, while resolution plans are prepared by the Single Resolution Board and national resolution authorities. In contrast, under the Dodd-Frank Act, banks must draft resolution plans and submit them to the Federal Reserve Board, the Financial Stability Oversight Council and the Federal Deposit Insurance Corporation.

48 Some scholars remain sceptical of the practical relevance of recovery and resolution planning. S.L. Schwarcz, Beyond Bankruptcy: Resolution as a Macroprudential Regulatory Tool, Notre Dame Law Review, Vol. 94, 2018, p. 719, commenting: 'In my many years as a workout and bankruptcy lawyer, I rarely saw a firm's failure that accurately reflected, much less closely resembled, expectations about the firm when it was profitable.'

enable efficient monitoring, timely early intervention, and the execution of resolution tools. Second, these plans play an educational and disciplining role, and improve the awareness of banks' own directors about potential problems or weaknesses.[49] As a result, they can serve as warning indicators and catalysts for addressing impediments to the resolvability of a credit institution or a banking group. This might involve improvements to the group's corporate and financial structure, business lines and task allocation. Third, crisis preparation and the disclosure of information in plans can 'clarify expectations and strengthen market confidence in the resolution actions of authorities'.[50] Fourth, living wills can help simplify relationships and reduce complexity within multi-layered and multi-national banking groups[51] – a complexity frequently driven by extensive intra-group transactions.[52]

10.28 Under EU law, group recovery plans should include a detailed description of the group's legal and financial structure, along with an explanation of internal (intra-group) interconnectedness. This 'interconnectedness' covers material intra-group exposures and financial arrangements, such as cross-guarantees, legal interconnectedness from material legally binding agreements between group companies and operational interconnectedness related to the division and centralisation of functions within the group, such as centralised IT, treasury, risk management or administrative functions critical to other entities in the group.[53]

---

49 M. Ventoruzzo and G. Sandrelli, O Tell Me the Truth about Bail-In: Theory and Practice, Journal of Business, Entrepreneurship and The Law, Vol. 13, 2020, p. 218.

50 FSB, Public Disclosure on Resolution Planning and Resolvability. Discussion Paper for Public Consultation, 3 June, 2019. In the EU, recovery and resolution plans are not publicly available. Yet, some information contained therein must be revealed, such as general terms of group financial support agreements. In the USA, resolution plans consist of a private section containing confidential supervisory and proprietary information that is not available to the public, and an open public section.

51 E. Avgouleas, C. Goodhart and D. Schoenmaker, Bank Resolution Plans as a catalyst for global financial reform, Journal of Financial Stability, Vol. 9, 2013, p. 211, attributing the complexity of banking group structures to banks' desire to exploit the benefits of the legal structure (e.g. regulatory and tax arbitrage) and take advantage of the synergies attached to operating as an integrated group (e.g. intra-group transactions).

52 J-H. Binder, Resolution Planning and Structural Bank Reform within the Banking Union, SAFE Working Paper No. 81, 2014, p. 6.

53 Commission Delegated Regulation (EU) 2016/1075 of 23 March 2016 supplementing Directive 2014/59/EU of the European Parliament and of the Council with regard to regulatory technical standards specifying the content of recovery plans, resolution plans and group resolution plans, the minimum criteria that the competent authority is to assess as regards recovery plans and group recovery plans, the conditions for group financial support, the requirements for independent valuers, the contractual recognition of write-down and conversion powers, the procedures and contents of notification requirements and of notice of suspension and the operational functioning of the resolution colleges [2016] OJ L 184/1, Article 7(1)(c).

The requirement to prepare living wills is not the only tool reflecting the post-GFC shift towards pre-emption. This shift is also evident in the way intra-group support and intra-group obligations are (pre-)arranged or (pre-) positioned within banking groups. Various mechanisms ensure that sufficient capital and liquidity are accessible to group members during a crisis. One such mechanism is a group financial support agreement introduced in the EU by the BRRD. Other preparatory strategies involve the pre-positioning of financial resources in subsidiaries and the use of organisational (structural) and contractual arrangements to support this positioning. These mechanisms aim to create a predictable and manageable framework for the recovery and resolution of banking groups. Whether they achieve this goal remains a subject of debate. It suffices to point out that advance planning differentiates them from the ad hoc (authorisation) and ex post (judicial review) strategies. **10.29**

10.3.2 Group financial support agreements under the BRRD

Intra-group financing within banking groups is described as 'large, volatile and heavily relied upon around the world'.[54] However, during the GFC, many jurisdictions imposed or tightened restrictions on intra-group asset transfers, limiting banking groups' ability to optimally reallocate funds from entities with excess capital and liquidity to those in need.[55] This was attributed to the policy of insulation and geographical ring-fencing, adopted by some states to protect local (national) interests (see the case of Icelandic banks in section 3.4.2). **10.30**

The BRRD acknowledges that financial support between entities within a cross-border banking group may encounter significant obstacles during a financial crisis.[56] Certain restrictions, such as the individual application of liquidity requirements and large exposure limits, are embedded in national and EU laws. These restrictions are designed to prevent crises, mitigate cross-border contagion, reduce intra-group exposures, protect local creditors and other stakeholders. In addition to these restrictions, general transaction avoidance rules, largely unharmonised across the EU, and the risk of directors' liability present more subtle but significant challenges to the continuity of **10.31**

---

54 D. Reinhardt and S.J. Riddiough, The Two Faces of Cross-Border Banking Flows, IMF Economic Review, Vol. 63, 2015, p. 781.

55 E. Cerutti et al., Bankers Without Borders? Implications of Ring-Fencing for European Cross-Border Banks, in L.L. Ong (ed), A Guide to IMF Stress Testing: Methods and Models, 2014, p. 152; EC, Study on the feasibility of reducing obstacles to the transfer of assets within a cross border banking group during a financial crisis, Final Report, 2010.

56 BRRD, Recital 38.

intra-group financing, when a party involved in such financing is on the brink of insolvency.[57]

10.32 In 2012, the European Commission recognised the problem and explored various responses, ranging from 'no policy change' (baseline), compulsory financial assistance, to the introduction of the concept of 'group interest' in the company laws of EU countries.[58] Another alternative considered was the conclusion of a voluntary agreement on group financial support and its supervisory approval. The results of a public consultation on these options were mixed. It was accepted that the introduction of 'group interest' in related-party transactions could blur the boundaries between group entities, while compulsory financial assistance was considered too intrusive and a departure from the doctrine of party autonomy. However, the establishment of a special tool in the form of a voluntary agreement for intra-group financing, referred to as a 'pre-emptive transaction', was generally supported.[59] It was observed that such a tool would alleviate concerns regarding directors' liability, minimise the risks of transaction avoidance and increase clarity for transacting parties. In line with this, the BRRD introduced a special framework called 'Group Financial Support Agreement' (GFSA).

10.33 A GFSA is concluded pre-emptively. It does not involve an immediate transfer of funds or the granting of a guarantee or collateral. Instead, it can be viewed as a commitment or promise to provide support if the conditions for such support are satisfied in the future. This is why a GFSA can only be concluded if the parties (i.e. group companies) do not meet the conditions for early intervention, such as the infringement or likely infringement of prudential or conduct of business requirements.[60] While the GFSA itself should be concluded pre-emptively, the actual provision of support must be carried out in an early intervention scenario. Hence, business-as-usual transfers do not fall within the

57 A. Campbell and P. Moffatt, Large Scale Bank Insolvencies and the Challenges Ahead, in M. Haentjens and B. Wessels (eds), Research Handbook on Crisis Management in the Banking Sector, Edward Elgar Publishing, 2015, p. 64, observing that in the context of banking groups, problems tend to arise 'where local transaction avoidance provisions render intra-group transactions (such as those relating to preferential payments, or the transfer of assets at an undervalue and so forth) void'. See also M. Haentjens and I. Kokorin, Bank Resolution and National Insolvency Law: The Case of Group Financing, Zeitschrift für Bankrecht und Bankwirtschaft, Vol. 36(1), 2024, pp. 8–15.

58 Impact Assessment accompanying the document – Proposal for a Directive establishing a framework for the recovery and resolution of credit institutions and investment firms, SWD(2012) 166 final.

59 Ibid.

60 BRRD, Articles 19(8) and 27(1). EBA, Guidelines on triggers for use of early intervention measures pursuant to Article 27(4) of Directive 2014/59/EU, 2015.

scope of the BRRD's protective regime for intra-group financial support.[61] Let us look into the key features of this supranational regime.

First, the rationale behind GFSAs should be clarified. The BRRD recognises the need for a special regulatory framework to ensure the financial stability of banking groups.[62] Without it, the rules of national law may restrict the ability of group entities to support each other in times of financial distress. Consequently, the efficient use of group resources could be hindered. Some group entities may be cash-rich and able to provide funds to other group members, helping them navigate through asymmetric and idiosyncratic shocks. The political dimension is also important. The GFC revealed home-host state tensions and exposed local ring-fencing, challenging the practice of centralised capital and liquidity management by cross-border banking groups.[63] A pre-arranged and approved support agreement, such as a GFSA, could, in theory, encourage cooperation between competent authorities in a crisis. **10.34**

Second, once a GFSA is concluded and approved, Member States must 'remove any legal impediment in national law to intra-group financial support transactions that are undertaken in accordance' with a GFSA.[64] This regime creates a safe harbour against various impediments, including those arising from insolvency-related transaction avoidance. **10.35**

Third, intra-group support may only be provided if several conditions are met. For instance, there should be a reasonable prospect that the support will redress the financial difficulties of the receiving group company.[65] The support should aim to preserve or restore the financial stability of the entire group or any of its members, and it must be in the interests of the group member providing support.[66] Importantly, when assessing the interests of the providing entity (i.e. the grantor of financial support), both direct and *indirect* benefits arising from the restoration of financial soundness of the receiving entity and the preservation of group synergies can be considered. The EBA acknowledges that indirect benefits are difficult to quantify, for instance, when they concern limiting potential damage to the franchise and reputation that could occur if **10.36**

61 BRRD, Article 19(3), stating that a GFSA shall not constitute a prerequisite to provide group financial support to a distressed group entity 'on a case-by-case basis and according to the group policies if it does not represent a risk for the whole group'.

62 BRRD, Recital 38.

63 D. Schoenmaker, Governance of International Banking: The Financial Trilemma, OUP, 2013, Ch. 4.2; P. Davies, Resolution of cross-border groups, in M. Haentjens and B. Wessels (eds), Research Handbook on Crisis Management in the Banking Sector, Edward Elgar Publishing, 2015, pp. 263-265.

64 BRRD, Article 19(4).

65 BRRD, Article 23(1)(a).

66 BRRD, Article 23(1)(b).

a group member is allowed to fail.[67] Finally, the liquidity and solvency of the providing entity shall not be compromised as a result of extending support.[68] Therefore, the providing entity should not sacrifice itself and its creditors for the sake of group interests (section 3.5.1).

10.37 Fourth, the procedural side of GFSAs is complex[69] and involves two separate stages. The first stage concerns the approval of a GFSA. It commences with the parent entity submitting an application for the authorisation of the GFSA to the consolidating supervisor.[70] This application is then transmitted to the competent authorities of the entities involved, with the aim of reaching a joint decision.[71] If no decision is reached within four months, the consolidating supervisor must make its own decision on the application. The matter could also be referred to the EBA, which would then make the final decision. Following authorisation, the GFSA needs to be approved by the shareholders of the relevant group entities.[72] The second stage pertains to the approval of the actual extension of financial support (e.g. transfer of funds). It includes the decision by the management of both the providing entity and the receiving entity,[73] as well as non-opposition from the competent authorities (see Figure 10.2).[74]

10.38 To sum up, a GFSA offers a harmonised, relatively clear and transparent framework for intra-group financial support, which could contribute to the optimal allocation of resources within banking groups and ensure the continued operation of banking subsidiaries. Additionally, the process of drafting and approving group support agreements and of incorporating them into the group structure and in group recovery plans can also help address the problem of the lack of transparency and neglect of the corporate form, brought to light by the failure of the Lehman Brothers group.

---

67 EBA, Guidelines specifying the conditions for group financial support under Article 23 of Directive 2014/59/EU, 2015.

68 BRRD, Article 23(1)(e). Yet non-compliance with prudential requirements for capital, liquidity and large exposures can be authorised in exceptional circumstances. See BRRD, Article 23(1)(g).

69 M. Schillig, Resolution and Insolvency of Banks and Financial Institutions, OUP, 2016, p. 191, observing that the process for approving and executing group financial support agreements is 'unsuitable to adequately address a crisis situation'.

70 The consolidating supervisor is the lead supervisor in the group oversight context. Within the euro area, the ECB is the consolidating supervisor. For a definition, see Regulation (EU) No 575/2013 of the European Parliament and of the Council of 26 June 2013 on prudential requirements for credit institutions and investment firms and amending Regulation (EU) No 648/2012, Article 4(1)(41).

71 BRRD, Article 20.

72 BRRD, Article 21.

73 BRRD, Article 24.

74 BRRD, Article 25.

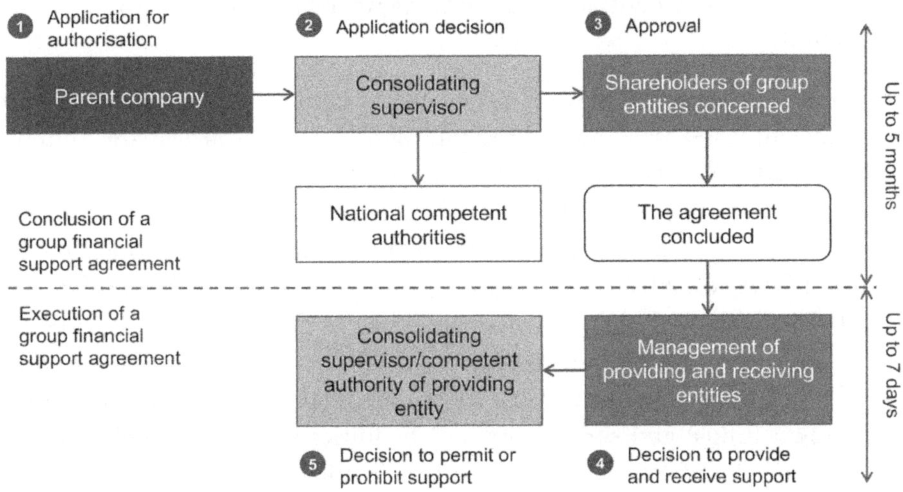

Figure 10.2 *Approval and authorisation of intra-group financial support under the BRRD*

However, writing in 2020, approximately five years after the BRRD entered into force, Gardella et al. concluded that the majority of banks active in the EU did not set up GFSAs, as they did not consider it a suitable tool.[75] This may be attributed to complex, cumbersome and inflexible rules governing the establishment and execution of GFSAs in crisis scenarios. Another drawback of the GFSA regime is that it does not oblige group entities to enter into GFSAs,[76] nor does it mandate their execution or empower supervisory authorities to demand intra-group support if the providing entity is not subject to early intervention.[77] Furthermore, the fact that a GFSA is concluded long before its potential execution can render it less suitable for a given crisis – a time-inconsistency problem.[78] **10.39**

75 A. Gardella, M. Rimarchi and D. Stroppa, Potential regulatory obstacles to cross-border mergers and acquisitions in the EU banking sector, EBA Staff Paper Series No. 7, 2020, p. 28.

76 M. Schillig, Resolution and Insolvency of Banks and Financial Institutions, OUP, 2016, para. 7.50, arguing that this is 'a major drawback in the BRRD regime'. EBA, Final Report on Recommendation on the coverage of entities in a group recovery plan, 2017, observing that the existence of a group support agreement would certainly help address the situation of financial distress and confirming that it is up to the institution to decide whether to include it as a recovery measure in a recovery plan.

77 D. Ramos Muñoz and M. Lamandini, Evolving key risks in the banking sector and related priorities for the SRB: the lack of an effective transfer-based bank crisis framework, November 2022, p. 9.

78 Time-inconsistency or dynamic inconsistency problem occurs when 'the best policy planned currently for some future period is no longer the best when that period arrives'. A. Cukierman, Central Bank Strategy, Credibility, and Independence: Theory and Evidence, MIT Press, 1992, p. 15.

10.3.3 Structural and contractual arrangements related to intra-group support

10.40 Many national legal frameworks applicable to banks are designed to ensure that sufficient loss-absorbing and recapitalisation capacity is available in resolution, so that the costs of a bank's failure are borne by its investors (i.e. shareholders and creditors) rather than depositors or taxpayers. The principle of loss internalisation is a major pillar of modern bank resolution frameworks. To this end, the BRRD establishes the Minimum Requirement for Own Funds and Eligible Liabilities (MREL),[79] while the FSB has developed similar rules for global systemically important banks, called Total Loss-Absorbing Capacity (TLAC).[80] Concretely, banks must meet these standards, so that regulatory capital (own funds) and certain types of liabilities (so-called eligible liabilities, primarily bonds) can be written down or converted into equity in cases of financial distress. These eligible debt instruments may be issued either to external investors – investors outside the banking group ('external MREL'), or to a parent entity within the group ('internal MREL' or 'iMREL').

10.41 In principle, loss-absorbing capacity – like capital and liquidity requirements – applies on an individual entity level, in line with the principle of entity separateness. A full prepositioning of loss-absorbing capacity, and capital and liquidity, on an entity-by-entity basis can be costly and does not per se result in the provision of fresh funds when a group entity urgently needs them.[81] In the EU, the current legal framework does not oblige parent companies to provide additional liquidity to their subsidiaries.[82]

10.42 Recent amendments to the BRRD (BRRD 2)[83] and the SRMR (SRMR 2)[84] make it possible to substitute the costly option of pre-positioning within

79 BRRD, Article 45.

80 FSB, Principles on Loss-absorbing and Recapitalisation Capacity of G-SIBs in Resolution. Total Loss-absorbing Capacity (TLAC) Term Sheet, 2015.

81 E. König, Single Point of Entry – a resolution strategy addressing the home–host issue in Europe's Banking Union, The SRB Blog, 22 April 2021, commenting that while the BRRD sets a prudent internal MREL requirement, it comes at a price, 'as it may lead to the fragmentation of the financial resources of internationally active groups'. See also I. Kokorin, Preemptive financing arrangements within cross-border banking groups: between flexibility and legal certainty, in L Böffel and J. Schürger (eds), Digitalisation, Sustainability, and the Banking and Capital Markets Union: Thoughts on Current Issues of EU Financial Regulation, Palgrave Macmillan, 2022, pp. 377–395.

82 M. Dewatripont, M. Montigny and G. Nguyen, When trust is not enough: Bank resolution, SPE, Ring-fencing and group support, ECGI Finance Working Paper No. 759/2021, 2021, p. 11.

83 Directive (EU) 2019/879 of 20 May 2019 amending Directive 2014/59/EU as regards the loss-absorbing and recapitalisation capacity of credit institutions and investment firms.

84 Regulation (EU) 2019/877 of the European Parliament and of the Council of 20 May 2019 amending Regulation (EU) No 806/2014 as regards the loss-absorbing and recapitalisation capacity of credit institutions and investment firms.

banking group entities with a less costly commitment of a top company (resolution entity) to financially assist its subsidiary. Accordingly, the resolution authority of the subsidiary (a non-resolution entity) can waive internal MREL for that subsidiary under certain conditions.[85] Such a waiver is possible if: (i) both the resolution entity and its subsidiary are established in the same EU Member State (which substantially limits the applicability of this option); (ii) they are part of the same resolution group; and (iii) 'there is no current or foreseen material practical or legal impediment to the prompt transfer of funds or repayment of liabilities by the resolution entity to the subsidiary'.[86]

The law does not clarify what constitutes 'material practical or legal impediments', which has led to disputes brought before the SRB Appeal Panel.[87] The latter has cited factors such as national company and insolvency laws, the legal structure of the banking group, by-laws and shareholder agreements that may obstruct the transfer of funds or repayment of liabilities by the parent company.[88] Thus, even with these amendments, the legal framework does not solve the current legal diversity and uncertainty in national corporate and insolvency laws regarding intra-group financing. It does not impose an obligation on group entities to support each other in a crisis or grant competent authorities the power to force one non-defaulting group member to provide financial assistance to another group member. Consequently, it neither replaces GFSAs nor establishes a comprehensive framework for intra-group financial support. **10.43**

In the US, intra-group support within banking groups is facilitated through contractually binding mechanisms (CBMs), security interests and penalties for non-compliance. CBMs take the form of secured support agreements (SSAs), whereby a non-operating holding company – referred to as an intermediate holding company (IHC) – undertakes to extend pre-bankruptcy support to material subsidiaries. This support is backed by perfected security interests in collateral granted by the IHC. To enable this arrangement, the IHC is pre-funded with resources from a parent company and maintains a liquidity and capital buffer that can be deployed upon a resolution event. The primary **10.44**

85 Internal MREL relates to the capacity to upstream losses from operating subsidiaries to the resolution entity. It requires the issuance (prepositioning) of 'loss-absorbing' debt instruments from the former to the latter. These instruments should be capable of being written off, if required, allowing losses to be passed to the resolution entity. Viewed from this perspective, internal MREL may be considered a type of intra-group support, because it entails upstreaming of losses from the subsidiary to the parent or resolution entity.

86 BRRD 2, Article 45f; SRMR 2, Article 12h.

87 SRB Appeal Panel, Final decision, Case 1/2021, 29 June 2022; SRB Appeal Panel, Final decision, Case 2/2021, 27 January 2022; SRB Appeal Panel, Final decision, Case 3/2021, 8 June 2022.

88 SRB, Minimum requirement for own funds and eligible liabilities (MREL), June 2022, Annex II.

objective of this structural setup is to ensure the uninterrupted operation of subsidiaries throughout the resolution process. SSAs are in line with the Single Point of Entry (SPOE) bank resolution model, which is prevalent among large US banks. Under the SPOE model, resolution powers (e.g. bail-in, bridge institution tool) are applied at the level of a holding company at the top of the banking group (or a sub-group), leaving the operating subsidiaries intact.[89]

10.45 SSAs are adopted by many global systemically important banks, including Bank of America,[90] Citigroup,[91] JPMorgan Chase & Co,[92] Goldman Sachs,[93] Morgan Stanley[94] and Bank of New York Mellon.[95] All these institutions follow the SPOE model, which fosters legal, managerial and financial centralisation.

10.46 For illustrative purposes, Figure 10.3 shows the functioning of the Support Agreement as presented in the resolution plan of JPMorgan Chase & Co. According to it,

1. Before the parent company's board votes to file a Chapter 11 petition, the parent company is contractually obliged to downstream certain of its remaining assets to IHC;
2. IHC undertakes to provide the necessary capital and/or liquidity support to the main bank and other key subsidiaries whose pre-positioned resources are insufficient to meet the needs for capital and liquidity in resolution; and
3. IHC's obligations to provide capital and/or liquidity support are secured by a security interest over its assets, ensuring that a breach of the Support Agreement would give rise to a secured claim based on an agreed-upon damages provision, which would be at least equal to, and potentially exceed, the support obligations. This ensures that any breach of the agreement would cause significant detriment to IHC.

10.47 The legal and operational structure of a banking group and the overall approach to resolution cannot be dealt with in isolation.[96] The SPOE model is preferable when the operations of group entities are integrated and when there

---

89 FSB, Recovery and Resolution Planning for Systemically Important Financial Institutions: Guidance on Developing Effective Resolution Strategies (2013) 12.

90 Bank of America Corporation 2023 Resolution Plan Submission.

91 Citigroup Inc. 2023 Resolution Plan, Public Section, 1 July, 2023.

92 JPMorgan Chase & Co, 2023 Resolution Plan Public Filing.

93 The Goldman Sachs Group, Inc. 2023 Resolution Plan, Public Section.

94 Morgan Stanley 2023 Resolution Plan, Public Section.

95 BNY Mellon, Resolution Plan, Public Section, 1 July 2023. Interestingly, BNY Mellon used the MPOE model in the 2015 Resolution Plan but opted for the SPOE model in its 2016 resolution plan submission. The same transition to the SPOE model was also made by Wells Fargo in its 2019 plan.

96 D. Schoenmaker, The impact of the legal and operational structures of euro-area banks on their resolvability, Policy Contribution, Issue 23, 2016, p. 6; P. Bolton and M. Oehmke, Bank Resolution and the

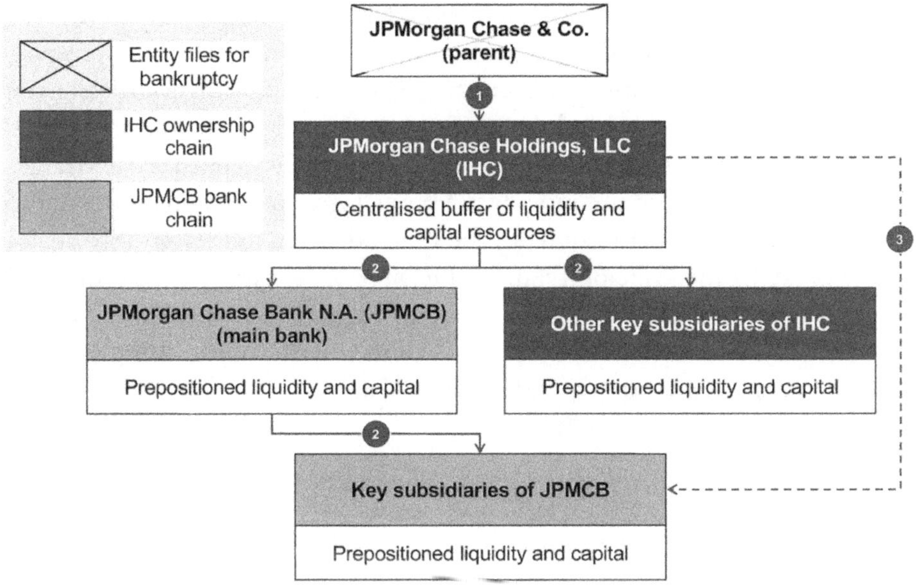

Note: This figure is based on JPMorgan Chase & Co, 2023 Targeted Resolution Plan, Public Filing, p. 40.

Figure 10.3 Support agreement under the resolution plan of JPMorgan Chase & Co

is a potential for group-wide contagion. This is common in groups that have centralised corporate and financial structures. For example, in the USA, banking groups have historically been organised with a top-level holding company whose capital structure includes bonds and other long-term unsecured debt, while short-term debt and operations are concentrated in subsidiaries.[97] In contrast, the Multiple Points of Entry (MPOE) model, which involves the intervention of multiple resolution authorities and the application of resolution tools at the level of operating companies, may be more appropriate for decentralised banking groups. Under this model, intra-group support agreements, such as SSAs or intercompany guarantees, might be less feasible, since the MPOE model seeks to limit financial interconnections and preserve the separateness of entities in resolution.

Structure of Global Banks, The Review of Financial Studies, Vol. 32, 2019, p. 2415, highlighting the need for complementarity between a bank resolution strategy and the structure of global banks.

97 D.A. Skeel, Single Point of Entry and the Bankruptcy Alternative, in M.N. Baily and J.B. Taylor (eds), Across the Great Divide: New Perspectives on the Financial Crisis, Hoover Press, 2014, p. 313, noting that this structure of the US financial groups 'is in large part a historical accident, caused by restrictions on banks' ability to branch across state lines and other regulatory obstacles'.

10.48 Apart from these observations, one should keep in mind that contractual arrangements are intended to complement, rather than replace, the pre-positioning of resources within group entities. They serve to enhance the existing MREL/TLAC regime by introducing flexibility and freeing some resources to be directed where and when they are needed. Arguably, contractual arrangements, such as SSAs, do not provide the same degree of certainty and predictability as pre-positioned resources. Their effectiveness hinges on two critical assumptions: (i) the availability and sufficiency of resources to be transferred from the parent to its subsidiaries, ensuring seamless operations; and (ii) the enforceability of support agreements and their insolvency-proofness, which depend on applicable contract and insolvency law.

10.4 CONCLUSIONS AND SUGGESTIONS

10.4.1 Overview of main findings

10.49 Regulating financial support within enterprise groups is a difficult task due to the complexity of intra-group relations, the variety of operational and financial arrangements among group members, entity bias in company and insolvency law and the risk of opportunistic behaviour by group members. The preceding chapters have identified two issues specific to intra-group financing. Chapter 6 explored the effects of the statutory subordination of intra-group loans, while Chapter 7 shed light on the challenges of ex post review of transactions involving group members. Both statutory subordination and transaction avoidance significantly increase the risk for parties extending financing. This chapter discussed two strategies that may be used to facilitate efficient intra-group rescue financing: safe harbours and pre-emptive structural and contractual arrangements.

10.50 English law does not have a well-developed statutory framework promoting rescue financing. In contrast, Dutch and US laws contain rules on ex ante authorisation of rescue financing, applicable in WHOA schemes and Chapter 11 plans. Dutch law permits the court to approve a legal act necessary to sustain the debtor's operations during WHOA plan preparation. Once approved, this act gains immunity from transaction avoidance. However, as I have shown, the court's approval of a legal act, such as a loan to the principal debtor (a scheme company), does not necessarily protect any accompanying transaction, such as a guarantee extended by a group member, which itself is not subject to the WHOA scheme. Should such a guarantor subsequently face bankruptcy, the likelihood of the guarantee being contested is considerable. The US law contains detailed rules on DIP financing, which equally apply to intra-group DIP financing. However, transactions involving affiliates are subject to heightened scrutiny based on the 'entire fairness' standard. Notably, US courts allow DIP financing to be organised and sanctioned at a group level. Typically, this occurs when group entities file bankruptcy petitions in one go and request the court to issue a first-day order approving DIP financing for the entire group, at least on a preliminary basis.

The second part of this chapter analysed various crisis preparation and pre-emption strategies. These strategies mainly apply to banking groups, as banks are subject to specific prudential and resolution requirements, including obligations related to the pre-positioning of resources and liabilities in group companies. The need to promote the efficient allocation of capital and liquidity within a banking group has led to a plethora of tools and strategies, ranging from the detailed framework for group financial support agreements (GFSAs) set out in the BRRD, to structural and contractual arrangements affecting intra-group financing. The latter include the establishment of 'buffer' intermediate holding companies, intra-group guarantees and secured support agreements. **10.51**

These pre-emptive strategies reflect two, at times conflicting, perspectives. One perspective facilitates the integrated management of capital and liquidity in the banking group, allowing resources to be allocated where they are most needed. This is the perspective of *flexibility and efficiency* of intra-group financing, better served by contractual support arrangements, which are common among large US banks. However, questions remain about their effectiveness and enforceability during a crisis. Another perspective prioritises *legal certainty and predictability*, which is promoted by pre-positioning, where resources are locked up in separate group entities. While this approach facilitates resolvability, ensures certainty and enhances the protection of national financial interests, it may also freeze resources that could otherwise be used more freely within the group. When choosing between these two perspectives, one is effectively navigating between Scylla and Charybdis. **10.52**

10.4.2 Suggestions on dealing with intra-group rescue financing

Based on an overview of different approaches to intra-group rescue financing and building on the findings outlined above, and in Chapters 6 and 7, the following suggestions regarding intra-group rescue financing in an insolvency context can be made. **10.53**

First, when applying transaction avoidance rules to transactions involving group members, such as cross-guarantees, and specifically when determining **10.54**

the associated benefits and detriments of any given transaction, group considerations and group interest should be taken into account. This group-conscious application of the law is necessarily fact-intensive and involves the assessment of various characteristics of a group and its financial distress. Factors that may be considered include:

- group integration and interconnectedness;
- the allocation of roles and functions among companies within the group;
- the presence of other guarantors and *in rem* security interests, which can benefit the guarantor and reduce its risks (e.g. due to subrogation or indemnity claims);
- the economic viability of an entity receiving financial support;
- external and internal causes contributing to financial difficulties;
- current market conditions and potential adverse trends; and
- the likely consequences of extending and withholding financial support.

10.55 When reviewing these factors, it is important to bear in mind that group interest alone cannot warrant the deprivation or sacrifice of the rights and interests of creditors of individual group members (section 3.5.2).

10.56 **Second**, even if group considerations are integrated into the analysis and facilitate efficient intra-group financing, thereby promoting the principle of group value maximisation, they cannot eliminate the legal uncertainty inherent in ex post judicial review. The greater the complexity of the legal assessment and the number of factors involved, the more scope there is for judicial discretion. To promote the principle of protection of legitimate expectations and trust (section 4.2.4), a strategy of ex ante authorisation of legal acts may be embraced. Once authorised, a legal act (e.g. an intra-group loan or a cross-guarantee securing it) is shielded from future avoidance actions. This legal act falls within a 'safe harbour'. If prescribed, the authorisation can also 'deactivate' statutory subordination or even confer priority to rescue financing.

10.57 When designing a safe harbour, different rules should be formulated for financing necessary to continue the debtor's operations during negotiations with creditors (i.e. interim financing) and for financing required to implement a restructuring plan (i.e. new financing). While decision-making power over interim financing, due to its urgency, could be vested in the court, the approval of new financing should be primarily left to the affected creditors. This is because these creditors are the ultimate risk-bearers. In other words, they have 'skin in the game' and stand to incur losses if the group restructuring fails. Moreover, in a situation of uncertainty, decision theory suggests that a collective decision made by a large and diverse group of persons, like creditors, is preferred to a decision made by a single expert, like a judge.[98]

Bork and Veder criticise restructuring privileges and ex ante authorisation of transactions.[99] Their critique primarily revolves around two key points. **10.58**

First, they observe that, in view of the rescue financier's awareness of the debtor's substantive insolvency, which is interpreted to include likely insolvency at some point in the future, the principle of protection of trust and legitimate expectations of creditors is triggered to a lesser degree, if at all.[100] While it is true that the existence of the risk itself is foreseeable and undisputed, determining its extent could be challenging. It should be noted that the awareness of the debtor's financial distress or prospective insolvency, or the fact that the counterparty is another group member, does not render creditor expectations less legitimate. The predicament lies in legal uncertainty and increased credit risk. The main question is how to deal with such uncertainty and risk to encourage *efficient* rescue financing. I believe that the absence of ex ante authorisation might lead to foregone rescue attempts (the problem of underinvestment, see section 6.5) ultimately harming estate value maximisation. **10.59**

Second, Bork and Veder question whether any ex ante control of rescue financing is capable of incorporating the assessment of avoidance prerequisites at a later point in time.[101] This critique may be less compelling for interim financing, which aims to ensure the continuity of business operations during restructuring negotiations. In any event, one should weigh the anticipated benefits of rescue financing against potential detriments. These benefits have to be evaluated at the time of court authorisation, rather than when the rescue effort fails, if it does at some point in the future. Given the uncertainty of the future, establishing legal certainty through court or creditor approval may be the only means to secure rescue financing 'here and now'. **10.60**

98 S. Madaus, On decision-making in rescue cases: why creditors and shareholders should decide about a rescue plan, in B. Santen and D. van Offeren (eds), Perspectives on International Insolvency Law: A Tribute to Bob Wessels, Kluwer: Deventer, 2014, pp. 215–227. The decisive role of creditors in decisions concerning rescue financing is supported by Tsioli. See L. Tsioli, Rescue Financing under a 'Viability Spotlight', Journal of Corporate Law Studies, Vol. 22, 2022, p. 876, arguing for an approach in which 'terms of the rescue financing would have to be considered by the entirety of the debtor's creditors in a process that imitates the "give-and-take" bargaining dynamics of the market-based model of rescue financing, albeit within an otherwise statutorily-organised framework'.

99 R. Bork and M. Veder, Harmonisation of Transactions Avoidance Laws, 1st edn, Intersentia, 2022, paras 4.119–4.122.

100 Ibid., para. 4.121.

101 Ibid., para. 4.122.

10.61 A properly structured safe harbour for rescue financing can be a valuable tool in the group restructuring toolbox. Implementing ex-ante authorisation within a controlled and supervised process is suitable, necessary and proportionate. The extensive experience with DIP financing in the USA and the limited, yet promising, use of Dutch WHOA schemes reinforces this conclusion. A statutory framework that encourages rescue financing can be particularly useful in jurisdictions lacking a developed rescue financing market. In these jurisdictions, the market may fail to seize opportunities to invest in viable businesses (market failure) unless supported by statutory intervention.

10.62 **Third**, the efficiency of a safe harbour regime will depend on its ability to adequately address group financial distress. A narrow focus on an individual entity within a group (e.g. an entity seeking rescue financing) is unlikely to capture the full picture.

10.63 If reorganisation is a collaborative 'group effort' and several group members are involved in securing rescue financing by acting as guarantors, co-borrowers or collateral providers, then all intra-group financial support transactions should ideally be included in a safe harbour. In the case of such an 'extended' safe harbour, it is crucial to ensure that the rights and interests of creditors of the group entities involved are protected. This approach is balanced and proportionate as it: (i) fosters efficient, value-preserving and value-enhancing rescue attempts, addressing underinvestment while contributing to value preservation and maximisation; (ii) ensures legal certainty and upholds trust; (iii) guarantees finality and prevents protracted litigation, thereby facilitating procedural efficiency and reducing costs; and (iv) when coupled with prior notice and a court hearing or a creditor vote on the proposed financial package, ensures procedural fairness and provides safeguards against group opportunism, including asset stripping and gambling for resurrection.

10.64 **Fourth**, this chapter demonstrates the challenges of balancing flexibility and legal certainty in the context of intra-group financial support within international banking groups. This is an area where supranational rules intersect with national corporate, contract and insolvency laws, and where various political issues, such as the home/host debate, are at stake. As a result, multiple obstacles and uncertainties can arise regarding intra-group asset transfers. This is why having a pre-emptive and predictable financial arrangement, like a GFSA, would bring clarity and efficiency to intra-group financing within banking groups.[102] It will reinforce trust, legal certainty and credibility, all of which are essential for any effective cross-border resolution regime.

When it comes to non-financial enterprises, certain pre-emptive strategies **10.65**
common in banking groups are worth considering and learning from. These strategies include the preparation of group recovery plans, the allocation (prepositioning) of resources to key group companies and entering into group support agreements to ensure financing of these key companies in a stress situation. Pre-emptive strategies are particularly relevant and proportionate for significant non-financial enterprises – companies and enterprise groups whose failure can produce significant negative social and economic externalities, impacting a large number of people and firms, increasing state expenditures, prompting bailouts and potentially disrupting vital public services.[103] Notable examples include the bankruptcies of Chrysler and General Motors in 2009, as well as the more recent liquidations of Carillion and British Steel. For these enterprises, both increased state intervention and a shift from reactive, ad hoc responses to proactive measures, preparation and pre-emption – on both individual entity and group levels – are entirely justified.[104]

102 I. Kokorin, Preemptive Financing Arrangements within Cross-Border Banking Groups: Between Flexibility and Legal Certainty, in L. Böffel and J. Schürger (eds), Digitalisation, Sustainability, and the Banking and Capital Markets Union, Palgrave Macmillan Cham, 2022, pp. 377–395. Creation of such a legal regime is also supported by D. Ramos Muñoz and M. Lamandini, Evolving key risks in the banking sector and related priorities for the SRB: the lack of an effective transfer-based bank crisis framework, November 2022, p. 16.

103 P. van Asperen and H. Koster, Leveranciers van elektriciteit en warmte in financiële moeilijkheden: een verkenning van de wettelijke regelingen, O&F 2020, Vol. 4, pp. 70–93.

104 For a discussion on the application of bank resolution-inspired tools to significant non-financial enterprises, see I. Kokorin, Insolvency of Significant Non-Financial Enterprises: Lessons from Bank Failures and Bank Resolution, European Business Law Review, Vol. 32, 2021, pp. 521–556.

PART VI

CONCLUSION

11

KEY FINDINGS AND OBSERVATIONS

11.1 FORCES OF CHANGE AND GROUP INSOLVENCIES

11.01 Writing in 2009 on the subject of insolvencies within multinational enterprise groups, Mevorach emphasised that 'thus far, legal regimes have refrained from explicitly tackling the problem [of group insolvencies]'.[1] However, she pointed out that the 'winds of change' were blowing – primarily referring to the work undertaken by UNCITRAL Working Group V on the topic of groups. Such winds were expected to impact the prevailing views and approaches to handling insolvencies of corporate groups. She was right. Since 2009, various initiatives have emerged aiming to modernise insolvency law to ensure the effective and efficient administration of insolvency proceedings in the context of enterprise groups. In Chapter 3, this new phase was referred to as the third generation of insolvency law – insolvency law 3.0. It was preceded by two generations: the first, when there were no rules targeting group failures and cross-border insolvencies (insolvency law 1.0); and the second, when some rules emerged addressing international insolvencies but generally on a single-entity basis (insolvency law 2.0).

11.02 Insolvency law 3.0 is represented by such instruments as the Dutch WHOA, German StaRUG and Singapore's IRDA schemes (national level), the BRRD

1 I. Mevorach, Insolvency within Multinational Enterprise Groups, OUP, 2009, p. 326.

and the EIR Recast (regional, European level), and the FSB Key Attributes and MLEGI (international level). Notably, all these instruments were adopted within the span of a single decade. This represents the fastest and most spectacular progress of insolvency law in history, at least in its domain dealing with the insolvencies of enterprise groups. I believe that insolvency law 3.0 is the result of two major forces of change.

11.03 The global financial crisis and the proliferation of the so-called 'rescue culture' over the past decade have facilitated the realisation and recognition that many global enterprises 'live' as groups of interconnected and interdependent (yet legally separate) companies – a group reality. When these enterprises 'die', the group reality should be recognised as well. Failure to do so might threaten financial stability, especially in the case of banking groups, or lead to a significant loss of value due to a breakup of important intra-group ties and the destruction of group synergies. The cases of Lehman Brothers, Nortel Networks and Oi Brazil, introduced in Chapter 1, clearly illustrate this point. They reveal the complexities of resolving financial distress within the multilayered and international structures of groups of companies.

11.04 These complexities arise, inter alia, from the ways groups arrange financing both externally and internally. Financing from third parties, such as bondholders and credit institutions, is typically accompanied by cross-guarantees, co-debtorship and collateral arrangements, as well as specific types of contractual clauses that create a correlation between entities within the group, namely intercompany ipso facto and cross-default clauses. In turn, once funds are available to a group entity, they can be transferred internally through intragroup loans and centralised cash management. While a corporate group is solvent and there is no default on obligations, these arrangements usually do not pose any problems. In contrast, in insolvency, they may result in disputes over the validity of pre-insolvency intra-group transfers (Oi Brazil), the calculation, attribution and enforcement of intercompany claims (Lehman Brothers, Nortel Networks, Oi Brazil), access to funds and valuable commercial information (Lehman Brothers), the treatment of cross-guarantees for the purposes of value allocation and distribution (Nortel Networks, Lehman Brothers), and the threat of substantive consolidation, which eliminates intercompany claims (Lehman Brothers, Nortel Networks, Oi Brazil). Thus, both intra-group liability arrangements and the challenges they create in a situation of financial distress and insolvency are ubiquitous.

11.05 An important factor to consider is that enterprise groups are different from each other. These differences concern economic, financial, operational and managerial structures. Furthermore, from a legal standpoint, there is no consistent or uniform definition of a corporate group. Such definition varies across jurisdictions and between different contexts and areas of law (section 2.3). Chapter 2 demonstrates that some groups take the form of integrated, pyramid-shaped enterprises with centralised management, while others lack hierarchical structures and instead operate in a more heterarchical manner, characterised by decentralised, flatter corporate networks with largely autonomous and self-sustaining units. This diversity in corporate and operational structures, group financing, management and ownership patterns complicates or even makes it impossible to develop a one-size-fits-all approach to their regulation, including regulation in situations of financial distress and insolvency.

The question of how group reality, recognised as a unique set of legal, economic and social norms and facts, brought into the spotlight by the forces of change, can be reconciled with the treatment of group-specific financial arrangements in insolvency, is part of the puzzle that this book seeks to resolve. It offers an overview and analysis of intra-group financial arrangements in the context of group insolvencies, viewed through the lens of legal principles. Among the most relevant legal principles are equal treatment of creditors, estate value preservation and maximisation and the protection of legitimate expectations and party autonomy (Chapter 4). When these principles collide – as they often do – a balancing and proportionality analysis is required, which is inherently context- and case-specific (section 4.4). However, this does not mean that it is impossible to identify general or typical factors that influence the proportionality analysis. Discovering these factors lies at the heart of this book, as it examines when group-mindful tools and solutions are justified. **11.06**

11.2 INTRA-GROUP FINANCING AND GROUP INSOLVENCY: CHALLENGES AND SOLUTIONS

11.2.1 Group economic and legal realities

The main challenge in dealing with insolvencies within enterprise groups is reconciling the group economic reality with the legal reality of entity separateness. While individual members of an enterprise group are recognised in law, the group itself is not treated as a distinct legal entity. Unlike certain other areas of law (e.g. competition law), where the (economic) concept of an enterprise or undertaking transcends the boundaries of a single legal entity, insolvency law traditionally operates on an entity-by-entity basis; this is referred to as the entity bias. The division of a single enterprise into separate legal entities with their own interests, governance, pools of assets and creditors, **11.07** is underpinned by the doctrines of limited liability and entity shielding. The former protects shareholders from liability for debts incurred by the legal entities they establish or invest in, while the latter ensures that the shareholder's own creditors do not have direct recourse against the assets of their companies.

11.08 Without disputing the importance of limited liability – though its rationale for highly integrated groups remains questionable – I argue that entity separateness does not and should not automatically result in complete entity insulation. Hence, it should not prevent legal responses that recognise and address group dynamics without contravening the corporate form (section 2.5). Insolvency law must respond to the legal reality of entity separateness and the economic reality of group integration. The greater the implications of or incursions into limited liability and asset partitioning, the more stringent the requirements become for applying a specific legal tool (section 3.6). This is why, for instance, substantive consolidation – a legal tool that leads to a complete disregard of the corporate form and eliminates intercompany claims – is typically limited to rare cases involving the intermingling of assets and liabilities within a group or cases of fraud and abuse of the corporate form.

11.09 The mismatch between group commercial and legal realities is further exacerbated by the prevalence of intra-group financial arrangements. In the legal sense, these arrangements do not undermine entity separateness, as group entities retain their independent existence and interests. In practice, however, they are often driven by the interests of the group as a whole. Such arrangements promote group interdependence and weaken the protection afforded by corporate shields, which, at least in theory, should uphold the separateness of the legal entities comprising the enterprise group. Undoubtedly, intercompany liability arrangements, including cross-guarantees and co-debtorship, serve protective, risk control and risk mitigation functions (section 5.4). They can also contribute to lowering the cost of debt. Nevertheless, in situations of financial distress, these arrangements may contribute to contagion across the group (domino effect), trigger holdout behaviour of some creditors and discourage early measures to avoid insolvency (section 5.6). The conflict between a single enterprise (economic form) and a single entity (legal form) becomes especially acute.

11.10 Take, for example, cross-guarantees – one of the most pervasive elements of many financial transactions. Should these guarantees be assessed in view of the group reality, or should their benefit be calculated based solely on the position of the guarantor, without regard to a broader group context? This question is discussed in Chapter 7. The answer to this question is of great practical relevance, as it is likely to determine whether a cross-guarantee can be avoided in insolvency. It is demonstrated that under UK, US and Dutch law, group considerations can, in principle, be taken into account by courts. Yet, the application of transaction avoidance rules to transactions involving group members and the evaluation of group interest are plagued by legal uncertainty. The problem relates to the calculation of reasonably equivalent value of a guarantee and the indirect benefits for a group guarantor, co-debtor or collateral provider (section 7.3). I support a group-mindful application of transaction avoidance rules that take into consideration group characteristics and intra-group relations and dependencies. At the same time, it should be emphasised that group interest alone, however defined, cannot justify the deprivation or sacrifice of the rights and interests of creditors of individual group companies (section 3.5.2).

Williamson observes that '[t]ransactions that are subject to *ex post* opportunism will benefit if appropriate safeguards can be devised *ex ante*'.[2] I agree. Considering the heightened risk of group opportunism, the far-reaching effects of insolvency transaction avoidance, and the inherent legal uncertainty of ex post review of transactions, it is prudent to explore alternative strategies (Chapter 10). These strategies include ex ante approval or a safe harbour (section 10.2) and pre-emptive structural and contractual support arrangements, akin to those adopted in many banking groups (section 10.3). They can promote efficient intra-group rescue financing and mitigate the problem of underinvestment, especially if such rescue financing is exempted from statutory subordination (Chapter 6). They provide a degree of legal certainty within an environment characterised by legal and economic uncertainty while shielding existing creditors from group opportunism. 11.11

11.2.2 'Extension effect' in insolvency law

The limitations of a single-entity approach and the necessity of a group-mindful approach become even more evident when group restructuring and the preservation of group synergies (group value) are at stake. Chapters 8 and 9 examine various legal tools designed to safeguard group value and address the disruptive consequences of intra-group financial arrangements. What these tools have in common is their ability to extend the effects of insolvency law rules and protections to third (non-debtor) parties. In other words, they create an 'extension effect' in insolvency law by (i) enabling the restructuring of group 11.12

2 O.E. Williamson, Opportunism and its Critics, Managerial and Decision Economics, Vol. 14, 1993, p. 105.

liabilities in a single procedure (third-party releases), and (ii) providing a temporary respite from enforcement actions to facilitate a group-oriented solution (extension of a bankruptcy stay to the debtor's affiliates).

11.13 These legal tools bridge economic and legal realities, preserving the separate legal identities of group companies while avoiding their complete insulation. Nonetheless, they inevitably raise questions about compliance with fundamental legal principles, such as the equal treatment of creditors, protection of legitimate expectations and party autonomy. The most acute conflict typically arises between the preservation and maximisation of estate value, on the one hand, and the protection of legitimate expectations and freedom of contract, on the other.

11.14 When a debtor files for bankruptcy, it gains access to numerous insolvency law protections but is subject to a certain level of scrutiny mandated by the insolvency process. This process may also involve reputational costs for the debtor. Yet, third parties benefiting from the 'extension effect' (non-debtor group members) may escape such scrutiny. For this reason, the application of legal tools with an extension effect must be carefully balanced and checked against the proportionality principle. The outcomes of this balancing exercise and my specific suggestions are outlined in the concluding sections of the chapters in Part V of this book: section 8.3 (third-party releases) and section 9.4 (extension of an enforcement stay to group affiliates). Some of these suggestions are further elaborated below.

11.15 *Third-party releases.* Chapter 5 describes how the 'triangle of rights and liabilities' – principal debtor ↔ guarantor ↔ creditor – complicates restructuring efforts due to: (i) the existence of a recourse or ricochet claim (e.g. indemnity, contribution) of the paying guarantor (i.e. 'ricochet problem'), or (ii) the fact that enforcement against the guarantor could lead to its collapse, potentially undermining the effectiveness of the principal debtor's restructuring (i.e. 'orphan restructuring problem'). In response, group debt deleveraging and debt adjustment can be carried out through a third-party release. This tool provides a practical solution for resolving some complexities of group financing, aligning legal responses with actual business and group financing models.

11.16 Third-party releases are the subject of heated debate because they affect the rights of creditors against third (non-debtor) parties and their obligations, without opening separate proceedings against them. This is one of the reasons why countries adopt divergent approaches to third-party releases. While English courts adhere to a pro-release approach and consider third-party releases a common practice in schemes of arrangement, and the Netherlands permits third-party releases in WHOA schemes involving group restructuring (though not necessarily outside them), the US Supreme Court has recently clarified that non-consensual non-debtor releases included in the company's Chapter 11 plan were impermissible under the US Bankruptcy Code.

Third-party releases are a valuable addition to the restructuring toolbox. They can help safeguard the continuity of a group enterprise by mitigating the destabilising effects of cross-guarantees and other cross-entity liability arrangements. The simultaneous enforcement of group guarantees could create additional costs, result in conflicting judgments, complicate group-wide reorganisation and ultimately lead to the destruction of enterprise value. The case of Oi Brazil perfectly illustrates this (section 1.1.3). While acknowledging the practical utility of third-party releases, it is emphasised that they must not strip group guarantees of their protective function. Therefore, I suggest the introduction of a 'group best-interest-of-creditors test', which would ensure that a guaranteed creditor is not deprived of its baseline entitlements and the benefits afforded by a valid security arrangement and property rights (i.e. a claim against a third party). It is also stressed that the case for a third-party release is stronger if the release is consensual, pertains to the debtor's own claim, or if the non-debtor third party is entitled to pursue a full recourse claim against the debtor, potentially undermining restructuring efforts (section 8.3.2). 11.17

Extension of enforcement stays. A less far-reaching tool addressing the 'triangle of rights and liabilities' is the extension of an enforcement stay to the debtor's affiliates (Chapter 9). Unlike a release, a stay does not definitively adjudicate rights; rather, it preserves the status quo and the potential for restructuring. The availability, design and scope of a stay vary significantly across jurisdictions, and sometimes within the same jurisdiction, depending on the applicable procedure. Among the national laws examined in this book, the automatic stay under the US Bankruptcy Code stands out as the most potent, given its extremely broad scope. Dutch law provides for a stay in bankruptcy and suspension of payments procedures but does not affect the rights of secured creditors. These 'separatist' creditors can enforce their security rights as if no bankruptcy proceedings were in place. UK law, by contrast, offers a patchwork of different rules and procedures, that might be used on a stand-alone basis or in combination with other procedures. 11.18

The unresolved question is whether a stay can and should be extended to non-debtor group entities, such as those acting as guarantors, co-debtors or collateral providers. I argue that, given the group economic reality, extending 11.19

the protective shield of an enforcement stay to the debtor's affiliates may be necessary to facilitate the efficient restructuring of an enterprise group. Such an extension aims to preserve key group synergies, maintain the operational continuity of group companies and strengthen the debtor's bargaining power. UK law does not seem to permit such an extension. US and Dutch law, to one extent or another, grant courts the authority to extend the stay to enjoin actions against third parties (section 9.3). However, considering that a stay encroaches on creditors' enforcement rights, its extension should not be automatic. Importantly, it must not unfairly prejudice the rights of affected creditors or cause substantial detriment to them. The extension of a stay to non-debtor parties should be accompanied by adequate protections to prevent potential abuse. This may require mirroring the protections inherent in the original stay and allowing for the possibility to lift the extended stay if its continuation harms the creditor. For instance, this could occur if the value of collateral provided by the third party declines, or if the third party attempts to conceal assets or engages in other forms of opportunistic behaviour (section 9.4.2).

11.20 The case for an intra-group operation of an insolvency stay appears to be stronger when the enterprise group is integrated, and a non-debtor group company plays an integral part in the debtor's restructuring, or when the restructuring involves a third-party release. In both cases, extending the stay becomes essential for the efficiency of the reorganisation. But even in cases involving asset sales, the extension of a stay may contribute to value maximisation insofar as it preserves the group's asset pool, which, as a whole, is worth more than the assets of individual group companies sold separately, on an entity-by-entity basis. An illustrative example is the bankruptcy of Nortel Networks (section 1.1.2), where the aggregate sale of assets belonging to different group companies helped to secure the highest purchase price.

11.3 KEY OBSERVATIONS: GUIDING FACTORS

11.3.1 In search of guiding factors

11.21 In her insightful book, Pistor describes how modern enterprises, such as Lehman Brothers, have turned the 'legal partitioning of assets with the help of corporate law into an art form'.[3] The division of a firm, representing a single interconnected economic ecosystem, into dozens, if not hundreds, of legal shells is a modern corporate reality. Be that as it may, insolvencies of

3 K. Pistor, The Code of Capital: How the Law Creates Wealth and Inequality, Princeton University Press, 2019, p. 54.

giants like Lehman Brothers, Nortel Networks, Oi Brazil, and more recently LATAM Airlines, Hertz and FTX, attest to the fact that group companies not only live together but also die (or recover) together. These cases demonstrate that many subsidiaries can hardly survive or raise funds without support from other group members. This support translates, among other things, into various intra-group liability arrangements, such as group guarantees and co-debtorships, which undermine or diminish what is often praised as the greatest privilege that shareholders enjoy – limited liability. While not all intra-group financing has the effect of perforating the corporate veil, it tends to increase group interdependence and thereby weaken the persuasiveness of the entity separateness narrative.

This book explores how insolvency law can better respond to the economic realities of corporate groups and their financial arrangements. Based on this exploration, I aim to dissect a number of general considerations or factors that play a role in determining whether a group-mindful approach should be adopted. Without claiming to have identified all the relevant factors, I highlight those that transpire throughout the entire book. They do not pre-determine any concrete result and should not be seen as rigid instructions. Instead, they could serve as key indicators, suggesting a direction or informing a decision, while allowing for flexibility and case-specific considerations. **11.22**

11.3.2 Group integration and interdependence

The first factor or theme that can guide the application of various legal tools tackling intra-group financing is group integration and interdependence. This integration can be backed by a wide range of operational and financial elements. Among them are reliance on the group for business commitments (such as supply of essential materials, provision of licences and know-how, leasing of premises, etc.), access to funds (e.g. intra-group loans, cross-guarantees, cash pooling), services (e.g. data management, IT, marketing), and other forms of collaboration (information sharing, development and implementation of a business plan or strategy). Examples of highly integrated groups include Lehman Brothers, Nortel Networks and Oi Brazil. **11.23**

For fully integrated businesses, where group entities essentially engage in a common business and depend on each other, and where the collapse of one company is likely to lead to the failure of other group companies or the entire group, context-specific tools and solutions tailored to the group's circumstances are justified. The factor of group integration appears throughout this book, when discussing transaction avoidance and the recognition of indirect benefits in intra-group financing (Chapters 7 and 10), group debt deleveraging and **11.24** adjustment via third-party releases addressing ricochet and orphan restructuring problems (Chapters 5, 8), and the preservation of group synergies and value through the extension of an insolvency stay to debtor's group affiliates (Chapter 9).

11.25 The Guide to MLEGI recognises that a widely based, possibly group-wide insolvency solution 'may be of particular importance where the business of the enterprise group is conducted in a closely integrated manner'.[4] The relevance of group integration should come as no surprise, as the discussed tools or solutions aim to leverage synergies across the group and connect the group economic reality with the legal reality of entity separateness. By contrast, what is justified and proportionate for integrated and interconnected enterprise groups may be less feasible or even disproportionate for groups with a significant degree of decentralisation and independence. For these groups, where individual group companies are not dependent on each other and, as a result, the failure of one is unlikely to spill over to other parts of the group – in other words, where entity separateness is strong – the use of group-sensitive insolvency law tools is less necessary from the proportionality perspective (section 4.4.2).

11.3.3 Financial situation of non-debtor group entities

11.26 The second factor relates to the financial situation of a group company seeking the benefits of extended insolvency law safeguards. If such a company is solvent and does not face cash flow or balance sheet insolvency due to a creditor action, the argument for using insolvency law 'superpowers' and extending insolvency law protections, including debt discharge and adjustment, and an enforcement stay, becomes weak.

11.27 After all, it is insolvency law and its principles – such as equal treatment of creditors, but most importantly, value preservation and maximisation – that serve to justify encroachment on creditors' property and contractual rights. Without insolvency risk, sustaining this justification becomes difficult, and freedom of contract, in its broadest sense, should prevail. Alongside matters of value preservation and maximisation, an insolvency process seeks to guarantee procedural and substantive fairness, underpinned by transparency, participation rights and equitable distribution of value. This is why the justification for a third-party release might be called into question when the third party benefiting from insolvency law tools does not subject itself to the requirements

4 Guide to MLEGI, para. 69.

of an insolvency process and is not financially distressed, either before or as a result of the enforcement of a creditor's claim under a guarantee, co-debtorship or collateral arrangement (see section 8.3.2). Similar observations were made regarding the extension of an enforcement stay to non-debtor group entities (section 9.4.2).

There may be cases where the enforcement of a creditor's right against a solvent group entity, acting as a group guarantor, co-obligor or collateral provider, damages or even dismantles group synergies and value, without serving a legitimate objective or the creditor's interests. In situations like this, a certain degree of flexibility could be considered. Among the jurisdictions examined in this book, the USA has the most flexible bankruptcy law. This is evidenced in the absence of any mandatory threshold of material insolvency or financial distress for accessing Chapter 11 – the principal restructuring framework. This enables the participation of different group entities, whether solvent or insolvent, in a reorganisation. The absence of an insolvency requirement, together with the affiliate-filing rule, flexible jurisdictional standards and other important benefits offered by the US Bankruptcy Code (e.g. DIP financing regime, powerful automatic stay), has made the USA a favoured destination for restructurings of enterprise groups, including foreign ones. However, it is important to note that when group companies, whether insolvent or solvent, file for bankruptcy in US courts, they subject themselves to the obligations and requirements of the bankruptcy process, including transparency. The flexibility and lack of an insolvency threshold have also contributed to the attractiveness of English schemes of arrangement. Despite the limited toolbox of schemes compared to US Chapter 11 (e.g. no automatic stay, no cross-class cram down), they have become a popular instrument for group (financial) restructuring. 11.28

11.3.4 Purpose and nature of the procedure

The third factor refers to the purpose and nature of the procedure. Two different scenarios should be distinguished concerning the purpose. The first scenario involves (i) financial and/or operational restructurings, where the business remains with the debtor company or a group of companies, or (ii) a going concern sale of the business to outside investors. Hence, the first scenario encompasses both 'restructuring' per se, which removes debt from the business, and 'asset-deal restructuring', which removes the business from its debt. The second scenario entails a piecemeal liquidation and closing down of the business. It does not matter whether such liquidation is accomplished through a Chapter 11 plan, a WHOA scheme or any other procedure. 11.29

11.30 Third-party releases, extended enforcement stays, and restrictions on certain contract terms aim to preserve the going concern value of the debtor and of its enterprise group – value that would otherwise be lost if creditors were allowed to enforce their rights against members of the enterprise group. That being said, in the context of a piecemeal liquidation, the rationale for preserving the debtor's or the group's going concern value is less compelling. Therefore, the discussed tools become less feasible or indeed unnecessary, as they would not achieve the goals for which they were designed. However, there may be some exceptions. For example, the extension of a stay to non-debtor group companies may be warranted even in a liquidation and asset sale scenario, provided that it facilitates an orderly liquidation of an enterprise group and the coordinated sale of its assets. Assets of separate group entities may be worth more if sold together. The case in point is the bankruptcy of Nortel Networks. This case demonstrates that the preservation of assets spread across different group companies, and their coordinated, global sale could secure the highest purchase price, in full compliance with the principle of value maximisation.

11.31 When it comes to the nature of the procedure, a distinction should also be made between, on the one hand, a 'light touch' or 'skinny' financial restructuring,[5] which primarily targets the company's debts (rather than assets) and involves well-informed, sophisticated and strongly adjusting creditors, such as bondholders and bank lenders, and, on the other hand, a full-fledged financial and operational restructuring that impacts the debtor's assets and affects the rights of less sophisticated parties, including employees, trade partners and tort victims. Schemes and scheme-like procedures are often used to deleverage complex financial capital structures.[6] Schemes are associated with additional flexibility, embraced to accommodate the realities of group financing, and provide legal tools to achieve group-mindful solutions.

11.32 In the UK, for instance, schemes of arrangement and third-party releases contained therein are commonly used to restructure group financial obligations under cross-guarantees and co-debtorship arrangements.[7] In the Netherlands,

5 I. Mevorach and A. Walters, The Characterization of Pre-insolvency Proceedings in Private International Law, EBOR, Vol. 21, 2020, pp. 855–894.

6 S. Paterson, Corporate Reorganization Law and Forces of Change, OUP, 2020, exploring the proliferation of a new type of corporate restructuring, one that only implicates financial liability and certain participants. This form of financial restructuring ensures the preservation of the group's cash flow, as the activities of operating companies and claims of trade creditors and employees remain unaffected by the restructuring process.

7 The restructurings of the Dutch retailer HEMA, Switzerland-headquartered aviation services company Swissport, vending machine operator Selecta and Spain's multinational group devoted to entertainment and leisure Codere, to name a few, have been carried out with the involvement of financial restructuring in the UK.

third-party releases and extended stays or cooling-off periods within WHOA schemes are directed at group financial arrangements, which frequently involve creditors who are professional financiers. Importantly, intra-group financing and the corresponding insolvency law tools rarely encroach upon the rights of vulnerable constituencies. This could justify some flexibility in the application of legal tools to implement financial restructuring and address complex financial arrangements.

Parties involved in intra-group financing tend to be better risk bearers, as they can negotiate a legal arrangement aligned with the assumed levels of risk and expected return. These parties are the ones who typically benefit from intra-group liability arrangements, such as intra-group guarantees, and have a clear understanding that they are effectively transacting with the entire group. This perception is reinforced by the existence of cross-entity liability arrangements, as pointed out by US courts in the Oi Brazil case. Why is this important? When a sophisticated party engages with a group enterprise, it should be able to foresee that if the group requires deleveraging or is on the brink of failure, group-specific legal tools like third-party releases might be invoked. This has to do with the protection of legitimate expectations (section 4.3.2). Guided by the principle of proportionality, I argue that group-mindful legal tools are more defensible and justifiable in cases of financial restructuring involving group entities and sophisticated financial creditors, as opposed to non-adjusting or poorly-adjusting creditors. Perhaps this is the reason why third-party releases have recently come under fire in cases involving mass torts (e.g. Purdue Pharma, Boy Scouts of America, USA Gymnastics), but have encountered less criticism in cases of the restructuring of intra-group financial obligations. 11.33

11.3.5 Prevalence of public interest

Traditionally, insolvency law has been seen as an instrument to resolve conflicts arising within a single entity – conflicts between the company and its investors, such as shareholders and creditors.[8] Insolvency law, therefore, is, for the most part: (i) microprudential: single entity-focused and designed to protect the interests of individual debtors and their creditors; (ii) contractarian: implementing the idea of the creditor's bargain and addressing the coordination problem between creditors of a single entity; and (iii) reactive: centred around post-crisis asset realisation and the allocation of proceeds among creditors. The situation is different for the resolution of financial institutions 11.34

8 S.L. Schwarcz, Beyond Bankruptcy: Resolution as a Macroprudential Regulatory Tool, Notre Dame Law Review, Vol. 92, 2018, p. 729.

– a difference that became apparent in the aftermath of the Global Financial Crisis. It was then that policymakers realised a new approach was needed to prevent bank bailouts, preserve financial stability and mitigate social harm and public unrest. In this respect, Lubben contends that the primary aim of bank resolution is not adjudicatory (i.e. the collective handling of claims and their enforcement) but rather regulatory.[9]

11.35 It is observed that the more prominent the role of the public interest, the greater the likelihood that the law will acknowledge and give effect to a group's reality in one way or another. In economic terms, the issue at stake is the degree of negative externalities created by a certain behaviour. The larger these externalities, the higher the public interest concerns, and the more likely the 'groupness' will be recognised and acted upon. This is why areas of law that tackle negative externalities and serve the public interest (e.g. tax, competition, anticorruption law) tend to look beyond the fiction of entity shells.[10] Said differently, group-mindful solutions are powered by public interest.

11.36 The considerations of public interest underpin many post-GFC reforms in the field of bank resolution, fostering the development of legal tools and mechanisms at a group rather than at an individual entity level. These tools include, inter alia, group recovery and resolution plans, group financial support agreements under the BRRD – a legal regime that explicitly recognises group interest (section 10.3.2), SPOE and MPOE models of bank resolution, and the related requirements for pre-positioning of resources within banking groups (section 10.3.3). When designing insolvency laws for enterprise groups, it is crucial to draw lessons from the regulation of banking groups, which tends to be more advanced and group-oriented, for good reasons.

11.37 The coordinated resolution of financial distress in banking groups and financial conglomerates is logical, as resolving a single company without considering its interconnectedness with other group entities and its integration in the financial system can be short-sighted and may create systemic risk. Some preemptive strategies, including the preparation of group recovery plans, entering

9 S.J. Lubben, A Functional Analysis of SIFI Insolvency, Texas Law Review, Vol. 96, 2018, p. 1396.

10 For example, EU competition law relies on the notion of an 'undertaking' that covers 'any entity engaged in an economic activity, irrespective of the legal status of that entity and the way in which it is financed, and thus defines an economic unit even if in law that economic unit consists of several persons, natural or legal'. C-516/15, *Akzo Nobel and Others v. Commission*, 27 April 2017, para. 48. As a result, formal boundaries between the legal entities within a single economic unit and their separate legal personalities – separate in a sense of being insulated – lose their salience when dealing with conduct that constitutes an infringement of competition law. Case C-882/19, *Sumal SL v. Mercedes Benz Trucks España SL*, 6 October 2021, extending liability from a parent company to a subsidiary within the same 'economic unit'.

into group support agreements to ensure the financing of key group companies in stress situations, and insulating them from insolvency through the prepositioning of resources, should also be considered for non-financial enterprises (section 10.4.2). These strategies are particularly relevant and proportionate for firms whose insolvency poses questions related to the provision of vital public services and raises concerns about employment, environmental, health and safety issues. For these significant non-financial enterprises, public interest may play a role in balancing conflicting legal principles.

The enterprise group is one of the primary forms of organising economic activity. In fact, virtually every major firm is organised as a group. From early precursors of business groups, such as the Medici system of partnerships in the fifteenth and sixteenth centuries and the European colonial trading empires of the seventeenth century (e.g. the Dutch and English East India Companies), to the emergence at the end of the nineteenth century of the first modern groups of companies characterised by multi-layered and hierarchical structures of ownership and control, groups have played an important role in both the economic and political life of societies. Yet, the enterprise group is a curious case. It combines separate entities and (often) an integrated business, sometimes pierced or perforated by an elaborate network of intra-group financial arrangements and dependencies. The study of corporate groups is complicated by the diversity of their types and features, as well as the multiple levels of regulation (international, regional and national) that reflect the international character of most groups. It is hoped that this book will contribute to a better understanding of enterprise groups, intra-group financing and their intersection with insolvency and restructuring law. **11.38**

INDEX